W9-BSF-206

THE DREAD DISEASE

Cartoon booklet from the 1950s. From the National Library of Medicine, Bethesda, Maryland.

THE DREAD DISEASE

Cancer and Modern American Culture

JAMES T. PATTERSON

HARVARD UNIVERSITY PRESS

CAMBRIDGE, MASSACHUSETTS

LONDON, ENGLAND

1987

Printed in the United States of America
10 9 8 7 6 5 4 3 2 1

Design by Joyce C. Weston

This book is printed on acid-free paper, and its binding materials have been chosen for strength and durability.

Library of Congress Cataloging in Publication Data

Patterson, James T.
The dread disease.

Bibliography: p.
Includes index.
1. Cancer—United States—History—20th century. 2. Cancer—United States—Public opinion. 3. Public opinion—United States. I. Title. [DNLM: 1. Attitude to Health—history—United States. 2. Culture—United States. 3. Neoplasms—history—United States. QZ 11 AA1 P3d]
RC276.P38 1987 362.1'96994'00973 87-160
ISBN 0-674-21625-3 (alk. paper)

Contents

Preface

EACH YEAR during the past century cancer has killed an ever increasing number of Americans. Since the 1920s it has been the second most common cause of death, behind heart ailments, in the United States. In 1985 the many forms of cancer—characterized by uncontrolled growth of abnormal cells—caused the death of an estimated 462,000 people in the United States, one every 68 seconds. Experts say that almost a third of the American population living in 1987 can expect to develop the disease.

But cancer has evoked popular fears that transcend its deadliness. Invested with feral personalities, cancers have been seen as "insidious," "mysterious," "lawless," "savage," and above all "relentless." At the turn of the century one physician described cancer as a "loathsome beast, which seized upon the breast, drove its long claws into the surrounding tissues, derived its sustenance by sucking out the juices of its victims, and never even relaxed its hold in death." Reactions such as these reveal that cancerphobia is deeply rooted in American culture.

The study of the history of disease can reveal much about patterns of thought and behavior in society. In this book I explore cancer in the context of American culture from the 1880s to the present. I draw heavily on the substantial archival and secondary literature about cancer research, therapy, and care. But I stress that I am writing a cultural history of cancer in the United States, not a detailed study of cancer research, of therapy, or of the experiences of patients. These are subjects for very different books. I am a historian, not a scientist or a physician: although I discuss various theories and therapies, I claim no medical expertise and offer no simple answers. Rather, I concentrate on elucidating the ways that the dread disease has reflected social and personal concerns during the modern, industrial era of United States history: concerns about illness, health, medical practices, and death and dying. Attitudes toward cancer have sometimes conformed to, and sometimes contradicted, cherished ideals of "civilization" and the good life since the 1880s.

I begin the story with the illness and death from cancer of Ulysses S. Grant in 1884–85. Medical and popular reactions to his deteriorating health, which received unprecedented public exposure, offer an unusually revealing portrait of American attitudes toward cancer, as well as toward disease, doctors, and death, in the early years of modern medical practice. Over the next three decades important social, intellectual, and medical developments gradually altered such attitudes. In the late nineteenth century Americans greatly feared deadly communicable diseases such as tuberculosis. But by 1915 many of these illnesses were coming under control, and the life expectancy of Americans was rapidly increasing. Chronic illnesses such as heart ailments and cancer, which especially afflicted older people, thereafter loomed as the most alarming and challenging medical problems of the age. During these same years the American medical profession gained unprecedented respectability, especially among the upper-middle, professional classes, who increasingly placed their faith in expert, scientific solutions to public problems. Cancer, the experts reiterated optimistically, could be conquered. The middle classes, having attained greater affluence and personal comfort, nourished expanding expectations about good health and betrayed increasing dread of early death.

These developments led to the development by 1915 of what I call the alliance against cancer, a slowly widening and ever more self-assured coalition of upper-middle-class groups. Led at first by an elite of surgeons and gynecologists, it came to include laboratory researchers, epidemiologists, and journalists. Though the allies had few effective answers, they expressed a characteristically American faith in the power of positive thinking. Then and later they emphasized the medical blessings of early detection, surgery, and scientific research into causes and cures for the disease. In

1937 Congress joined the alliance by establishing the National Cancer Institute, the first (and always the biggest) of the government's many research empires that today constitute the National Institutes of Health in Bethesda, Maryland.

The history of cancer in America is also a history of social and cultural tensions. Set against the optimistic anticancer alliance were a variety of people, many of them relatively poor and ill educated. Though enormously different from one another in their beliefs and backgrounds, these Americans together constituted what I call a cancer counterculture, skeptical about orthodox medical notions of disease and about the claims to expert knowledge by what they came to call the Cancer Establishment. Some of these doubters relied on home remedies, others on "quacks," folk wisdom, or religious faith. Many clung defiantly to ideas about cancer that were scorned by the majority of scientists. Still others were simply terrified: the persistence and growth of popular cancerphobia are central themes of the book. Most of these Americans, as well as many general practitioners, were bewildered and pessimistic. All have a place in my story.

The counterculture clashed often with the confident, optimistic allies against cancer. Indeed, the tension between the two groups illustrates durable social and cultural divisions in modern America. The cultural history of cancer during the past century reveals many changes in thought and behavior, but especially striking are the continuities, among them the power of class conflicts, ideological divisions, and popular resistance to centralized, paternalistic direction of people's affairs.

In the incomparably affluent years after 1945 Americans became more driven than ever by dreams of good health, of conquering disease, and of escaping early death. Drawing on these large expectations, the allies against cancer employed modern, quintessentially American techniques of public relations and salesmanship. They greatly enlarged their network of supporters and created well-financed research empires. Influential media preached the virtues of science, medical technology, and professionalism, and the federal government impetuously declared a "war" on cancer in 1971.

But even in the face of this onslaught the disbelievers and doubters did not disappear. Especially in times of cultural disarray, such as the late 1970s, they boldly challenged the research emphases of the Cancer Establishment. Some insisted that the best weapon against cancer was not high-tech research and therapy, but prevention: control pollution, eat carefully, drink less, above all stop smoking. Others deplored exaggerated claims in the media, the commercialization of the research establishment, the flaws of the medical profession, and the deterioration of the environment. Many of these people considered cancer not only a scourge but also a metaphor for catastrophic economic and industrial growth. Life as we live it, they seemed to be saying, caused cancer.

The persistence of substantial fears and doubts exposes the extent of social, cultural, and ideological divisions in the United States during the past century: American society has been considerably less consensual than many people have imagined. It indicates, too, that millions of Americans have remained ambivalent about modern medicine. Despite enormous changes in American life and thought during the industrial age, much has remained the same.

A final word: much of the time I use the word "cancer" as if it were a single, easily defined disease. Scientists, by contrast, have enumerated as many as two hundred different varieties of cancer, each with its own natural history. Though I honor the medical precision of such distinctions, I often talk about attitudes toward "cancer" in the singular. This is the way that most laymen, as well as many doctors, have tended to describe the various cancerous diseases that afflict the human body.

Acknowledgments

I COULD NOT HAVE WRITTEN this book without the assistance of a large number of people. Scholars who gave me helpful advice in the early stages include Gerald Grob of Rutgers University, Harry Marks of the Harvard Medical School, James Cassedy of the National Library of Medicine, Nancy Erdey of Case-Western Reserve, Wyndham Miles of the National Library of Medicine, David Courtwright of the University of Hartford, Albert Wessen of Brown University, Sheila Rothman of Columbia University, Morton Keller of Brandeis University, Patricia Spain Ward of the University of Illinois at Chicago, William Leuchtenburg of the University of North Carolina, Chapel Hill, and Joan Austoker of the Wellcome Institute, University of Oxford. My friend Dr. John Glick of the University of Pennsylvania Cancer Center offered early encouragement; he and his wife, Jane Glick, also provided welcome hospitality. Wendi Berkowitz and Jon Rees, Brown undergraduates, were intelligent and hardworking research assistants in the summers of 1984 and 1985, respectively.

Archivists who went out of their way to help are Kenneth Thibodeau of the National Cancer Institute, Dr. Sourya Henderson of the American Cancer Society Library, Inge Dupont of the New York Academy of Medicine, Richard Wolfe of the Countway Library of the Harvard Medical School, Janet Golden and Diana Long Hall of the College of Physicians of Philadelphia, Stephen Catlett of the American Philosophical Society, Manfred Wasserman of the National Library of Medicine, Thomas Rosenbaum of the Rockefeller Archives at Pocantico Hills, N.Y., Aloha South of the National Archives, and Micaela Sullivan of the American Medical Association. I placed special demands on the staff of the Interlibrary Loan office at Brown University. I received research and travel assistance from the Francis C. Wood Institute of the College of Physicians of Philadelphia. The Faculty Development Fund at Brown enabled me to pay for illustrations and permissions. Skilled editorial help came from Aida Donald, Elizabeth Suttell, and Kate Schmit of Harvard University Press.

Many people took the time to criticize parts of the manuscript in one or more of its many stages. These include Al Dahlberg, David Brautigan, and Peter Shank of Brown University—scientists who tried to protect me from errors concerning biological research. Drs. Edwin Forman and Georges Peter of the Brown University Medical School considerably enhanced my understanding of medical matters. Friends who carefully criticized sections of the book are Joseph Perrott of Penn Charter School, Philadelphia, John Rowett of Brasenose College, Oxford, and John Thompson, now of Bath, Maine. My son, Stephen, gave useful reactions to two chapters.

William McFeely, then at Mt. Holyoke College, and Paul Boyer, of the University of Wisconsin, provided expert comments on portions of the manuscript. Barbara Gutmann Rosenkrantz of Harvard, David Musto of Yale, Barbara Sicherman of Trinity College, and Philip Benedict, James Morone, Roger Cobb, and Thomas Anton of Brown constructively evaluated related papers that I gave to seminars, conferences, and professional meetings. Louise Newman, a doctoral candidate in history at Brown, helped me greatly with one chapter. Donald Fleming of Harvard took time to read one of my innumerable drafts.

I am especially grateful to a number of unusually perceptive critics: my colleague Mary Gluck, whose intelligent comments forced me to rethink several of my ideas; Dr. H. Denman Scott, director of the Rhode Island Department of Health, who gave a careful reading to several chapters and offered steady encouragement; James Harvey Young of Emory University, who evaluated the entire manuscript at an early stage; John Cairns of the department of cancer biology at the Harvard School of Public Health, who offered rigorous criticism of most of my chapters; and Charles Rosenberg of the University of Pennsylvania, who did much to improve my manuscript, especially the first few chapters.

A few scholars did me the great favor of reading complete drafts of the manuscript and deluging me with suggestions for revision. These include John Thomas, my colleague in the Brown department of history; Dr. Alan Morrison of Brown University, a critical and knowledgeable epidemiologist; Dr. Michael Shimkin, a cancer scientist and historian of cancer research who gave special encouragement to my work; Allan Brandt of Harvard, a thoughtful historian of science and medicine; and James Jones of the University of Houston, a friend and historian of medicine who pushed me to write such a book and gave a careful reading to an early draft of it.

Final and special thanks go to my wife, Cynthia, who listened to my ideas about this book and who read all my chapters in draft. Her intelligence and encouragement made the long process worthwhile and happy.

THE DREAD DISEASE

PROLOGUE

The Travail of General Grant

IN FEBRUARY 1885 America's most famous author, Mark Twain, arrived in New York City to call on General Ulysses S. Grant, the nation's most revered war hero. His visit was partly social—Twain admired the stolid, simple soldier who had led the Union troops to victory in the Civil War—but it was prompted mainly by concerns of business. Twain, acting as publisher, came to an arrangement with Grant that greatly satisfied both parties: handsome advances to the financially hard-pressed ex-president for the war memoirs he was writing, and lucrative publication rights to Twain.[1]

Twain knew that the sixty-two-year-old Grant had not been well. In June 1884 the general had complained of dryness and pain in his throat, and later that summer and fall he belatedly sought medical help. Slow to diagnose his problem, the doctors were unable to arrest his illness. By January 1885 his condition had deteriorated, and rumors circulated that the general—for twenty-three years a heavy smoker of cigars—had cancer of the mouth. His physicians publicly denied such rumors. Grant, one of them announced, had had a bothersome tooth removed and had given up smoking. "The improvement in his condition since then is marvelous." On February 20, the day before Twain's visit, the *New York World* reported that "all the more serious symptoms" of Grant's illness were gone and that he suffered from "chronic superficial inflammation of the tongue," probably caused by excessive smoking.[2]

When Twain saw Grant, however, he was shocked by his frail appearance. The press was obviously not printing the whole story. Indeed, two days earlier the doctors had thoroughly examined

Grant at his comfortable town house at 3 East Sixty-sixth Street, within sight of Central Park. Their tests confirmed an earlier diagnosis: Grant had a form of cancer. "The disease," they concluded privately, "was an epithelioma, or epithelial cancer of the malignant type, that was sure to end fatally."[3]

Grant, in fact, had a squamous-cell carcinoma, a virulent malignancy. The tumor had been readily observable as early as October, when Dr. John Hancock Douglas, a renowned New York City throat specialist, had examined him. Four months later it had spread from the tonsil to the mouth, the neck, and the soft palate. Surgery at this late date would probably have necessitated removal of most of the soft palate, all of the tongue, and considerable glandular structure under the lower jaw. Severe hemorrhaging might have followed—this in a day when surgeons could not safely manage blood transfusions. Moreover, Grant was already so weak by February that Dr. George Shrady, a noted surgeon who had joined Douglas in attending, was afraid that an operation would send him into shock. Infection, all too common a result of surgery in those times, was a distinct threat. These and other specialists recognized that Grant had a fatal illness and that they dared do nothing for him except try to relieve his suffering.[4]

When the doctors gave Grant the news, he responded calmly, in part because he had long suspected as much. Ruthlessly realistic about his health, he told his family that he had cancer. Newspapermen, however, showed no such calm. By the end of February rumors of Grant's condition became insistent, and reporters pressed the doctors for the full story. By March 1 they had it. The *New York Times* headline that day was typical: SINKING INTO THE GRAVE / GEN. GRANT'S FRIENDS GIVE UP HOPE: DYING SLOWLY FROM CANCER—WORKING CALMLY ON HIS BOOK IN SPITE OF PAIN—SYMPATHY FROM EVERY SIDE. The story carried on in the same vein: "It was agreed that the trouble from which the General was suffering was cancer, and the only difference of opinion was as to the probable rapidity of its development." The doctors had given him opiates to dull the discomfort, but his throat was "much enlarged" and "very painful . . . during the past week he suffered a great deal."

"General Grant," the *Times* noted, "has been most patient during his sickness. Even while sitting up with bandages about his head, which was throbbing with pain, with a resigned calm expression, he would listen to the reading of his book." Grant, indeed, showed remarkable determination in working on his memoirs—at one sitting, Twain marveled, he dictated ten thousand words.[5] The newspaper added that Grant was touched by the concern of the many friends and relatives who gathered every day in the long parlor on the first floor. But nothing could arrest the "insidious disease with which the old hero is struggling." His doctors held out "no hope or expectation of permanent betterment. Their opinion seems to be that the gallant old warrior has at the most only a few months to live, and that his death may occur in a short time."[6]

The report was but one of many in highly competitive newspapers, most of which covered the story in clinical detail over the next few months. Unconstrained by concerns for factual precision, eager to advance circulation, the papers reveled in the macabre. That his illness was a lingering, painful form of cancer, which exercised a special hold on the popular imagination, added to the power of the drama. But the papers had relatively little to say about the causes or cures of cancer—these mystified the commentators. Some observers, Twain among them, speculated that smoking had provoked Grant's illness. Dr. Douglas, however, was quoted as surmising that a recent financial crisis—Grant had been bilked by swindlers—had left him vulnerable to the disease. "Depression and distress of mind," Douglas surmised, "was a more important factor."[7]

Baffled by the phenomenon of cancer, American journalists reflected the dread and revulsion common to popular attitudes concerning the disease. Ghoulish prose highlighted those relatively rare stories about cancer that managed to find their way into the newspapers of the time. A few months earlier the *Times* had broken customary reticence on the subject by describing an autopsy on the body of a doctor's twelve-year-old son. The doctors found "an immense cancer, weighing five pounds, surrounding the heart . . . The heart had been compressed into one-half its normal size, and the left lung was badly crushed. It is believed that the action of the cancer was the severest towards the end. Hence the pain the boy suffered." Not to be outdone, the *Tribune* wrote about the illness of a coal miner from St. Louis found to have an operable cancer at the base of the tongue. His ailment seemed to resemble Grant's. According to the paper, surgeons applied anesthesia, cut into the windpipe, and slit open the cheek. With "two sharp cuts in the jawbone" they took out parts of the bone, chin, and tongue from its base. The man was expected to recover, "horribly disfigured for life."[8]

Stories like these reflected the alarm and apprehension aroused by mention of cancer in America. But public use of the word was in fact uncommon. Most people in the 1880s remained squeamish about public discussion of frightening ailments. Rarely did reporters have an opportunity to describe the disease as experienced by a famous living person. For these and other reasons newspaper space given to cancer fell far short of what it was to become fifty or a hundred years later.

The great exception to this virtual conspiracy of silence was the illness of Grant. Once the story broke that he had a malignant tumor, there was no sating the appetite of the reporters. Within a few weeks the major dailies had joined the wire services to take over a nearby house on Madison Avenue. There the reporters congregated, often in shifts, around the clock; special wires ran directly to home editorial offices. Newsmen paced the street in front of the general's home, interviewing the stream of famous people—Leland Stanford, John Jacob Astor, Joseph Pulitzer, Confederate and Union generals, Twain—who came to pay their respects. Until President Ronald Reagan developed a malignancy in his colon a century later, no case of cancer received more thorough coverage in the press.

The newspaper stories prompted an outpouring of popular concern for the nation's greatest living hero. Throughout the country stores displayed large pictures of Grant and posted the latest health bulletins. Crowds gathered across the street from his house, watching "hushed" carriages pull carefully to a stop and discharge the dignitaries of the day. As if aware of the people's concerns, Grant sometimes sat near the window of his sickroom. "Many people," one account said, "were visibly affected by the sight of his calm patient face, and walked away with bowed heads."[9]

For reporters the vigil was long and the competition fierce. To meet the demands of their editors they resorted to a number of ruses. A few, simulating the symptoms of throat cancer, went to the offices of Grant's doctors in the hope of getting a scoop. One newsman was said to court a maid in a home across the street so as to secure a better view of the sickroom. More generally, they simply wrote vivid, creative reports.[10] No stories outdid those by the *Times* reporter in late March and early April, during the first of periodic crises that appeared to presage the end. Under the headline GEN. GRANT'S SUFFERINGS, one article described a "violent and alarming fit of coughing" that overwhelmed the general at 1:30 in the morning. Doctors hurried to his side; the family was summoned. Grant, discovering unexpected energy, "suddenly sprang from his bed, overcoming the efforts of his valet to restrain him, and exclaimed in a choking voice, which was scarcely audible, 'I can't stand it! I'm going to die!'" A few nights later he awoke again, this time at 3:30 A.M., coughing "violently and spasmodically." Attendants alerted the family and sent for Dr. Shrady, who summoned a horse and carriage and tore out of his front door shouting, "this is a case of life or death." The news account elaborated:

> The words had scarcely been uttered when the lash fell upon the smoking flanks of the horse. The animal broke into a wild gallop and, urged by voice and whip, dashed through Madison Avenue and into 66th St. at a racing gait. Reeking with sweat, the horse was almost thrown upon its haunches by the sudden stop he was compelled to make in front of Gen. Grant's residence.

Shrady, the paper was happy to add, arrived in time to discover that the worst was over. Having coughed some of the blockage away, Grant survived.[11]

Recognizing the advanced state of Grant's illness, physicians adhered to the conservative therapy that they had settled on in February. That consisted mainly of having the patient gargle, usually with a mixture of permanganate of potash and brewers' yeast, and administering various painkillers, including codeine, morphine, and brandy.[12] They also resorted to cocaine, then a relatively new drug. Their frequent statements reveal that they were deeply concerned, but not panicked. Not so the headlines: GEN. GRANT MUCH WORSE, THE END THOUGHT TO BE AT HAND. News stories relied heavily on doomsaying by Grant's visitors. Ex-senator Jerome Chaffee of Colorado emerged from the house early one morning and said, "General Grant is dying. He is sinking very fast. The doctors give no hope." The *Times* reporter then took it upon himself to deliver the verdict on the patient: "he sat awaiting the end, which he knew could not be far off."[13]

The resourceful reporters imagined the drama in the sickroom itself. Several accounts portrayed Grant, an unreligious man, as trusting deeply in the ministrations of the Rev. Dr. John Newman, who ingratiated himself with the family and relished the attention of reporters. "The scene," one story went, "was a most touching one . . . The General was sitting up. Any other posture would have hastened the end. Yet as he sat the halo of death enwrapped him. He held out his hand to the Pastor. Then in a voice of hope and comfort the clergyman said, 'Does the future look bright and pleasant?' The General pressed his friend's hand and looked trustingly into his eyes. There was an instant of silence, when the General said, in tones low but clear. 'Perfectly. I am impatient to go, with regret only at leaving my family.'" Shaken, Mrs. Grant and other ladies "hurried weeping from the room." Only Nellie, his adoring daughter, stayed to comfort her gasping parent. She "went tearfully over to her father and kissed him."[14]

Confounding the alarmists, Grant rallied, leading one of his doctors to observe privately that he would "live until next winter unless new casualties may occur."[15] His remission was largely a mystery. Some hailed the beneficence of prayer and the faith of the Rev. Dr. Newman. Others attributed his improvement to the brandy. (This theory, when printed in the papers, enraged the temperance societies.) Newman managed to credit a blend of both hypotheses. "When the family were summoned," he told reporters on April 4, "the doctor said that Grant had not five minutes to live. We all knelt in prayer. Then we prayed again, when, as by a flash of inspiration, Dr. Shrady thought of the hypodermic of brandy, and the tide of life flowed in again. Our prayer had been answered."[16]

What of Grant himself amid these tribulations? All indications were that he was a model patient: trusting, undemanding, considerate to friends, servants, and family. Knowing that he was mortally ill, he feared choking to death and insisted on sitting up in an easy chair, his feet propped on another chair in front of him. He did his best to take whatever sustenance, mostly fluids, that his swollen and painful mouth and throat could tolerate. But nonetheless he lost weight steadily: at the end he weighed around one hundred pounds, little more than half the amount his sturdy frame had once carried. Although he sometimes was able to walk about the house and even to be taken for carriage rides, he seldom strayed far from his chairs. His was a harsh and confining illness.

Grant's consuming passion was to finish his memoirs, which he saw as the solution to his financial plight. To that end he worked steadily, writing, sometimes dictating (until his voice gave out in late spring), constantly editing. His persistence was later rewarded: his direct, compelling prose greatly appealed to readers. The two-volume set of memoirs sold more than 300,000 copies in the next ten years—an astonishing sale (*Huckleberry Finn* sold 500,000 copies)—and earned Grant's widow close to $500,000.[17] This accomplishment, given the circumstances of his illness, was one of the most remarkable and dramatic in the history of American publishing.

GRANT SEEMED TO improve in late April and May. Though the papers carried daily bulletins, they gradually relegated the information to inside pages. The crowds thinned on Sixty-sixth Street and the reporters relaxed their vigil. But in early June his health deteriorated. The right side of his neck began to swell, indicating that the cancer had invaded deep-seated tissues. Finding it increasingly painful to swallow or to talk, he began scribbling short notes to the doctors. The papers of Dr. Douglas, housed in the Library of Congress, contain many such messages scrawled in pencil on scraps of light brown paper.

By mid-June it grew hot and humid in the city, and it was decided to move the patient to a cooler site. A philanthropist, Joseph Drexel, offered Grant the use of his cottage on Mount McGregor in the Adirondacks, and William Vanderbilt, a friend, tendered his private railroad car for the trip. After a trying journey to Saratoga

Springs, Grant was cheered by one hundred members of the Grand Army of the Republic. Upon finally reaching Mount McGregor, he walked to the sweeping veranda of the cottage where he was to stay. One of the ever-present reporters drew close enough to determine that the general's voice was scarcely audible and that he was "grim, haggard, silent, thinking of what."[18]

While at the cottage Grant occasionally took short walks or was carried in a kind of rickshaw to enjoy the mountain vistas. Usually, however, he stayed home, often on the porch. He dressed formally, a silk scarf wrapped tightly about his neck and tucked into a stovepipe hat—cover for his swelling and protection against the air and other painful sensations. Every now and then, forced by his family to rest, he played desultorily at solitaire, but he spent most of his time working hard, pad and pencil on his lap, at editing his memoirs, the first volume of which went off to Twain on July 11. Occasionally he looked up from his labors to peer into the shadowy depths under the tall trees surrounding the porch. As one reporter described the scene, Grant sat "in his easy chair, his hands resting on his knees, gazing silently into the mist and gloom. He made a touching and melancholy picture."[19]

Unfortunately for Grant, he was not allowed to face his agony in private. Thanks to the newspapers, his whereabouts and condition were known to all who took the trouble to glance at the front pages. Hundreds of Americans came to stare at Grant's bundled and impassive countenance on the veranda. Friends and acquaintances, generals and common soldiers, and delegations of schoolchildren proffering bouquets made the pilgrimage. Many circled the cottage taking pictures of the scene. "Before the season is over," the *Tribune* reported, "there will not be a square inch of the General's cottage that has not been photographed dozens of times."[20]

Most of the onlookers were polite and deferential. Some, like Twain, were welcomed into the entourage of family, doctors, and servants. But a few bold strangers strode to the porch to take pictures or even to talk. On one such occasion Grant, annoyed, managed to rise and to disappear inside. "They will talk me to death," he complained to his son.[21] On another occasion a man described as a "vendor of patent medicines" marched, with "a degree of brazen assurance which no simile could do justice to," onto the steps of the porch and placed in Grant's lap a "package of chewing gum, with some supposed medical property."[22]

Grant managed his illness stoically during these distracting times. Occasionally, of course, he grew silent, moody, and depressed. As Dr. Shrady put it later, the Great Commander was "quietly fighting a battle with himself."[23] The pain in his throat had to be countered with larger and more frequent doses of opiates. Some of the notes Grant wrote during this period were despairing. "I feel quite weak in the stomach this morning. The least effort to clear my head would make me gag or vomit. I do not know but it will be the best thing to die." A few days later he added, "If it is within God's providence that I should go now I am ready to obey His call without a murmer. I should prefer going now to enduring my present suffering for a single day without hope of recovery." Other notes poignantly revealed his resignation: "I think I am a verb instead of a

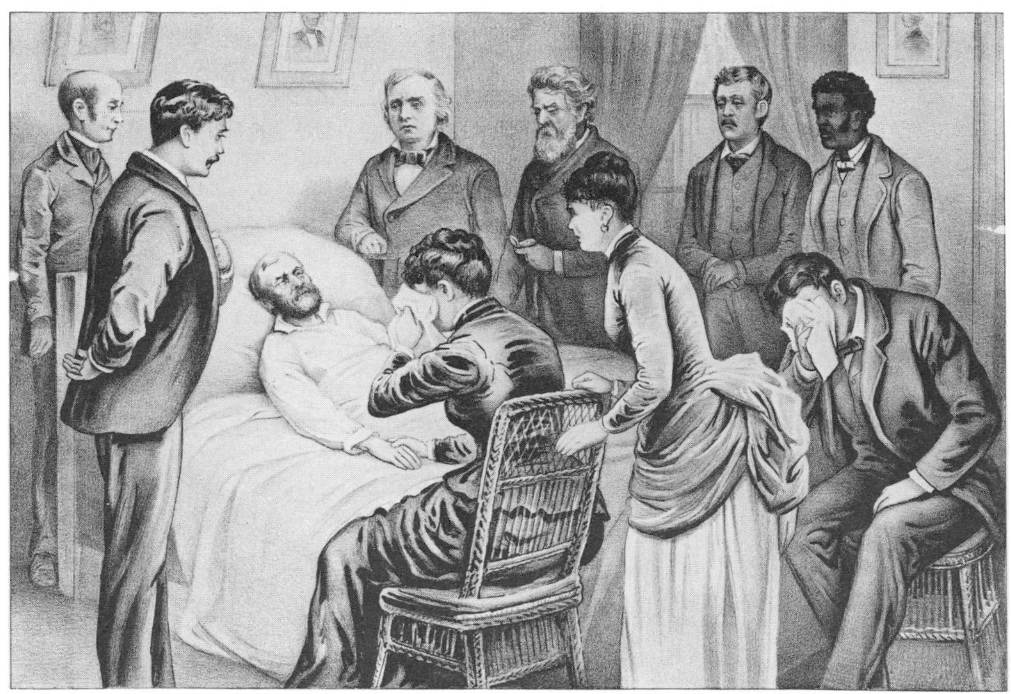

"The Death of General Grant," by Currier and Ives. The Rev. Dr. Newman and Dr. Douglas (holding a pocket watch) stand on the far side of the bed. From the Library of Congress, #LC-US Z62-2313.

personal pronoun. A verb is anything that signifies to be; to do; or to suffer. I signify all three."[24]

But the notes showed that Grant remained coolly analytical, as commanding in dying as in battle. "I have tried to study the function of the use of cocain," he wrote, "as impartially as possible considering that I am the person affected by its use. The conclusion I have come to in my case is, taken properly, it gives a wonderful amount of relief from pain." In one of his longest messages he told Douglas:

> I can feel plainly that my system is preparing for dissolution in one of three ways: one by hemorrhage; one by strangulation; and the third by exhaustion. The first and second are liable to come at any moment to relieve me of my earthly sufferings. The time of the third can be computed with almost mathematical certainty. With an increase in daily food, I have fallen off in weight and strength very rapidly in the past two weeks. There cannot be hope of going far beyond this period. All my physicians, or any number of them can do for me now, is to make my burden of pain as light as possible. I do not want any physician but yourself, but I tell you, so that if you are unwilling to have me go without consultation with other professional men, you can send for them. I dread them, however, knowing that it means another desperate effort to save me, and more suffering.[25]

A few days later, with heat oppressing the mountains, Grant began to fail. DEATH APPARENTLY NEAR, the *Times* proclaimed on July 22. GEN. GRANT MUCH WORSE, the *Tribune* echoed. During that day and the next he remained inside, cut off from visitors, heavily sedated with brandy and morphine, fanned constantly by his two male nurses. Perhaps aware that the end was near, he asked to be taken from his easy chairs and placed in bed. The *Times* described the scene: "General Grant has lost his desire to live. His intense discomfort has brought about this condition. As the air that he takes with every breath passes through the inflamed growths in his throat, it is almost as if a dull saw were hacking away at his flesh, and most intense pain follows."[26]

Death came at last at 8:08 on the morning of July 23. According to Dr. Douglas, who took notes, it arrived undramatically after a night during which Grant—speechless and sedated—slowly lost his struggle to live. "The breathing," Douglas wrote, "each instant became feebler and feebler, and soon ceased altogether. There was no expiring sigh. Life passed away so quietly, so peacefully, that, to be sure it had terminated, we waited a minute."[27]

American newspapers devoted enormous amounts of space to the story of his death. Many of the stories were given heavy black borders. GEN. GRANT'S STRUGGLE OVER, the *Tribune* proclaimed, observing that it had been nine months since Grant had first seen Dr. Douglas and been told he had epithelioma. During this time there had "hardly been a moment" when Grant had been "free from the pain that always accompanies cancer."[28] The *Tribune* wrung from the occasion every bit of melodrama it could. As Grant lay dying, it reported, beams of early morning light "trickled through the pine trees" into the room, and fixed on a picture of the "sad face of Lincoln" hanging on the wall above the patient's bed. "As the sun rose higher in the heavens, the beams of light moved slowly downward, and at the moment when the last tinge of sunlight slipped off the picture the spirit of the great commander left its tenement of clay and took its flight to that unknown country, the dwelling place of the soul."[29]

1

Cancerphobia in the Late Nineteenth Century

GRANT'S CONTEMPORARIES were fascinated by death and the macabre, and they relished the drama surrounding the dying of the famous. How much of the inflated journalism the public read cannot be estimated, nor can one assume that the reporters' views exactly reflected popular opinions. Still, no other case of cancer received greater coverage. From that coverage—the words used, the assumptions made, the things left unsaid—it is possible to explore in some depth the cultural meaning of cancer in late-nineteenth-century America.

Medically speaking, the meaning of cancer was agreed upon by most informed doctors and lay people in the 1880s, who knew that cancer was as old as the origins of multicellular evolution. Ancient Egyptian papyri had referred to the disease, and sarcomas, cancers originating in connective tissues or bones, had been found in mummies. The word can be traced to Hippocrates, who in the fifth century B.C. likened the long, distended veins radiating from lumps in the breast to crabs—*karkinoma* in Greek, *cancer* in Latin. The term seemed especially apt to later commentators, who emphasized that cancers, like crabs, crept along, eating away at the flesh.[1]

To the ancients, as to those who were to battle the disease for centuries thereafter, cancers were indeed like crabs: voracious, insidious, and relentless. They responded to no ready remedies. Hippocrates all but threw up his hands in despair, counseling against heroic therapy. "It is better," he advised, "not to apply any treatment in cases of occult [hidden] cancer; for if treated, the patients die quickly; but if not treated, they hold out for a long time."

Other ancient physicians performed surgery, including amputation of the female breast, but like Hippocrates they recognized that cancer was a disease of runaway growth: unless excised very early it was virtually certain to reappear. Some operations, indeed, might hasten the spreading that they knew was basic to the disease. Celsus, a renowned Roman doctor of the first century A.D., offered a widely held medical view: "only the beginning of a cancer admits of a cure; but when 'tis settled and confirmed, 'tis incurable and must die under a cold sweat."[2]

Even in Hippocrates's time several other things were known about the disease: it usually invaded adjacent tissue or metastasized to distant sites; it was exceedingly difficult to treat unless detected very early, which was very hard to do; surgery, while useless or worse in advanced cases, was probably the only reliable therapy for tumors in their early stages. Most orthodox physicians in Grant's time agreed with all these conclusions.

The ancients had also emphasized that cancer posed a special threat to women. Though reliable statistics did not exist to substantiate this perception, it was clear that the disease often struck at the breasts, uteri, and other internal organs of females. For women, indeed, the disease was not only medically lethal but also emotionally devastating. Ashamed, embarrassed, in their minds de-sexed, women with such forms of cancer often clung desperately to their awful secret. In doing so they heightened a virtual conspiracy of silence that surrounded the disease throughout history.

By the 1880s informed people knew more about cancer. They dimly understood, first of all, that environmental conditions and personal habits were associated with some forms of cancer. As early as 1700 the Italian Bernardino Ramazzini had observed an unusually high incidence of breast cancer among nuns. "You seldom find," he wrote, "a convent that does not harbor this accursed pest, cancer, within its walls."[3] He also thought that workers in some occupations were especially prone. "Various and manifold," he said, "is the harvest of diseases reaped by certain workers from the crafts that they pursue. All the profit that they get is fatal injury to their health."[4] Better known to American doc-

These developments in bacteriology were exciting, front-page news. They did much to destroy earlier notions about the sources of infectious disease—among which had been the belief that epidemics stemmed from "miasma" emanating from decaying organic matter. The germ theory also encouraged surgeons to use antiseptic procedures while operating. By the late 1880s American physicians were widely employing the antiseptic methods originally developed by the English surgeon Joseph Lister in the late 1860s. In the 1890s and 1900s surgeons adopted aseptic techniques—first the sterilization of instruments, then the use of surgical gloves and gowns, then the more or less complete sterilization of operating rooms. Gone by then were the days of surgeons wearing street clothes in operating rooms and probing incisions with germ-covered fingers. The possibilities for successful cancer surgery were obviously much enchanced.[14]

An understanding of cells and gradual acceptance of the germ theory made yet another contribution to the study of diseases in general and of cancer in particular: the idea that illnesses had specific etiologies, or causes. Earlier in the nineteenth century most doctors and patients had believed differently. Individuals, they thought, were specially "predisposed" to develop particular ailments, and most diseases were constitutional. Illness stemmed from general breakdown in the necessary balance between an individual's body and the environment. Recovery depended on restoring the balance—by administering drugs, herbs, or bleeding or by adopting public-health measures to improve the environment. As the century progressed and physicians came to reject heroic therapies such as bleeding and purging, some of the many competing medical sects emphasized the virtue of letting sick people alone and allowing nature to work its course. Other sects stressed the importance of proper regimens and diets that might counter an individual's predisposition to illness and promote equilibrium. By the late 1880s, however, most informed physicians assumed that diseases had local, observable mechanisms and specific etiologies.[15] By no means fully accepted at the time of Grant's illness—many physicians still doubted monocausal explanations for such apparently constitutional ailments as tuberculosis—this new view was nonetheless ascendant. It was to form a bedrock for doctors' claims to specialized expertise in coming years.

Many people were later to complain bitterly that the notion of specific etiology led to an increasingly specialized medical profession, to reliance on impersonal medical technology, and—most lamentably—to the neglect of methods, including public-health reforms, for prevention of diseases. Society, they insisted, was becoming "medicalized," doctors worshipped, the environment ignored. Many diseases stemmed not from identifiable single causes, they said, but from constellations of circumstances requiring complex, sometimes nonmedical responses.[16] But arguments like these were not heard in the 1880s and 1890s, when one dramatic breakthrough after another—the identification of germs, the introduction of new surgical techniques, the greater control of infection, indeed the potential eradication of the bane of infectious diseases—began to revolutionize the standing of doctors in American culture.

ALTHOUGH PROGRESS in scientific medicine was to prove considerable after 1885, it was slow to be reflected in the practice of ordinary doctors or to undermine long-held popular notions about diseases. In fact, it was still widely believed at the time that doctors did not know what they were doing. Statements to that effect had rung like a litany throughout the nineteenth century. Jacob Bigelow, a prominent doctor at Harvard, conceded in the 1830s that the "amount of death and disaster in the world would be less, if all disease were left to itself." At the same time Dr. Oliver Wendell Holmes added, "if the whole *materia medica,* as now used, could be sunk to the bottom of the sea, it would be better for mankind—and all the worse for the fishes." Though most people of means consulted physicians when they fell sick, many Americans shared the popular wisdom that there was a considerable difference between a good doctor and a bad one, but hardly any difference between a good doctor and none at all.[17]

Some of this skepticism—indeed hostility—stemmed from a Jacksonian distrust of elites and of claims for expertise. But it derived also from the accurate perceptions of patients. They knew from often bitter experience that physicians were poorly educated, if at all; that the varied sects to which they gave allegiance warred loudly among one another; that many doctors charged high fees; that medical "cures" were sometimes worse than the diseases; and that the majority knew almost nothing of contemporary developments in medical science.[18]

Americans in the 1880s were especially doubtful about surgery. With the widespread use of asepsis a few years in the future, patients understandably recoiled from the often radical cutting, painful cauterizing, and infections associated with the operating table. As one harsh critic noted later, surgery before 1900 "was hardly an asset to the patients; it speeded their deaths. They were like guinea pigs sacrificed for the benefit of future patients." Wise doctors, indeed, simply refused to tackle operations involving many internal organs. A leading practitioner noted in the 1890s that "even in the eighties *noli me tangere* [do not touch me] was written large on the head, chest, and abdomen, and their contained organs were still held as sanctuaries which no one dared to open with unhallowed hands."[19]

The sad state of surgery was especially well known to Americans in the 1880s as a result of the shooting on July 2, 1881, of President James Garfield. A number of prominent physicians probed for the lodged bullet with their fingers, virtually guaranteeing the development of infection. Lacking the skill to cut safely into the lung area, they simply hoped the wound would heal. Instead, the wound continued to fester and to "discharge healthy pus," at which point the doctors decided to make incisions so as to help the drainage. Their efforts were in vain, and President Garfield died on September 19, more than two months after the shooting.[20] The scandal caused by this most public of medical incompetencies, which did much to besmirch an already widely discredited medical fraternity, helps explain the aggressiveness of the press with regard to Grant's ailment three-and-a-half years later.

The ordinary practitioner, of course, made little pretense of expertise in surgery or in other specialties. Chances were that he had a very brief medical education. He was likely to have a fuzzy view at best of the causes of illnesses and to be able to diagnose only the simplest of ailments. His prescriptions, mainly for sore throats, fevers, coughs, and diarrheas, depended heavily on sugar pills and other placebos. Aspirin was just beginning to be widely prescribed. For some high fevers he resorted to quinine. Narcotics such as opium and morphine were his main weapons against acute pain, insomnia, and diarrhea. By the 1890s Americans were using half a million pounds of crude opium per year.[21]

Nothing more clearly revealed the popular fear of doctors in that era than the ubiquity of patent medicines and of unorthodox healers—or quacks, as regular practitioners called them.[22] There was no distinction in the 1880s between prescription and over-the-counter drugs; anyone could go to a pharmacy and buy opium. Newspapers and magazines depended heavily on ads for self-dosage. While the front pages of the papers were carrying melodramatic bulletins about Grant's sickness, the inside columns were full of claims for patent medicines. Especially boosted were "cathartic pills," "cocaine tablets—for hay fever," "pillow inhalers" featuring "vapors" against "catarrh, asthma, and consumption," and "effervescent seltzer aperients" for use against "chronic constipation." Other ads asserted the virtues of sodium hypochlorite for treatment of cholera, diphtheria, fevers, and malaria; "R. R. R.—Radway's Ready Relief—A CURE FOR ALL BOWEL COMPLAINTS"; and "Hard's Sarsparilla," which could relieve that "extreme tired feeling . . . humors will be expelled from the blood."[23]

Millions of Americans in the late nineteenth century were too poorly educated to read the ads, let alone one of the many books recommending home cures. For them the antidote to sickness was fortitude, religious faith, or perhaps a folk remedy. Some people wound a string about a dead man's finger and then tied the string to the tumor needing treatment. Others held that the dead person's hand itself should be placed on the growth, which would then rot away; still others said that a dead mole or toad ought to be applied. European remedies carried to America called for using crows' feet, crude brimstone, or white arsenic. One cure advised a "broth of crayfish boiled in asses' milk drunk five days successively, and this course repeated seven times." Another prescribed "the head of a puppy a month old, cut off and dried and powdered, mixed with honey, and laid on an ulcerous cancer."[24] Wearing one's clothes inside out, walking backwards, throwing things over the shoulder, and cutting one's fingernails on a Friday during a waning moon were also among the hundreds of contemporary folk practices and rituals used against cancer. Many of these remedies, setting one malignant force to battle another, were psychologically plausible and reassuring. The wide extent to which they were practiced revealed the existence of what might be called a considerable though amorphous cancer counterculture.[25]

Unorthodox cancer cures flourished also because many Americans were afraid to confront the reality of the disease. To consult a doctor about a lump or discharge was to risk an unpleasant diagnosis—and possibly surgery. The promise of relief from pain was then and always one of the strongest drawing cards of unorthodox practitioners. Some people shrank from consulting physicians because they did not want anyone to know they had the disease. They were sure that cancer was unmentionable—perhaps contagious, perhaps hereditary, surely insidious and fatal. Better to face one's fate in private, or to treat the illness oneself with potions available by mail or vendor.

For all these reasons cancer "cures" had always supported a brisk business. Many treatments, reflecting the power of religious beliefs in the nineteenth century, relied on the laying on of hands by faith healers. Others were chemicals of one kind or another. In 1748 the House of Burgesses in Virginia awarded a woman a prize of one hundred pounds for her "receipt for curing cancers," a remedy which featured a mix of garden sorrel, celandine, and the "inner bark of a persimon from the south side of a tree."[26]

Leeches, sandalwood, and turpentine, the virtues of which had been celebrated since the time of Galen, were hailed as panaceas; ointments, salves, and caustics that claimed to eat away surface tumors were especially popular. Among the many patent medicine vendors of the 1800s was John D. Rockefeller's father, whose handbills read, "Dr. William A. Rockefeller, the Celebrated Cancer Specialist. Here for One Day Only. All Cases of Cancer Cured unless too far gone and then they can be greatly benefitted." His remedy was a liquid concoction that sold for up to twenty-five dollars a bottle.[27]

Unorthodox healers pushed their way almost to the bedside of Grant himself. The stranger who accosted him on the porch at Mount McGregor was not the only one who tried to cash in on the general's distress. On the day after Grant's death, amid the columns of print devoted to the great hero's life, the newspapers carried an ad for "Swift's Specific." The ad featured a testimonial from a Mrs. Mary Comer, who maintained that the nostrum had cured an awful cancer of the mouth that had proved resistant to the efforts of "six or seven of the best physicians of the country." Their failure had transformed her from a "hearty, robust woman of 150 pounds . . . to a mere frame of skin and bones, almost unable to turn myself in bed." Finally, after two-and-a-half years of suffering, she found Swift's Specific, whereupon she gained fifty pounds and was able to walk again. The end of the ad left no one in doubt that Grant's doctors had failed. "CANCER OF TONGUE," it proclaimed, "A CASE RESEMBLING THAT OF GEN. GRANT."[28]

WITH MEDICAL SCIENCE in such an uncertain and defensive state, the topic of cancer was riddled with controversy and bewilderment in the 1880s and 1890s. At the root of the bewilderment was one intractable reality—scientists did not know how or why cancer cells broke loose on their destructive paths. Samuel Gross, a leading Philadelphia surgeon who wrote of his experiences at mid-century, confessed his ignorance with admirable candor: "all we know, with any degree of certainty, is, that we know nothing."[29] Some writers hypothesized that cancer cells were the offspring of normal cells, others that they were *sui generis.* A few experts thought that cancer cells began as imperfections in the embryo, others that they developed only later. But the careful writers, like Gross, admitted that answers to the basic biological questions—what were cancer cells, and how did they develop?—were simply beyond the capacity of contemporary medical science.

One impediment to researchers was the paucity of reliable information. In most instances of death caused by disease attending doctors did not ask for autopsies but attributed the death to vague causes, such as "old age." Even if they suspected cancer, they were often begged by surviving relatives to list on the death certificate another, less stigmatizing cause. Moreover, pathologists still had far to go in the demanding task of classifying tumors. For these reasons it was difficult for people of Grant's generation to know if the disease was becoming more widespread or to reach intelligent conclusions about the origins of the illness in individual patients.

A lack of research facilities paralleled the dearth of clinical resources. About the time Grant first felt symptoms of his cancer in May 1884, workmen laid the cornerstone for the New York Cancer Hospital at 106th Street and Central Park West, the first such specialized hospital in America. (The first in the world is thought to have been founded in Rheims, France, in 1740; Middlesex Hospital in London, beginning in 1792, had special cancer wards). In the 1880s there were no special laboratories for medical research in the United States, and no governmental support—local, state, or national—for biological scientists. When the *Boston Medical and Surgical Journal* attempted to arouse interest in cancer research in 1881, by sponsoring a competition awarding one thousand dollars for the best essay on the "Cure for Malignant Disease," it received only three entries. Appalled, the journal reopened the competition in 1882 and allowed entrants extra time to submit their ideas. No one turned in a creditable essay, a fact that the journal attributed sadly to the "comparative barrenness of American researchers in the field of medical science."[30]

With cancer research in disorder, the field was wide open for the promulgation of theories. One of these was the notion that germs caused cancer. Indeed, the search for such organisms as the source of the disease created a stir during the heyday of microbiology in the late 1880s and early 1890s. As one historian later observed, it "appeared to have been a question, not so much as to the infectious origin of cancer, but rather as to which of the many parasites was the real causative agent."[31] Pursuing this line of research, scientists produced a considerable literature dealing with parasites, viruses, bacilli, molds, and protozoa.

A logical corollary of the germ theory was the notion that cancer might be contagious. This ancient idea relied partly on the belief in "cancer streets," "villages," and "families." Napoleon was supposed to have belonged to one such family. Many people thought that cancer was related to venereal disease and that victims should be barred from hospitals. When Mr. and Mrs. John Jacob Astor tried to give the Woman's Hospital of New York a cancer pavilion in 1884, their offer was coolly received, in part because hospital board members thought the malady was incurable, but also because they were frightened of having cancer patients in the same facility with other women. "Cancer may not be contagious," one trustee was supposed to have said, "but the name is." Another demanded to know "whether or not cancer is contagious, or infectious, or could injuriously affect patients in other pavilions." Irritated, the Astors decided to set up a new facility for cancer patients. Thus did fear of contagion help give birth to the nation's first cancer hospital, which opened—for women only—in 1887.[32] Among the doctors on its original staff were three of Grant's physicians, including Dr. George Shrady.

Another contemporary theory stressed the role of heredity. Many general practitioners simply assumed that the illness was transmitted from one generation to the next. Their first question of patients was, "Is there cancer in your family?" Told no, physicians breathed a sigh of relief: chances were, they assured patients, that cancer was not the problem. There was much commonsense evidence to refute such notions. Cancer, after all, appeared to strike randomly.[33] Like the contagion theory, however, hereditarian hypotheses persisted, particularly in the popular mind. The durability of both notions revealed the power of hereditarian ideas in the age of Darwin and the extent of popular alarm about contagion in an era when infectious diseases—tuberculosis, cholera, yellow fever—often ran rampant. It attested also to the lack of consensus behind any other theory. So long as cancer remained a mystery, theories must proliferate.[34]

Still another hypothesis attributed cancer to the rise of industrial civilization. Advocates of this common view, like hydropathists and other sectarian medical practitioners earlier in the century, drew upon a long tradition in America of holistic ideas about health. Urban civilization, they thought, destroyed the all-important balance between human beings and their "natural" environments, thereby causing a host of ailments, cancer among them. Proponents of such ideas differed, often sharply, among themselves. Many, however, emphasized that people were losing touch with the rugged virtues necessary for good health. Americans, they said, were stuffing themselves with rich foods and falling victim to luxurious living. These alarmists argued that cancer did not afflict primitive societies. "Luxurious living," one physician wrote, "and particularly excess in animal food, increases the waste products of the body, and, if coupled with insufficient exercise, the waste products are retained in the system and have a tendency to produce abnormal growths."[35]

Intimately related to this view was another blaming cancer on emotional or mental stress. This general idea, too, was not new. Galen had seen cancer on the increase among "melancholy" women ("black bile" is the translation for the Greek *melan chole*). An early definition (1601) added that "cancer is a swelling or some coming of *melancholy* blood, about which the veins appeare of a black or swert colour spread in the manner of a creifish claws."[36] Sir Astley Cooper emphasized in 1826 that carcinoma of the rectum frequently followed mental distress and that breast cancer evolved from grief or anxiety. A few years later the eminent British authority Walter Walsh wrote that cancer often derived from the "influence of mental misery, sudden reverses of fortune, and habitual gloomings of the temper on the disposition of carcinomatous matter. If systematic writers can be credited, these constitute the most powerful cause of the disease."[37]

Advocates of the stress hypothesis were elaborating on the increasingly popular view that urban, industrial life, carrying with it class conflict and social misery, threatened not only the peace and future of the Republic but also the health of its citizens. Many of the most devastating nineteenth-century illnesses—tuberculosis, typhus, cholera, typhoid—indeed flourished amid the dirt, pollution, and poor nutrition of slums.[38] Other ailments, notably the apparently epidemic rise of neurasthenia and other forms of mental illness, also seemed closely linked to the pressures of contemporary urban civilization. Americans who singled out civilization and stress as the villains believed that human beings possessed only a finite amount of energy, much of which could be drained as a result of excessive mental or emotional effort.[39]

Contemporary physicians who published their notes on cancer patients also began to emphasize the baneful role of stress. One was Willard Parker of New York, who studied 397 cases of breast cancer and in 1885 related them to "mental care, affliction or sorrow." Parker thought that there was a close physiological connection between surface cells and the ends of nerve fibers; if the nervous system went awry, it could not monitor epithelial cells, which then veered off in an "abnormal direction." He concluded that "great mental depression, particularly grief, induces a predisposition to such a disease as cancer, or becomes an exciting cause under circumstances where the predisposition had already been acquired."[40]

The writings of Sir Herbert Snow were also known to some American doctors of the 1880s. After interviewing 250 cancer patients in a London hospital, Snow concluded that the disease stemmed from flaws in the nervous system. Malignant tumors of the breast and uterus, he said, were likely to afflict women who had recently lost a close relative. Snow admitted that his evidence was sketchy—it was based entirely on the interviews—but he nonetheless insisted that stress explained why cancer was more prevalent among nervous women, why it was more common in cities than in the country, and why it afflicted older people more than the young.[41]

The stress hypothesis rested on still other broad suppositions. Just as some Americans continued to think that disease stemmed from a breakdown in the relationship between body and environment, they also tended to believe in a vital dependence of each part of the body on all other parts. A distracted mind could curdle the stomach, and an upset stomach could disturb the mind.[42] It was further thought that individuals were responsible for their own health. If a person fell sick, it was his or her own fault. This tendency to "blame the victim"—to stigmatize the sick—can be identified throughout the cultural history of cancer in modern America.

Later researchers were to support various versions of stress theories. Holists have insisted that it is arbitrary to separate body and mind and, more specifically, that the central nervous system may control the immune system, which in turn may affect cancer. Many diseases, they have added, are not mainly local in origin but are instead systemic.[43] But neither in the 1880s nor later were researchers able to offer convincing validation of the effects of stress and other emotional states in causing cancer. Many who supported the stress theory, like those who emphasized contagion, heredity, and civilization, were expressing cultural concerns rather than experimentally verifiable theories. Like other frightened Americans in the new urban age, they feared that the rise of industrial civilization was unraveling the bonds of society, prompting emotional stress and trauma and harming the physical well-being of the citizenry. Cancer, a mysteriously invasive disease of runaway growth, seemed in the human body to be a metaphor for the fate of industrial society at large.[44]

WHILE THESE IDEAS enjoyed some popular support in the late 1800s, none (save the germ theory) generated much enthusiasm in orthodox medical circles. Most regular physicians resisted grand hypotheses and holistic theories. They rejected strictly environmental or psychological models of illness, seeking instead local, observable physical causes and effects. Their conclusion, following Virchow, was that "irritation" in some way provoked not only cancer, but also other ailments for which physicians had no certain explanations.

To some doctors, like Parker, irritation could mean almost anything, including blows to the body or even chafing from the tight stays and dresses of the time, which exerted "habitual pressure" and caused "injury to the mammary gland" that could turn malignant.[45] Most, like Snow, dismissed the idea that blows caused cancer—this was always a notion more popular with the public than with physicians—and argued that the "exciting" (as opposed to "predisposing") cause of cancer was "always some continued mechanical irritant." Snow and many of his contemporaries held that syphilitic warts and ulcers were easily irritated and were "almost always sure to result in malignant disease." They warned especially of the dangers of placing sharp objects, such as pipes, in the mouth and of the potentially cancerous irritation caused by jagged teeth.[46]

These doctors also cautioned against taking snuff and excessive smoking, but not because they thought these habits caused cancer of the lung or any of the multitude of ailments, including heart disease and emphysema, later associated with tobacco. At that time some three-fifths of known cancer victims were women, the vast majority of whom did not smoke, and cancer of the lung was virtually an unknown disease. Nor did doctors express much alarm about smoke inhalation: most smokers before 1900 used pipes or cigars. It was not until 1884 that W. Duke and Sons perfected the Bonsack cigarette-making machine and revolutionized the smoking habits of millions of Americans.[47]

Rather, the doctors were concerned about the effect of smoking on accessible organs, especially the tongue, the mouth, and the throat. Pipes, they thought, rubbed against and irritated the tender skin of the mouth. The searing heat of smoking, whether of cigars or pipes, damaged the mouth and caused cancer. A hostility to smoking was shared by many Americans at the time. The editor Horace Greeley (who had run for the presidency against Grant in 1872) defined a cigar as a "fire at one end and a fool at the other."[48] Twain, a heavy smoker, was well aware of contemporary medical views and was sure that cigars were the ruination of Grant. Even Dr. Douglas, while emphasizing the role of emotional stress, stated publicly in March that "smoking was the exciting cause" of Grant's cancer, "though there have been many contributing causes since."[49]

Not all medical authorities subscribed to this hypothesis. Dr. Frank Abbott, who extracted two of Grant's teeth in late 1884, responded in April that "every anti-tobacco crank in the country" had jumped to the conclusion that the "disease that is slowly but surely eating out the life of the most distinguished man of his age is the direct fruit of the cigar." On the contrary, Abbott said, "tobacco probably had little or nothing to do with the origin of the tumor." He attributed the "constant irritation" that caused Grant's troubles to the "rough and ragged surfaces of a broken tooth."[50]

As Grant weakened, however, less was heard about his teeth, stress, or other causes. The villain, at least in the eyes of his doctors, was the constant irritation caused by tobacco. No one asserted this opinion more emphatically than Dr. Shrady, who in summarizing medical findings a week after Grant's death stated that epithelioma

> as a rule starts from local irritation, and unlike other forms of cancer, is not dependent upon hereditary predisposition to the disease. There must, however, aside from this, be a latent tendency toward cancerous troubles which is more pronounced in some individuals than in others . . . It is quite probable that the irritation of smoking was the

> active cause of the cancer in General Grant's case, or, at least, it is fair to presume that he would not have had the disease if his habit had not been carried to excess. This assumption is made in the face of the fact that, of the thousands who smoke, but a very small proportion suffer from the disease.[51]

AMID THE PROLIFERATION of theories about cancer there was inevitably an equally large supply of competing therapies. Most general practitioners had been told little or nothing about the malady during their brief medical educations. They were unable to diagnose the disease when it afflicted internal organs or to determine whether externally visible lumps were benign or malignant. If they suspected cancer, they often waited for weeks or months to be sure, meanwhile doing little or nothing for it. Ulcerating skin diseases—whether cancerous or otherwise—were sometimes burned or scraped off. Parker prescribed leeching and a compound of lead iodide for one woman.[52] Some treatments, by quacks as well as by orthodox physicians, were extraordinarily painful and disfiguring. It was no wonder that anything promising relief from pain proved popular, or that a popular notion about cancer—"the treatment is as bad as the disease"—was already widespread.[53]

Those few doctors who made an effort to study cancer, however, were virtually unanimous—then and for many years thereafter—in their preferred treatment: detection as early as possible, followed immediately by surgery to cut away accessible external growths. For cancers discovered late or those affecting most internal organs, they continued to counsel in Hippocratic terms: leave the tumor alone. But surgery, where warranted, ought to be as thorough—as "radical"—as possible, so as to get out all the tumors in time. Snow favored the "old method of searing off the breast with a red-hot knife."[54] Though frightened, most educated Americans did not doubt the wisdom of surgical treatment. The fear of metastasis, central to popular perceptions of the disease, surfaced again and again, not only in medical discussions but also in the everyday discourse of American life. In 1894 the Socialist leader Eugene Debs, urging radical change in the United States, called forth an appropriate metaphor: "You can cover [injustice] with a poultice, but the cancer continues to spread. You must apply the knife and root it out if you expect relief."[55]

It was one thing to advise early diagnosis of cancer, however, and quite another to succeed in detecting it. Often deep and slow-growing and painless in the early stages, cancers could be extremely difficult to see or to feel. And people who suspected cancer tended to procrastinate before consulting a doctor. Grant, awaiting the return from vacation of his personal physician, wasted four months before seeing a competent specialist. Even knowledgeable physicians rarely had the chance to detect cancer early or to prevent its spread. Early detection, which was to become a litany of the medical profession in the twentieth century—one of many historical continuities surrounding the illness—remained the goal, not the reality for the vast majority of patients.

Nor was surgery a welcome prospect to the patient of 1885. Surgeons who bothered to look at journals could read an unusually thorough statistical account of the results of surgery for breast cancer. The world-renowned Albert Christian Theodor Billroth of Vienna, reporting on the outcome of 170 operations that he had performed between 1867 and 1876, attempted to show that cancer, contrary to the opinions of doomsayers, could in fact be cured with the knife. But what statistics! Only 4.7 percent of the women were alive three years later.[56]

Confronted with such odds—and with failure after failure in their own practice—most physicians did not place much faith in surgery. They agreed with Sir James Paget, who advised, "I will not say such a thing as cure is impossible, but it is so highly improbable that a hope of this occurring in any single instance cannot be reasonably entertained." Another expert, Charles Childe, writing in 1906, added that "some of the older surgeons of even the present time say they have never seen a case of cure of cancer." Referring to an "eminent London surgeon" who twenty years earlier had admitted, "I never use the word cancer to my patient," Childe wrote: "How eloquent of the attitude of the medical profession towards this disease less than a generation ago! Hopeless in the eyes of the patient; hopeless in the eyes of the surgeon; afraid even to use the word."[57]

GRANT'S TREATMENT, by his doctors and by the press, suggests that Childe's retrospective judgment on medicine in the 1880s was slightly exaggerated. It was not true, for instance, that everyone was afraid to use the word. Newspaper accounts of Grant's health mentioned cancer from time to time and were almost brutally graphic in describing its effects. The *Tribune* reported in March that "a genuine case of malignant cancer is incurable, and sooner or later will prove fatal . . . this is the situation in the case of General Grant."[58] Shrady was pleased to see this relative openness in the press. Thanks to the coverage, he said, "the terms epithelioma, malignancy, and infiltration will be as well understood as in former times were those of suppuration, pus-track, and bullet-cysts."[59]

But for the most part Childe described accurately the fear inspired by the disease. Public use of the word remained relatively rare, and newspapers ordinarily employed such euphemisms as "long illness" in their obituaries. Doctors, too, were reticent. Douglas admitted that even when pressed by Grant he "avoided the use of the word 'Cancer.'" Three months later, Douglas informed the press that Grant did not have cancer but an "inflammation of the epithelial membrane of the mouth."[60]

The reasons for these fearful reactions were both powerful and of long standing. Cancer, doctors recognized, caricatured life itself. A disease of runaway growth, it mimicked normal development, as if in some cruel mockery of human pretensions. Obscure in origin and progression, it seemed as omnipresent and as uncontrollable as other broad and impersonal forces, such as industrialization and bureaucracy, which also challenged the natural order. Then and later fear of cancer reflected a range of broader social concerns. Cancer, moreover, was especially humbling to physicians who were claiming the skill to define the causes and mechanisms of disease. The mystery of cancer was infuriatingly to refute the more grandiose claims of modern medicine and to confirm the inevitability of human suffering.

More directly, fears of the disease stemmed from the belief by doctors and laymen alike that it was an alien and living invader that gave little or no warning before "eating" into people. Unlike most infectious diseases, it apparently assaulted at random, caring not whether the victim was rich or poor, male or female, black or white, fit or unfit. There seemed to be nothing one could do to prevent it. And when it came, it stayed, "lurking" as an evil and surreptitious monster on the prowl. Even when it seemed to be cured, it was likely to come back. Cancer, in fact, was relentless, a virtual death sentence. "There is, perhaps, no disease," one authority wrote in 1853, "which has carried off its victims with more unerring certainty than cancer. For centuries it has been the dread of the human race . . . Its distinctive character has rendered its very name significant of malignancy; the ancient leprosy could scarcely have been regarded with more terror."[61]

The disease was also feared for its "sinister" aspect. Cancer, people thought, tore at the flesh, often ravaging one's private organs and leaving victims feeling dirty, betrayed by their bodies, without control over themselves. It was a "fire" burning, an "army" invading, a "criminal" attacking. Many Americans feared that bumps, bruises, and sores could develop into cancer. Some worried that tumors, like venereal disease, stemmed from sinful sexual activity or some other form of misbehavior. Popular notions such as these helped account for the guilt and isolation felt by many patients and for the special stigma often assigned to victims, especially women.

Above all, people imagined cancers to be living, moving creatures in themselves—uninvited beasts which surreptitiously ganged up on the body. One writer likened cancer to a "newcomer" arriving at the family dinner table. It began by eating "all the food and finally the family itself. It starts very quietly, is small at first, but gradually grows until it destroys the very tissues that feed it." Rudyard Kipling, writing in 1893, similarly described the disease: "Cancer the Crab lies so still that you might think he was asleep if you did not see the ceaseless play and winnowing motion of the feathery branches round his mouth. That movement never ceases. It is like the eating of a smothering fire into rotten timber in that it is noiseless and without haste."[62]

Two changes in attitude in the late nineteenth century may have reinforced these fears. One was the sense that cancer was becoming a more common cause of death. Whether this was so could not be proved, for reliable mortality statistics on the disease did not exist until after 1900. Why cancer might be spreading was much debated; some blamed urban civilization, while others pointed out that as longevity increased so too would ailments that strike the elderly, such as cancer. But doctors and others frequently published estimates of mortality from various diseases, and all asserted that cancer, while far behind tuberculosis, pneumonia, and other infectious diseases as a cause of death, was becoming an even greater threat. Later statistics lent some tentative support to these suppositions: cancer annually may have killed some 50 people per 100,000 population in the 1880s, as compared with perhaps only 15 or 20 per 100,000 in the 1840s. It caused the death in 1900 of more than 64 Americans per 100,000 population—or 48,000 people—the eighth leading cause of death in the United States.[63] Many more people suffered from the disease at any particular time. By the turn of the century many millions of adult Americans either developed cancer at some point in their lives or (much more commonly) knew someone who did.

The second change in attitude concerned expectations about old age and death. Until the nineteenth century most Americans fatalistically accepted illness, pain, and early death as unavoidable aspects of human existence. Life-threatening diseases struck without warning or favor and had to be accepted as the will of God or of fate. Sometimes death was welcomed as a deliverance from worldly suffering. By the late 1800s, however, many developments were slowly altering the resignation with which people faced illness and death. Narcotics and analgesics could prevent extreme pain. Improved diets and sanitation were extending the span and the quality of life. Religious ideas counseling acceptance of early death were losing hold. Perhaps most important, the ever larger middle classes were enjoying amenities that softened the struggle for daily existence, thereby making life all the more cherished. Amid these developments death more loudly announced its sting. To many people it became something dirty and disgusting—a fate to be dreaded and denied. Cancer, which often killed slowly, "wasting" its victims, aroused particular apprehension. No contemporary malady seemed a more certain sentence of death.[64]

The denial of death was especially strong in the United States, land of perceived opportunity, technological progress, and economic growth. It manifested a distinctively American quest for good health, which became central to the good life. It helped account for many responses to cancer in the United States during the twentieth century, including a readiness to entertain promises of "magic bullets" and to spare no financial resources in the attempt to find a cure. In no other nation have cancerphobia and "wars" against cancer been more pronounced than in the United States.

ALTHOUGH fear of the disease was pervasive, in two ways it was relatively restrained—less extreme, for example, than it was to become in the middle decades of the twentieth century. First, for all its frightening aspects, cancer did not excite hysteria about epidemics. Unlike scarlet fever and diphtheria, it did not take aim primarily at children or young people: on the contrary, it was known as an older person's ailment. Cancer patients, while often shunned and stigmatized, did not inspire the same loathing or panic that had systematically isolated victims of leprosy, the plague, and other repulsive, communicable diseases.[65]

To many, in fact, cancer aroused less dread than tuberculosis. The "great destroyer" or "white plague," as tuberculosis was called, resembled cancer in some ways: its origin was mysterious; it appeared to start in one place before creeping through other healthy organs; it "consumed" people and slowly killed them. Worst of all, tuberculosis was then the greatest killer in Western civilization, especially of the poor and undernourished living in industrial slums. In 1900 it killed some 200 Americans per 100,000 population, or more than three times the number thought to be claimed by cancer. It tended to afflict young and middle-aged people. It had no known medical cure—Koch had found the bacillus, but failed to discover a cure for it—and, after Koch, it was understood to be contagious. People with advanced cases of the malady were pale, emaciated, short of breath, racked with coughing. Easily recognized, they were feared and shunned as "lungers." Even in 1905 one newspaper commented on the "unfounded and often hysterical fear" and the "insane dread" that people had of the disease. A historian added later that "social taboos against discussing, much less admitting to having tuberculosis were almost unbelievable—among the lower classes much stronger than Victorian resistances against sex."[66]

The second restraint on fear of cancer in the 1880s and 1890s was the sense that it was apparently a random killer. Most people free from cancer dreaded the illness in the abstract, but had no special reason to expect that they would get it—at least not until old age. Denying that they might develop the disease, they could relegate fear of it to the fringes of their day-to-day consciousness. This capacity for denial was to remain a powerful psychological defense.

Patients and their families of course had no such options. For them cancer was indeed a dread disease which stripped away one's defenses and exposed all concerned to a wide range of emotions—rage, depression, guilt, self-pity, loneliness, and resignation.[67] But many patients maintained a courageous and even down-to-earth acceptance of their fate. Grant was but the most public of the brave; learning that he was ill, he recognized that he had two tasks to do—to write and to die. He did both well.

There were thousands more who responded as Grant did. Dr. Childe told of one fifty-year-old woman who had been bleeding irregularly for three or four months. Advised to have a special examination, she demurred. When the doctors told her elliptically that postponement of the test might be a "question of life or death," she guessed their meaning and replied abruptly, "Well, if it is cancer, nothing can be done for me. I would rather not know it." Alice James, sister of the novelist Henry James, learned in 1891 that she had cancer of the breast. No one, she wrote, could welcome such an "uncompromising verdict" or "choose such an ugly and gruesome method of progression down the dark Valley of the Shadow of Death." Yet it was something of a relief to her to know the cause of her trouble, and she grew resigned to her fate. The doctor, she wrote a friend, had told her that "a lump I have had in one of my breasts for three months, which has given me a great deal of pain, is a tumor; that nothing can be done for me but to alleviate the pain; that it is only a question of time, etc."[68]

The resignation with which people face terminal illness is timeless, and millions of later cancer patients courageously endured their trials. These things do not change. Moreover some Americans, most of them in the more optimistic middle classes, soon began to think that cancer could be beaten. After 1900 medical researchers grew more confident about their abilities, and reporters and magazine writers started to publicize their claims. At the same time, most of the major infectious diseases came under better control in the United States, thereby provoking demands that cancer be conquered next. In these ways the coexistence of traditional fears of cancer, of rising alarm about cancer death rates, and of mounting medical claims soon intensified popular pressure, mainly from middle-class believers, for a war aginst the disease. Cancer, once a gruesome but inescapable fact of life, became more and more a social—and ultimately a political—"problem" to be solved.

2

The Rise of the Doctors

EIGHT YEARS after Grant's death Grover Cleveland became the first president to fall ill with cancer while in office. (The second and third—so far as is known—were Lyndon Johnson, whose skin cancer in 1967 was not disclosed, and Ronald Reagan, whose malignancy in the colon and skin cancer on the nose was widely reported.)[1] For Cleveland the diagnosis—cancer of the jaw—was alarming, the more so because in 1893 the country was in the grip of a depression and a financial panic that threatened to undermine the credibility of the Treasury. If it were to become known that the president was seriously ill, public confidence in the currency might cease and economic catastrophe ensue.

Traveling secretly to the Battery in New York City, Cleveland boarded a yacht under cover of darkness. As the boat cruised eastward into Long Island Sound, the president underwent surgery for the removal of two upper teeth and most of his upper left jaw. The one-and-a-half-hour operation was an ordeal for the president, who later told a friend, "My God, they almost killed me!" But he recovered well, and, because the incision was inside his mouth, the surgery left no visible scar.

Five days later, on July 5, 1893, Cleveland reappeared, walking unassisted off the yacht to begin a vacation on Buzzards Bay. Spokesmen attributed his haggard appearance to a flare-up of rheumatism in his foot and knee. Twelve days later doctors cut away more suspicious-looking tissue, again in secret at sea. Specialists then fitted him with a vulcanized rubber jaw. It worked beautifully, and on August 7 a poised president gave a deeply reassuring address to Congress. No one noticed any flaws in his delivery.[2]

To Cleveland and his doctors the operation was a notable triumph for surgery.[3] Equally remarkable was the success of the campaign for secrecy. Early in July rumors of the operation began circulating, and in late August reporters divulged the truth. But Cleveland's doctors and White House spokesmen angrily and repeatedly denied it. Cleveland, they said, had had only a "very trifling" operation on his teeth. They denounced the *Philadelphia Press,* which had broken the true story, as a "*malignant*" paper.[4] After a while the rumors abated. It was not until 1917, nine years after Cleveland had died of heart trouble and twenty-four years after the surgery, that one of his doctors told the whole story in print.[5]

Cleveland's decision for secrecy stemmed only in part from wanting to conceal that he had cancer. Given the social unrest at the time, he would probably have hidden any serious illness. And the subsequent concealment was understandable: why confess to so elaborate and deliberate a ruse? Yet the reticence and fear that cancer aroused remained powerful. During these years a wide variety of pessimists continued to challenge those optimists who announced modern, "expert" theories and therapies against the disease. The conflict between traditional beliefs and new "scientific" approaches was to remain a dominant, largely unchanging feature of America's experience with cancer between the 1880s and the 1980s.

TRADITIONAL RESPONSES to cancer persisted throughout the Progressive Era. Various well-known figures—the novelist Alexandre Dumas, the poet James Russell Lowell—died of cancer in the 1890s, without public acknowledgment of the cause of death. The statesman William Gladstone fell victim in 1898; the obituary spoke only of his "incurable" illness.[6] Six years later doctors in Philadelphia opened a hospital for cancer patients, but to avoid frightening the public they named it the American Oncologic Hospital. (The word stemmed from the Greek *onkos,* meaning "bulk" or "mass.") And in 1906 Dr. Charles P. Childe, a British authority on the disease, was forbidden by his publishers from using the word "cancer" in the main title of his book, *The Control of a Scourge.*[7]

Hereditarian notions also persisted in the popular consciousness—and in some medical circles.[8] The fear that cancer is hereditary, while speculative at that time, turned out to have some validity: statistics later showed that a few forms of cancer, notably of the breast, tend to occur with greater frequency among certain families than among the population at large. In that sense, some people seem genetically more susceptible than others to certain cancers.[9] But those who put forth hereditarian hypotheses at the turn of the century had no good evidence to rely on. Many uncritically embraced the contemporary vogue for genetic explanations and for eugenics. They stood ready to believe that cancer—like other social ills such as hysteria, alcoholism, imbecility, drug addiction, vagrancy, and criminality—was a sign of degeneration that was genetically transmitted.[10] Hereditarian notions about cancer, moreover, promoted fatalism; if the problem was in the genes, there was little one could do about it. Pessimistic and ashamed, many relatives of cancer victims considered it a familial disease to be kept under wraps at all costs. Survivors not only denied that their relatives had cancer but also burned or buried the clothes of their dead. In 1915 an editorial in the *Scientific American* denounced people who "think there must be some taint handed down from one generation to another which causes cancer to flourish in certain families . . . This belief may well cause a feeling that it is somehow shameful to have the disease."[11]

The notion that cancer was contagious lingered too. At the New York Cancer Hospital financial difficulties in the 1890s forced the authorities to admit large numbers of patients not believed to have cancer, and until 1913 cancer patients were partitioned from those in the other wards. To many New Yorkers, in fact, the hospital—which featured large circular towers to let light into the wards—was a fortress, the "Bastille" of uptown Manhattan.[12] Pedestrians and cab drivers often gave the hospital a wide berth, as if the virulent germs of cancer were able to penetrate the walls and contaminate the surroundings.

Though most doctors rejected such fears, many Americans refused to discard them. After all, communicable illnesses like tuberculosis continued to take thousands of lives each year, and the press still featured stories about "cancer cities" and "cancer houses." One New York headline in 1914 proclaimed, LONDON EXPERT ASSERTS CANCER IS INFECTIOUS. The story described what appeared to be an epidemic of cancer in a Norwegian village.[13]

Fear of contagion was worldwide, as a Connecticut woman discovered in 1913, when her husband died of cancer in a Swiss hotel. The hotel keeper, sure that cancer germs were spreading through his establishment, destroyed the bedroom furniture and sued the widow for $255 in damages. The judge, unsure how to proceed, finally rebuked him for besmirching the worldwide reputation of Swiss hostelry. That, he said, was worth far more than money. But he compromised on the issue of contagion: the innkeeper was awarded $155.[14]

Popular concerns also promoted the unabated proliferation of patent medicines and other unorthodox therapies for cancer. Indeed, the 1890s and early 1900s may be called the golden age of "quackeries," as they were branded by orthodox practitioners. The muckraking journalist Samuel Hopkins Adams exposed cancer quacks in a series of widely noted articles on the "Great American Fraud" in *Collier's Weekly* in 1905 and 1906. The so-called Propaganda Department of the American Medical Association followed suit in 1911 by publishing the first of several volumes devoted to the denunciation of quackery. And federal officials, acting under

Cancer Cured at Home

I have so perfected my Mild Combination Treatment that patients may use it at their home with practically as good results as though it were applied at my offices. I will gladly furnish to every sufferer positive and indisputable proofs that my treatment Does Cure Cancer. I will furnish ample evidence of my integrity, honesty, financial and professional ability. No matter how serious your case may be—no matter how many operations you have had—no matter what treatments you have tried, do not give up hope, but write for my book, "Cancer and Its Cure." It will cost you nothing and will tell you how you can be cured at home. Address,

DR. JOHNSON REMEDY CO., SUITE 341 1233 GRAND AVE. KANSAS CITY, MO.

Have you a friend suffering from Cancer? Do them a favor they'll never forget by sending them this ad"

From the Historical Health Fraud Collection at the American Medical Association, Chicago.

regulatory legislation passed in 1906 (partly as a result of pressure following Adams's articles), haled a famous cancer quack, Dr. A. O. Johnson of Kansas City, into court for his claims of producing "the most successful cure for cancer known to medical science." The case reached the Supreme Court in 1911, which ruled that the 1906 law outlawed false and misleading labeling of contents, but not inaccurate therapeutic claims. In 1912 Congress enacted a law that covered therapeutic claims on labels, but it saddled government with the burden of proving such claims false and fraudulent, and the law had little effect.

Newsworthy events like these demonstrate that cancer quackery was lucrative even amid bountiful sales of other patent medicines (estimated by Adams to be worth $75 million per year). The freedom to advertise also dealt a severe blow to federal officials who sought to bring suit against self-proclaimed cancer doctors. Henceforth healers had to label their products accurately if they wished to sell them in interstate commerce. But they could and did continue to make unverified claims for their products in newspapers and magazines, which depended on them to a large extent for revenue.[15]

The inability of orthodox doctors to cure most forms of cancer further played into the hands of quacks, including some charlatans of dash and spirit. Rupert Wells of Saint Louis, a self-styled "Professor of Radio-therapy" at the "Postgraduate College of Electro-therapeutics," hailed the blessings of "Radol," or "Radiatized Fluid," which Adams said contained "exactly as much radium as dishwater does." Unperturbed, Wells's newspaper ads proclaimed, "I have discovered a new and seemingly unfailing cure for the deadly cancer. I have made some most astonishing cures. I believe every person with cancer should know of this marvellous medicine and its wonderful cures, and I will be glad to give full information free to all who write me and tell me about their case." According to Adams, a careful reporter, Wells earned around $70,000 in 1908.[16]

Wells was an amateur advertiser compared to a Mr. Isham (from Isham Spring, California), who sang the praises of his "California Waters of Life" (which Adams, on analysis, discovered to be regular water). Isham explained that his water was the same that sprang from the rock smote by Moses. It would not only cure cancer within thirty days; it would also stop diabetes and Bright's disease and bring hair to the bald. In time, Isham was arrested and convicted for mislabeling. Adams commented that he was "either of unsound mind or the most arrant and blasphemous faker before the public."[17]

Other quacks also promoted remedies that ranged far from the orthodoxies of the day. They included Andral Kilmer of Binghampton, New York, whose CanCertorium featured treatments with a substance consisting primarily of alcohol; Dr. D. M. Bye of Indianapolis, who advertised a "Combination Oil Cure" that promised to absorb "Cancer and Other Malignant Diseases"; and Albert Adams, who attracted attention in 1910 for "spondylotherapy." In spondylotherapy the patient was to deposit a drop of blood on an electrical "dynamizer"—sold, of course, by Mr. Adams—and then place an electrode from the dynamizer on the forehead of a healthy person, who would face to the west in a dim light. Exit cancer.[18]

Unorthodox healers (like many orthodox physicians) were quick to make use of promising technological developments. Seizing upon claims for the therapeutic value of radium, they advertised so-called variants of the substance in their compounds. They made great claims for "electrotherapy," which was supposed to restore the vitality of degenerating bodies. Others, however, continued to extol traditional folk remedies, including herbal plasters, liquid paraffin, mineral waters, molasses, turpentine, ox gall, thyroid extract, violet leaves, and soap solutions.[19] In 1908 the *New York Times* reported that a Massachusetts druggist had died after applying live frogs to a cancer on his neck. It also told of a Buffalo physician, Dr. Hiram Walker, whose seven years of research purported to show that cancer came from parasites that "oozed" out of earthworms onto vegetables. Walker explained that "all the suffering and death caused by cancer can be prevented by refraining from eating such vegetables as cabbage, celery, onions, and lettuce which have been infected by these parasites."[20]

The commercial success of many such remedies should not be seen as a sign only of popular gullibility; it also exposed the continuing distrust of orthodox medicine, which could claim credit for few cures. Regular practitioners asserted the virtues of surgery; quacks, by contrast, promised to help people escape pain. One

Cancer Cured at Kellam Hospital

The Kellam Hospital is without parallel in the cure of Cancers, Tumors, Ulcers, X-Ray Burns, Chronic Sores and all Skin Diseases. We want every man and woman in the United States to know that we have cured without the use of the knife, X-ray, radium or acids over 90 per cent. of the many hundreds of sufferers treated during the past 18 years.

KELLAM HOSPITAL, Inc.

1617 West Main Street RICHMOND, VA.

Long Distance Phone Mad. 4614

From the National Archives, Public Health Service Records, Record Group 90, file 2236.

newspaper ad proclaimed a cure that was "The Greatest Discovery and Wonder of the World—Without Knife or Pain." Another advertised "Cancer—Treated at Home or at the Cedar Hill Sanitarium Without the Knife, Without Risk, and Without Danger." In these and in many other ads cancer was depicted as a living, purposeful thing, usually visible on or near the skin. If patients would rub on this or that ointment or salve, or ingest this or that potion, the offending malignancy would lose its crablike tenacity and dissolve without pain to the once ravaged host.[21]

Along with popular notions about heredity and contagion and widespread reliance on quackery, nineteenth-century beliefs that civilization caused cancer lingered in America in the early 1900s, although a slight change in emphasis accompanied the return of better times in 1897. Thereafter a few writers worried that people in the age of telephones and automobiles were "living faster" and were therefore subject to "stress," making them prone not only to cancer but also to apoplexy, arteriosclerosis, and heart attacks.[22] But many writers were less obsessed with stress than they had been in the tension-ridden 1880s and 1890s. Instead they focused more sharply on "softness" and "luxurious living," which they thought were sapping the vitality of middle-class citizens. Their laments echoed earlier criticisms of materialism in American life—often loudest in times of relative prosperity.

Worries that America was going "soft" were by no means limited to writers about cancer. The appeal of Frederick Jackson Turner's frontier thesis, enunciated in 1893, testified to a broadening concern that the hardy virtues associated with the frontier were vanishing. As if to compensate, many urban, middle-class Americans convinced themselves of the necessity for vigorous physical exercise, including hiking, rowing, gymnastics, and bicycling. Theodore Roosevelt disparaged the "over-civilized man, who has lost the great, fighting, masterful virtues," and called for a return to the "strenuous life."[23]

The sense that "luxurious living" caused cancer (and many other ailments) flourished within this broader cultural context at the turn of the century. One writer, noting that cancer mortality was on the rise among men, argued that "want of proper exercise and changed surroundings" were emasculating men and leaving them subject to "women's diseases."[24] Some cited anthropological writings about the simplicity and hardiness of "primitive" people, who did not suffer from "civilized" diseases such as cancer. (Others, however, asserted that South Sea islanders, whose lives were thought to be blissfully free of hard work, also were spared from cancer.) A few doctors shared the tendency to indict civilization. Cancer, one argued in 1918, "selects its victims in an apparently lawless and erratic manner but following an indefinite law by which the most civilized races are the most liable to its ravages."[25]

Still other commentators contrasted cancer with tuberculosis in their effort to associate malignant tumors with the ease of civilized life. One wrote that "the Captain of the Men of Death," tuberculosis, "takes his victims mostly from humanity's submerged strata, the starved, the ill-clad, the poorly housed." The "Crab," however, "is wont to stretch out its tentacles [*sic*] for the life tissues of the well-to-do in civilization." Another authority added that cancer "accompanies certain conditions of rich and luxurious living, so that in a general way we can say that the idle rich are more apt to be attacked by cancer than they are by tuberculosis, while the opposite is also true."[26]

Some critics of luxurious living focused on diet, arguing mainly that people overstuffed themselves, "autointoxicating" their bodies and "irritating" internal organs which then contracted cancer. "Too much nourishing food," one magazine article said in 1900, "has to do with the production of the cancerous disposition." Cancer's "most notorious victims are well-nourished persons who live well and do not work off their waste products." Dr. William Mayo, of the famed Mayo brothers clinic, noted a few years later that one-third of all cancers in civilized countries afflicted the stomach. This rate was apparently considerably higher than that in less advanced countries. "It seems not improbable that the taking of very hot food and drink by civilized people may be the cause of this." Frederick Hoffman, the leading health statistician of his day, tended to agree. "Overeating," he wrote, "and even more overnutrition are unquestionably most important contributory causes in cancer occurrence." The low rate of cancer among orthodox Jews, he suggested, stemmed from their adherence to simple diets.[27]

Others singled out excessive meat eating as the bane of modern civilization. Heirs to a considerable vegetarian tradition, they correlated increased consumption of flesh in "civilized" societies with rising cancer mortality. One intriguing study—which received fairly wide coverage in magazines and newspapers—associated the eating habits of various ethnic groups in Chicago with their susceptibility to cancer. Heavy meat eaters—Germans, Irish, Scandinavians—apparently had high rates of cancer mortality, but pasta-consuming Italians and rice-eating Chinese had low rates. Though the survey was crude, it was more thorough than many of its kind (it studied some 4,600 cases over a seven-year stretch from 1900 to 1907). Its conclusions concerning the potential risk of eating too much meat crudely anticipated those of many experts eighty years later.[28]

Epidemiological studies such as these were part of a broader passion for statistics that transformed social as well as medical science in the nineteenth century. But few of the studies at that time were carefully designed; fewer still related presumed causes to specific types or sites of cancer or took fully into account the lapse of time often necessary to detect carcinogenic effects. The proliferation of studies linking cancer to civilization, and more specifically to luxury or diet, said more about contemporary cultural concerns than about the disease.

No one did a better job at demolishing such unorthodox studies than Dr. Charles Childe, whose book *Control of a Scourge* (1906) was by far the best exposition of cancer written by a reputable physician for the general public. An Englishman, Childe nonetheless expressed the views of leading American physicians and popular writers like Samuel Hopkins Adams, whose message would have been familiar to Grant's physicians: detect the disease early and, if possible, cut it out.

With this no-nonsense attitude Childe was quick to denounce hereditarian and contagionist theories about cancer and to ridicule all manner of quacks. He scorned those who blamed the "stress" associated with "civilization." What, he asked, was meant by "stress"? Was it something sudden or catastrophic, or was it akin to chronic anxiety? How much stress, and for how long, must one endure before cancer afflicts? Doctors and clergymen, he said, held notably stressful positions, yet their susceptibility to cancer was low. Old people were most likely to get cancer: was senescence especially stressful? He concluded by noting that the world was full of stress and anxiety and always had been but that it was silly to link them to cancer. "Of all the theories of the origin of cancer, I

surgeons did not dare to operate on the stomach or the colon. Even with aseptic procedures they still faced the threat of infection following surgery—a source of distress until the dawn of antibiotics in the mid-1930s. Most general practitioners were careful to recommend surgery only when absolutely necessary.[43]

Medicine in the Progressive Era changed far less in practice than in rhetoric. While John D. Rockefeller, Jr., was spending millions to improve medical education, his father kept as his personal physician a homeopath who was ignorant of contemporary medical science. (Rockefeller lived to the age of ninety-seven.) Recognizing their limitations, the better general practitioners still employed what was called "supportive treatment." That consisted, Lewis Thomas explained later, of "plain common sense: good nursing care; appropriate bed rest; a sensible diet; avoidance of traditional nostrums and patent medicine; and a measured degree of trust that nature, in taking its course, would very often bring things to a satisfactory conclusion."[44]

Despite these limitations, the medical profession enjoyed a revolutionary rise in status during the early twentieth century. Greater respect for physicians stemmed from improvements in the training and competence of physicians and from cultural changes that enhanced the value of doctors' claims for expertise and the blessings of personal health. Together, these developments placed doctors in a position from which they felt confident in seizing ownership not only of the cancer problem, but of a wide range of ills afflicting American life.

The medical improvements, while less dramatic than some publicists proclaimed, nonetheless were important. Medical educators began to emphasize up-to-date findings of laboratory science; clinicians applied the methods of physiology, pathology, and chemistry to the study of human diseases; medical schools became centers for research; weak schools disappeared; licensing of doctors became more than a formality.[45]

Researchers, meanwhile, announced one discovery after another. In 1901 they identified the mosquitoes that carried yellow fever; in 1906 they found the bacterium that caused whooping cough; in 1908 they developed a serum against meningitis; in 1909 they learned that lice carried the epidemic typhus; and in the same year

Paul Ehrlich finally—after trying 606 different compounds—found a substance, Salvarsan, that seemed to combat syphilis. Ehrlich's announcement unleashed a popular fascination for the "magic bullets" of chemotherapy. One observer marveled that "the chancre, the rash, the Wasserman reaction, all cleared up like magic. People . . . were astounded . . . It was a miracle."[46]

Surgeons made further claims. As early as 1889 the eminent Johns Hopkins surgeon William Halsted performed the first radical mastectomy and claimed remarkable improvements in survival rates. The Mayo brothers developed a surgical practice in Minnesota that attracted national attention; by 1912 their office handled some 15,000 patients a year.[47]

Most accomplishments heralded in the press were in the realm of applied science or involved specialized surgical procedures affecting few patients. The remarkable improvement in life expectancy resulted less from medical intervention than from better diets, sanitation, and reforms in public health.[48] Still, by around 1910 Americans could safely assume that most of the terrifying infectious diseases—yellow fever, smallpox, typhus, cholera—had been relegated to history, at least in their epidemic form in the United States. It is hard to exaggerate the magnitude of this accomplishment.

The attention given scientific advances was especially great in a culture that had always placed a high value on tangible results. Physicians, it seemed, were at last exhibiting the "can-do" dexterity that was the essence of American ingenuity. In the words of Lawrence Henderson, an eminent social scientist, "somewhere between 1910 and 1912 in this country, a random patient, with a random disease, consulting a doctor chosen at random, had, *for the first time* in the history of mankind, a better than fifty-fifty chance of profiting from the encounter."[49]

So great was the rise in the prestige of scientific medicine that common metaphors took on a medical instead of a moral tone. Afflictions once thought to stem from personal failing—drunkenness, madness, idiocy, criminality, homosexuality, even poverty—came by 1915 to be described as forms of sickness. People were less likely to be called "immoral" or "depraved"; they were "ill." The shift in terms did not mean that the "sick" received great new waves of sympathy. On the contrary, to be ill in a society that glorified achievement and the work ethic was to be negligent, useless, even deviant. Still, the transformation of language revealed the extent to which the practice of medicine, once ridiculed and maligned, was achieving unprecedented authority in middle-class circles.[50]

All these developments naturally enhanced the confidence of doctors themselves. Like American professionals in other fields, they demonstrated their confidence by organizing into increasingly exclusive and specialized groups. The biggest by far for doctors was the American Medical Association: its membership at the turn of the century was only 8,400, but ten years later had swelled to more than 70,000. By 1920 it claimed the adherence of about 60 percent of practicing physicians in the United States. From this period dated the rise of "organized medicine" in America. No development more graphically demonstrated the astonishing rise in the professional self-consciousness of doctors in the early years of the century.[51]

The accelerating rise in the status of organized medicine, however, did not result entirely from true accomplishments—which in fact were exaggerated at the time. It stemmed also from the way that the perceived achievements of medical science reinforced cultural values, for example, the growing faith in professional expertise. By 1900 respect accorded religious leaders and values had substantially declined. At the same time, the ever larger and more assertive middle classes saluted the virtues of efficiency, organization, and specialized expertise. They deeply admired professionalism—in medicine, in business management, in social work, even in motherhood and childrearing. "The spirit of science," Osler wrote, "was brooding on the waters." This spirit offered Americans a new faith to replace the breakdown of religious certainties. Heroic "microbe hunters" battling disease, like Sinclair Lewis's Martin Arrowsmith in the 1920s, became priests and ministers of the new culture. They were unselfish and embattled evangelists crusading for a new age of science.[52]

Middle-class advocates of science and efficiency were activists, progressives who hoped to reform society—or at least prevent it from falling apart under the dangerous stresses of industrialization, immigration, and urbanization. Psychiatrists began to claim that they could cure social problems such as alcoholism, crime, prostitution, and criminality—all of which were described in the metaphors of illness. Doctors in other fields were equally self-confident: weren't they now getting scientific training in the medical schools and clinical expertise in the hospitals? Their optimism at the turn of the century was but one manifestation of the growing self-assurance of the urban middle classes once they had put the frightening doubts of the 1890s behind them. It was at one with the progressive mentality of growing segments of middle-class culture.[53]

Progressive doctors collaborated with community leaders to command a variety of crusades aimed at preventing disease. Far and away the most effective collaboration—a model for the subsequent struggle against cancer—was the National Association for the Study and Prevention of Tuberculosis, founded in 1904. It relied in part on arousing fear of the disease. To this end saloonkeepers erected exhibits of tuberculous lungs in formaldehyde and big painted skeletons showing the damage done by the disease. Lights flashed at intervals to symbolize the entrance of yet another poor wasted soul to the hereafter. Later, the association enlisted the help of the Red Cross and promoted Christmas Seals drives, which by 1919 involved the participation of some three million children.[54]

The tuberculosis crusaders were followed by other national organizations for preventing or eradicating various diseases. By 1913, in fact, the passion for organization, and for management of mass opinion, led the AMA to call a conference aimed at "eliminating unnecessary organizations." There were fifty-seven national organizations in 1917 devoted at least in part to the improvement of health.[55]

By then it seemed that concern for good health was becoming almost a national obsession among the urban middle classes. A cult of exercise and physical fitness attracted many thousands of people. Magazines and newspapers featured stories on the necessity of keeping fit, and writers produced How to Stay Healthy books for willing publishers and readers. The publications stressed the importance of sound personal hygiene and prevention. As one public-health official put it, "My plea is that you live health, talk health, and think health. Sell it alike to young and old. Sell it by example and by precept; by good health news published in the right way; through the press; by the motion pictures, the radio, slogan, and poster, or in any other way that you will. But *sell it.*"[56]

Popular definitions of good health were also changing during this era. Until then most Americans thought that to be healthy was not to feel sick. Health was the absence of what later observers called the "Three Ds" of Disease, Disability, and Death. By 1900, however, many people, especially in the more favored classes, expected much more from life than the absence of sickness. One indication of this view was the growing fear and denial of early, "premature" death. Another was a gathering quest for freedom from two other "Ds"—Discomfort and Dissatisfaction. Still another was the rise, especially noticeable after 1900, of the idea that people could not only be free from illness but could also be spiritually, psychically, and emotionally happy. One historian estimated that there were more than one hundred magazines and newspapers calling for "mind cures" in 1910. Even the main-line Protestant churches took up modified versions of this transcendental quest for personal fulfillment that led a few decades later to the phenomenal popularity of preachers such as Norman Vincent Peale.[57]

Such broad definitions of good health were not altogether new. Since de Tocqueville observers had noted the periodic rise and fall of health and exercise fads and quests for spiritual peace and social regeneration. The rapid spread of health movements at the turn of the century owed something, as well, to social changes. Americans taking on professional and white-collar tasks in the cities began to chafe at the confining routines that regulated their lives. Living in a society of ever greater abundance, they rejected restraints. They began to think that there might be no limit to the potential of the body, no finite amount of energy to be harnessed and utilized. On the contrary, physical activity might regenerate the "soft," "overcivilized" white races of the world.[58] Physicians, who now had "scientific" answers, might take the lead to improve national vitality.

It was the immense good fortune of the medical profession that all these scientific and cultural forces came together at much the same time. That dynamic process transformed the status of doctors and in the long run led toward greater acceptance, especially among the middle classes, of the role of orthodox physicians in combatting disease. In the shorter run this process also gave leaders of the profession the confidence to challenge the deep-seated popular pessimism about cancer and to seize command of an alliance against it.

3

The Alliance against Cancer

THE DOCTORS who launched the campaign against cancer after 1900 recognized that they confronted a number of disadvantages, chief among them their inability either to explain the origin and development of the many forms of the disease or to cure most of them. Millions of Americans, aware of these limitations, continued to resist the predominantly middle-class world of modern medicine. They succumbed to the fear or the fatalism that had characterized reactions toward cancer since time immemorial. Deeply held cultural attitudes changed slowly, if at all.

But at the same time leading doctors were able to recruit many allies in their fight against these attitudes. Most of these allies were upper-middle-class people of optimistic, progressive temperament: philanthropists, statisticians, and—to some degree—the press. An elite corps of doctors then carried the campaign forward, establishing a broader, more secure alliance by the 1920s.

WHENEVER theories proliferate about a disease, it is a safe bet that no one knows its causes. This was the case with theories about cancer. Aside from the many obvious quacks who continued to do a thriving business, a steady stream of men and women of science proposed "answers" to the ancient enigma.

One answer focused on aging. This theory assumed that aging was a degenerative process that led to a "predisposing disability." "The functions of life," one authority wrote, "increase for a time in strength, range and complexity, pass through a period of comparative repose, and finally break up and disappear." By this reckoning cancer, a disease that especially afflicted the aging, stemmed from an intrinsic errancy of cells that accompanies advanced age. It was an illness of "degeneration"—a specially gruesome complication of the ultimately retrogressive pattern to life.[1]

This theory had its attractions. It accorded with a widely held medical view that cancer started from inherent imperfections in human cells. It also reinforced commonsense observations of general practitioners. Older people, whose numbers were growing rapidly (from 3.1 million aged sixty-five or more in 1900 to 6.6 million in 1930) as life expectancy increased (from forty-seven years at birth to sixty), obviously had the most severe physical problems, cancer high among them.[2] It was logical to conclude that the increases in the number of older people and the growth of mortality from cancer were not merely correlated statistically but also the result of the process of aging itself.

Some scientists also believed that aging created hormonal changes that, if controlled, might slow down the process. Researchers found that breast cancers could be prevented in female mice if their ovaries were removed. This work made it seem possible that human cancers, many of which afflicted sexual organs, could be hormonally controlled.[3] By the early 1920s this idea attracted a number of evangelists claiming to have the secret to eternal youth. "We need no longer succumb to the encroachments of senility," one said. "If the years assail us, we can stand up and fight back." Sigmund Freud underwent a vasectomy in 1923, a few months after having been diagnosed as having cancer of the mouth. (He, like Grant and Cleveland, was a heavy smoker of cigars.) At age sixty-seven Freud was not concerned about fathering children; he believed that the operation could improve his hormonal balance, combat the cancer, and allow him a longer life.[4]

These people were correct in associating the growth in cancer mortality with the increase in the number of older people: cancer had always afflicted the elderly much more than it did the young. Some later researchers were also to suggest that the aging of the population was more than coincidentally associated with cancer; old age, they speculated, caused a breakdown in the body's defense mechanisms, thereby opening the door to cancer.[5] But the attempt to see the physiological process of aging as a main cause of cancer lacked solid evidence early in the century. Critics pointed out that the aging theory had trouble explaining why cancer also struck many children (defenders blamed unusual genetic or environmental forces), or why the malady was becoming a more frequent cause of death among all age groups.[6] Critics noted also that cancers tended to attack only a few of the body's organs, whereas the aging process affected practically all bodily tissues, and they stressed that many elderly people showed no signs of cancer. For these reasons few scientists paid the aging theory much attention in these years.

Another questionable lead was the hereditarian hypothesis. For a brief time after 1900, when the rediscovery of Mendel's work gave great impetus to genetic hypotheses, there was a resurgence of research on the hereditary transmission of cancer. One of the most dedicated researchers was Maud Slye, the "mouse lady" of Chicago. Beginning in 1900, when she began selectively breeding mice in makeshift quarters at the University of Chicago, Slye worked obsessively for forty years at proving the hereditarian thesis. At first she asserted that cancer stemmed from recessive genes that could be controlled after two generations of proper breeding. Later, under sharp attack from other scientists, she softened her thesis, but still insisted that cancer was hereditary.[7] "Romance," she argued in 1937, "was the only thing that stood in the way" of selective human breeding against cancer.[8]

Hereditarian arguments, drawing on broader fascination with eugenic explanations, never died out in the popular mind: typical was a story in *Collier's* in 1952 entitled, "Is Cancer Hereditary?" Hereditarian ideas also commanded some attention among researchers. While doubting theories about direct inheritance of cancer, scientists continued to suspect that many people were "predisposed"—a key word in the literature—by their genetic makeup to develop the disease. How else to explain, they were later to argue, why some smokers fell victim to lung cancer while many others did not. Cancer, they concluded, was not so random or so indiscriminate as it appeared.[9]

But few biological scientists before 1925 were attracted to the research of Slye and others. Most followed different leads, pursuing research into virology and chemical carcinogenesis. Those who tried to replicate Slye's work failed, and many argued that her research was irrelevant in any event, for human mating over many generations could not be controlled the way it was in mice. It was therefore impossible to predict the probability of cancer in children of a particular man and woman.[10]

The idea that cancer arose from some sort of virus or bacterium also seemed promising early in the century, when the bacteriological discoveries of the 1880s and 1890s were still fresh. Dr. Peyton Rous, of the newly established Rockefeller Institute, created a stir in 1910–11 by reporting that he had succeeded in running tumors from chickens through filters that blocked normal cells, isolating tiny particles, or "filtrable agents." These cell-free agents, when injected into healthy chickens, produced tumors. The experiment suggested that some type of filtrable virus either provoked or was associated with cancer, at least in chickens.[11] Rous and a few other intrepid researchers continued to believe in the viral transmission of cancer—a theory that (thanks in part to sensational revelations about polio virus) regained credibility in the 1950s and 1960s. In 1966 Rous finally received a Nobel Prize for his work.[12]

Rous, however, struggled against the tide of contemporary cancer research. A few scientists maintained that he had injected the chickens with cancer cells, not a cell-free virus. More important, Rous and others were unable to discover viruses associated with cancer in human beings. Such viruses were not identified until the late 1970s. Meanwhile, bacterial explanations also met with severe criticism. Transplants of cancer cells to animals, scientists noted, did not infect surrounding cells. On the contrary, transplanted cancer cells divided and multiplied on their own, displacing and thereby damaging neighboring cells. Cancers, critics added, were not contagious. Healthy animals placed near cancerous ones did not develop the disease. Neither did doctors and nurses who attended cancer patients. For all these reasons theories attributing cancer to the work of infectious agents lost favor among leading scientists during the early twentieth century.[13]

Still another theory—that trout-filled waters caused cancer—received considerable attention between 1908 and 1910, to the extent that President William Howard Taft called on Congress to appropriate $50,000 to support a research lab to investigate the idea. In making this recommendation Taft was following the advice of Dr.

H. R. Gaylord, director of the New York State Institute for the Study of Malignant Disease, who had concluded that "cancer in man is most prevalent in the well-wooded, well-watered, and mountainous regions or in poorly drained areas with alluvial soil." It was an "astonishing coincidence," he added, "that the distribution of this variety of fish [trout] and the concentration of cancer in man in this country are almost identical. A map of one might well be taken as a map of the other."[14]

This imaginative theory appealed not only to Taft, but to others as well; it received the approval of the *New York Times,* which devoted eight columns to the idea the Sunday following Taft's message. The president's proposal, the paper said, was "the greatest stroke so far toward the conquest of the dread disease . . . a scourge that is second only to tuberculosis."[15] Gaylord later claimed that "100,000,000 state trout had cancer" and that people who drank trout-inhabited water ran the risk of dying from the disease.[16] But no other scientists seemed to share his distrust of the noble trout. Congress sent the proposal to the Committee on Fisheries, and that was the end of that.

Rejecting these varied explanations, most researchers turned to the line of thinking that dominated cancer science then and for many years afterwards: the "irritation" theory. Childe said that "local irritation is undoubtedly directly or indirectly a cause of it." Samuel Hopkins Adams reported in the *Ladies Home Journal* the consensus among scientists that "irritation, while not the cause of cancer, is usually, if not invariably the occasion for it." Dr. William Mayo weighed in with the public statement that "chronic irritation is the most important condition which predisposes tissue to cancerous growths." And the eminent pathologist James Ewing, in his definitive tome on the subject, *Neoplastic Diseases* (1919), concluded that "without previous chronic inflammation cancer does not exist . . . the cumulative effects of chronic irritation alter the nutrition and growth activity of cells so that when they become isolated they are not normal cells but are in a state of disturbed equilibrium with a tendency toward exaggerated growth."[17]

This theory made sense to many Americans, who had always assumed that cancer stemmed from irritated bumps, bruises, or sores—in other words, had confused causes with symptoms. More significantly, it led cancer researchers to intensify a search for specific irritants. In 1915 their work began to show results. In that year two Japanese researchers provoked cancer in rabbits by painting their ears with coal tar. Though they did not know what specific chemicals in the tar had caused the cancer—others began isolating these in the 1920s--their work was wonderfully exciting. It showed researchers how to induce cancer at will in various kinds of animals, greatly assisting laboratory study of the growth of tumors and giving enormous impetus to a main line of subsequent research: experimental oncology. It confirmed previous suspicions: man-made chemicals could excite the disease, at least in rabbits.[18]

The emphasis on irritation rested on other discoveries as well. Clinicians treating cancer with X-rays discovered that these, too, provoked cancer. Epidemiologists showed that women in India who chewed betel nuts were especially susceptible to cancer of the cheeks and that Kashmir natives who held warming pans of charcoal next to their bodies developed cancer of the abdomen. Scientists reminded Americans of Dr. Percivall Pott, who had proved in 1775 that soot caused cancer of the scrotum among chimney sweeps.

No single irritant received more contemporary attention than tobacco. Early in the century the medical opponents of smoking hardly needed to raise the specter of mouth cancers, such as those that had afflicted both Grant and Cleveland. They could rely on a much broader cultural revulsion against the growing addiction of people to cigarettes, or the "weed." Some of this revulsion expressed moral concerns. A contemporary song warned of the danger from "cigarettes and whiskey and wild wild women." Other observers emphasized the dangers to health. Magazine articles spoke of the "cigarette fiend," the "servitude" and the "disastrous evil" associated with smoking. A governmental study explained that "inhaling tobacco smoke brings carbon monoxide directly into the blood-stream. It is found that smoking increases blood pressure, which in fact possibly explains the reduction in endurance." Determined opponents of smoking enacted restrictive legislation in fifteen states by 1909.[19]

Despite this crusade against tobacco, smoking increased in America, especially after the high point of restriction in 1909. Cigarette companies introduced milder, tastier tobaccos and launched expensive advertising campaigns. "I'd Walk a Mile for a Camel," the best-seller proclaimed. Soldiers in World War One seemed almost desperate for a smoke. "You ask me what we need to win this war," General "Black Jack" Pershing said. "I answer tobacco as much as bullets." In 1910 adult Americans (mainly men) smoked 85.5 cigarettes per capita; ten years later they consumed 470.9. By 1925, 50 percent of adult men, along with growing numbers of "liberated" women, were smoking. The warnings of their antitobacco contemporaries had fallen on deaf ears.[20]

It was not surprising that smokers persisted, for the irritation theory left much unexplained. No one then suspected that smoking caused cancer of the lung, which one authority in 1912 said was "among the rarest forms of the disease."[21] Nor could anyone demonstrate the biological processes by which irritation from smoking actually caused cancer. After all, while some habitual smokers developed the disease, the vast majority did not. Few women smoked, yet cancer afflicted them more than men. Until lung cancer became a medically recognized disease in the 1930s and epidemiologists in the 1940s and 1950s found correlations between cigarettes and cancer, the tobacco companies scarcely bothered responding to the few "cranks" who maintained that tobacco was carcinogenic.

Irritation theories, moreover, in general left some unanswered questions. What was meant biologically by "irritation"? Was it a "predisposing" or an "exciting" cause? How much irritation was bad for the health? Why did irritants cause cancer in some people but not in others? Experts like Ewing, while asserting the role of irritation, conceded that they did not know the answers to these questions. The cellular changes associated with cancer remained mysterious: they stemmed from "numerous etiologic factors" that provoked many different types of tumors in many different organs. Researchers, Ewing cautioned, must abandon the notion that there was a "universal causative agent" behind cancer.[22]

Ewing was one of several experts who frankly admitted how much remained to be learned about the disease. Childe was another. "The cause of the disease," he wrote, "is at present unknown. It is neither salt nor cider, beer nor tomatoes. Its scientific cure or prevention, therefore, is not within the scope of practical politics."[23]

Cancer scientists, indeed, continued to be baffled. Their research between 1900 and 1925 did more to complicate existing theories than to propose satisfactory new ones. This fact, as much as any other contemporary aspect of the cancer conundrum, deterred Americans from enlisting enthusiastically in the doctors' optimistic war against the disease.

CANCER therapies, as problematic as cancer theories, multiplied to an almost bewildering extent in these years, periodically evoking enthusiastic commentary in the press and raising and then dashing the hopes of patients and their relatives. This pattern was particularly clear in the United States, where it mirrored a tendency of American culture to embrace whatever was new, especially if it seemed to rest on advanced science and technology and if it promised to have immediate practical utility. It was to become a common—and increasingly commercialized—feature of the American struggle against cancer.

Many therapies were indeed both new and technologically dramatic. Some proposed electrical answers. Electrical "fulguration," one of these ideas, involved application to tumors of "five-inch electrical sparks of an insulated probe, charged with a high frequency current of 60,000 to 200,000 volts." French physicians jolted patients with electrical charges to raise cancerous tissue to 55 degrees Centigrade. The New York Skin and Cancer Hospital meanwhile was testing the use of "lucidescent light of 500 candle power" as a possible treatment.[24] But these treatments did not do anything for patients, and few doctors prescribed them. "Electricity as a cancer cure," a group of French researchers told the *New York Times* in 1909, "is destined to disappear with the foolish serum method whose uselessness to science has been demonstrated."[25]

Other therapies involved a virtually endless variety of mineral and vegetable remedies. There were periodic enthusiasms for eosin, selenium, autolysin, trypsin, and colloidal copper. Dr. William Coley of New York attracted special attention between 1895 and 1908 for his claims that injections of the bacteria causing erysipelas, a streptococcal infection, killed advanced forms of inoperable cancer.[26]

Some of these ideas advanced "chemotherapy." Healers had long promoted caustics, such as arsenic or zinc chloride, rubbed into surface cancers in the belief that the chemicals would eat away the tumors. In this sense the reliance on chemical therapy was not new. But the chemotherapists of the new century brought a special zeal to their cause. They believed their magic bullets would be the salvation of humanity. When Ehrlich succeeded in 1909 in finding a useful chemical weapon against venereal disease, the quest for new remedies became intense. Ehrlich himself turned to cancer work after 1911. Other cancer researchers took to injecting cancerous rats and mice with a range of compounds, and drug companies began advertising products with "striking therapeutic effects."[27]

But chemotherapy, too, proved deeply disappointing. Many of the new drugs seemed to have little effect. Others were highly toxic, killing the mice and rats as fast as or faster than the cancers. Understandably, practicing physicians were reluctant to use them on their patients. Although chemotherapeutic research continued, it generated relatively little support from physicians until the late 1940s and 1950s.

Therapeutic use of X-rays or radium attracted much greater attention in these years. The vogue for X-radiation came first, immediately following discovery of the X-ray in 1895. An X-ray "cure" for a cancer patient was reported as early as 1899. But before long the enthusiasm for radiotherapy faded. Physicians could not standardize the doses, and they did not know enough about the biological results of the rays. It soon became clear that the rays themselves caused cancer. By 1911 a book documented some fifty-four cases of death or serious illness owing to exposure in one way or another to technologically exciting but dangerous radiation. A number of the victims were X-ray technicians or doctors.[28] Researchers continued to seek better ways of applying radiotherapy—one scientist reported enthusiastically in 1914 that he had developed an X-ray machine that could shoot beams through two-and-a-half inches of beefsteak without any loss of strength in the rays—but they, like the chemotherapists, enjoyed only cautious support in American medical circles for many years.[29]

The use of radium, by contrast, seemed more promising. Unlike X-rays, one account emphasized, "radium gives a beautifully consistent and uniform supply of rays." By 1905 doctors were not only applying radium directly to surface cancers; they were conserving the precious substance by embedding, usually in beads of glass or metal, small quantities of radon—a gas derived from the disintegration of radium—into cancerous growths.[30]

Excitement about radium peaked in 1913 and early 1914. CANCERS VANISH WITHIN A MONTH—*Wonderful Effects of The Radium Treatment,* the *New York Times* proclaimed in January 1914. Its story noted that thirty-two of sixty-eight cancer patients treated with radium at a London Hospital had been discharged, as opposed to a mortality of 100 percent among people subjected to other therapies.[31] At the same time newspapers eagerly followed the case of United States Representative Robert Bremner of New Jersey, a friend of President Woodrow Wilson. Bremner found a Baltimore doctor who somehow procured $100,000 worth of radium, which he injected into Bremner's shoulder on Christmas Day, 1913. "If experimenting on me has added a new fact to science," Bremner said, "then my life has not been in vain, but has helped the race . . . I am ready for the scrap heap, but feel that the cutting and the doctoring have added to the knowledge of how best to fight cancer. Some poor souls who come after me may benefit." Three weeks later Bremner was dead at the age of thirty-nine.[32]

No one was more enthusiastic about the potential of radium than James Douglas, Chairman of the Phelps-Dodge Copper Mining Company. Douglas founded the National Radium Institute in collaboration with the United States Bureau of Mines in 1913. Between 1913 and 1918 he gave $600,000, as well as supplies of radium, to General Memorial Hospital in New York and emphasized that he expected the staff to make optimum use of radium therapy. A zealot, Douglas used it on his daughter, who nonetheless died of cancer, and mixed it into an ointment that he rubbed on his wife's feet. He kept a pitcher of radium-charged water on his desk and invited visitors to drink of it. He died in 1918 of pernicious anemia that some people thought had been caused by radium poisoning.[33]

The hospital followed Douglas's instructions, treating thousands of patients with radium by 1924. It became renowned for its emphasis on this form of treatment.[34] But though radium excited patients, who hailed it as a painless alternative to surgery, it met with a cooler reception from physicians. Some stressed correctly that it was useful mainly for certain "superficial" skin cancers. Others complained of the very considerable cost of the precious material—which prevented all but a handful of hospitals from acquiring any. Still others noted that the vogue for radium encouraged a new wave of quackery and stopped patients from undergoing necessary surgery.

Following the dashed expectations aroused in the Bremner case of 1914, criticism from medical authorities grew more insistent. Dr. Francis Carter Wood, head of the cancer institute at Columbia University, grumbled that "it is now not always possible to get patients to submit to surgery for the removal of a tumor, they are so anxious to be treated with radium." A Boston doctor added, "Radium hysteria is a disease that is likely to set back the proper treatment of cancer, and the inevitable failure of radium as at present exploited as a cure will add acute mental suffering to the physical tortures resulting from the disease."[35] The visit to the United States in 1921 of Marie Curie, Nobel Prize winner and pioneer in research on radium, launched a new wave of popular enthusiasm for radiotherapy. One researcher at that time claimed that radium could "extend life, restore vigor of youth, prevent wrinkles, produce new hair on bald heads, and possibly a third set of natural teeth."[36] But most scientists and clinicians were much more cautious: they knew that radium, like X-radiation, was of little use in alleviating, much less curing, the vast majority of common cancers.

Having offered reservations about all these therapies—electricity, chemotherapy, X-rays, radium—leaders in the field of cancer therapy relied on the same answers that doctors had recommended in the nineteenth century: early diagnosis and surgery. "No cancer is hopeless when discovered early," Samuel Hopkins Adams counseled in a widely reprinted article in 1913. "Most cancer, discovered early, is curable. The only cure is the knife." The story of President Cleveland's successful operation, revealed at last in 1917, received wide play in the press. A popular guide to health in 1918 added that people who showed any sign of cancer (fatigue, loss of weight, persistent indigestion, growing warts or moles, lumps in the breast) should see a doctor *"at once."* "THE CURE OF CANCER CONSISTS IN THE COMPLETE SURGICAL REMOVAL OF THE GROWTH AT THE EARLIEST POSSIBLE MOMENT."[37]

As the advice literature made clear, the surgery must be radical as well as quick, for cancer, once started, raced madly through the body. "It may be accepted as a safe rule," one writer observed in 1915, "that when in doubt about symptoms in patients at the cancer age: *Don't wait, explore!*" Another doctor counseled, "the early operation is the effective one. Do not perform less radical operations on favorable cases than you do on unfavorable ones. Make wide dissections." A leading surgeon concluded, "in regard to tumors . . . lynch law is by far the better procedure than 'due process.'"[38]

The faith in radical removal of tumors rested on widely touted improvements in surgical pathology and practice. Tumor committees were formed in the larger hospitals. Physicians and surgeons made special efforts to help women learn the early symptoms of breast cancer, which had always provoked special fears. Medical claims for the impressive results of radical mastectomies—almost universally thought to be the proper response to the disease—appeared in ladies' magazines, and helped sustain the special status enjoyed by surgeons in these and later years.

But the orthodoxy of early detection and surgery did not much change the habits of general practitioners. Most doctors still had received little or no exposure to cancer in medical school and shared a widespread belief that it was a hopeless, incurable disease. Many others remained unable to distinguish benign from malignant growths. Still other physicians shunned the "delicate" (and mostly unproductive) task of giving rectal or vaginal examinations. Rockefeller's medical adviser observed privately in 1925, "it is very little use in educating the public until the general practitioner knows more about cancer than he does."[39] When Massachusetts became the first state, in 1926, to support a cancer hospital, it urged the state health department to formulate a public-health effort against the disease, "with or without the cooperation [of] . . . local physicians."[40]

The practitioners' lack of enthusiasm for the gospel of early detection made a good deal of sense. Although early detection of surface tumors was then possible, physicians recognized that it continued to be very difficult to detect cancers in their formative stages. "By the time there are any 'signs' of cancer visible to the naked eye," one doctor complained in 1916, "or to the touch, or that can be detected from the patient's symptoms, the cancerous process is already well established, and has been going on for weeks or months."[41] It was not until much later in the century, when Pap smears, mammograms, and fiber optics became available, that physicians were able to detect major forms of cancer in their early stages.

Even with these later advances the gains from early detection were to remain rather limited. John Cairns, an informed writer-researcher, explained to lay readers in 1978 what medical specialists had recognized for some time: it was wrong to assume that the "natural history of every cancer consists of a growth to a size at which diagnosis becomes possible, followed inevitably by metastasis after some constant interval of time." On the contrary, he said, there are many kinds of cancers, some of which metastasize while still too small to be detected. He estimated that early diagnosis could reduce mortality from cervical cancer (a relatively uncommon form of the disease) by as much as 50 percent, but that for most of the more common cancers the possible reduction was usually "much less."[42]

The gospel of early detection had another major drawback: it was undramatic. Researchers, politicians, and the media could grow excited about technological "breakthroughs" in the fields of chemotherapy or radiotherapy, which offered the promise of a quick fix. But except for some surface cancers, detection of cancer's "danger signals" often called for worrisome self-examination or expensive medical checkups. Few Americans knew much about self-detection or wanted to spend the time to take regular examinations.

Physicians rejected the advice of the experts for another reason: they doubted the value of surgery. They knew that most of their patients were terrified of the knife and of the often zealous surgeons who wielded it. They were sure that the disease was relentless and insidious—that surgery in most cases would merely prolong the suffering or, worse, accelerate metastasis. This gulf separating the elite of the medical profession from the much larger and scattered group of general practitioners (and their patients) persisted for many years.

Pessimistic attitudes among physicians were grounded ultimately in fear. Sharing the concerns of their patients, many doctors conspired with frightened relatives to hide the "awful truth" of cancer. They relied on deception—or shots of morphine—to control suffering. As in the past, the conspiracy of silence extended to death certificates and to obituaries and added to the mystique of cancer.

For all these reasons most Americans did not respond any more enthusiastically to the new therapies of the day than they did to theories about the disease. The vast majority could not afford to go to doctors with any regularity, if at all. Most never saw the inside of a hospital, let alone a research center. What they knew about cancer they learned from watching friends or loved ones turn sick and die from it, sometimes slowly, expensively, and agonizingly. That was all that was needed to make them wonder if the medical establishment, whether the elite or the general practitioners, had anything helpful to offer. Skepticism, sometimes bitter, ran deep in the minds of millions of people who lived outside the mostly middle-class world of modern medical culture.

Despite the impediments to their efforts, the top leaders of the profession persisted in their positive thinking. They employed to their advantage the argument that the conquest of cancer was the next great challenge facing medical science. Many of the great killers of the nineteenth century, such as yellow fever and cholera, seemed under control in the United States. Even tuberculosis, many thought, would someday succumb. These improvements left chronic diseases as the field to explore. One leading researcher explained in 1914 that "cancer is today the most intriguing subject that claims the attention of surgeons, since tuberculosis is being mastered."[43]

By the 1920s this challenge was especially inviting. John D. Rockefeller, Jr.'s, medical adviser reported privately that cancer was "practically the only disease left that the medical profession does not know (1) the cause, (2) the treatment, (3) the cure, and (4) the prevention." He concluded, "here is a unique field. Here is the outstanding disease, not only in this country, but the whole world . . .

I cannot think of anything that would be more '*popular*' for Mr. Rockefeller to do than to become vitally interested in this cancer field."[44]

With characteristically American optimism researchers insisted between 1900 and 1925 that they now had some useful scientific weapons at their disposal. They pointed especially to exciting new developments in laboratory research using animals. This kind of work attracted especially great enthusiasm after 1903, when a Danish veterinarian succeeded in transplanting cancerous tumors into mice; it seemed enormously promising, not only because it enabled researchers to observe the growth of cancer, but also because in animals such as mice, which had a short life span, tumors grew much more rapidly than in human beings. Laboratory experiments of this kind henceforth became a major form of cancer research.[45] In 1911 biological scientists hailed another breakthrough in research, the development of "tissue culture"—the demonstration that cells (cancerous and otherwise) could be nurtured in test tubes. Four years later came the report from Japan that coal tars were carcinogenic, at least in rabbits. The frontiers of biological science, it seemed, were boundless.[46]

Emphasizing the glorious potential of medical research, scientists began to attract philanthropists to the support of cancer research. As early as 1898 Dr. Roswell Park, a Buffalo physician, had convinced New York State to appropriate $10,000 to establish the State Institute for the Study of Malignant Disease (later named the Roswell Park Institute). The cure, Dr. Park promised, "was just around the corner." A year later Caroline Brewer Croft, whose father had died of cancer, donated $100,000 to establish a Cancer Commission at Harvard University.[47] She stipulated that the money be used to search for "some remedy or means of cure for certain diseases generally supposed to be difficult or incapable of cure, such as cancer." Additions to this initial gift permitted construction in 1912 of the Collis P. Huntington Memorial Hospital for Cancer Research in Boston.[48]

Many other research institutions and hospitals were established in this age of faith in science: the Collis Huntington Fund for Cancer Research given to General Memorial Hospital in New York (1902); the American Oncologic Hospital of Philadelphia (1904);

the St. Louis Skin and Cancer Hospital (1905), the only one west of the Mississippi before 1938; and the American Association for Cancer Research (1907). In 1910 Columbia University received the largest bequest to that time, following the death of George Crocker, a western rancher and entrepreneur whose wife had died of the disease (as did he). The gift of $1.5 million made possible the Institute of Cancer Research, for years one of the major establishments in the United States.[49]

Nineteen thirteen marked the completion of the first wave of organization and philanthropy in the field of cancer research. In that year James Douglas started to give enormous sums of money to the General Memorial Hospital in New York. Thanks to his gifts, the hospital again concentrated on cancer medicine and research. Dr. James Ewing, an eccentric, demanding professor at the nearby Cornell University Medical College, became president of the hospital's medical board. Already a widely respected pathologist, Ewing was to become the most eminent person in the cancer field for the next twenty-five years. The philanthropies of Douglas and others, the stature of Ewing, and the connections that Ewing established between research and clinical work made the Memorial Hospital the most prestigious cancer center in the United States, if not in the world.[50]

These activities were part of the larger transformation of American medicine, which, sustained by the "new philanthropy" of science, helped to place the United States nearer the forefront of cancer research worldwide. At the turn of the century Europe led the way. As early as 1896 the first journal devoted to cancer had appeared in France. (The first in the United States, the *Journal of Cancer Research,* started in 1916.) In 1900 the Central Committee for the Study and Control of Cancer was founded in Germany, and in 1902 the Imperial Cancer Research Institute opened in England. The gifts of Crocker, Douglas, and others then helped to advance the United States. Thereafter American scientists began to take on important roles in the many international conferences and symposia that marked the rise of cancer research as a recognized specialty.[51]

Another major event of 1913 was the formation of the American Society for the Control of Cancer, whose goal was "to disseminate knowledge concerning the symptoms, diagnosis, treatment, and prevention of cancer, to investigate the conditions under which cancer is found and to compile statistics in regard thereto." This organization did not engage in research. Its goal, like many others in the Progressive Era, was to educate the public, to break down the reticence—and consequently the mythology—that had long surrounded the disease. For the next thirty-two years (and thereafter as the rechristened American Cancer Society) it joined hands with leading doctors in calling for the essence of medical orthodoxy: early detection and surgery.[52]

The founding of the ASCC, like that of other voluntary health organizations of the era, depended first of all upon the philanthropy of a few concerned citizens—in this case mainly Mrs. Robert G. Mead, the wealthy daughter of a New York gynecologist, Dr. Clement Cleveland, at whose home some of the early meetings were held. Mead was a friend of John D. Rockefeller, Jr., who became a major benefactor of the society. (Rockefeller's personal counsel, Thomas Debevoise, was a long-time secretary of the organization.)[53] For years the ASCC was a very small operation which relied heavily on the contributions of a few wealthy people and which had little visibility outside the Northeast. RICH WOMEN BEGIN A WAR ON CANCER, the *New York Times* announced.[54] In its size, funding, and influence the society bore little resemblance to the much richer National Tuberculosis Association or to the polished and powerful pressure group that the American Cancer Society was to become in the late 1940s.[55]

As was true of many health organizations in those years, the ASCC was dominated by doctors and more particularly by surgeons. Seventeen of its twenty-member (all-male) executive committee in 1914 were physicians, as were forty-six of its sixty-seven directors (six were women) in 1915. Its leaders were closely connected with two elite organizations of the East Coast in the United States, the American College of Surgeons and the American Medical Association. It was not until the 1940s, when advertising and public-relations executives staged a virtual coup to take control of the society, that it managed to reach far outside medical circles and become a potent lobby for cancer research and prevention.[56]

The society resembled other health organizations in an additional important respect: its reliance on pamphlets, speakers, and magazine articles to spread the word of early detection. ASCC leaders, like other progressives, believed that the people would listen to the experts, that publicity could do much to combat the dangers of cancer. An early recruit, Samuel Hopkins Adams, was briefed carefully on the goals of the organization and published a much reprinted article in the May 1913 issue of the *Ladies Home Journal,* "What Can We Do About Cancer?: The Most Vital and Insistent Question in the Medical World." It emphasized the growing menace of the disease and urged people to see their doctors at the slightest hint of trouble.

For the next thirty years ASCC speakers and pamphlets tirelessly reiterated this message. One pamphlet, issued in 1915, was entitled, "CANCER, and What You Should Know About THIS DISEASE OF MIDDLE LIFE AND OLD AGE." Another was "CANCER POINTERS: Signs That Should Be Known and Heeded." A third, entitled

CANCER, TREATED IN TIME, IS CURABLE!

By Dr. William Brady.

Physicians frequently pass over cancer symptoms at the first examination. Eternal vigilance from patient and thoroughness from doctor is the price of safety. Below are the danger signals of incipient cancer. (The World assumes no responsibility for Dr. Brady's statements, presenting them merely as the opinions of an expert.)

ONE in every eight women, one in every eleven men past the age of thirty-five dies of cancer. After middle life cancer kills more women than any other disease.

Cancer may well be called the living death, for it creeps upon its victims insidiously, drags them down to despair before they realize the meaning of its deceptive early signs.

In the United States the prevalence of cancer has multiplied nearly eightfold in thirty years. Seventy-five thousand deaths were attributed to this malignant disease in the registration area during the single year of 1909—a figure which probably represents about two-thirds of the actual death rate.

From "Clippings on Cancer, 1913–14," compiled by Frederick Hoffman, Historical Collections of the Library, College of Physicians of Philadelphia.

"Breast Cancer," explained "How a wise woman won the battle against cancer. She had faith in her physician. He had confidence in his power. LOSE NO TIME."[57] The message was clear: trust the doctors, they know the answers. "The best Preventive," one writer emphasized, "is a Thorough Physical Examination. At Least Once a Year. In China, doctors are paid to keep People Well, not to cure them after they get sick. *Don't Wait Until It's Too Late.*" Another common warning was aimed against quacks: "Medical cancer cures are all bogus. Barring the use of radium or similar means for the small affairs of the skin, surgical operation is the only cure for cancer."[58]

Many educational efforts spoke to women. From the start gynecological surgeons were prominent in the ASCC. They were alarmed by the prevalence of cervical, uterine, and breast cancer, which were responsible for the deaths of roughly one-eighth of all women over forty-five years of age. They were equally distressed by the stigma that was still attached to cancers in these "secret," "private" parts. All too often, specialists recognized, women blamed themselves for such tumors and refused to seek professional help. With these concerns in mind the gynecologists developed close relations with women's clubs and nurses' organizations and turned to the women's magazines for help. Adams's piece in the *Ladies Home Journal* was only one of a spate of such articles over the years.[59]

In preaching the virtues of early detection and reliance on doctors, ASCC members had the help of insurance executives. None was so involved as Frederick Hoffman, the energetic, self-assured, and methodical chief statistician for the Prudential Insurance Company. Hoffman had long interested himself in the incidence of and mortality from various diseases, and in 1912–13 he turned his curious eye on cancer. He discovered that the Metropolitan Life Insurance Company in 1912 had documented the death from cancer of 4.9 percent of male policyholders and 9.8 percent of female policyholders. The total cost of these deaths to the company was $717,000. Hoffman ascribed to the popular belief that cancer tended to hit the middle and upper classes—the very people who could best afford insurance.[60]

Like the gynecologists Hoffman was also alarmed about the dangers of cancer to women. Addressing the annual convention of the

American Gynecological Society in March 1913, he spoke on "The Menace of Cancer." This speech, widely circulated, helped inspire formation of the ASCC a month later, and Hoffman became one of the few nonmedical members of the ASCC board. In the early years Hoffman was a key figure in gathering statistics and in securing the help of the insurance companies—who needed little prodding—in disseminating ASCC literature. No individual was more central to the ASCC in its infancy.[61]

Modeling their efforts on the educational work of the National Tuberculosis Association, leaders of the ASCC focused on securing the support of other organizations—state health departments, women's clubs, the American Public Health Association, nurses, and above all the press. "Public sentiment," the society's house organ said, "must be thoroughly aroused and organized. Scientific light on the cancer problem and public sentiment must go hand in hand, if we hope to realize any results toward the eradication of cancer. When the people really know what to do to get rid of cancer, we are sure they will do it."[62]

In spreading the word leaders of the ASCC faced a special problem of strategy that was to spark a continuing debate: how to publicize the issue so that people would take steps to detect the disease. They discovered that any approach was controversial. If they put out sober messages about the virtues of early detection and medical intervention, they ran the risk of boring their audience. But if they tried to dramatize things by emphasizing the horrors of the disease—the so-called Chicken Little approach—they might be accused of frightening people. "To warn the public," the AMA complained in 1921, "that 'moles, excrescences, fistulas, and warts' are the 'first signs of cancer' is to erect a specter capable of shattering even a normal mentality."[63] "Cancerphobia," the AMA said, made people even more reluctant to admit that they had symptoms or to seek medical help.

The society sometimes risked this kind of criticism and dramatized the cancer problem, particularly in statistical articles highlighting the rise of cancer mortality. Its "14 Points about Cancer," issued in 1919 to echo Wilson's Fourteen Points for peace, reminded people that more Americans died from cancer between April 1917 and November 1918 than had been lost on the battlefields of World War One.[64] Other pamphlets were entitled "Cancer—The Most Dreaded of All Diseases," "Cancer the Outlaw," and "Cancer the Menace." A poster in 1921 resorted to melodrama, showing a woman with children on her lap reading a pamphlet on the disease. The caption read, "If Daddy had only known this!"[65]

In its first few years, however, the society mainly opted for restraint. Far from trying to shock people, it attempted to bring cancer out in the open and soberly to overturn the conspiracy of fear and silence that had so long surrounded the disease. It emphasized that cancer was not inherited or contagious, that it was nothing to be ashamed of, above all that it was a disease of observable local origin for which there was a "Message of Hope"—early detection—available to all Americans.[66] Though mixed from time to time with appeals to fear, the Message of Hope became a dominant, consistent feature of the alliance's struggle against cancer in the twentieth century.

Pursuing this strategy, the ASCC embarked on a new track in the early 1920s: National Cancer Weeks. For these campaigns the society produced a deluge of pamphlets and other forms of propaganda. During the Cancer Week of 1921 it claimed to send out five million pieces of literature and to reach ten million people "either directly or indirectly with the simple facts of cancer control."[67] It enlisted the endorsement of leading citizens, including President Warren Harding, and tapped their distinctively American faith in public education. No comparable excitement, let alone public-relations expertise, characterized contemporary European responses to the disease.

The popular impact of these campaigns cannot be measured exactly, but it was surely slight, especially among the less educated classes and among people who did not live near the East Coast. The ASCC remained small, precariously funded, and elitist in membership. In 1921 its expenditures totalled only $12,000, and by 1923 it still had only two thousand members.[68] Even those middle-class easterners who might have been reached by the society seemed to pay the message little attention. Deluged with health propaganda, they largely ignored the warnings. (Tuberculosis, after all, was still a more serious threat.) Other Americans, reflecting the long-

If Daddy had only known this!

The right way to attack cancer—

Go immediately to a reputable physician and insist upon a thorough examination when you notice:

1. Any lump, especially in the breast.
2. Any irregular bleeding or discharge.
3. Any sore that does not heal, particularly about the tongue, mouth or lips.
4. Persistent indigestion with loss of weight.

The wrong way, waisting precious time and money

1. Waiting to see if the condition won't go away of itself.
2. Using "Patent Medicines."
3. Allowing advertising "Cancer Specialists" and "Quack Doctors" to treat you.
4. Being guided by anybody except a thoroughly competent physician.

The Right Way is the Only Safe Way

This poster was prepared and printed by the National Safety Council from material provided by the American Society for the Control of Cancer.

Reprinted with permission from *ASCC Campaign Notes,* 3, no. 4 (1921) 4; © 1921 American Cancer Society.

standing sense that cancer was incurable, appeared to see little point in going to the doctor. They questioned the Message of Hope.

The formation of the ASCC was nonetheless a sign of changing times. Its creation, together with the contemporaneous spread of cancer hospitals and research institutes, showed that doctors were moving aggressively to control cancer. Increasingly secure in their professionalism and social status, many physicians were self-confident and optimistic. Having taken the lead in what was becoming a many-sided war against cancer, they were not to relinquish it—then or ever—without a struggle.

ALTHOUGH MEDICAL EXPERTS were the major force in the gathering drive against cancer, they were aided by other specialists. Statisticians and epidemiologists offered evidence of a different kind of scientific certainty, that cancer was increasingly threatening the world. This message lent urgency to the campaigns of the ASCC and others fighting the disease.

Before 1900 scattered statistics had suggested that cancer was becoming more widespread. But scattered they were, based on small and unreliable samples and seldom controlled for the age of the population. "In the early 1900s," one writer noted later, "a suggestion that statisticians could make substantial contributions to the pathogenesis of cancer would have been looked on as utopian as a trip to the moon."[69] To that time epidemiological work had concentrated on the feared infectious diseases. It was not until the 1900 census that the United States began publishing useful mortality statistics on cancer. These were based on death certificates filled out by physicians in the ten states (accounting for 25 percent of the total population) that defined the Death Registration Area of the country.

On the basis of these data various studies began to argue that cancer mortality was indeed rising. Among the most careful of these was a census report of 1906, which asserted that there was a "steady increase in the death rates due to cancer." A government report in 1909 concluded that cancer of all kinds accounted for 4.4 percent of deaths in the United States—eighth among the leading killers, behind tuberculosis of the lungs (9.9 percent), heart disease

(8.1), diarhhea and enteritis (7.7), violence (7.5), pneumonia (7), Bright's disease (5.6), and apoplexy (4.4). Ranking behind cancer were such ailments as congenital debility, old age, premature birth, typhoid, meningitis, diphtheria, and acute bronchitis.[70]

It fell to the indefatigable Hoffman to pull these and other statistics together. In a series of publications after 1912, including *The Mortality from Cancer throughout the World* (1915), Hoffman did much to establish the orthodox view that cancer was not merely increasing, but becoming a threat to Western civilization. He stressed: "*The actual frequency of malignant disease throughout the civilized world has been ascertained to be much more of a menace to the welfare of mankind than has generally been assumed to be the case . . . cancer remains one of the few diseases actually and persistently on the increase in practically all of the countries and large cities for which trustworthy data are obtainable.*"[71]

Supporting this conclusion was an impressive array of statistics. Some may have provided a measure of grim satisfaction for American readers. Hoffman wrote that there were no important differences in the incidence or mortality from cancer between whites and blacks or between people living in cities and rural areas; that neither heredity nor contagion caused the malady; and that mortality rates from cancer were higher in many "civilized" parts of the world (England, Holland, Bavaria, Switzerland) than in the United States.[72]

The rest of his news was depressing. Hoffman argued that more adults were afflicted by cancer than by tuberculosis, typhoid, pneumonia, and digestive disease combined, all of which were becoming less and less life-threatening, and that it killed 7 percent of American males and 16 percent of females between the ages of forty-five and sixty-four, or more than 75,000 per year. Worse, mortality from cancer was increasing in the United States at the rate of 2.5 percent per year—faster for males than for females. Hoffman calculated that cancer mortality for women had risen from 79.7 per 100,000 population in 1900 to 97.2 per 100,000 in 1913, and for men from 43.6 to 56.7 per 100,000. The figures for both sexes were 62.9 per 100,000 in 1900 and 78.9 in 1913. Were it not for improvements in cancer surgery, Hoffman noted, the picture would be worse.[73]

Even as he wrote, however, Hoffman recognized that there were many who challenged his conclusions. Some writers replied that the increase in cancer mortality signified only that people were living longer, as a result of better nutrition and the much reduced threat from infectious diseases. More Americans, they said, were approaching the allotted three-score-and-ten and then dying of diseases of old age. Hoffman's critics added that women, thanks in part to reduced mortality from childbearing, were living longer than men—a reversal of the pattern that had prevailed in the past. Large numbers of women were simply growing old enough to succumb to the malady.

Hoffman answered his critics by explaining that his statistics on cancer death rates were adjusted for age. The age-adjusted rates, he asserted correctly, were increasing, though much more gradually than total cancer death rates.[74] It was nonetheless true that much of the increase in total annual cancer deaths—from perhaps 48,000 in 1900 to 85,000 in 1915—depended on the rapidly growing number of Americans who were escaping infectious diseases to reach middle and old age. Then and later, those who would dramatize the onslaught of cancer tended to cite these alarming numbers, not the more gradual increases in age-adjusted mortality rates.

Others attacked Hoffman's pessimism from a different perspective, arguing that much of the reported rise in cancer mortality was artificial. Better detection of the disease, they said, was inflating the number of cancer cases; better analyses by medical examiners and pathologists were hiking total reported cancer deaths. "The verdict as to the increase of cancer in modern times," Childe concluded as early as 1906, "must be the cautious Scotch one, 'not proven.'"[75]

Many observers shared Childe's uncertainty. Indeed, debate over cancer statistics was almost as heated at that time—and as fraught with importance for cancer policy—as it was to become in later years. Questions about diagnoses, moreover, were both understandable and important. In the census of 1900, when useful time series on cancer began, 38 percent of the deaths in the Death Registration Area had no cause listed. Some of these deaths were the result of hard-to-detect malignancies; many others may have been caused by cancers but were recorded as "old age" by doctors anxious not to stigmatize surviving relatives. If properly identified, such cases would have added to the number of cancer deaths in 1900 and thereby minimized the subsequent "increase" perceived by Hoffman and others.[76]

Data from a special census study of 1916 also qualified Hoffman's findings. This study, done at the request of the ASCC, relied on questionnaires asking doctors to review the diagnoses of 52,420 deaths attributed to cancer in 1914 in the twenty-five states that by then comprised the Death Registration Area. The responses showed that only 11 percent of the cases were confirmed by necropsies or operations. Only 58.3 percent could be labeled "diagnosis reasonably certain." Of the remaining cases 27.5 percent were classified as "diagnosis uncertain," 14.2 percent as "diagnosis unknown."[77] Imprecision in diagnosing disease and in certifying deaths, if given greater emphasis by writers like Hoffman, might have undermined some of the expanded claims for medical science at the time. It revealed the very real constraints under which epidemiologists then had to operate.

Partly as a result of evidence such as this, Hoffman, acting as statistical director of the ASCC, grew slightly more tentative in his conclusions after 1916. The society's publications for the next decade normally conceded that increasing mortality from cancer owed something to more accurate diagnosis and reporting of causes of death. "As the rate rises," it noted in 1922, "it does not mean that any more people are dying of cancer, but merely that we know more accurately of what they are dying."[78] Yet Hoffman and others in the ASCC did not back down from their major conclusions. While admitting some ambiguities, they insisted repeatedly that cancer mortality was on the upswing, both in total numbers (which almost everyone conceded) and after adjustments for the aging of the population.

The ASCC view seemed vindicated by another census study, in 1920, which concluded that age-adjusted cancer mortality rates in the original ten Death Registration states had increased from 60.9 per 100,000 population in 1900 to 87.8 per 100,000 in 1920; it was further supported by a special examination of the problem published in 1925 by the United States Public Health Service. Accepting the figures of the 1920 study, the PHS estimated that only one-third of the reported rise in cancer deaths for people over forty stemmed from better diagnosis and certification of death. The other two-thirds represented a real increase in the danger from cancer, which by then was the fourth leading cause of death. The study concluded that "while man has been greatly strengthening his defenses against the gamut of diseases which decimate childhood and early man and womanhood, these lives are later overhung with an ever-darkening shadow of increased liability to what seems, though slow-moving, the grimmest and most inexorable malady of all."[79]

Most of these studies tended to consider "cancer" in the singular—as if breast cancers, for instance, stemmed from the same forces that provoked stomach or brain cancers. Because all cancers featured uncontrolled and invasive cell growth, this was an understandable and arguable practice. But it necessarily resulted in the publicizing of large and frightening numbers. Had cancers been enumerated separately—as by type or site—the numbers might not have seemed so alarming.

Still, these reports were generally accurate in emphasizing the increasing threat of cancer in the United States. Hoffman and others were clearly correct in arguing that the once terrifying infectious diseases were no longer so threatening and that the chronic ailments, notably cancer and heart disease, were becoming the major causes of mortality: in 1924 recorded deaths from cancer for the first time outnumbered those attributed to tuberculosis. So Hoffman's original conclusions, if excessively alarming, continued to be used to reinforce the efforts of the doctors and the ASCC and to dramatize the cancer issue to the public.[80]

DID THEY SUCCEED in their efforts? The effectiveness of the alliance depended on many things, among them the way in which contemporary newspapers and magazines treated the arguments put forth.

Although coverage of cancer news was much more extensive than it had been in the late nineteenth century, when culturally enforced reticence prevailed, it was by no means common or widespread after 1900. The *Readers' Guide to Periodical Literature* reported only 13 articles about cancer between 1900 and 1904. Tuberculo-

NEW CANCER POSTER

The National Safety Council, cooperating through its Health Service Section, with the American Society for the Control of Cancer has just published a poster on cancer, of which the text is given below. Additional copies of this poster may be obtained at cost from the National Safety Council, Chicago, Ill.

About Cancer

One Out of Every Ten Persons Over Forty Dies of Cancer

Cancer Is Curable If Treated Early

Cancer begins as a local disease. *If recognized in time it can often be completely removed and the patient cured.* If neglected, it spreads through the body with fatal results. No medicine will cure cancer. Early diagnosis is all important, but pain rarely gives the first warning.

Danger Signals--

[1] Any lump, especially in the breast.
[2] Any irregular bleeding or discharge.
[3] Any sore that does not heal, particularly about the mouth, lip or tongue.
[4] Persistent indigestion with loss of weight.

These signs do not necessarily mean cancer, but any one of them should take you to a competent doctor for a thorough examination. Don't wait until you are sure it is cancer. It may then be too late.

Reprinted with permission from *ASCC Campaign Notes*, 1, no. 16 (1919), 4;

sis, by contrast, was the main subject of 102 articles. Thereafter, as medical interest in cancer grew, the pattern changed a little. Between 1910 and 1914, 74 articles appeared on the problem of cancer, compared to 143 on tuberculosis. Though coverage of cancer then slackened somewhat—to only 72 articles in the next decade—the magazines devoted more attention to cancer than to any other disease except tuberculosis.[81] References in the *New York Times* index showed a similar pattern in these years.

The content of the articles was of two very different sorts. One type emphasized the Message of Hope. The *New York Times* wrote in 1907 that "the cancer problem may be likened to an impregnable citadel," but that "professional opinion sanctions the belief that it will ultimately fall." It devoted several articles to favorable reports on the potential of trypsin, a digestive juice of the pancreas with which a Scottish doctor had been inoculating animals. "The most amazing thing I have ever seen," a visiting American physician gushed.[82] Two years later, reporting on researchers who were vaccinating dogs with slow-growing tumors to render them immune to malignancy, the *Times* cited experts who prophesied that "the beginning of the end of the cancer problem is in sight." In 1910 it lauded the work of a scientist who was injecting fluid from a recovered cancer patient into another victim, and described the experiment as "one of the most important ever made in connection with the treatment of this dread malady."[83] And in 1913 a page-wide headline announced, CAUSE OF CANCER FOUND AT LAST. The cause, it turned out, was an "inorganic poison" in the system.[84]

This sort of reporting was credulous, to say the least. It regularly reflected an entirely uncritical and breathless regurgitation of preliminary research.[85] More careful observers, needless to say, were appalled by the misrepresentation and exaggeration. As early as 1906 Childe complained, "the cure of cancer has been times out of number proclaimed to the public in the lay press . . . A doctor, for instance, has only to read a paper before one of the medical societies . . . and we see immediately in the columns of some of the daily papers a sensational article under the heading, 'Cancer Cured at Last,' 'The Death Blow to Cancer,' or something of that kind."[86]

The other form of coverage was quite the reverse. Scare stories in lurid language followed headlines like BIG INCREASE IN CANCER

CAUSE OF CANCER FOUND AT LAST BY BOSTON SCIENTIST

Not a Germ but an Inorganic Chemical Poison, Isolated from Malignant Tumors After Many Experiments by Dr. Howard W. Nowell, Boston University School of Medicine.

THE NEW YORK TIMES, SUNDAY, APRIL 20, 1913.

By Van Buren Thorne, M. D.

DR. HOWARD W. NOWELL, instructor in pathology in the Boston University School of Medicine, has achieved a notable triumph in the domain of medicine by discovering a cause of cancer. The active agent which he has succeeded in isolating, after years of patient laboratory work, is an inorganic poison and is derived from human carcinoma, the latter being the name by which true cancer is designated in scientific nomenclature.

The reason Dr. Nowell is sure he has really found a cause of cancer is that a solution of this inorganic chemical substance produces carcinoma, or true cancer, when injected into the bodies of healthy animals.

The writer of this article visited The Robert Dawson Evans Department of Clinical Research and Preventive Medicine in Boston, where the experiments destined to attract world-wide attention by their brilliant results have been conducted, on Monday last, and, through the courtesy of Dr. Nowell, was permitted to examine animals which were the subjects of experimentation. They presented the clinical evidences of cancer. Tumors which had been removed in autopsy from rabbits presented the usual macroscopic appearance of malignant growths taken from human beings. Sections of these tumors, stained and mounted on glass slides, were revealed under the microscope as true carcinomatous growths, differing in no respect from similar sections of cancerous tumor as found in the human subject.

Dr. Nowell has done a good deal more, however, than isolate an inorganic toxic agent from human carcinoma as the result of his long series of bio-chemical studies, although he wishes it to be distinctly understood that he does not assert that he has found a cure for cancer. By the

From "Clippings on Cancer, 1913–14," compiled by Frederick Hoffman, Historical Collections of the Library, College of Physicians of Philadelphia.

DEATHS. The *New York World* reported that cancer "may well be called the living death, for it creeps upon its victims insidiously, and drags them down to desperation before they realize the meaning of its deceptive early signs." Not to be outdone, another journalist branded it a "living thing . . . a veritable Frankenstein's monster, bent on the destruction of its host." A writer for the *Independent* described "the sunken cheek, the hollow eye and wasted flesh, the loss of appetite and strength, the pain, the restless nights and the hopeless days—these are all fully known, but at this stage little can be done to relieve the sufferer and absolutely nothing to save him from death."[87]

These two very different emphases—the one carrying a message of hope, the other depicting the depredations of the disease—often coexisted. Authors dramatized the horrors of cancer in order to deliver the moral: seek medical help before it was too late. The two-sided message showed that the dilemma faced by writers for the ASCC was never resolved.

Whether these stories had much effect is very hard to say. Judging by the relatively modest amount of coverage given the disease, it is logical to conclude that editors—who can be presumed to have some feel for the public pulse—regarded the issue as but one of many concerns of their readers. And people who took the trouble to scan the stories may have been confused by what they read. On the one hand cancer was about to be cured, and on the other hand it loomed as the epidemic disease of the twentieth century. Either way, it appeared that people—especially the millions who could not afford regular medical care—could do little about it. For these reasons it is doubtful that the media profoundly altered cultural responses to cancer in America in the early years of the alliance.

Still, it remained true that more stories appeared than in the past, many of them in one way or another treating the disease as a growing threat to civilization. At least some people were aroused to demand action from researchers and public authorities. One writer, responding to an account in the *New York Times* of high rates of cancer in New Jersey, insisted that "it seems high time for science to explain these cancer belts." In 1915 Massachusetts legislators pushed through resolutions calling on the government to do more than amass statistics.[88] We can conclude that the press, along with the doctors and the statisticians, were beginning to arouse demands for action, even though the alliance had less impact than it hoped to have. Later, under changing political and social circumstances, the alliance was to become a major force in promoting campaigns against cancer in the United States.

4
The Wilderness Years

ON MAY 18, 1928, Senator Matthew Neely of West Virginia rose from his seat to warn his colleagues about cancer. His stirring address, "Cancer—Humanity's Greatest Scourge," opened a campaign to bring the federal government into the alliance against cancer; it also symbolized a decade and more of groping for answers. Neely's metaphors were characteristic, if overblown. "I propose," he said,

> to speak of a monster that is more insatiable than the guillotine; more destructive to life and health than the mightiest army that ever marched to battle; more terrifying than any scourge that has ever threatened the existence of the human race. The monster of which I speak . . . has fed and feasted and fattened . . . on the flesh and blood and brains and bones of men and children in every land. The sighs and sobs and shrieks that it has exhorted from perishing humanity would, if they were tangible things, make a mountain. The tears that it has wrung from weeping women's eyes would make an ocean. The blood that it has shed would redden every wave that rolls on every sea. The name of this loathsome, deadly, and insatiate monster is "cancer."

Lest his fellow senators miss the point, Neely waved a copy of Hoffman's book on cancer mortality and added that the number of cancer deaths in the United States had increased from 86,000 in 1921 to 95,000 in 1926. "If the rapid increase in cancer fatalities should persist in the future," he said, "the cancer curse would in a few centuries depopulate the earth."[1] The number of deaths was bad enough, but "even more horrible is the fact that in its later stages cancer inflicts upon its wretched victims suffering greater than any ever devised by American Indians, agony more intolerable than any ever inflicted by the fanatical fiends of the Dark Ages." The disease, he emphasized to an efficiency-oriented audience, cost the country $800 million a year, of which $110 million represented the cost of medical care and the rest the value of contributions withheld from the economy by people disabled by the disease. Yet the government, its priorities askew, spent $10 million a year to eradicate the corn borer and $5 million to investigate tuberculosis in animals, but nothing whatever on cancer.[2]

Neely's goal was to secure passage of a bill to give $100,000 in federal funds to the National Academy of Sciences for cancer research. Neely admitted the failure of the legislation he had introduced in 1927 offering a $5 million reward for a successful cure. That effort (which had failed in the Senate) had managed only to attract an avalanche of 2,500 letters from quacks, one urging victims to place an "anointed hanky over the cancer, in the name of Jesus . . . If this doesn't do you any good, it is because you have no faith," another recommending "10 grains of arsenic, the white of one egg, enough soot from a wood stove to make a thick paste—applied twice a day." Neely concluded that "letters like the foregoing convince me that the plan to offer a reward for a cancer cure was imperfect, if not utterly futile." It was time, instead, to turn to modern medical research.

A colleague objected to Neely's statistics. Wasn't the increase in mortality, he asked, somewhat artificial—the result of better diagnosis over time? At this point Senator Royal Copeland of New York, a physician, jumped in to support Neely's stance. "Whether due to our habits of civilization," he said, "or what it may be . . . the fact remains that cancer is increasing." Finally, the Senate unanimously passed an amended version of Neely's bill that reduced the initial appropriation to $50,000.

To Neely's dismay the bill died in House committee, the victim not only of frugality in the lower house, but also of lack of enthusiasm from the Public Health Service. Congressmen clearly did not share Neely's urgency about cancer. Despite the maneuvers of the alliance against cancer over the previous fifteen years, Congress was not yet ready to bring the resources of the federal government into the battle.

Neely's efforts were reiterated in many subsequent calls for action, all of which were frustrated for another decade. The striking aspect of the 1920s and 1930s was the groping, often desperate, quest for a solution to the ever enigmatic problem of cancer. Despite continuing research, warriors against cancer did not produce convincing theories or therapies. On the contrary, the allies had to admit that millions of people—even doctors—distrusted their message. Some, clinging to religious faith, persisted in relying on preachers, not on physicians or any other "experts." Others, as in the past, depended on folk wisdom, quacks, and patent medicines. A much larger number of doubters were poor and had little to do with doctors. They were largely deaf to the optimistic Message of Hope advanced by the pundits of positive thinking—for so they were often perceived—who led the alliance against cancer.

This was a very diffuse but stubbornly persistent cancer counterculture, one of many constants in the modern social history of cancer in the United States. It revealed the continuing existence of a gulf between the optimism of Neely and the scientists on the one hand and a host of popular doubts and fears on the other—about doctors in general and orthodox cancer therapy in particular—that perhaps sharpened in the depression-ridden 1930s. Given its depth, it was not surprising that middle-class exponents of modern medical ideas often despaired during the interwar years.

THE HEART of the alliance, the ASCC, continued to devote much of its energy to publicizing the virtues of early detection, orthodox medical care, and, if necessary, surgery. Cooperating with the AMA, it pressed its endless campaign against quacks.[3] Advances in public-relations techniques were put to use in films such as "This Great Peril," the story of an honorable young doctor who leaves his hometown for a two-year specialization in cancer work. His fiancée, angry that he left, breaks off the engagement. Her mother then falls sick, follows the advice of a quack, and ends up in a sanitarium. The daughter belatedly comes to her senses and begs the good doctor to help. After insisting first that the quack be dismissed, the doctor performs an operation that, though dangerously late, is nonetheless successful, and everyone lives happily ever after.[4]

The ASCC's use of film showed that, like other professional

groups during the interwar years, it was ready to embrace some of the new techniques of advertising and public relations that accompanied the growth of an urban, commercial culture in the United States. But film represented only a small part of the society's overall publicity effort; it continued to rely heavily on lecturers and pamphlets. One pamphlet, "What Every Woman Should Know about Cancer," was distributed not only by the ASCC but also by the General Federation of Womens Clubs, the YWCA, and the Metropolitan Life Insurance Company. The society estimated that 668,000 people received the pamphlet in 1929.[5]

The allies against cancer still perceived the disease as especially dangerous to women. No one held that view more firmly than Dr. Joseph Bloodgood, an eminent Johns Hopkins surgeon and medical adviser to the ASCC. (It was Bloodgood to whom Neely and other senators turned in the late 1920s for advice on cancer.) He was certain that women could be taught to detect cancer early and therefore to protect themselves against it. "I have never seen a beautiful woman in whom cancer of the face developed." This was because women were "jealous of their lovely skins, and therefore the moment a persistent blemish of the skin becomes noticeable, they seek a physician."[6] Vastly underestimating the fear and shame that many women felt when they suspected cancer, Bloodgood believed that the modern zeal for cleanliness and beauty would advance the campaign for self-examination.

In this spirit the society in 1927 had already adopted as its official slogan "Fight Cancer with Knowledge." It kept its progressive faith in the power of education, in the belief that experts could manage public opinion. It also emphasized the military metaphor implicit in much of its earlier publicity. Henceforth the society regularly featured on its stationery, pamphlets, and posters a zealous crusader—often St. George taking his sword to a dragon labeled "Cancer." It proclaimed proudly in 1929 that its posters bedecked all the trains and streetcars of New York. "While passengers are waiting in the tubes, the silver sword flames forth with its message of hope—'to come early' and, 'in early discovery lies the hope for permanent recovery.'"[7]

While public education remained the focus of the ASCC, the society also took the lead in promoting clinical diagnosis and treat-

Reprinted with permission from *History of the American Society for the Control of Cancer, 1913–1944*, p. 1927; © 1944 American Cancer Society.

FOR FREE INFORMATION WRITE TO

AMERICAN SOCIETY FOR THE CONTROL OF CANCER

25 WEST 43RD STREET

NEW YORK, N. Y.

Reprinted with permission; © 1932 American Cancer Society.

ment of the disease. This new emphasis came at the urging of Dr. George Soper, a sanitary engineer and public-health officer who became managing director of the society in 1923. Soper stressed the need for more clinical facilities and for the doctors to man them. In 1930 the Board of Regents of the American College of Surgeons lent a hand by endorsing the society's call for cancer clinics at approved general hospitals. With pressure from the surgeons, who dominated many hospitals, clinics spread at a rapid pace. In the early 1920s there had been fewer than 15; by 1934 there were 181, and by 1940, 345. That represented 20 percent of approved hospitals with 100 or more beds in the United States and Canada.[8] By 1931 more than 500 hospitals also offered deep X-ray therapy for cancer patients. At the same time there were 17 skin and cancer hospitals with 1,272 beds (of a total of 4,302 hospitals with 371,609 beds in the nation). The most influential continued to be Memorial Hospital in New York, with 103 beds. These figures show a significant increase over the total of 949 beds in cancer hospitals in 1927.[9]

Though the society took pride in these developments, they were modest. The vast majority of people still lived nowhere near a clinic, and many people who did lacked the funds or the nerve to go to one. The number of cancer hospitals, and of beds for cancer patients, was tiny compared to the need. It was estimated that by the late 1930s close to 150,000 Americans died of cancer each year, or more than one per 1,000 people. Perhaps five times that number were suffering from it at any given time.[10] No one in the know had to be reminded of the shortage of clinical resources, or of the cost of cancer care, which shattered the family finances of many victims.

One reason for this paucity of treatment facilities was the power of fee-for-service practitioners, many of whom resisted the campaign for public clinics. Another was continuing pessimism about the value of early diagnosis and therapy: why go to clinics, or "waste" money to set them up, when doctors only rarely were able to detect or to treat the disease? Under these conditions clinics attracted less support than did experimental laboratory research.

Moreover, the ASCC had little influence in these years. It remained a small, ill-funded organization dominated by doctors; its branches outside New York were weak, and it had virtually no mass visibility or appeal. It scarcely existed west of the Mississippi. Although it added substantially to its endowment, which exceeded $1 million by 1937, it could not spend much more than $50,000 annually in the depression years. Most of this money went for salaries for the director, staff, and a small group (usually four) of field agents. Funds from annual contributions were pathetically limited, usually less than $5,000 per year, and dues brought in little more, usually less than $10,000.[11] To see the ASCC as a powerful lobby behind a war against cancer during the interwar years is to give far too much credence to the society's handouts.

PRIOR TO 1925 the ASCC relied heavily on the sobering statistics compiled by Hoffman and others, whose work lent credibility and urgency to the doctors' cause. During the next fifteen years statisticians continued to argue that cancer and other chronic diseases represented major threats to health. Census calculations indicated that age-adjusted death rates from cancer increased almost as rapidly in the 1920s and 1930s as they had from 1900 to 1920, from slightly less than 100 per 100,000 population in 1920 to 120 in 1940, or from an estimated 88,000 deaths to 158,000.[12] Cancer was by then solidly established as the second leading cause of mortality, well ahead of tuberculosis. (By the 1930s some local tuberculosis societies used Christmas Seal money to fight cancer.)[13] Only heart and blood vessel ailments took more lives (approximately twice as many). These two chronic illnesses were joined by automobile accidents and diabetes as the only major causes of increased age-adjusted mortality rates during these years.[14]

The statisticians emphasized the impact of cancer on various regions and groups of the population. Studies showed first of all that the malady continued to strike older people with special force. By 1939 50 percent of those who died from the disease were aged 50 to 69; 75 percent were aged 40 to 79.[15] Mortality rates from the disease appeared to be higher in the urban Northeast than in rural areas of the South.[16] The most striking findings concerned mortality by gender. By the mid-1930s it was clear that age-adjusted cancer death rates for women were stabilizing, while those for men, though still slightly lower, were increasing substantially.[17] By 1938 men accounted for 47 percent of cancer deaths, as opposed to perhaps 35 percent at the turn of the century.[18] Men seemed especially prone to develop tumors of the digestive tract, which caused almost 50 percent of cancer mortality for males in the late 1930s. Women still suffered heavily from malignancies of the uterus (20 percent of female cancer mortality) and the breast (18 percent). Not much discussed at the time, but starkly clear to later students of cancer epidemiology, was a perceptible rise in the incidence of cancers affecting the respiratory system. The increase in mortality from such cancers between 1900 and 1935, reflecting the response to the epidemic of cigarette smoking that had begun early in the century, amounted to an estimated 52 percent for men and 39 percent for women.[19]

Statistics such as these might well have prompted popular outcries for action—federal or otherwise—against cancer. A common response, however, was to challenge the figures. One expert argued in 1932 that "the general evidence tends more and more to . . . prove that the apparent increase in the disease is due to improved methods of diagnosis by which more cases are discovered, and to the greater longevity of the human race, by which more people attain the cancer age." Louis Dublin, an insurance company executive who joined Hoffman as a leading expert on the subject in the 1930s, gradually but unmistakably took a more sanguine view of the recent history of cancer. In the late 1920s and early 1930s he shared Hoffman's gloom—"cancer as a cause of disability and death," he said in 1926, "is increasing. There is no longer any room for doubt about that." But in 1937 he was more optimistic. "I am convinced that cancer as a cause of death is no longer increasing in the United States."[20]

In retrospect it is clear that Dublin was essentially correct in 1937. Cancer, while beginning to kill many thousands of smokers, was not—once the aging of the population and better diagnosis were considered—a much greater threat to life than it had been in the mid-1920s. By the 1930s, however, the statisticians had apparently debated the question to a standstill. Those people who took the trouble to follow the arguments, which appeared mainly in specialized journals, could not easily determine which side was correct. Moreover, most Americans understood the cancer problem not from statistics, but from the increasingly common personal experience of watching a close friend or relative suffer from the ailment. Having escaped the infectious diseases that had killed so many of their forebears, they sensed as they advanced beyond middle age that they might well fall victim to cancer. To that extent they were ready to heed the prophets of doom.

Unable to stir the public to action with statistics, the crusaders hoped for support from the newspapers and magazines of the day. Many publications indeed devoted greater space to cancer stories. Coverage in the *New York Times* increased from an average of around forty or fifty stories per year during the 1920s to nearly one hundred per year in the mid-1930s. The number of magazine articles listed in the *Readers' Guide to Periodical Literature* rose from 10 to 15 per year (on the average) in the 1920s to roughly twice that number by the mid-1930s. By that time cancer drew more attention in both the papers and the magazines than did tuberculosis, and no other illnesses—not even heart diseases, far and away the largest cause of death—even approached the coverage given these two.[21]

It was clear from this imbalance in coverage that cancer continued to exercise a hold on the popular imagination out of proportion to its danger to life. Though the heart had a special mystique of its own—people had "fighting" hearts, "kind" hearts, "big" hearts—it could also be thought of more dispassionately, like a mechanical pump that could be repaired when it broke down. Cancer, by contrast, was "The Common Enemy," "The Great Peril," "The Greatest Scourge in the World."[22] To most Americans it remained an insidious, mysterious, indiscriminating, impoverishing, and painfully wasting disease that could hit anywhere, anytime, and could not be arrested once it appeared.

As if to counter such fears, many of the stories grossly exaggerated promising developments in research. Cures for cancer, it seemed, were forever being announced.[23] Sensationalism aside, however, the subject of cancer was rarely front-page news. The papers ordinarily put cancer stories on the inside pages—often next to news aimed at women—and kept them short. Adolph Ochs of the *New York Times,* according to one source, was willing to devote the first six pages of his paper to news of a cancer cure—"no matter if the United States is being defeated in a war."[24] But that "cure" never came, so Ochs, like other publishers, waited.

The prevailing attitude made good sense from a publisher's standpoint, which deemed that many people did not want to read about unpleasant matters such as cancer; they just skipped over articles that troubled them. Moreover, until there was a "war" against cancer to write about—and victories to be reported—American publishers recognized that their readers might tire of the monotonous positive thinking pushed by the allies. Like the doctors in the ASCC and the statisticians, they were not yet ready to seek the aid of government. The alliance held, but it had yet to assume the power that it was to enjoy in later decades.

ALTHOUGH there still were no persuasive explanations of the causes of the disease, and few cures, these realities did not stop some researchers from predicting imminent breakthroughs.[25] Newspapers gave special attention in 1925 to a report in the British medical journal, *Lancet,* that a virus caused cancer. *Lancet's* editors called the research "an event in the history of medicine," adding that it might "represent a solution of the central problem of cancer."[26] The announcement, the *New Republic* declared two weeks later, "produced a furor that would do credit to a minor war." Peyton Rous of the Rockefeller Institute, whose work on chicken viruses had inspired the British researchers, was deluged with requests for tumor material. One "able man," Rous marveled, came to see him and walked off with a live specimen clutched under his arm.[27]

Rous was pleased that his work was again attracting attention, and he struck up a long correspondence with William Gye, the British researcher. But Rous was nonetheless worried, for he anticipated much controversy that would discredit viral research in general.[28] His reservations were justified: other scientists could not confirm the work abroad, and important researchers in America were suspicious, indeed scornful, from the start. Bacterial theories, Francis Carter Wood of the Institute of Cancer Research at Columbia pointed out, had "always been the darling of crackpots and dabblers." Privately, Wood told a friend that Gye had a "touch of the swelled head." He added, "I can't get it at all, and I should be very grateful to Gye if, instead of talking about a cure in human beings, he had kept his mouth shut and cured *one hen* first, and there is no evidence that he has done that. I may be dyspeptic, but these are my views."[29]

By 1926 criticisms of Gye and his collaborators again relegated viral and bacterial theories to the fringes of cancer research, leaving the experts with their old standby, that cancer was activated by "irritation."[30] This notion received further support from revelations of work-related tumors. The jaw cancers of five women in New Jersey were attributed to their occupation as painters of radium watch dials. The women had "pointed" their radium-covered paint brushes by placing them in their mouths.[31] Other research demonstrated the carcinogenic activity of certain lubricating oils used in cotton mills. And in the late 1920s British scientists began identifying the specific carcinogenic agents in dyes and coal tars.[32]

Although during the depression environmental approaches to cancer research generated slightly more scholarly interest than they had in the past, these important studies did not attract great popular attention. American cancer scientists, in fact, had to look hard for financial assistance. Even with continuing support from the Rockefeller Foundation, the sums available for cancer research from foundations, universities, contributions, and public sources did not exceed $700,000 per year in the mid-1930s. This was less than one-third of the money, *Fortune* magazine complained in 1937, that the public spent in an afternoon to watch one major football game.[33]

Everywhere cancer fighters looked they encountered discouraging facts. The only chair of oncology in the country was at Cornell-Memorial Hospital—held by Ewing. Cancer research held few attractions for the ablest young scientists. "Cancer," one recalled, "was not considered a very respectable thing to study because no progress was being made in it." Wood added that "there are no rewards for such work, and in many cases the discoveries are of a type which have no value in getting a man an academic position."[34] A leading medical historian commented that "if a great scientist at the end of a brilliant career wants to make a fool of himself, he takes up the problem of cancer."[35]

This remark suggested the most demoralizing fact of all: the disease remained a mystery. "Nobody knew what the cancer problem was, which way it should go, and what should be supported and what shouldn't," one researcher recalled. The *Index Catalogue of the Library of the Surgeon General's Office*, the major reference work for medical research, listed some 8,500 articles on cancer published between 1923 and 1938—there was no dearth of output, scholarly and otherwise, on the subject—but the articles ran the gamut of hypotheses. "Causes" included civilization, filth, population density, air pollution, diets, sex life, emotional trauma, occupation, geophysical radiation, tea drinking, heredity (many entrants), nerves, social status, injury, and chronic irritation.[36]

Cancer therapies, too, offered little hope. Groping for novel approaches, researchers publicized a wide range of experiments, some of them on human beings. Injections of hormones and electrical charges passed through cancer cells were tried. One imaginative scientist thought that injections of typhoid fever would cure the disease (his patient died four days later).[37] Another assumed that cancer spread in the "warmer" regions of the body and that tumors could therefore be "frozen out." Patients, *Time* reported, were "stripped, placed on beds, and piled high with crushed ice, like frozen fish."

> An electric fan blew chill winds through the cold room, and soon, the first numbing pain of the ice obliterated by anesthetics, they fell into a frozen slumber. For five days, they remained in a coma. Their pulse beats almost stopped, their stomachs, kidneys, and bowels ceased functioning, their general body temperatures fell from a normal 98.6°F to 90°, a record sustained low.[38]

Though the patients seemed better when they awoke—the tumors appeared to have shrunk—they all died within a few months. According to the doctors, death stemmed from the advanced state of the malignancies.

Most physicians, of course, eschewed such dramatics, relying instead on more tested therapeutics such as X-rays, radium, and surgery. But none of these appeared to be any more promising than in the past. X-radiation, though frequently employed in conjunction with surgical operations, still seemed unpredictable. Careful observers continued to point out that the rays did little for most cancers afflicting internal organs.[39] Radium, while also used widely, evoked little more official enthusiasm—it did not seem to control the vast majority of tumors. It was also expensive.

Surgery remained the best hope. It enjoyed great status as a speciality in the treatment of many ailments in these years.[40] But it, too, seldom cured cancers. (Freud had twenty-five painful operations on cancerous tissue in his mouth between 1923 and 1937, and ultimately died of the disease in 1939.) Many patients died on the table. A careful assessment in 1927 revealed that breast surgery—employed at an early stage—was fairly safe. It was by far the most common surgical procedure (skin cancers excepted) in cancer cases. By contrast, there were only one-fifth as many resections of the colon, stomach, and intestine, and mortality in these cases exceeded 50 percent.[41]

Surgeons emphasized that their biggest handicap, aside from the dangers of infection or shock, continued to be the advanced state of the vast majority of cancers that finally came to their attention. Most internal cancers still could not be detected in their early stages. ASCC leaders pointed out that many people persisted in procrastinating—out of fear as well as out of ignorance—before going to a doctor about suspicious symptoms.[42] Wood repeatedly estimated that fewer than 20 percent of cases were operable.[43]

Some experts felt general practitioners were to blame. Cancer victims, Wood estimated, amounted to but 5 percent of patients in general hospitals; many doctors did not know cancer when they saw it. Even pathologists, he said, needed better training.[44] Another cancer expert, who agreed with Wood's pessimistic view, described an all too typical approach of nonspecialists: "I have been watching a bump on a woman's breast for about a year," a practitioner wrote him, "and I think it may be time for you to see it." Predictably, the cancer was by then inoperable.[45]

The majority of doctors, moreover, continued to be fatalistic. Unlike later physicians, they did not think there were cures for very many ailments. The smallest part of medical school training, in fact, concerned treatment; most of it dealt with the identification and classification of diseases. As Lewis Thomas said of his experience as a medical student in the early 1930s, "it gradually dawned on us that we didn't know much that was really useful, that we could do nothing to change the course of the great majority of the diseases we were so busy analyzing, that medicine, for all its facade as a learned profession, was in real life a profoundly ignorant occupation."[46] Although Thomas exaggerated slightly, overlooking some real advances of the previous forty years, he was correct in stressing the pessimism that overtook many of his contemporaries.

For these reasons cancer therapy, too, remained a demoralizing business. And some of the experts—resisting the positive thinking so dear to middle-class American culture—were not afraid to say so. Characteristically, Ewing took the lead in emphasizing this prudent view. "Too much," he said in 1940, "has been expected from the prevention of cancer . . . It is certain that efforts in this field have thus far been quite desultory and inefficient. No new curative agent or method will be found in the near future."[47] Others, including Wood at Columbia, agreed. The experts knew that there was far too much yet to be learned about the basic biology of cells before the disease could be prevented or before the victims of cancer could get effective therapy.

Understandably, many patients and their relatives were as fatalistic as those facing cancer in generations past. Their emotions were varied, complex, and changing. No one, perhaps, portrayed these emotions more tellingly than the novelist Thomas Wolfe, one of the few major writers to deal with cancer in his fiction. In *Of Time and the River* (1935) a key character, Gant, suffers horribly from cancer, which Wolfe describes in graphic terms. When Gant's blood finally gushes all over the bed, his wife, expressing a folk wisdom of the ages, tells her daughter that all will now be well, that the cancer had bled itself right out of his system. "Nature has taken its own course . . . nature is the best physician in the end!" The daughter, reflecting a more modern sensibility, counters such self-delusion by remarking that the doctor had predicted the end. Not so, the mother persists. "It won't be the first time that a doctor has been wrong . . . It's always been my opinion that they're wrong about as often as they're right—only you can't prove it on 'em. They *bury* their mistakes."[48]

ATTITUDES SUCH AS THESE, among experts and common folk, thrived within a broader ideological context that identified the environment, not heredity, as the key to understanding the world. Culture, many intellectuals thought, determined the circumstances of one's life.[49] And "civilization" itself—at least for some people in the middle classes—was noxious. To Ezra Pound civilization was "an old bitch gone in the teeth." To T. S. Eliot it was a "Wasteland." Amory Blaine, a protagonist in a work by F. Scott Fitzgerald, imagined himself caught "in his underwear, so to speak," by the "crude, vulgar air of western civilization." Anthropologists, led by Margaret Mead, contrasted the freedom and ease of the South Seas with the tenseness and competitiveness of Western culture.[50] These were scattered signs that some middle-class Americans in the urban, commercial world following World War I were alienated by the "civilization" of their own times and yearned for a simpler, freer existence.

Within this cultural context it was not surprising that contemporary writers reiterated the historically durable idea that cancer was *the* disease of civilization. Many echoed the view that the "stress" of civilization was a threat to health. Some of these writers drew their inspiration from the growing vogue for psychosomatic medicine, which popularized the idea that people would be healthier if they learned to relax and avoid tension.[51] Others borrowed from Jung and Freud to denounce "repression."[52] The poet W. H. Auden wondered if cancer followed discouragement:

> Doctor Thomas sat over his dinner
> Though his wife was waiting to ring,
> Rolling his bread into pellets;
> Said, "Cancer's a funny thing.
>
> "Nobody knows what the cause is,
> Though some pretend they do
> It's like some hidden assassin
> Waiting to strike at you.
>
> "Childless men get it,
> And men when they retire;
> It's as if there had to be some outlet
> For their foiled creative fire."[53]

Other writers stressed above all that people in industrial society were eating the wrong foods. Nutritional prescriptions, enhanced by discoveries of vitamins, flourished in the interwar years.[54] No one was more insistent on the role of diets than J. Ellis Barker, an Englishman whose *Cancer: How It Is Caused, How It Can Be Prevented* (1924) set the tone for some later writings.[55] Barker was certain that cancer stemmed from "autointoxication of the bowel. Apparently civilization and constipation go hand in hand." He attributed the prevalence of cancers in the alimentary canal to constipation, which in turn stemmed from stress, repression, the overuse of food preservatives, and—ultimately—the emancipation of women, who were too busy working to cook carefully or to prepare "natural foods." Barker campaigned for greater consumption of uncooked vegetables and undried meats. He opposed the use of toilets and toilet seats; squatting, he felt, would assist bowel movements. "In suitable places," he said, there should be inscribed:

> Three visits a day
> Keep illness away
> Things too sweet and too hot
> Cause our insides to rot.
>
> Cancer is a disease of civilization
> It is caused by bowel poisons, chemical poisons, and faked food.
> Give Nature a chance.[56]

Barker's enthusiasms were undisciplined. So, too, were those of his countryman, John Cope. In his *Cancer: Civilization and Degeneration* (1932), Cope worried about "repression and the overregulation of the food instinct." He found fault with porridges, milk puddings, and many liquids and encouraged a diet of meat, fruits, and nuts. To advance such habits, Cope said, people should abolish the spoon! And they should enjoy plenty of sex, to keep sexual organs from falling into the "disuse" that prompted cancer.[57]

Orthodox writers angrily rejected these ideas. It was unclear, they reiterated, that "primitive" societies were free of cancer. On the contrary, the available evidence suggested that cancer afflicted all people and all races: better statistics on non-Western societies would show that to be clear.[58] Heaping scorn on the cancer-civilization connection, *Fortune* insisted that there existed "no trustworthy evidence, experimental, clinical, or statistical, of a causal relationship between cancer and the absence or presence of any particular constituent of the human diet."[59] Although the orthodox view prevailed in the prestigious magazines and journals, it could not prevent the undercurrent of popular opposition. Even a few epidemiologists advanced dietary arguments. Hoffman came out with a 767-page book on the subject in 1937. While none of these studies convinced the alliance against cancer, they were evidence that many people continued to believe in a correlation between cancer and nutrition.

Most critics of the allies against cancer emphasized one thing: that more attention be paid to strategies of prevention. They argued that control of the disease depended not only on laboratory research into basic cellular processes but also on identifying the "external causes," such as poor diets, that set cells on the rampage. "Some of the factors concerned in the aetiology of cancer," one observer explained in 1934, "are of a rather banal nature, which one can avoid. There is no reason to regard the problem as an impenetrable mystery."[60] But preventive approaches commanded relatively little attention among leading researchers in the 1920s and 1930s, who correctly pointed out the dearth of solid scientific evidence documenting a major role for life styles, including diets, or for environmental carcinogens. It was not until the 1970s that arguments relating cancer and nutrition attracted much support among orthodox experts on the disease.

Beliefs that stress, civilization, and diet caused cancer were only a few of the vast array of popular notions and superstitions about medicine in general and cancer in particular in these years. When the sociologists Robert and Helen Lynd conducted their study of Muncie, Indiana, in the 1920s, they discovered that many working-class people thought the doctor was "something of a magician from whom the patient dares expect only a small part of the truth and no explanation of it."[61] The Lynds found that the majority of people were too poor to go to a physician and that many others relied on folk wisdoms and incantations. Some went to a healer whom residents referred to as "the old nigger out in——, an outlying village." He was known to wave his hands before his visitors and drive diseases through the feet and into the ground. A barber "regularly takes patients into a back room for magical treatment for everything from headache to cancer." Mothers wrapped old leather hatbands about each breast after childbirth to avoid all sorts of breast trouble and tied shoestrings about their children's necks to prevent croup. When folk remedies failed, there were always patent medicines to help out. The Lynds counted sixty-eight advertisements of one inch or larger in the morning paper one day. Thirty-seven of them plugged salves, soaps, and remedies.[62]

As earlier, cancer "cures" were main staples of newspaper ads—and of the unorthodox healers who peddled them, some of whom operated on a grand scale. Norman Baker of Iowa, advertising between 1929 and 1932 that "Cancer is Conquered," peddled what appeared to be an arsenic compound for rubbing onto external tumors. With the help of a magazine, *TNT* ("The Naked Truth"), and especially a radio station, KTNT, he struck it rich, collecting an estimated million dollars in the next few years. Sure of his powers, Baker had no qualms about explaining his work to federal authorities. The Surgeon General, who at first expressed only "reserve and skepticism" about his claims, later joined other governmental agencies in a protracted legal struggle against Baker.[63] The suit forced Baker to flee to Mexico in 1937.[64] He was later prosecuted for mail fraud and was imprisoned at Leavenworth between 1941 and 1944.

Still more famous was Harry Hoxsey, an itinerant cancer specialist in the 1920s and early 1930s who touted his Hoxide Treatment as a cure for malignant tumors. His medication for palpable growths consisted mainly of arsenic; for internal tumors it featured potassium iodide, along with varying amounts of red clover, poke root, prickly ash bark, and other herbal aids. Though repeatedly denounced by the medical profession, Hoxsey opened a clinic in Dallas in 1936, where he prospered for twenty-four years—one estimate said he treated 8,000 patients and grossed $1.5 million in 1956. Led by the Food and Drug Administration, whose authority was enhanced by new regulatory legislation in 1938, the government mounted a legal attack on Hoxsey in the 1940s and 1950s. But the wheels of justice turned slowly and closed up his operation only in 1960.

The popularity of healers like Baker and Hoxsey derived from more than their skill as charlatans. Both men appealed to class and religious feelings, especially among the poor and ill-educated. Baker

This Man Offers $5000.00

Norman Baker, perfecter of the simple Baker Cancer Treatments and founder of the Baker Hospitals, sitting in his special designed desk, the only one of its kind in the world.

And Challenges All Doctors

WITHOUT OPERATIONS, RADIUM OR X-RAY

LAREDO, TEXAS
1016 FLORES AVE.

MUSCATINE, IOWA
407 EAST FRONT ST.

From the Historical Health Fraud Collection at the American Medical Association, Chicago.

presented himself for a while as something of a populist, running in 1932 as a Farmer-Labor candidate for governor of Iowa. Hoxsey, too, depicted himself as a man of the common people. "We are not fighting for ourselves," he said, "but for those poor old victims who live at the forks of the creek; who till the soil with a mule." Appealing to the religious faith of the rural poor, Hoxsey compared himself with Christ, who had been persecuted for trying to help the needy. "Jesus Christ was crucified and yet he was the only man who ever cured the lepers."[65]

Baker, Hoxsey, and others capitalized especially on the enduring hostility of many Americans to orthodox medical professionals. Though this hostility was geographically widespread, it seemed especially sharp in the economically impoverished areas of the rural South and West—the areas most removed from the modern medical culture of twentieth-century America. Baker was abrasive in his hostility, branding the AMA as the American Meatcutters Association and M.D. as "More Dough." He circulated a pamphlet entitled, "Doctors, Dynamiters, and Gunmen." He added, "Do not believe all they publish about their cures, but look back and see if you can recall one relative, one friend or acquaintance that was ever permanently cured by operations, radium, and X-ray—that tells the TRUE STORY."[66]

Hoxsey and Baker were charlatans of magnificent bravado. Many others operated on a smaller scale. Salesman of aluminum pots and pans worked the cancer angle by assuring housewives that aluminum, unlike old-fashioned kitchenware, would not cause tumors. Faith healers and those who promoted home "remedies" continued to flourish. Peyton Rous heard from a man who had a "wound around the juglar vein" and couldn't talk for three years. After spending $6,000 on radium treatments, the victim turned to a healer who "drew that cancer out of his throat in less than three days." The patient remained in good health for a year, but then died "of paralysis from the effect of the large amount of radium treatments he had received."[67] Another correspondent told Rous that she had "cured one man he had been five months bed fast passing blood and puss day and night for three months he had to wear a napkin like a baby." She then asked if there was a reward for his remedy. Rous penciled on the letter, "Not answered . . . How could it be?"[68]

The records of the Public Health Service show that healers were quick to write the White House. One sent Warren Harding a copy of his pamphlet, "Natural Laws That Govern Health," and said he had a remedy that could "purify the blood and make a person's flesh look as pure as a baby's, which I believe will cure cancer." Another told of a "genuine cancer cure which was left to me (by my Father) and it has been in the Family back four generations which was got from the Indians." He had tried it "on the brest of a ladie" and "the cancer came out and she is very near healed up. I have the cancer in alcohol and the Ladie as evidence."[69]

Nothing so clearly exposed the groping for answers, and the sociocultural gulf separating medical orthodoxy from many popular views, as the excitement over cancer prizes sponsored in 1927 by William Saunders, chairman of the board of Ingersoll-Rand Company and director of the Federal Reserve Bank of New York. Saunders was explicit in doubting the wisdom of orthodox medical practitioners. "Discoveries," he said, "are not always made by experts; physicians like businessmen are not always the best workers. Through the lure of a reward this serious problem might be solved through the genius of a lay mind, by chemists, or through unknown and unorganized sources." Saunders offered to pay $50,000 for a cure and $50,000 for discovery of the causes of cancer.[70]

The response of orthodox medical leaders to the idea of the rewards was predictably negative. Senator Copeland of New York, who supported governmental funding of cancer research, claimed that such a competition would only "stimulate all sorts of cranks and frauds to apply for it immediately. After all, what is needed is more brains rather than more money, and the brains best suited to this kind of work appear to be devoted to it already."[71] Saunders, however, was not easy to ignore. He asked the ASCC to administer and judge the competition. The board split over the issue. Ewing, ever the medical professional, scorned the proposal. "No discovery of value in medicine," he said, "has ever been made by a layman." But other board members felt they could not reject the offer out of hand. Soper helped break the impasse by recommending that the society do as Saunders had asked. "If it did nothing more," he advised, "it would be an opportunity to demonstrate the futility of seeking to solve the cancer problem through the offer of a money reward."[72] This lukewarm endorsement won over the doctors who dominated the society.

More than 3,500 claims inundated the society by early 1928, when a deadline mercifully ended the competition. A thoroughly disgusted Soper, in an article announcing that no one deserved the prizes, categorized the first 1,500 entrants. Three hundred fifteen claims came from Europe, and 24 countries in all were represented. Soper mordantly observed that "555 were illiterate, 565 were indefinite, and 291 were mercenary." Sixty-six of the applicants had dietary cures in mind, 42 religious answers. Many writers thought that Saunders had cancer and was looking to cure himself. Most of the "mercenary" applicants wanted cash on delivery, their remedies to be supplied in return.[73] Soper complained bitterly of the "low mentality, the lack of ordinary sense, shown by many of the writers." He listed at great length the home remedies advanced by the applicants.

> It was curious to see what confidence was placed in the authority which age and decrepitude impart; in the beneficent gifts which mother nature offers to her children in the form of herbs; in the power of poisons, acids and alkalis; in the healing qualities of such uncanny objects as living moles, crabs and toads; in the green of copper vessels, the sting of insects and bites of serpents. Some of the cures were exceedingly simple. Others were highly complicated. A few were disgusting.

Soper found patterns behind the apparently unrelated popular responses. First, the people who entered the contest—many of them unlettered—assumed that "a common element was at work in the production of all cancers." Many Americans, only dimly aware of efforts to classify the various forms of cancer, considered cancer a single disease. Second, the respondents openly denigrated doctors. "The opinion was frequently expressed," Soper noted, "that the medical profession had a closed mind in regard to the cause and cure of cancer." Third, people imagined cancer to be caused by bruises, sores, or "parasites" and saw it as an affliction that could be treated by rubbing in one kind of compound or another. As Soper noted, this belief flew in the face of statistics, which showed that only 3 percent of cancers affected the skin, as opposed to 34 percent which attacked the stomach.

COMPARABLY BEWILDERED NOTIONS about cancer persisted in the 1930s. A public-opinion poll in 1939 revealed that 41 percent of respondents thought cancer might be contagious. Doctors at Harvard heard from a woman who wanted to know what to do with the "personal effects" of her aunt, who had recently died of the disease. "In the absence of definite knowledge," she wrote, "I feel that extraordinary precautions are justified . . . will sunlight be enough or should they be destroyed?" Another woman begged to know if her brothers and sisters should consider marrying anyone who had ever had cancer in the family, adding that "it is very humiliating to be publicly branded as 'diseased.'"[74]

As this letter suggested, many Americans still considered cancer a stigmatizing illness to be kept quiet at all costs. Herbert Lombard, a pioneering cancer epidemiologist and public-health officer in Massachusetts, felt that his lecture audiences often looked bored: they were waiting for him to talk about the "real" cause of the disease, syphilis.[75] A Michigan physician agreed. "Cancer," he noted, "entails a social stigma; thus physicians are prevailed upon to falsify death returns."[76] Another doctor urged that cancer clinics be named "tumor clinics." "Many patients," he said, "do not wish to be seen in an institution labeled as a cancer hospital. The word 'cancer' should not be employed in contacts with patients, even though a tacit understanding exists as to the nature of the disease being treated."[77]

Many people were so upset by the thought of cancer that they scarcely wished to think of it, much less read stories about it. The editors of *Life* discovered this continuing capacity for self-censorship in 1937, when they broke ground journalistically by including graphic photographs in a lead story about cancer. "I burned up my copy," one subscriber wrote angrily. "I can't imagine anything more repulsive." Another added, "LIFE has doubtless succeeded in scaring a lot of readers, caused mental anguish, helped no one." A third respondent, after complaining of the "horrible and revolting pictures," explained that "fortunately I was able to clip them before the issue reached my wife, who is particularly sensitive to such gory specimens."[78]

When people did talk about cancer, they used the same vivid language that had long provided clues to their deeper feelings. Some similes were relatively gentle—cancer, one expert said, was like a weed. "As a dandelion scatters its seeds to distant places, so the cancer may scatter its seeds along the blood stream."[79] Most were more frightening. Many Americans saw cancer as an invading army or—reflecting the contemporary fascination with organized crime—as a "gangster disease, for it strikes ruthlessly, without warning and in the dark, carrying fear to the heart of the possible victim, which means any human being." The enemy, this writer added, should come "out into the open. Any of us would rather meet such a killer in broad daylight on a public highway and protected with a good weapon than to encounter him unarmed in a dark alley at midnight."[80]

By the 1930s cancer had surpassed tuberculosis as the "dread disease" in the country. A Gallup poll in 1939 listed four illnesses and asked people, "Which of these diseases would you hate most to have?" Seventy-six percent named cancer, 13 percent tuberculosis, 9 percent heart trouble, and 2 percent pneumonia. When asked why, respondents emphasized that cancer almost always killed, that its victims suffered more, that it was a lingering disease. The poll confirmed what many observers had long been saying. "Many people," one doctor said, "are afraid to even mention the name. They still endow the condition with an aura of mysticism and hopelessness and throw in the sponge at the mere mention of the dread word."[81]

It is obvious in retrospect—and was clear to many close observers at the time—that to "throw in the sponge" about cancer was in some ways to exaggerate the threat from the disease. Cancer ranked well behind heart and circulatory ailments as a killer, and its mortality rate, when adjusted for age, was increasing only slightly. Contrary to popular opinion, it was not always painful or disabling—some heart ailments were worse in these respects. The popular dread of cancer, as before and later, was in all these ways a little irrational. But people who feared cancer were correct on two important points: the large majority (probably four-fifths) of cancer patients did die from the disease, sometimes slowly, miserably, and at enormous emotional and economic cost to their families; moreover, popular attitudes toward disease are rarely defined by reactions to statistics. The feeling that Western civilization was helpless in the grip of a vicious gangster was unnerving, especially in a society that prided itself on its ability to solve all kinds of social, economic, and medical problems. Cancer cruelly contradicted American optimism.

To the aggressive, middle-class allies—the doctors, the statisticians, some of the media, politicians like Neely—the mystery of cancer demanded vigorous counterattack. But millions of Americans, especially the poor and ill-educated, paid them little heed. Their inattention can be explained. Cancer was indeed to be feared, but—unlike cholera or yellow fever in the nineteenth century or influenza in 1919—it was not a terrorizing epidemic that could wipe out one's family and friends overnight. Unlike polio in the 1940s, it did not seem so highly contagious as to threaten one's children. People feared cancer but, save for patients and their families, they ordinarily did so at some distance. Denying that they would develop the disease, they were not ready to demand public action against it. Dread is different from terror.

Finally, Americans in that era did not expect as much—from doctors, from the government, from life in general—as they were to demand in the very different, more affluent age of higher expectations following World War Two. The poor and the blue-collar classes, a majority before 1940, had never had much, and with the Depression further impoverishing their lives they coped from day to day without great hopes for the future. So it was that the more elite groups in the anticancer alliance made little headway with their fellow Americans in the wilderness years of the 1920s and 1930s.

5

Government Joins the Fight

IN JULY 1937 a small but determined group of scientists and politicians succeeded where Senator Neely had failed in 1928. The group secured unanimous passage of legislation authorizing $700,000 in federal funds to support cancer research in the coming fiscal year and an additional $750,000 to build a National Cancer Institute in Bethesda, Maryland. The authorization strongly committed the federal government to cancer research in the United States, which henceforth was to assume world leadership in the field.[1] Surgeon General Thomas Parran exulted that the law was "as broad as all outdoors," sanctioning virtually total freedom for the administrators and scientists who now joined the alliance against cancer. Important in itself, the law was a model for much governmental activity that followed World War Two—such as the institutes for heart ailments, mental illness, and other health problems.[2]

The congressional rhetoric that ushered in this remarkable piece of legislation was almost as vivid as Neely's had been a decade earlier. The major sponsor in the Senate, Homer Bone, a progressive Democrat from Washington, pointed out that the dread disease killed more people in two years—270,000—than had been lost in all of America's foreign wars. "If 140,000 persons in this country were burned over slow fires every year," he declaimed, "it would stagger the moral conscience of the world; and yet here, we, a body with our fingers on the purse strings, have it in our power at least to try to do something to stamp out a disease which not only takes 140,000 lives each year but which claims them in such a hideous fashion."[3] The key sponsor in the House, liberal Maury Maverick of Texas, avoided bombastic language and instead aroused his colleagues' personal unease about the illness. "Sixty members of the present Congress," he remarked, "will die of cancer. So this is bringing it close to home. One out of every eight persons over 40 who die, die of cancer. As most of us are over 40, I have figured there will be around 60 of us who thus meet death."[4]

When the legislation passed Bone and Maverick were understandably pleased, but it is difficult to argue that their rhetoric—which added little to what the congressmen already knew about the disease—overwhelmed their colleagues. Indeed, given the impotence of the anticancer alliance through the early 1930s, it seems surprising in retrospect that the statute made it through Congress. That the bill passed unanimously seems especially remarkable in view of what authorities on cancer were saying in 1937. By then many experts were openly doubting the earlier opinion—widely held at the time of Neely's appeal in 1928—that the age-adjusted cancer mortality rate was rapidly increasing. And leading scientists remained doubtful about the effectiveness of organized drives to conquer the disease. As Ewing put it at the time, "there is not the slightest indication that the nature of malignant growth will be unravelled in the present state of biological knowledge." The answer to cancer, he said, "will come when science is ready for it and cannot be hastened by pouring sums of money into the effort."[5]

Why then did this legislation pass in 1937? Given the later significance of the law—no act did more over time to dramatize the search for a magic bullet against the disease—that is an important, though still intriguing, question.

ONE REASON for the greater support given cancer research was the still growing reputation—mainly among the politically influential middle classes—of the profession of medicine. As in the past the rise in status rested in part on some real achievements. Researchers in the early 1920s discovered that insulin could restore comatose diabetics to consciousness; this dramatic step was properly hailed as a "miracle of modern medicine."[6] In 1936 came early reports of the potential of sulfa drugs, which—doctors marveled—

might make it possible to cure or control a host of ancient diseases, including lobar pneumonia, meningitis, and septicemias of various types. As Lewis Thomas put it later (exaggerating slightly), the sulfa drugs (and, in the 1940s, penicillin) created a "revolution in medical practice . . . it was a totally new world. Doctors could now *cure* disease, and this was astonishing, most of all to the doctors themselves."[7]

Significant in themselves, these advances seemed the more impressive in a culture that greatly feared early death and valued good health. The quest for an ever healthier society had intensified during World War One, when millions of young men failed their physicals for the draft: much obviously remained to be done. Thereafter—to judge from the popular press and from the AMA's magazine for the general audience, *Hygeia,* started in 1923—Americans became increasingly concerned about obesity and nutrition. The potential of vitamins aroused great interest. People demanded not only freedom from disease and disability, but also the right to be comfortable. To be healthy, they thought, was to live the good life. It followed that society must assure this right to all who were willing to pay for it.[8]

In this cultural context the reputation of doctors flourished. By the 1920s the white-coated physician emerged as chief salesman in ads for a wide range of goods available to the burgeoning consumer society. "Your Doctor KNOWS, Ask Him!" read advertisements for "Vitamine Bread." Doctors appeared in ads for cosmetics, toothpaste, cars, even (and especially) cigarettes.[9] The use of physicians as authority figures, while hard to assess as an advertising gimmick—the Lynds, among others, still doubted that working-class families had much faith in doctors—testified to the deference of the culturally influential middle classes to experts in general and to doctors and medical scientists in particular.

Even the Depression, which damaged the prestige of other professional groups—lawyers, businessmen, financiers—did not dull the image of the medical profession among many middle-class Americans. Magazines and newspapers identified physicians as disinterested, expert men of science.[10] Films presented noble portrayals of doctors, such as Paul Muni's performance as Louis Pasteur, which won him the Academy Award in 1936. By 1937 the family incomes of physicians were two to three times the average of other Americans. Their social standing and economic power—marginal only a half century earlier—were solidly established in American life.

Philanthropists also showed greater faith in the medical profession. Just before Congress voted its support of the anticancer crusade, two notable gifts were announced. In 1936 John D. Rockefeller, Jr., bestowed $3 million, plus land valued at $900,000 between East Sixty-seventh and Sixty-eighth streets in Manhattan, for a new building for Memorial Hospital. Descriptions of the proposed twelve-story structure, which was completed in 1939, made it clear that it was to be far and away the most impressive and well-equipped facility of its kind in the world.[11] A few months later Starling Childs, a New York utilities magnate whose wife Jane Coffin Childs died of cancer in 1936, established a $10 million endowment in her name at Yale University.[12] This was by far the largest single gift in the history of cancer philanthropy.

Both Rockefeller and Childs stressed their confidence in the abilities of medical researchers and clinicians. Their largesse was ample testimony to the faith of America's leading citizens in the potential of scientific medicine. This confidence was an underlying if elusive source of support for those who wanted to bring government into the anticancer alliance.

A SECOND SOURCE of support for centralized research against cancer was the growing readiness of Americans to turn to government—both state and federal—for solutions to societal problems. Greatly strengthened by the Depression, this tendency was substantial by 1937, and the anticancer alliance took advantage of it.

A governmental beachhead in medical research, although distinctly limited in activity prior to the 1930s, had long existed. As early as 1887 the government's Hygienic Laboratory, which conducted research into infectious diseases, was opened on Staten Island. In 1891 it moved to Washington, where it merged with the Public Health Service, which Congress established in legislation in 1902 and 1912. The PHS henceforth took the lead in federal activity against diseases; research teams of the PHS in Washington and at the Harvard Medical School in Boston began basic investigations of the biological effects of radiation on malignant cells and of the biochemistry of cancer cells.[13] State and local health departments, while poorly funded, were providing periodic medical and dental examinations for schoolchildren and cooperating with private groups to mitigate hookworm, pellagra, venereal disease, and tuberculosis.[14]

To public-health advocates these scattered efforts were far from adequate.[15] The PHS in the 1920s had budgets of only $300,000 per year. Located in the Treasury Department, it attracted little attention. It concerned itself less with chronic illnesses like cancer than with venereal disease, Rocky Mountain spotted fever, and other communicable ailments.[16] Unhappy with this state of affairs, leaders of the anticancer alliance urged the government to get more deeply involved. Hoffman as early as 1920 called for publicly assisted clinics and cancer hospitals.[17] In 1928 Ewing spoke for many experts who welcomed governmental support of cancer institutes. He explained that he "would be willing to accept almost any degree of socialization if we could only get some results in the field of cancer."[18]

In the 1920s public pressure for state action against cancer became especially strong in Massachusetts, where it was reported that cancer mortality had increased by 50 percent in the previous fifty years. The Bay State, it seemed, had the highest cancer death rates in the country. Pressure peaked in 1926, with news of the plight of Wilbur Trussell, a telegraph operator and father of eight. Trussell cared for his mother-in-law, ailing from cancer, in his crowded home. His neighbors, fearful that cancer was contagious, ostracized him and his family. Trussell had no place to turn, and the lady finally died at his home.[19] Thanks in part to publicity about the Trussells, the legislature in 1926 provided for state-aided clinics and appropriated $20,000 for the purchase of radium. Most significant, it funded (at a cost of some $100,000) the renovation of an unused facility in Pondville as the first state-operated cancer hospital in America. The hospital had 115 beds and served 1,000 or more patients per year soon after opening in 1927.[20]

Having been pushed into the cancer business, Bay State officials soon developed enthusiasm for the cause. They helped Massachusetts join New York, which had funded cancer research on a small scale since 1898, as a leader in publicly supported work against cancer. Connecticut followed in 1935, establishing the nation's first "tumor registry," which collected statistics concerning the incidence and mortality from different kinds of tumors.[21] But few other states followed suit, especially after depression conditions forced a squeeze on revenues. In 1936 only four states (New Hampshire was the fourth) appropriated state funds for cancer programs. The total in state money at the time was less than $1 million a year.[22]

In the late 1920s pressure for public action against disease mounted at the federal level. Following Neely's abortive quest for federal aid in 1928, other Democrats pursued his vision. When Neely failed to be reelected in 1928, his friend and colleague, Senator William Harris of Georgia, introduced a likeness of Neely's bill calling for $100,000 in government support of cancer research. It passed the Senate in early 1930, only to die in the House.[23] But in the same year Congress authorized $750,000—a considerable sum at the time—to facilitate construction of and equipment for a National Institute of Health, which was to replace and greatly enlarge the Hygienic Laboratory.[24]

Creation of the NIH was the result of pressure from chemists and medical researchers and of lobbying by the mild-mannered but persuasive Assistant Surgeon General Lewis ("Jimmy") Thompson, a veteran bureaucrat with friendly contacts on Capitol Hill. More broadly, passage of the NIH bill stemmed from the sense in the 1920s that private aid for health research was inadequate. Establishment of the NIH signified that federal aid to medical research had found a small place on the cluttered political agenda of the national government.[25]

Federally supported cancer scientists—the same who had been quietly pursuing their separate investigations in Boston and Washington since 1922—came under the wing of the NIH after 1930.[26] Though the Depression trimmed their already modest funding from $106,000 in 1933 to a low of $85,000 in 1934, they managed to carry on their work.[27] Indeed, America's public support for cancer research was not ungenerous in comparison with government funding in other Western nations. There, as in the United States, the commitment of public funds was small.[28]

More important still in promoting federal aid to health was the administration of President Franklin D. Roosevelt and the New

Deal. Roosevelt himself was not a strong advocate of health legislation. On the contrary, "in matters of health and medicine," his Surgeon General Thomas Parran recalled, "he was quite conservative. He was almost the country squire in his conservatism about what the government should do in terms of health."[29] Roosevelt did little to assist the Public Health Service, whose total appropriation for research in 1938 was only $2.8 million. (By contrast, research funds for the Agriculture Department—beneficiary of potent political lobbies—amounted to $26.3 million.)[30] But the overall thrust of the New Deal was both activist and humanitarian. It stood generally for increasing federal involvement in American life, particularly to help people who could not help themselves. In this broad sense the 1930s were congenial times for federal support of national health. Roosevelt's top adviser, Harry Hopkins, had headed New York's tuberculosis society before 1929. As chief relief administrator from 1933 through 1938 Hopkins expanded federal health services such as home visits by nurses, free physical examinations and immunizations, and school lunches for the poor.[31] Hopkins and others also lobbied effectively for including in the Social Security Act a section (Title 6) that provided for federal support of research into diseases.[32]

As finally funded, the Social Security Act set aside only $375,000 for Title 6 in fiscal 1936, hardly a munificent sum, but the New Dealers had nonetheless accepted a visible role for government in health issues. When Bone, Maverick, and others enlisted the anticancer alliance in support of federal assistance in 1937, they were building upon a number of legislative precedents, both state and federal, for public aid.

THE SUCCESS of the NCI bill, however, is still not explained. Why create an institute for cancer? Why not concentrate on some other threat to health—such as arterial and heart diseases, which killed twice as many people as cancer?

In the broadest sense congressmen chose cancer because they, like their constituents, felt a special dread of the disease. As *Time* explained during the debate, "more than any other disease, cancer has horrified the imagination of mankind. It kills slowly, painfully, and science does not yet know its causes or mechanism."[33] Many heart diseases, by contrast, had *known* causes, including obesity, which people could take steps to prevent. Heart ailments—evoking the comparably benign image of a malfunctioning pump as opposed to a voracious crab—aroused less popular alarm.

But dread of cancer, hardly new in 1937, was an insufficient explanation of passage of the NCI. Congressmen acted then because purposeful individuals took advantage both of the broadening consensus behind governmental support of medical research and of specific events that brought cancer more vividly into the public consciousness in 1936 and 1937.

Chief among these individuals was Clarence Cook ("Pete") Little, who took over as head of the ASCC from Soper in 1930. Only forty-two at that time, Little was a self-possessed Harvard graduate who had served as a researcher for the Harvard Cancer Commission in the 1910s and had become known as an authority on the genetics of cancer. He also had a national reputation as a spokesman for birth control and eugenics and as an educator: in the 1920s he served as president of the University of Maine and the University of Michigan.[34] In 1929, shortly before taking command of the cancer society, Little returned to Maine to head what became known as the Roscoe B. Jackson Memorial Laboratory at Bar Harbor. The lab became an important site for research on cancer genetics and for the breeding and sale of special lines of mice for medical research.[35] While head of the ASCC Little shuttled from Maine to New York to push the society's educational campaign.[36]

At first Little did not do much to change the society, which until 1933 continued working for public education and the creation of cancer clinics. But Little then decided on a new strategy. Over the next two years he quietly laid the groundwork for this effort, mainly by wooing the leadership of the General Federation of Women's Clubs, which had a national membership of two million people.[37] "If we can get all the women talking about cancer," he explained later, "we will be in a fair way of controlling this tremendous cause of suffering and death."[38] When assured of the federation's support in late 1935, he set aside $5,000 to hire its health director, Marjorie Illig. A trained radiologist, Illig became an indefatigable organizer and promoter for the ASCC in the next few years.

With the federation's approval in early 1936, Little and Illig launched the Women's Field Army. Illig took over as National Commander, leading the "war" against the "stubborn foe" and issuing orders to state commanders and captains dressed in brown uniforms. Posters and handbills listed Eleanor Roosevelt and other national figures as honorary supporters and featured the ASCC's symbol, a flaming sword that glowed with spirit and determination. "There SHALL be light!" these proclaimed: ENLIST IN WOMEN'S FIELD ARMY![39] Thus armed, the officers hoped to build an army of foot soldiers who would carry the message of early detection and medical intervention into every home in the land.

From the beginning the WFA encountered sniping from various sources. Some local medical societies feared sharing their control with lay people.[40] Others regarded the WFA as a public-relations gambit without clearly stated goals. A few doctors worried that it was campaigning, as Soper had, for public care of indigent patients, which they saw as the spearhead for socialized medicine.[41] For the most part, however, the WFA flourished, securing solid footholds in twenty-five states by October 1936. It then readied itself for its long-planned major assault: an Enlistment Campaign scheduled for March 1937. Despite bad weather, the campaign was largely successful. Illig estimated later in the year that the army had distributed more than 233,000 pieces of literature, secured "over 100,000 enlistments," and raised $107,000.[42]

In the long run the WFA was a source of strength for the ASCC. Money raised from its recruits added to the society's revenue. By 1939 it had some 200,000 members throughout the country. It helped set up cancer clinics and, as doctors had feared, assisted cancer patients in poverty. Its efforts at the grass roots transformed the cancer society from an elite operation into a still small but more widely recognized national health organization.[43]

The WFA also had a modest success in challenging the conspiracy of silence, encouraging women to take more aggressive charge of their health. Illig, at least, thought so. One woman who had been "worried sick for over a year" that she had cancer, Illig said, was inspired by a WFA-sponsored talk on early detection: "I walked right out and up to my doctor. He examined me. I haven't got a cancer, and I feel twenty years younger." Another woman in her forties, Illig added,

> decided to consult a surgeon about lumps in her breast, which was beginning to discharge from the nipple. She had had these lumps for years, and had been living in a perfect terror of dread. The radio and newspaper articles on this subject made her screw her courage up to the point of going to the surgeon, who operated, removing her breast . . . So far there are no bad after-effects from the operation, and the woman is free from the dreadful horror which had been hanging over her head.[44]

It happened that the WFA mobilized its major offensive in 1937 at the very same time that Bone and Maverick were making their moves in Congress, but nothing indicates that their efforts were coordinated. Neither Little nor Illig articulated a clear vision of a national institute for cancer research and did not lend active support to it until it was virtually assured of passage. Nor is there evidence to suggest that the new recruits lobbied for federal action. Most of the foot soldiers were middle-class women with energy and time to join a worthy cause. They hoped to relieve suffering in their home communities, not to establish a research institution in far-off Bethesda.

Still, the activity of the Women's Field Army helped to spread the word about cancer into towns and cities throughout the country. It gave considerable publicity to the "menace" of cancer, some of it used by Bone and his allies during congressional deliberations on the cancer bill. More than anything the ASCC had ever done, the WFA campaign brought cancer education to substantial numbers of middle-class Americans. In these mundane and mostly unanticipated ways it facilitated the effort for federal involvement in 1937.

ALTHOUGH Little gave great emphasis to the Women's Field Army after 1936, he saw it as only part of a broader quest for publicity about cancer. To advance that aim he created another new office, that of publicity director, in October 1936. His choice for the job was Clifton Read, a knowledgeable operator. Read perceived the potential propaganda value of the WFA's campaign and early in 1937 set about making the most of it.[45] Touting the campaign as "United States Cancer Week," Read had astonishing success. During March alone stories about the enlistment drive—and more generally about the menace from cancer—appeared in *American Legion Monthly* (880,000 circulation), *Elks* magazine (487,000), *Women's Home Companion* (284,000), and many others. At the same time Read engineered a coast-to-coast radio hookup for broadcasts about cancer and its control.[46]

Read's greatest coup was to enlist the support of the important network of news outlets *Time, Life,* and *Fortune.* In February the "March of Time" newsreel series, shown in hundreds of American cinemas, focused on cancer. A month later *Fortune* devoted much of its issue to "The Great Darkness," a long, detailed, and illustrated story on cancer. Also in March, *Life* used a dramatic picture of laboratory mice to feature its story on Little, U.S. SCIENTIST WARS AGAINST AN UNKNOWN ENEMY; CANCER. Three weeks later it was *Time*'s turn. The popular weekly depicted Little, calmly smoking a pipe, on its cover.[47] *Newsweek* then followed in early April with a cancer cover story of its own, but its focus, oddly, was on Little's rival as a cancer geneticist, Maud Slye of Chicago.[48] Though the article praising Slye could only have irritated Little and his friends—it was not Read's doing—it was nonetheless publicity for cancer research. It completed a remarkable six-week splurge of prominent coverage in the major news magazines of America.

The stories did much to publicize the ASCC. *Fortune*'s circulation at the time was only 148,000, but *Time,* with 616,000, and *Life,* with 800,000, reached millions of Americans. The stories all used news of the WFA enlistment drive as a springboard of sorts and then ranged far afield. In so doing they managed to have it both ways. Cancer, it seemed, was both a looming threat to civilization and a disease that brilliant scientists were beginning to conquer. Thus *Fortune,* obscuring the qualifications of expert epidemiologists, prophesied that mortality from cancer would "continue to rise during the next thirty-five years, to become stationary at approximately one and one-half times the present rate." It then emphasized, however, that "society has within it the power, if not directly to call forth light from these spokesmen ["brilliant" researchers], at least to finance the brains and equipment by which it might be called forth."

Life, too, appealed simultaneously to dread and to hope. Though its photographs of very sick cancer victims sparked a barrage of outraged letters, its overall message was upbeat, and it placed great faith in the blessings of technology. The key to cure, it suggested, might be Columbia University's 1,250,000-volt X-ray machine, which *Life* depicted in all its imposing grandeur and described as the "biggest gun in the war" against cancer. Then as later the publications of Henry Luce were entranced by the potential of bigger and better machines to save the world.

The articles and others like them, reaching millions of Americans, inevitably excited many patients and their loved ones with the promise of deliverance from pain and anxiety. Desperate for help, readers sent clippings of the articles to researchers and pleaded for help and advice. "Let me know what your terms and rates are," one woman wrote the Harvard cancer group. "I think I need help have a lump in my left brest, it if is not too expencive." Another wrote, expressing interest in X-radiation, "as I have a breast cancer and would like to know more about this type of treatment. I haven't any faith in operations as so many who have had an operation for this only live a short while." A third simply begged, "please let me have a ray of hope as I am very desperate in my terrible position."[49] As these letters suggested, the popular expectations aroused by the press were both exaggerated and cruel.

Whether the publicity had much to do with congressional activity in 1937 is unclear. Nothing in the stories—which focused on the ASCC and the WFA—suggests that the ASCC had much interest in a federally supported cancer institute. Nor did journalists devote much attention to the cancer bills once they reached the floor of Congress in June and July, when the most exciting political controversy was Roosevelt's rash attempt to pack the Supreme Court.[50] When the cancer bill finally passed in late July, *Time* reported the story and included a photo of Senator Bone. But it was routine news, nothing like the splash that the magazines had given to cancer research in March. The *New York Times* carried the story of Roosevelt signing the bill in a thirteen-line story on page 19.[51]

Still, the blizzard of publicity, like the WFA campaign of which it was a part, was significant. It showed that important magazines were ready at last to join with some enthusiasm in the alliance against cancer, even to the extent of dramatizing the issue on their covers. That willingness, in turn, reflected more than the salesmanship of insiders like Little and Read. It suggested that at least a few news editors thought that stories about cancer had mass appeal.

The stories also contributed indirectly to Bone's effort in Congress. From the descriptions of the need for more cancer research money and praise for the work being done by existing institutes, congressmen could easily visualize the utility of federal funding. Surgeon General Parran noted the interest in the problem as early as March 30, when he wrote Little, an old friend, about federal developments. The PHS, Parran said, had not initiated any legislation against cancer, but "a number of Senators and Congressmen have been in touch with us from time to time, and their interest [was] apparently stimulated, in part, at least, by your recent publicizing of the cancer program."[52] In this unintended and roundabout manner, the burst of magazine stories about cancer in early 1937 was one of the many forces easing creation of the NCI a few months later.

SEVERAL OTHER ACTORS were important in advancing the cancer legislation between April and August. The featured performer was Senator Bone, who had been quietly currying support from the start of the 1937 session and who introduced the first of several congressional cancer bills on April 2. Why he became committed to the cause is obscure; some sources credit his secretary, Saul Haas, with educating him on the issue and with doing much of the legwork necessary to secure the backing of cosponsors.[53] But there was no doubting Bone's commitment in 1937. A progressive, Bone disputed a then common view of the disease—that it indiscriminatingly harmed the rich as well as the poor. On the contrary, Bone argued, cancer especially victimized the needy, who lacked the means to seek early medical diagnosis.[54] Using this argument, which had some appeal in the economically depressed 1930s, Bone managed to secure the cosponsorship of all his colleagues. This remark-

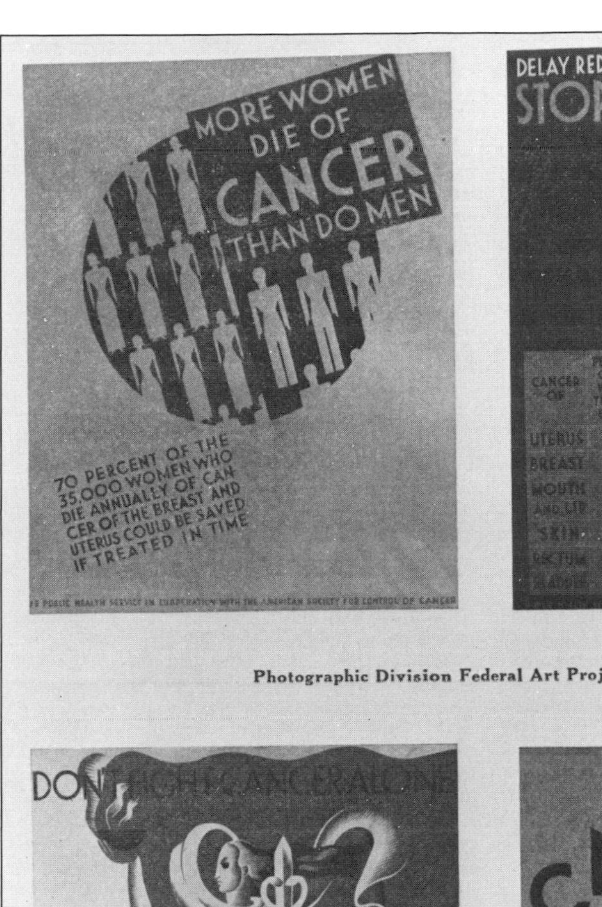

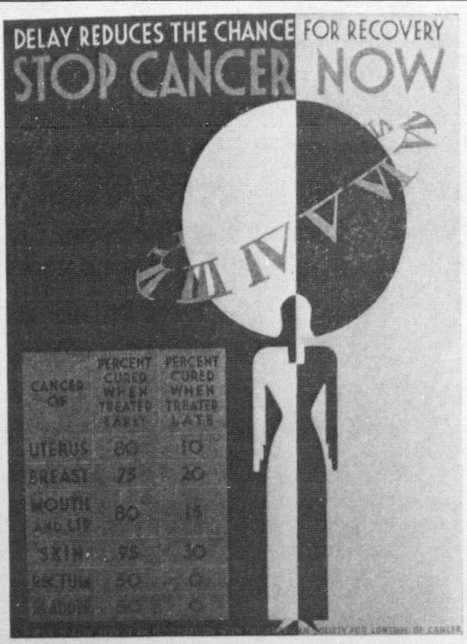

Photographic Division Federal Art Project W. P. A.

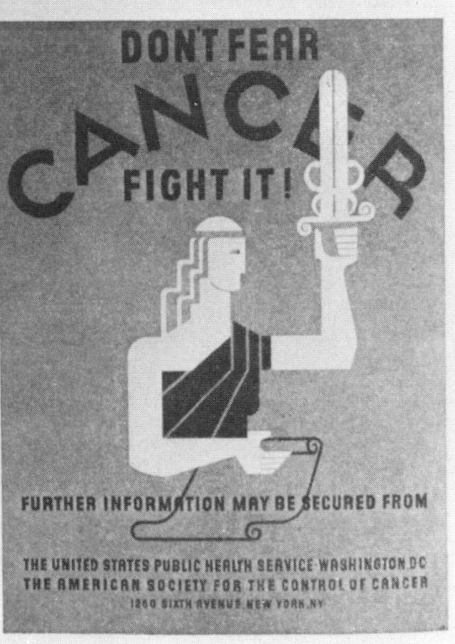

Reprinted with permission from *ASCC National Bulletin,* 20, no. 5 (1938), 10; © 1938 American Cancer Society.

able feat virtually assured passage in the upper chamber of some version of anticancer legislation in 1937.

A second key figure was very much an outsider. He was Dr. Dudley Jackson, a surgeon from San Antonio, Texas. Since the early 1930s Jackson had struggled on limited funds to carry out research into the carbohydrate metabolism of dogs—work that he thought could unravel the mysteries of human cancer. He turned to the PHS, which fended him off—experts like Ewing and Carter Wood belittled his research—before finally giving him $1,000 in 1935.[55] Endlessly persistent, Jackson then began to lobby for a federal institute for cancer research. In late 1936 he enlisted the enthusiastic support of Representative Maverick, his friend and congressman.[56] The next spring Jackson testified in House hearings on behalf of his dream, and when the NCI was finally funded, he was among the first to apply (mostly without success) for money.[57] In allotting credit for passage of the final NCI bill, several close observers placed Jackson behind only Bone.[58]

A third star in the cast of players was Surgeon General Parran. A veteran public-health officer and expert on venereal disease, Parran came to New York in 1930 as Governor Roosevelt's state health commissioner. When Surgeon General Hugh Cumming stepped down in 1936, Parran was President Roosevelt's choice for the post, which carried with it leadership of the Public Health Service and, under the PHS, of the NIH. Parran had a liberal, activist view of the government's role in public health. "We have reached a stage in our civilization," he said in 1937, "when we must accept as a major premise that citizens should have an equal opportunity for health as an inherent right with the right of liberty and the pursuit of happiness." "Whatever path we take," he added, "inevitably will conform to the governmental framework."[59] No statement better articulated the growing consensus of Americans behind an expansive definition of the right to good health and the responsibility of government to assure it.

To veteran leaders of the cancer alliance—Little, Ewing, Wood—Parran was a welcome choice. In 1929 his wife had died of cancer; in 1932 he had been elected to the board of directors of the ASCC; and in 1935–36 he had served as vice-president of the society. While Surgeon General in 1936–37 he continued as chairman of the

ASCC education committee.[60] He told Bone in March 1937 that cancer was, with venereal disease, tuberculosis, and pneumonia, one of the "four great public health problems." He added: "Although the cause of cancer as yet has baffled medical science, there is every reason to hope that in time this problem will be unraveled and that increasing expenditures for cancer research would pay very large dividends in the ultimate control of this disease."[61] Parran's support of the NCI bill symbolized his progressive faith in federal aid to health in general and to cancer research in particular.[62]

As the various cancer bills moved through the gauntlet of committee hearings and debate on the floor, they encountered some opposition. A few opponents were followers of healers who wrote in to say that they already knew the answers to the cancer problem. "What is the use of trying to find something," one man asked, "that has already been found?" He said he could tell "you folks of the Health Service" of a remedy which "will cure a stomach cancer, and that is going some. I suppose it will save the Govt a lot of money by using a cure that has already been found rather than trying to find one."[63] A woman urged President Roosevelt to give the money to a wonderful "bloodless surgeon" who had already cleared up her own "hard and cancerous liver, a condition the medical world considers incurable . . . now the cancer is breaking loose and being eliminated." If this doctor could get government aid, she concluded, "the quacks would die a natural death for lack of patients."[64]

Letters such as these were yet another manifestation of America's cancer counterculture. Then as earlier a stubborn minority of people held to their faith in folk remedies and in "painless," unorthodox cures. But it went without saying that their letters received perfunctory replies (if replies at all) from the scientists and politicians who were trying to enlist the government behind cancer research. Sure of their expertise, these scientists had little time for the often unlettered people who besieged them with claims for miracles.

A different kind of opposition to the cancer bills came from a handful of research scientists who feared that a national institute would create a bureaucratic "Supermind."[65] America, they feared, was developing what later critics called a "General Motors approach to science," which emphasized the role of centralized management at the expense of good basic research. Peyton Rous, still supporting out-of-fashion viral theories about cancer, was one of these skeptical opponents in 1937. He complained privately that he was not of the "'in' group" and predicted that a federal institute would mean "regimented direction." Observing the interest in the NCI of drug companies and of manufacturers of X-ray machines, he noted that "the guns of the powerful laboratories run by the electric and engineering companies at once began to say Boom! Boom!"[66]

When the NCI later became a vast and impersonal operation, Rous's concerns were shared by many others, including some leading scientists. The GM analogy, they agreed, was valid. In 1937, however, not many researchers publicly agreed with Rous. Those who labored in cancer specialities, like Jackson, were eager to promote federal funding. Others, such as Little and the elite of doctors who ran the ASCC, had never opposed federal aid to medical research. Little, in fact, had managed in the early 1930s to attract small sums of federal money for his mice-breeding efforts in Maine.[67] Most cancer researchers—whatever their doubts about creating a specialized federal institute—recognized that it was in their self-interest not to rock the boat. Their pressure helped feed the explosive growth of the agency after 1945.

Such noticeable opposition as developed in 1937 came not from quacks or from scientists but from a few private physicians and from Representative James Wadsworth, a thoughtful, articulate conservative from New York State. The doctors feared that a cancer institute would lead to socialized medicine. The AMA warned of the "danger of putting the government in the dominant position in relation to medical research."[68] Wadsworth explained to the House that cancer was "not the only disease in connection with which there is mystery. Infantile paralysis is another . . . the establishment of one Federal institute to study a given disease will be followed by the establishment of another and then another and then another."[69]

Wadsworth was prophetic: after World War Two Congress did establish "another and then another and then another" institute. But in 1937 his was a lone voice, all but silenced by the consensus behind federal aid. And the AMA, ordinarily a potent lobby, did not mobilize its forces. Its watch-and-wait attitude rested on an accurate perception of doctors' self-interest. Federal support for medical research might set dangerous precedents in the long run, but so long as it did not provide government-supported medical care—which would threaten fee-for-service payment—a cancer institute could be tolerated. Better to save the AMA's political strength to oppose other, more frightening legislation, such as national health insurance.

In this favorable political context some sort of cancer legislation seemed highly likely. It remained only for Maverick and Bone to reconcile their slightly different bills. With the overt help of Parran, Little, and Jackson, they did so in July. The result was a bill creating an institute to "provide for and foster the continuous study of the cause, the prevention, the diagnosis, and the treatment of cancer." The conferees settled for cuts in authorizations, and Congress later appropriated only $400,000 in first-year operating money, of which $200,000 might be spent on the purchase and distribution of radium. Passage of the authorizing legislation was unanimous in both houses.[70]

The bill set up a six-member National Advisory Cancer Council, which was expected to implement policies bringing some coherence to the open-ended mandate. Among the first members Parran named to this powerful council were the leading anticancer figures of the day: Ewing of Memorial, Wood of Columbia, and Little. The others were the nationally known physicist Arthur Compton of Chicago, Harvard president James Conant, and Ludvig Hektoen, chairman of the division of medical sciences of the National Research Council. A regular attendee was Assistant Surgeon General Thompson, who also served as head of the NIH, which oversaw the NCI. Presiding officer, as head of the PHS, was Surgeon General Parran.

This council of scientific insiders enjoyed remarkable freedom from political control, and it quickly shaped the future course of the institute.[71] The key, they agreed, was not to emphasize public education (that was the role of the ASCC, with which the NCI worked very closely from the beginning), or treatment (that was the province of physicians), or prevention (which was undramatic and, they thought, unpromising).[72] They were cool to the idea of pur-

SUNDAY, SEPTEMBER 19, 1937. LOS ANGELES EXAMINER---A PAPER FOR PEOPLE WHO THINK SUNDAY, SEPTEMBER 19, 1937.

The United States Public Health Service Speaks:

'Proposed National Cancer Institute Will Provide Maximum Study of Disease Which Takes Annual U.S. Toll of 140,000'

CHART SHOWING ELEVEN LEADING CAUSES OF DEATH

Increase in Deaths from Dread Ailment Could Be Retarded

By Dr. L. R. THOMPSON, M.D.,
Ast. Surgeon General, U. S. Public Health Service

CANCER is the second cause of death in the United States today, with only heart diseases outranking it. Last year approximately 140,000 persons died of cancer in this country, and there are 400,000 existing cases of cancer currently.

Unlike diphtheria, tuberculosis and scarlet fever, whose death rate is constantly declining, the death rate from cancer is increasing.

By 1960, according to tabulations based on our present figures, there will be a 50 per cent increase in deaths from cancer although there will be no change in the basic prevalence of the disease, because we will have a larger proportion of the population living long enough to die from the disease, which is primarily an ailment of older people.

Surely a disease which takes such a sweeping toll, and against which preventative measures are virtually useless, (since the cause of cancer may be said to be unknown), merits the maximum amount of research which can be given it.

It is the purpose of the proposed National Cancer Institute to gather, co-ordinate, and then disseminate all the existing information with relation to cancer which is available, or which will come to light as research and investigation progress.

Extensive Laboratory Investigation and Research of Cancer Causes and Treatments Will Be Fostered

Through appropriated funds, once the Institute itself is erected, equipped and staffed, the United States Government through the Public Health Service will be able to conduct experiments and investigations relating to the cause, diagnosis, and treatment of cancer, and assist and foster similar research activities by other agencies, both public and private, by the distribution of funds and the co-operation of personnel.

Laboratory research in the fields wherein lie present methods of investigation will be extensively carried out.

This includes the fields of pathology, radiology, advanced methods of cancer surgery, and research studies in bio-chemistry and bio-physics with their relation to the cancer problem.

While the National Cancer Institute, as created in the Public Health Service, comes under the jurisdiction of the Surgeon General, the bill signed by the President for the creation of a National Advisory Cancer Council of six members, to be appointed by the Surgeon General with the approval of the Secretary of the Treasury, and with the Surgeon General, ex-officio, as chairman.

These men, selected from leading medical or scientific authorities who are outstanding in the study, diagnosis or treatment of cancer in the United States, bring to the Institute the finest administrative and scientific minds available for the guidance of the Institute.

The people of the United States can look to them confidently for the most advanced thinking and ablest advice obtainable.

Two important functions of the National Cancer Institute, as provided in the bill, will be in relation to radium and in the training of personnel.

Ablest Advice Obtainable From Finest Scientific Minds Will Aid the Entire Nation

With the approval of the Secretary of the Treasury, the Surgeon General is authorized to purchase radium from time to time, and then make that radium available on loan to institutions engaged in the study of the cause, prevention, methods of diagnosis or treatment of cancer, or for the actual treatment of cancer.

There is, at present, in this country, only about 50 per cent of the radium needed for such research and treatment, and this function of the National Cancer Institute is of inestimable value.

The provision for the training of such persons as the Surgeon General considers properly equipped (by reason of previous technical training) in all technical matters relating to diagnosis and treatment of cancer, is also of paramount importance.

Leading cancer authorities have stated that, if all the knowledge which we now have on the subject of cancer were made available to all the people, 20 per cent of the deaths now occurring from the disease could be prevented.

The training of personnel, whose future function will be mainly utilizing the knowledge they have gained, and making it available to larger numbers of sufferers from cancer, should substantially aid in the reduction of fatalities.

It was brought out when the original plans were formulated for the establishment of the National Cancer Institute that its primary object was to be research and the dissemination of information which results from these research activities.

Correct Diagnosis of This Dread Disease in Its Earliest Stages Is the Goal of the Institute

Clarifying the stipulation further, it should be stated that the establishment of no hospital or working cancer clinic is contemplated in relation to the Institute. There is a very definite need, on the part of hospitals already existing, for the services of trained scientific personnel, money to further their own research and enlarge their own cancer laboratories, and for radium for the treatment of cancerous growths.

With its determined policy to augment research and support worthwhile and promising cancer studies already being carried on by other organizations or institutions, the Institute will attack this problem solely from that angle.

What the establishment of this National Cancer Institute can mean to the people of the United States is not by any means limited to those now suffering from cancer.

The correct diagnosis of the disease in its early stages, before it has made such inroads that death can only be postponed, has always been and is at the present time a critical handicap in the prevention of fatalities.

The advantage to the people in having a centralized point of training, where men going into the field are given the latest available data and the most up-to-date courses in how to recognize the symptoms of cancer quickly and surely, is an advantage of OVERWHELMING VALUE IN THE CONCERTED WARFARE AGAINST THE DISEASE.

Dr. L. R. THOMPSON, M. D.
Asst. Surgeon General, U. S. Public Health Service

Who Prophecies:

'Wider Diffusion of Knowledge to All People Will Save 28,000 Lives Every Year'

DR. THOMAS PARRAN, Jr., of New York, Surgeon General, U. S. Public Health Service.

Los Angeles Examiner, September 19, 1937. From the National Archives, National Institute of Health Records, Record Group 443, box 187.

chasing radium, for which they foresaw never-ending demand. They were equally cool to suggestions that the NCI support the building of a hospital, which they expected congressmen would try to fill with their ailing friends and constituents. Though the NCI spent small sums on clinical research and care at the Marine Hospital in Baltimore, it waited for more than a decade before adding extensive hospital facilities at Bethesda.[73]

Though the council held firm against big expenditures for radium, it gave its largest early grant (for $30,000) to the California physicist Ernest Lawrence, developer of the cyclotron. Radioactive materials created by the cyclotron, Lawrence said, could do better than X-rays in bombarding cancer cells.[74] The council was often to show its fascination with technological marvels—which captivated many Americans during and after World War Two—especially those resulting from work in atomic physics.[75]

Instead of funding education or treatment, the council emphasized the need for basic biological research, spending most of the institute's money on fellowships for research and training. Some of this research was to be conducted "in-house"—at the NCI's building in Bethesda when it was ready for occupancy in early 1940—by the PHS teams that had already been working in Boston and Washington. In these early years the Bethesda operation was small and manageable, housed in a three-story Georgian brick building. In early 1940 it supported twenty-eight in-house research fellows and a staff, including janitors, of around one hundred.[76]

Other research was to be done in outside labs by scientists who competed successfully for grants. At first these applicants were ranked by the council; later, when the agency mushroomed in size, they were recommended to Parran and his successors by study groups of peers. In its support of extramural medical research the act pioneered. This authorization, extended to other scientific investigators in the Public Health Act of 1944, was to have vast implications for universities and research institutions after World War Two.[77]

The NCI's focus on research reflected the influence of the scientists on the council, notably of Ewing, who continued to stress the enormous gaps in basic biological knowledge about malignant growth. He opposed dribbling out the money on scattered "five and

Reprinted with permission from *ASCC National Bulletin*, 21, no. 2 (1939), 9; © 1939 American Cancer Society. Jerry Costello in *The Knickerbocker News*.

ten cent grants," recommending instead that support go to scientists who would use existing research centers (such as Memorial Hospital).[78] In the years ahead the council continued to emphasize this approach, which greatly assisted scientists at Memorial and a handful of other large research complexes.

Thanks to the scientific prestige of the council, this concentration on long-range laboratory research aroused little controversy in the early years. Given the real and formidable obstacles to a strategy of prevention—what, after all, could people then do to prevent the illness?—it was a tenable emphasis. Even then, however, some of the members recognized that Congress, reflecting public anxiety about the disease, would someday expect tangible results, indeed a magic bullet, for the taxpayers' money. Compton urged his colleagues to consider spending some funds on radium. "Here is something," he said, "that we know will be of clinical, therapeutic value to the public." When they demurred, he reminded them that "if we are going to satisfy the public notions, we should do something for the alleviation of the patients."[79] Compton's comments exposed a problem that the NCI was later to face: how to justify long-range research to a lay public whose expectations were ever expanded by the promises of science and whose demands for a "cure" could only grow more strident.

HISTORIANS have advanced different theories for the success of the bill establishing the National Cancer Institute. One has emphasized the role of popular opinion stemming in part from the media blitz of March and April. "Public feeling and pressure on Congress," he concluded, "may have seemed overwhelming."[80] Another has spoken of a "wave of letters" arriving in congressional offices.[81] But it is doubtful that popular pressure made a great difference. Though Americans dreaded cancer, and though they were by then ready to accept the enhanced role of government in combatting it, they did not show special interest in the legislation or in the precedent-setting deliberations of the NCI council. They applied little public pressure to increase the NCI's appropriations, which grew only slightly in the early years.

The NCI owed its existence more to the ability of well-placed individuals, like Bone, who were able to articulate broad societal concerns and to use the political process to address them. Some of these concerns, such as dread of cancer, had existed for many years. Others, such as the right to good health, were relatively new in American society. Still others—the sense that government had a responsibility for health—grew considerably under the trauma of the Great Depression and the liberalism of the New Deal.

Working within these broad parameters favorable to federal action, a fairly small group of research scientists, public-health officials, progressive politicians, and—in the end—spokesmen for the cancer society, joined hands to support legislation that no one but the hard-hearted could resist. The scientists, taking firm command of the anticancer alliance, then implemented the law in ways that advanced their own laboratory research and institutional interests and that mainly dismissed preventive approaches. In later years, abetted by explosively expanding popular expectations and by much increased federal expenditures, they watched the NCI become the center of a large and politically powerful interest group. Almost no one in 1937—not Ewing, not Little, not Bone, not even Parran—had foreseen that.

6

Hymns to Science and Prayers to God

HATS OFF to the men of research," the *Milwaukee Journal* editorialized at the close of World War Two. "Science-explorers," the *St. Louis Post-Dispatch* added, "should never again be denied anything useful for their adventures."[1] These were but two of a chorus of hymns to science offered in the years following the war. They sang the praises of an age of faith in science and technology that profoundly influenced American society in general and the cultural milieu of cancer in particular.

Given the technological advances of the war this faith in science was understandable. Scientists designed and developed fantastic weapons, including radar and, of course, the bomb. By war's end they had discovered "wonder drugs" such as penicillin. The death rate from disease in the wartime army was far lower than ever before in history. American life expectancy, which had hardly changed in the previous decade, jumped by three years between 1939 and 1945.[2]

Thanks in part to the much greater affluence of the postwar era, these gains continued in the late 1940s and 1950s. Scientists, moreover, began to break new ground in biological research, most remarkably perhaps by elucidating the shape of DNA in 1953. These developments confirmed the faith in science that had grown so dramatically during the war. One contemporary cancer patient expressed this optimism with a wide-eyed wonder characteristic of many people at that time. Researchers, she admitted, could not decipher the puzzle of cancer. "But still science inches along and some day we will have the answer." Scientists, she added, "are like small, consecrated ants determined to tunnel through a mountain.

Persistently, blindly almost, they struggle on, turning over in ecstacy and wonderment each small particle of truth in the mountain of mud before them."[3]

The faith in medical science was such that millions of American families in 1954 voluntarily participated in double-blind tests of the Salk vaccine against polio, a contagious virus that terrified American parents in the 1940s and early 1950s. On April 12, 1955, when the epidemiologists announced that the vaccine worked, joy and relief overcame the country. "Thank you, Dr. Salk" signs proliferated; people wept in the streets; authorities closed schools and offices and flocked to the churches to give prayers of thanks. The vaccine was widely seen as a major victory for the wonder workers of science and medicine.[4]

While triumph over polio would have been celebrated in any age, it seemed especially exciting in a culture that was developing near-utopian expectations about the importance of good health. By the 1950s some 15 million Americans a year volunteered their time to health organizations such as the cancer society. Fundraisers for these agencies tapped citizens for remarkable sums—even the Christmas seals drive for tuberculosis, by then a much less frightening malady, raised more than $20 million in 1948.[5] The popular support for health organizations in the 1940s and 1950s, like the environmentalist movement in the 1970s and 1980s, stemmed from demands for good health that were becoming central to American society.

At the root of these demands was the unprecedented, indeed unimaginably greater prosperity that transformed the daily lives of the middle classes in postwar America. As one scholar put it later, "the more affluent a society becomes, the lower is its threshold for discomfort, and the greater the demands for relief of even the most minor indispositions."[6] Reflecting these feelings, health professionals explicitly broadened their definitions of what it meant to be well. The World Health Organization concluded that good health was far more than the absence of disease or infirmity. Rather, it was a "state of complete physical, mental, and social well-being."[7]

Similar feelings accentuated the fear and denial of early death, which had continued to intensify throughout the twentieth century. As people lived longer and enjoyed the pleasures of the burgeoning consumer culture, they cherished the Good Life. Less religious than their ancestors, they grew ever more afraid of dying before their time—or dying at all. Untimely death, moreover, flouted the prevailing faith in technology and science.[8] Fatal diseases—particularly a slow and "certain" killer such as cancer—were especially distressing to patients and their families. Premature death dulled the gloss of the affluent, technological society.

As later writers were to point out, such expansive notions about health, sickness, and death created profoundly unsettling problems, chief among them the large expectations they aroused, especially among the affluent. As good health became more central to the culture, it became almost synonymous with the Good Life. To be healthy was to be happy. To be sick was to feel useless and deviant. To be fatally ill was terrifying. In a world of "doing better and feeling worse," many people suffered the pangs of the "worried well."[9]

In the 1940s and 1950s, however, the problematic consequences of these expectations had not become clear. Indeed, the expectations well served physicians. The status of doctors rose to its peak in these years. People tipped their hats to physicians when they passed them on the streets. Public opinion polls revealed that doctors were admired more than all other occupational groups—even atomic scientists. Hollywood movies featured physicians not as cold or greedy technicians but as keen, wise, and caring professionals. The new and affecting medium of television was soon to bring physician-heroes like Dr. Kildare, Ben Casey, and Marcus Welby, M.D., into millions of living rooms.

Americans acted on this rapidly growing admiration of doctors. Thanks to affluence, and to the rise of organizations like Blue Cross, millions of middle-class Americans began buying private health insurance (to judge from ads for such insurance, fear of cancer prompted purchases), and to turn to their physicians with increasing confidence and regularity. After all, doctors now had the skills, and the drugs, to *cure*. As one contemporary observer noted sourly, "most patients are as completely under the supposedly scientific yoke of modern medicine as any primitive savage is under the superstitious serfdom of the tribal witch doctor."[10]

Critical views such as this suggested that many people did not have a positive view of science and medicine. Millions of poorer Americans still had little access to modern medicine and resented the wealth and power of physicians. Realistically, many expected relatively little from life. Thoughtful skeptics wondered if the limited extent of knowledge about cellular behavior justified expending huge resources on cancer research. But the doubters and the critics did not secure much of a hearing. The postwar years were increasingly prosperous, confident, and patriotic—years of assertive and distinctively American positive thinking—and most middle-class people celebrated the ability of experts to solve social and economic problems.

In the minds of many Americans the conquest of cancer was the next great challenge—to be met in same manner that the physicists had taken on the mysteries of the atom. Dr. Stafford Warren, medical research director of the Manhattan Project, told Congress in 1946 that "the cancer problem is no more impossible than the atomic bomb." Roscoe Spencer, head of the NCI, explained in *Reader's Digest* that the struggle against cancer required the same sort of effort as had been devoted to atomic research. The war, he added, had cost the government $317 billion while killing 280,000 Americans; during that same time (from the attack on Pearl Harbor to VJ Day in August 1945), the NCI had spent but $2 million to combat an enemy that felled 607,000 people, or roughly 160,000 per year.[11] A writer for the *Saturday Evening Post* resorted to this analogy in a typical fashion, while at the same time employing the hyperbolic language long used to fan cancerphobia. He reminded his readers that harnessing of the atom had required a "vast and perfectly organized effort." "In precisely the same way a solution will be found for the riddle of cancer—a scourge which, for thousands of years, has stalked the earth and lurked like a threatening shadow in the background of all our lives, particularly in the lives of women."[12]

Scientists, of course, knew that analogies linking the conquest of cancer to wonder drugs were spurious and dangerously misleading. Drugs such as penicillin attacked bacteria, not mammalian cells. Cancer cells, moreover, had the same underlying chemistry as normal cells: drugs used against cancer would affect normal cells as well. That was a fact that chemotherapists were to struggle with for years to come.[13]

Analogies to the bomb were equally inappropriate. The bomb, scientists emphasized, had been developed only after years of basic research had unlocked some of the mysteries of the atom. But no such advances in basic biological understanding had occurred to guide cancer scientists. "We cannot make a direct analogy between fabricating an atomic bomb and a cure for cancer," Surgeon General Parran warned. Another writer added, "the basic principles of atomic fission had been discovered in Germany long before we laid out a nickel for the Manhattan Project. The basic principles of the insidious biologic fission we call cancer, however, are still among the scientific unknowns."[14]

Even while expressing such reservations, however, Parran and other scientific leaders pressed for higher funding. In part they acted out of frustration with past disappointments: the failure to conquer cancer stood as a stinging rebuke to the claims of biological science. Yet they were honestly hopeful, believing the riddle could be solved. Their optimism fed popular expectations about cancer research. A Gallup poll in December 1949 found that 88 percent of respondents expected to see a cure for cancer within the next fifty years. By contrast only 15 percent thought that a man could be landed on the moon within that time. Polls in the 1950s revealed comparable optimism about the struggle against the dread disease.[15]

This confidence profoundly influenced philanthropists, whose unprecedented largesse in these affluent years helped to transform the field of cancer research into a big business by the 1950s. Thanks mainly to the Pew family of Pennsylvania, the Lankenau Hospital–Research Institute of Philadelphia, founded in 1927, was incorporated in 1945 as the Institute for Cancer Research. Between 1946 and 1957 its funding increased considerably, and its staff rose from 46 to 132.[16] In Houston, Randolph Lee Clark, an articulate and persuasive surgeon, attracted great infusions of money as director of the M. D. Anderson Hospital for Cancer Research. And in Boston Sidney Farber, a Harvard professor of pathology, established a children's cancer research foundation in 1946 and published important research concerning chemotherapeutic remedies for leukemia. A large, impressive man who developed key contacts with philanthropists and politicians, Farber used money-raising techniques such as the Jimmy Fund to sustain an ever-growing research empire.[17]

Walter Winchell, the popular radio broadcaster and syndicated columnist, lent his considerable powers of persuasion to generate support for cancer research. Immediately following the death from cancer in 1946 of the colorful Broadway reporter, Damon Runyon, Winchell launched the Damon Runyon Memorial Fund for cancer research and treatment. Winchell was friendly with show business personalities and induced many of them—Bob Hope, Dinah Shore, Jack Benny, Frank Sinatra, Benny Goodman—to stage benefits for the cause. Methods such as these—which involved little fund-raising bureaucracy or costly advertising—amassed more than a million dollars per year in the late 1940s and 1950s. The money went to cancer societies, hospitals, and research institutions.[18]

No cancer facility grew more impressively than Memorial Hospital in New York. The city contributed $1.5 million in 1945 to add a 300-bed unit (the James B. Ewing Hospital), and Memorial started a drive of its own for $4 million more. In August 1945 Alfred P. Sloan, Jr., chairman of the board of General Motors, and Charles Kettering, GM's vice-president and research director, announced a gift from the Sloan Foundation of $4 million to establish there the Sloan-Kettering Institute for Cancer Research. "Cancer," Sloan said, "now strikes one U.S. citizen in nine. Very rapid progress against this mysterious scourge could be made possible if the problem got the same amount of money, brains and planning that was devoted to developing the atomic bomb."[19] The Sloan-Kettering complex, a fourteen-floor structure ready in 1948, became the largest private cancer research facility in the world. It and other expanding cancer empires testified to the growing faith in science and medicine and the escalating expectations about good health that were transforming American society and culture in the affluent and confident postwar years.

HOW DID THESE social and cultural changes affect the way that Americans perceived cancer in the 1940s and early 1950s? One way to explore that question is to observe cancer reporting in newspapers and mass-circulation magazines. These years, before the massive spread of television, were a golden age for popular periodicals in the United States. Americans, more prosperous, more educated, had wide exposure to *Life, Time, Newsweek, Collier's, Saturday Evening Post, Look, Reader's Digest,* and a wide variety of women's, "true story," and romance publications. Lavishly illustrated and financed by advertisements, these disseminated and reflected many values of the era.

Among those values, of course, were the faith in science, modern technology, and doctors, and the desire for ever better, even perfect health. Most of the popular magazines gave these matters constant, almost reverential attention. More specifically, they singled out cancer for special scrutiny. Though coverage of cancer had expanded in the 1920s and 1930s, it grew to considerable proportions only in the 1940s and 1950s. Between 1943 and 1945 the *Reader's Guide* counted 53 articles on cancer. By 1945–47 the number had risen to 113, and by 1955–57 to a peak of 273. Similar increases in the number of stories about cancer—from 54 in 1940 to 144 in 1955—occurred in the *New York Times.* Not even polio attracted so much special attention in the press at the time. Only mental illnesses came close.

Of the several themes running through many of these articles, one received much more attention than in the past: cancer was a big killer of children. "In the fight to conquer cancer," *Newsweek* reminded its readers in 1947, "too little has been said of its danger to children." In 1948 *Collier's* ran a feature entitled CANCER, THE CHILD KILLER. *Saturday Evening Post* chimed in with a story headed, "Cancer Kills Children, Too." It emphasized that cancer, after accidents, was the number-one killer of children aged five to fourteen in the United States. Other stories stressed that cancer felled more children in this age group than were lost in America to scarlet fever, polio, diphtheria, dysentery, meningitis, peritonitis, diarrhea, and malaria combined.[20] The emphasis on children was heartrending, especially in a culture that celebrated the sweetness and innocence of the very young. It also revealed that the stigma attached to many cancers, such as those which afflicted the sexual organs of women, was not extended to cancers in children. No emphasis was better calculated to alarm readers or to induce them to join in the war against cancer.

Some stories pulled hard indeed on the emotions of readers. One, reprinted in many papers, featured a photograph of three winsome, pajama-clad children clutching blankets, dolls, and toys as they tottered through the special children's ward at Memorial. "Cancer Struck All Three" was the caption. Other articles emphasized that the wonders of science—if generously supported—could help such patients. "Cancer-Struck Baby Saved by Operation," one headline read. Another added, "Cancer Center Breathes Life into Tiny Baby Boy." Many of these stories emanated from hospitals and institutes which were increasingly competing among themselves for publicity and money.[21] Others originated in large part from reporters and editors, who aggressively sought out researchers and sometimes exaggerated the positive thinking that they heard.

Perhaps no story of this kind was more affecting than one that received widespread coverage in January 1946. It featured Charlie Hall, a three-year-old New Jersey boy whose cancerous leg had been amputated at Memorial three months earlier. But surgery had come too late. The child "sits in a wheelchair and rocks all day long," one story said. "No one has told him that he is about to die." The message was clear: people should give generously to the struggle against cancer, the child killer. Photographs showed Charlie sitting on his mother's lap, his lower body and leg covered by a sheet. "You see that door," he whispered, pointing to the operating room. "They're going to take me in there pretty soon and give me back my leg." His father echoed Charlie's determination: "People must stop just saying, 'This is awful!' They must do something to see that this thing is licked." When Charlie died in February, the father added, "My wife and I shall continue in the fight until the very end."[22]

Although these stories depended for their appeal on popular fears of the disease, they were almost always hopeful. More than in previous decades the magazines and newspapers extolled the researchers and predicted eventual success—especially if people gave money to the cause. The only word that can capture the flavor of these stories, which promised much more than the researchers could deliver, had not then been coined: Hype.

Newspaper headlines consistently displayed this positive thinking about medical progress against cancer. Some of the hundreds that appeared in the 1940s and 1950s were: "New Cancer Cure Believed Found" (1942), "Big Gains Made in Atom War Against Cancer" (1948), "Cancer Battle Takes Mighty Step Forward" (1953), "Search for Man's No. 2 Killer Cancer, Is Believed Paying Off" (1956), and "Cancer Like Weeds in Lawn / It Can Be Uprooted by Surgery or Burned Out" (1959). Accompanying many stories were photographs of white-coated scientists, magnificent medical technology, and miraculously cured patients.[23]

There were endless variations on this theme, many of them composed by reporters with little background in biological science. The *Saturday Evening Post* ran several articles praising the accomplishments of surgeons, who were ushering in a "new and brilliant era of lifesaving." "Thanks to the spectacular achievements of our surgeons and our researchers—today's victims have a real chance to survive." *U.S. News and World Report* added that improved methods of early detection would cut cancer death rates in half within five years, even if treatment did not change. "Now," it concluded, "millions of dollars, hundreds of scientists, and careful planning are being used in what authorities regard as medicine's counterpart of the wartime atom bomb project."[24]

A *Time* cover story in 1949 typified this cheerful approach. It featured Cornelius ("Dusty") Rhoads, the zealous, crewcut, and energetic pathologist who had succeeded Ewing as head of Memorial in 1939 and who more than any other cancer warrior in the 1940s and 1950s symbolized the official optimism about the new world of cancer research. For *Time*'s cover Rhoads wore a white coat and looked confidently upward, his sharp, keen eyes gleaming behind his glasses. Next to him was a glowing sword, symbol of the American Cancer Society, smashing through a fierce-looking crab. The story, entitled "Frontal Attack," concentrated on the work done at Memorial Sloan-Kettering, "a tower of hope." From his penthouse apartment atop the institute, *Time* said, Rhoads could view the work of

> the world's most impressive array of cancer-fighting weapons: the eggs with their little glass windows, the tubes of cancer tissue on their merry-go-rounds, the rows of deft-fingered girls with the squeaking, doomed white mice, the dangerous viruses, the green and white molds, the thousands upon thousands of chemical agents, the scholarly chemists, physicists, biologists, clinicians all working in unison to defeat the common enemy: cancer.

Careful readers could have learned that neither Rhoads nor Memorial Sloan-Kettering was close to a cure for cancer. But this reminder, a staple in articles of this kind, was all but buried beneath the paragraphs of positive thinking. Rhoads estimated that advances in surgery, combined with early diagnosis, could "save" (not prolong) the lives of one-third to one-half of the living Americans who, on the basis of statistics, would otherwise die of it. This was a saving of six to nine million people. Rhoads concluded with a statement that would have shaken Ewing, his prudent predecessor: "Some authorities think that we cannot solve the cancer problem until we have made a great, basic, unexpected discovery, perhaps in some apparently unrelated field. I disagree. I think we know enough to go ahead now and made a frontal attack with all our forces."[25]

Magazine stories in the 1950s repeated this positive message of hope, often with comparably warlike imagery. In 1953 William Laurence, a well-known science writer, wrote a story for *Look* in which he predicted that polio, cancer, and heart disease would be conquered within ten years. "Medical atomic bombs" and chemotherapy, he said, "will make us ten years younger." Two years later *Newsweek* informed its readers that scientists would probably develop a vaccine against cancer within a few years. In 1956 *Reader's Digest* reprinted a *McCall's* article rhapsodizing abut a typical day at Memorial Hospital. "On this average day," the article noted, "there have been hard fights lost—but *28 men, women, and children have left the Center completely cured of cancer or, for a time at least, restored to health and normal living.*"[26]

By then a few serious magazines—*Harper's, Nation, Saturday Review*—had tried to place this frenetic optimism in proper perspective by pointing out how little the scientists really knew. The world of cancer medicine, they added, was becoming excessively competitive and commercial. A writer for *Harper's* in 1952 denounced the "hoopla . . . of a particularly irresponsible kind" in the media. He continued by castigating as dangerously misleading the oft-used analogy of cancer research with development of the atomic bomb.[27]

Deaf to such warnings, writers for the popular magazines persisted in their optimism. In 1957 *Life* carried yet another of its many stories celebrating cancer technology—in this case an "electronic cancer spotter" developed at Sloan-Kettering. A year later, under the headline, CANCER—ON BRINK OF BREAKTHROUGHS, it quoted John ("Rod") Heller, then the head of the NCI, as saying, "I've spent many years in cancer research. Now I believe that I will see the end of it. We are on the verge of breakthroughs." *Reader's Digest* wrote approvingly of experiments being conducted on Ohio prisoners who volunteered for injections of cancerous cells to test their immunity. The article considered this experiment a "history-making research project that could lead to a breakthrough in the struggle to understand this dread killer."[28]

Many forces accounted for the eager attention that the postwar press gave to the problem of cancer. One was the increasingly vigorous competitiveness, both of cancer researchers and of the media, in the United States. This competition led to what June Goodfield, an English observer, correctly termed the "overheated atmosphere of American science"—which led further to bitter debates over the meaning of cancer statistics, exaggerated claims for therapies, and even falsification of data.[29] As researchers competed ever more avidly for funds, they felt obliged to highlight their expertise and to seek maximum publicity for their efforts. Competitive reporters, in turn, looked for "breakthroughs," which are rare indeed in science.

More broadly, postwar medical reporting in the United States mirrored the special optimism and positive thinking of American scientists. As Goodfield noted, English and American scientists were apt to react differently to research problems. English researchers, asked about their work, replied, "We are just wriggling along." American scientists, by contrast, said that their experiments were "marvellous, just fine." When English scientists were asked a tough question, they were likely to respond, "We don't know." Americans replied, "We are hurrying along with our investigations into just that problem."[30] The "can do" confidence of American scientists

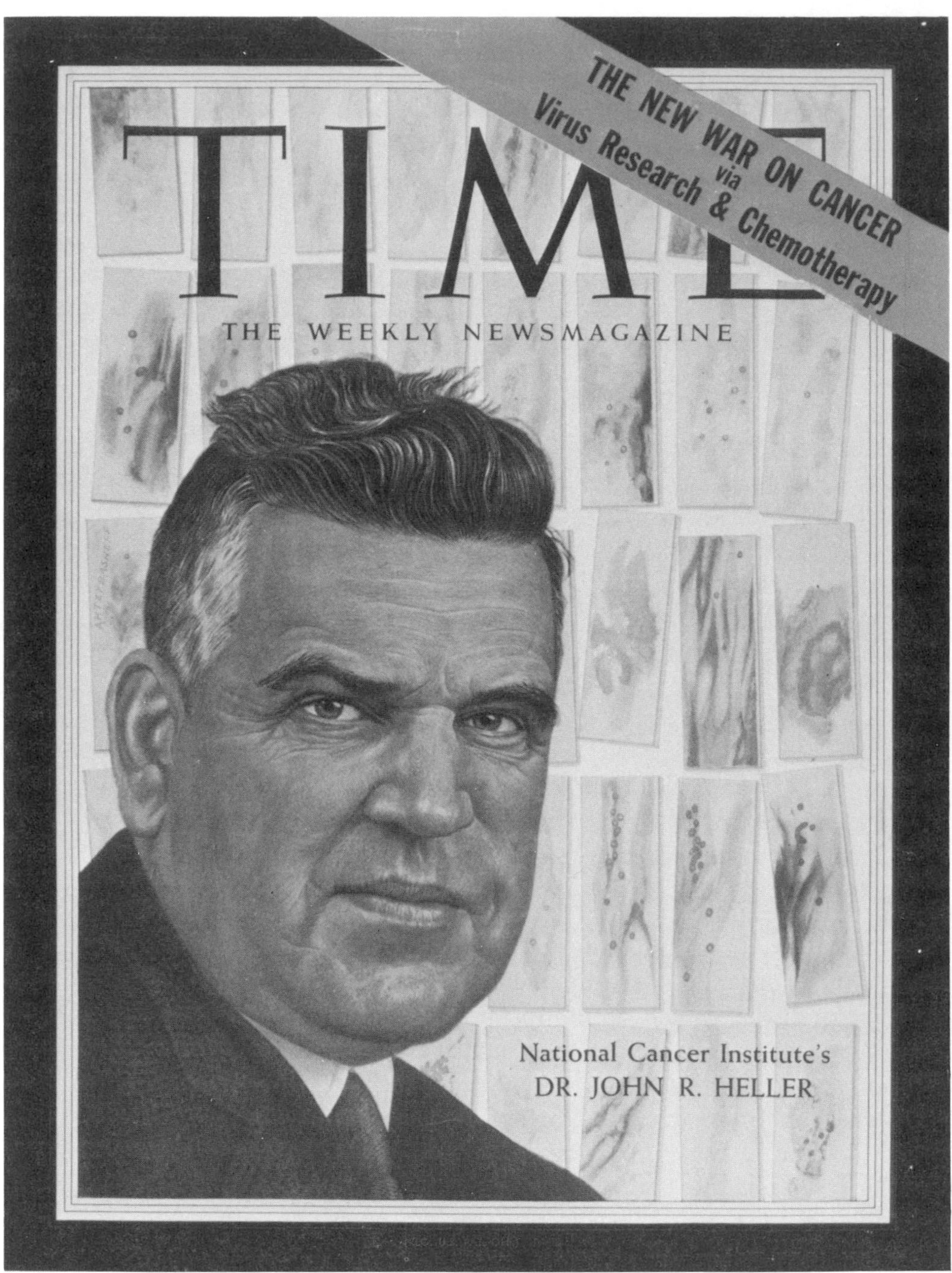

Reprinted with permission from *Time*, July 27, 1959.

reflected the faith in progress that characterized middle-class culture at large. It was likely to be deep and genuine. It was hardly surprising, therefore, that reporters, sharing such confidence in science and technology, accentuated the positive.

Accompanying these exaggerations in the media was another staple of the popular magazines of the era: "tell-all" tales by patients. These had surfaced first in the 1930s and early 1940s, when a few people—mainly women—dared at last to talk about the disease in print. Some proudly joined the "Cured Cancer Club," sponsored by the cancer society. "We all have to die sooner or later," one woman had written. "The knife is the surest, often the only way to avoid suffering." Proud to tell of her ordeal, she said, "No more whispering campaign about me." Another woman, saved by early detection, added "If ever *you* detect symptoms, don't wait! Oh, don't wait! For if you act quickly and intelligently, instead of locking the secret twenty layers down in your own heart, then, in the words of the Beloved Apostle, 'Let not your heart be troubled, nor let it be afraid!'"[31]

Such stories were printed primarily in health-oriented publications such as *Hygeia,* the AMA's general circulation magazine, until the late 1940s and 1950s. Then they appeared with increasing regularity in mass-circulation periodicals, first in women's magazines. Their message, like the Message of Hope, was aimed at breaking down the dread, stigma, and public reticence toward cancer, but that did not mean that all the stories ended on an upbeat. Some were so sad that they may have intensified the very fear they were supposed to banish. In 1949 the *Saturday Evening Post* carried a posthumous story by a man who had neglected to see a doctor in time, called "I Lost My Battle With Cancer."[32] In 1957 *Look* published perhaps the most sensational story of all: the tale of a woman who first helped her husband fight the disease and then helped him die. After overdoses of morphine failed to kill him, she watched approvingly as he slashed his wrists and bled to death. The moral: fight hard, but not forever.[33]

The vast majority of these stories, however, had happy endings. Typical was one that appeared in the *Ladies Home Journal* in 1947. Like many others, it was written by a woman and aimed at a female audience. Its goal was to promote candor about the malady, and specifically to counteract the special stigma that many people, women included, still felt attached to "defeminizing" cancers of the "private" parts. The author praised her husband for making her admit she had cancer. This was important, for "so many women of the last generation speak about cancer as if it were one of the social diseases—a taboo word never to be mentioned in polite company. As soon as people realize it is nothing to be afraid of, half the battle will be won."[34]

Many other articles promoted this struggle against the conspiracy of silence. In "Man Who Licked Cancer," published in 1951, *Reader's Digest* told the story of a man who was told that he had cancer of the kidney and no more than two weeks to live. But he did not despair. "The way I see it," he said, "hope is a thing for me to determine, not medicine. You just do your best for me and let me do the hoping . . . What the hell's this fear that gets everybody the minute they hear the word cancer?" Miraculously, he lived. "Believe in yourself, and in the Lord; that's the cure, if you want to call it that. The man who gives up hoping is a victim; the man who hopes can conquer cancer."[35]

Most tell-all stories preached the orthodox medical gospel of early detection, to be followed as quickly as possible by surgery. Avoid quacks. Don't be afraid. Bring the disease out into the open. Break down superstition and stigmatizing myths. Whether the stories achieved these goals was unclear—the repetition suggests that Americans either did not hear or still were not listening. For many people, indeed, public reticence about cancer served as a useful defense mechanism, helping to bolster denial. But the stories did prove that the conspiracy of silence was slowly relaxing. By 1955 *Life* not only carried a profusely illustrated article on a lung cancer operation; it also arranged to have the surgery shown live on commercial television, with the avowed goal of propagandizing for early detection and surgery.[36]

This survival literature also illustrated the growth of an attitude which was later to become more prominent: people not only must sustain hope, they must also demand the best possible care and treatment. In the 1950s that tended to mean acting quickly and finding a good doctor—much of the onus of recovery was on the patient. It was not until the more iconoclastic 1960s and 1970s, when the expertise of physicians came more critically under question, that many patients began to demand greater participation in managing their own treatment. By then growing numbers of patients, especially in the more affluent, educated classes, fought not only for their lives, but also for frankness from doctors, informed consent, and protection against malpractice. Although all sorts of patients joined in, the battle seemed to be waged with special tenacity by cancer patients, who began at last to throw off a little of their fatalism and to articulate their anger and impatience with the disease. Unintentionally, then, the newspapers and popular magazines of the 1940s and 1950s did more than help to break down public reticence. By reinforcing expectations about good health and long life and urging people to act aggressively to help themselves, they encouraged a few to become more informed, independent, and contentious.

AMONG THE magazine and newspaper stories about cancer during the 1950s were accounts of the disease as it afflicted various well-known Americans. Such accounts became relatively common in the postwar years for two reasons. The first was demographic: as cancer carried away increasing numbers of people, it was inevitable that some of them would be prominent. Among those acknowledged to die of the disease were Gertrude Stein (1946), Runyon (1946), Babe Ruth (1948), Eva Peron (1952), Senator Arthur Vandenberg (1951), the actress Gertrude Lawrence (1952), Senator Robert Taft (1953), Babe Didrikson Zaharias (1956), Humphrey Bogart (1957), Matthew Neely (1958), and John Foster Dulles (1959). Others, such as the radio star Arthur Godfrey and Tom Dooley, the celebrated thirty-four-year-old medical missionary to Laos, underwent well-publicized major surgery for cancer (both in 1959).[37]

Second and more important was the slow erosion of public reticence about the disease. Most of those who developed cancer before the 1940s were either not told they had it or tried to keep the news out of the papers. By the 1950s, however, some people, like Zaharias and Godfrey, chose to make public their plight, while others, though preferring privacy, found that they simply could not prevent the press from telling some of the truth. By the end of the decade the word "cancer" was finally appearing in some obituaries in place of euphemisms about "prolonged" or "serious" illness.

Reportage of Ruth's cancer was especially revealing of cultural attitudes. First hints that he might be seriously ill appeared in January 1947, when it was learned that the former New York Yankees baseball star had undergone a "serious operation" on his neck. Neither then nor in many subsequent stories about his uncertain physical condition in early 1947 was there specific mention of cancer. Though he seemed to be recovering only slowly, if at all, his poor health was attributed mainly to "bad weather."[38] Only in July 1948 was it reported that the fifty-three-year-old Sultan of Swat had entered Memorial Hospital to receive radiation treatment.

When Ruth's condition deteriorated in August, the press gave his struggle front-page exposure such as had not been seen since the travail of Ulysses S. Grant more than sixty years earlier. By August 13, three days before his death, generous coverage had enlisted a rush of national concern, and 13,000 letters and telegrams swamped the hospital staff. Sandlot baseball players interrupted their games to pray for the recovery of their idol. But there was a big difference between Grant's coverage and Ruth's. The Babe was never told that he had the disease. The public learned in these anxious days only that he had "pulmonary complications." Many Americans of course knew better—after all, Memorial was mainly a cancer hospital, and Ruth had been ill for a year and a half. Still, neither Ruth's family nor his doctors wanted to let the truth be known. The obituary observed with odd satisfaction that his cancer was "one of the best kept secrets in modern times."[39]

But Ruth's death on August 16 finally made such secrecy impossible to maintain, and the newspapers then explained that he had suffered and died from throat cancer. The *New York Times* added that "the powerful six-footer who had once electrified Americans with sixty homers in a season, had wasted away. The famous round face had become so hollowed that his snub nose looked long." The *Times* praised Ruth's splendid courage in fighting the "scourge that kills more than 170,000 Americans every year and is responsible for one out of every eight deaths."[40]

Five years later, in April 1953, Robert Taft of Ohio, Republican majority leader of the Senate, felt a pain in his left hip while playing golf in Georgia with President Eisenhower, who had bested him for the presidential nomination in 1952. He could not shake the pain and fatigue after he returned to Washington, and he finally checked into Walter Reed Hospital for tests in late May. But the battery of tests he endured failed to indicate what was wrong.[41] Pale, limping badly, and weak with pain, Taft traveled to a hospital in his hometown of Cincinnati, where his physicians found malignant growths. They told Taft that he had cancer, but that they did not know where it had originated, or what the best therapy—exploratory surgery, X-radiation, drugs?—might be. His cancer had been very hard to diagnose; when diagnosed, it had been equally hard to trace; and it left doctors unsure about the appropriate form of therapy.

Afraid to upset congressional politics, Taft went out of his way to hide the truth. He rejected the advice of friends that he go to Memorial Hospital for treatment. Instead, he checked into the adjacent New York Hospital under an assumed name. There the diagnosis of cancer was confirmed, but eleven eminent specialists, including Rhoads, could not be sure where the cancer had originated or how to attack the tumors. Taft checked out again—this was his third hospital in three weeks—and went back to Washington.

By this time he was not only ill, but also visibly in pain. In the Senate, where he had been a powerful figure for fifteen years, he swung awkwardly down the aisles on crutches. Soon he was again in and out of New York Hospital, now openly and under his own name, but without acknowledging publicly that he had cancer. After administering X-rays, transfusions, and drugs, the doctors finally tried exploratory surgery on July 8. They found cancer everywhere and closed him up. Death came at last, of a brain hemorrhage, on July 31.[42] Taft was sixty-three years old.

Again, only at death did the press disclose the truth. Quoting the doctors, the papers explained that Taft had died of "widespread, highly malignant, rapidly growing tumors, the first symptoms of which were pains in the legs, later localized in the left hip,"[43] and that they could not be sure where or why this very ferocious cancer had started.

At one level Taft's experience was another example of the continuing reticence—similar to the reportage of Ruth's illness—that marked the media's handling of cancer patients, especially when they were important political figures. At another level it helped congressional advocates of more generous government aid for cancer research (Taft had not been such an advocate), who used his suffering to force an increase in appropriations for the NCI. At still another level Taft's ordeal was typical of many people's experiences—the helplessness of the doctors in the face of the continuing mystery belied the drumbeat of official optimism.

At the same time that Taft was first experiencing pain on the golf course, America's most famous woman athlete, the Olympic track star turned professional golfer Babe Didrikson Zaharias, entered a hospital for a colostomy. The openness of reporting about her experiences, then and over the next three years, contrasted sharply with the obfuscations put out about Ruth and Taft. Though her doctors at first avoided the word "cancer," they soon made no serious attempt to hide the truth. "Babe," they said in stories that appeared on the front page of newspapers, was being operated on for a "rectal malignancy." Her physician praised her as a "gallant competitor," but pointed out that she now faced a "truly formidable opponent." He predicted that she would never play sports again, at least at the competitive level.[44]

The readiness of Zaharias and her doctors to talk openly of "malignancy," especially in such a private organ as the rectum, was little short of astonishing for that day and age. It testified to her unusually frank response to adversity and to a physical strength that surprised her doctors. Confounding their pessimism, Zaharias returned to the golf circuit and won the 1954 Ladies U.S. Open by twelve strokes. As *Reader's Digest* wrote admiringly, she triumphed "fifteen months after lying for three hours while [the doctors] performed a colostomy upon her cancer-wracked body." The article went on to capture the breeziness for which she was famous. When asked how she managed to hit a golf ball 250 yards, she replied, "'Brother, I just loosen my girdle and let 'er go! That's the way to lick golf or cancer or anything else. That, and a little thing called faith.'"[45]

For the next two years, as she coped with the spread of her cancer, Zaharias spoke optimistically about her illness. Indeed, her strong, open approach made her a cancer publicist's ideal. In 1955,

Saturday Evening Post carried an autobiography of sorts, "This Life I've Led," which highlighted her winning combat with cancer. By then newspaper and magazine stories about her used the word "cancer" almost as readily as they might have talked about heart disease, polio, or any other nonstigmatizing ailment.[46]

The press and public rooted heartily for Zaharias. Reporting on a hospital stay in January 1956—after a third recurrence of serious problems—the *New York Times* carried a characteristically optimistic headline: "Mrs. Zaharias, Cured / Quits Texas Hospital." And when she died in September of that year, at forty-five, the *Times* gave the story front-page coverage, saying that cancer "had ravaged her once-powerful body, but it never defeated her spirit."[47]

This upbeat response was common in reports of her death. Eisenhower paid tribute to the "woman who had won the admiration of all Americans both in her sports career and in her fight against cancer . . . She put up one of the kind of fights that inspired us all." The *Times* explained that her experience "will show a lot of people that they need not be afraid of an operation and can go on and lead a normal life."[48] Like other newspapers and magazines, the *Times* hoped that her candor would sweep away some of the reticence and mystique surrounding the disease.

Insofar as coverage in the media was concerned, that wish came true—to an extent. With Zaharias's determination as a model other well-known patients were a little readier to let their troubles be known, and the press was more aggressive in publishing the truth. Still, reporting depended mainly on the response of individual patients and doctors. When Humphrey Bogart, the heavy-smoking symbol of tough-guy masculinity, underwent an operation for cancer in February 1956, the papers first noted only that he had had a "slight obstruction" removed from his esophagus and would leave the hospital in a week.

Though the newspapers described Bogart's operation as "major surgery" a few days later, it was not until November, when he had to reenter the hospital "for treatment of nerve root pressure," that they reported he had cancer. Thereafter the movie idol sank rapidly and died, at the age of fifty-seven, in January 1957. No one at that time made much of his heavy tobacco habit, but there was by then no hiding the fact that cancer had killed him. His widow, Lauren

Bacall, made that clear. Like many survivors in later years, she asked that people wishing to make commemorations send donations to the American Cancer Society.[49]

As Bogart grew weak in November 1956, Secretary of State John Foster Dulles checked into the hospital for cancer surgery on his intestine. It was an unusually tense time in American policy making, with crises in Hungary and the Suez Canal threatening world peace, and neither Dulles nor his doctors were anxious to make his illness public. But when the operation confirmed the diagnosis of cancer, they did not hide it. Instead, they emphasized that all had gone well. The cancer had been cut out, and the secretary was going to recover. Subsequent bulletins over the next two years kept track of Dulles's regular checkups and repeated the optimistic message.[50]

When Dulles's condition deteriorated in late 1958, the press at first carried similarly reassuring stories. His hospitalization, newspapers said, was caused by "inflammation of the colon"; doctors could find no new malignancies. But in February 1959 he was operated on again, and journalists grew restive when the doctors were slow to give them a definitive report. "Overnight, the nation's and world's fears mounted steadily," *Time* wrote. "Why the delay in a report routinely quick in every up-to-date operating room?"[51] Reporters, their sensitivities heightened during President Eisenhower's serious ailments a few years earlier, were becoming considerably more inquisitive about cases of cancer in politicians than they had been about Taft's case, only six years earlier.

They were also becoming more blunt. *Newsweek* made it unmistakably clear that Dulles would soon die. Two months later, when the patient resigned as secretary and returned to Walter Reed Hospital for radiation treatments, it reported that he was "visibly in the most ravaging stage of his dreadful illness." Eisenhower observed that his trusted adviser had become "absolutely incapacitated." The *New York Times* devoted an entire page to a detailed review of his protracted ordeal and to his treatment, which had featured not only surgery and extensive radiation therapy (from a "gleaming metal, one-million volt" machine) but also an injection of radioactive gold.[52]

When Dulles, aged seventy-one, died a few weeks later, the newspapers and magazines eulogized him. *Time* described him as a "tough old warrior" who had fought against the enemy of cancer as courageously as he had fought for freedom throughout the world. *Newsweek* predicted accurately that his death would lead to greatly increased congressional appropriations for cancer research. "All over Washington," it said, "and all across the United States the death of the fifty-third Secretary of State seemed to forge a new and iron dedication in the assault on the nation's Number Two killer."[53]

What was the cultural meaning of these five stories of the 1940s and 1950s? From the vantage point of the 1980s—when the press all but photographed the cancer in President Reagan's colon—it may seem that the articles of that more decorous era were written by reporters wearing kid gloves. Indeed, the struggle of the media against public reticence (and obfuscation) was slow and halting. Though 72 percent of Americans told a Gallup poll in 1949 that they "would not mind" if newspapers used the word "cancer" in death notices about their relatives, obituaries for thousands of people, including those who died at Memorial, still used familiar euphemisms to avoid the stigma of the disease.[54]

Yet cultural change is slow and gradual. If the media's handling of these cases was in many ways reticent, it was nonetheless much more candid than cancer coverage had been in the past. It is far less clear, however, that the efforts of the media actually succeeded in weakening the enduring mystique of cancer, which—like many things in the cultural history of the disease in America—changed only slowly if at all. Readers who thought carefully about the articles on these famous patients could not help but observe that cancer struck in unfathomable and different ways. It was not one disease, but many, each with its own distinctive forms of invasiveness and progression. Each required a different and sometimes complex blend of therapies. There were no simple answers.

Observant readers also had to recognize that doctors and scientists were far less able to deal with the disease than optimistic stories were suggesting. Though various therapies had kept the victims alive for a time, none had worked in the end. All five patients had received difficult and sometimes painful treatments and had undergone surgery at least once. Ruth had died young, only thirteen years after hitting his last home run in 1935. Taft had been struck down with bewildering speed. Bogart had seemed to waste away. Dulles had suffered greatly. Only Zaharias, a relatively young and splendidly conditioned athlete, had survived for more than two-and-a-half years following initial surgery (and for only a year more than that). To the millions of less-favored Americans who had seen how cancer afflicted friends and relatives, these stories probably seemed all too familiar. To the poor, the elderly, and people at high risk they must have been especially frightening. The ordeals of all five demonstrated anew the power of the dread disease.

THOUGH THESE ARTICLES about cancer reached many readers, they did not fall into the hands of all—or even a majority—of the people. Even in the 1950s millions of Americans remained too poor to buy magazines or too ill-educated to learn much from a newspaper. Television sets were as yet beyond their means. Millions of other Americans resisted the problem-solving positive thinking of editors and experts. To explore the attitudes of such people, a declining but still substantial minority of the population, is to recognize that American society remained divided along a complex range of regional, racial, religious, and class lines; it was nowhere near so consensual or so amenable to professional advice as optimists liked to think. Millions of doubters either did not hear or did not pay attention to the hype. Their attitudes changed slowly if at all amid the rapid transformation of postwar America.

To be sure, some evidence about popular attitudes seemed to suggest otherwise. Polls indicated that large majorities of Americans were more hopeful about cancer than they had been earlier. Again and again 70 to 90 percent of people polled said that they favored generous government spending for cancer research. Slightly smaller majorities continued to think that a cure could soon be found. Other polls revealed that 95 percent of Americans saw "nothing shameful" about the disease and that 97 percent would want doctors to tell them the truth if they developed it.[55] Though some of these polls were slanted and predictable—who was likely to oppose appropriations to make people healthy or to admit shame of the disease?—they all appeared to point in the same modern direction. They suggested that a substantial majority of people, presumably including sizable numbers of the poorer and ill-educated classes, were less fearful and fatalistic than their forebears had been earlier in the century.

There were in fact reasons for guarded optimism. There may not have been great advances in research—no "breakthroughs"—but reassuring conclusions could be drawn from statistics on cancer mortality. To be sure, some of these statistics seemed to point to a continuation of earlier, apparently alarming trends. Primarily because of the aging of the population (in 1960 there were 16.7 million Americans aged sixty-five or older, or 9.2 percent of the population, as opposed to 6.7 million, or 5.4 percent, in 1930),[56] ever larger numbers of people were developing cancer. Roughly 170,000 a year died of it by 1950. Cancer deaths, thanks in part to better control of other diseases, rose as a percentage of total deaths, to more than 15 percent by the early 1960s. Cancer continued to rank second, well behind heart ailments, as a cause of mortality in the United States. But there were more optimistic ways of understanding the statistics. In fact, age-adjusted cancer mortality rates in the 1940s and 1950s were rising only very slowly. Significant decreases in deaths from certain tumors (mainly of the stomach and the cervix) were compensating for increases in lung cancer. Age-adjusted cancer death rates for women were declining. Indeed, cancer then afflicted more men than women. And five-year "cure-rates," thanks to a greater frequency of early diagnosis and to more significant advances in surgery, were a little better each year.[57] Louis Dublin, still a leading expert on the subject, took pains to disseminate this balanced statistical view. "With due consideration for the aging of the population," he explained in *Women's Home Companion* in 1947, "the peak of the mortality has passed. The picture ahead is increasingly hopeful."[58]

Dublin and others pointed to other aspects of cancer that placed it in a slightly less threatening perspective. Because cancer mainly afflicted older people, they argued, it did not greatly shorten overall life expectancy in America: if the disease were eradicated from the country, life expectancy would increase by less than three years. (Thousands of people, however, died in their forties and fifties from the disease.) They added that other ailments, including a variety of heart problems, caused more pain and limitations on physical activity than did cancer. Some of the many forms of cancer, they stressed, were neither debilitating nor life-threatening, and a few could be cured. Cancer, one writer pointed out in 1955, was not a "single and dreadful disease." Some kinds were "no harder to live with" or "to die with" than were many other afflictions.[59]

There is little evidence, however, to suggest that the majority of Americans adopted either the optimism of the Message of Hope or the reasoned explanations of the epidemiologists. On the contrary, millions of American adults in the 1940s and 1950s had to confront cancer directly, either as patients or as relatives or close friends of patients. Others, particularly those at risk, often worried about developing it. As in the past, many people with sores, bumps, and bruises—or who felt tired and run-down—were ready to fear the worse. Skeptical about the official line, they continued to dread the disease.[60]

A quantitative measure of these concerns is available from surveys of public opinion. Typical was a Gallup poll in 1947 which asked, "What disease or illness would you dread having most?" A total of 67 percent of respondents named cancer (compared to 76 percent who had done so in the poll of 1939). Other diseases mentioned in 1947 were tuberculosis (15 percent), heart trouble (5 percent), polio (5 percent), and venereal disease (2 percent). In 1956 little had changed. When Charles Cameron, scientific director of the cancer society, asked 100 newspaper editors what headline they thought their readers most wanted to see, several answered, CURE FOR CANCER FOUND.[61]

The metaphors of everyday speech also show the special anxiety generated by cancer. The author John Gunther, whose son died of a brain tumor, called it a "vicious invader," a "gangster outbreak of misplaced cells," and a "monster of productivity." Harry Hoxsey, still an immensely successful quack, called it a "horrible crab-like disease" and a "loathsome scavenger slowly and inexorably consuming you alive." The advertising genius Bruce Barton drew back in horror from the "teeth and claws of the awful thing." Cancer, he said, was "something more terrible than words can describe." These descriptions, and the more general use of metaphor—"a cancerous slum," " a cancer on the body politic," "the cancer of pollution," "the fire spread like a cancer"—revealed the especially vivid hold that the illness continued to have on the popular imagination.[62]

Another manifestation of popular fears was the continuing proliferation of unorthodox ideas about the disease. "Not a day passes," the head of the NCI complained privately in 1947, "that we don't get one or two letters with new theories from people . . . who know nothing about cancer biology . . . We have to have some kind of policy for simple protection against lunatic fringe ideas." A journalist in 1950 estimated that the commercial intake of such ideas was $8 million. Cameron added in 1956 that the "catalogue of misconceptions is long. It varies from the inane, the silly, the pathetic, the supernatural, the ludicrous, on to the dangerous and the sinister."[63]

As in the past some of these notions derived from deeply held religious feelings. If some Americans listened to Norman Vincent Peale proclaim a vaguely secularized "power of positive thinking," millions of others clung to faiths which rejected his facile optimism. Several million still belonged to deeply conservative or fundamentalist denominations. Other believers, uprooted from their rural roots and buffeted by the rapid social change of the postwar years, turned to such faiths in order to bring some certitude and stability to their lives. While only a few faiths, such as Christian Science, tended to reject doctors, many counseled people to believe literally in the Word of God (or His earthly representatives), not in the siren songs of modernity, science included. Some, led by charismatic evangelists such as Oral Roberts, championed faith healing. Cancer, these preachers said, afflicted those who did not believe; it was a scourge to sinners from an angry God.

Many true believers were quick to express their views to cancer specialists. Dr. James Murphy, a leading cancer researcher at the Rockefeller Institute, heard from one woman who said that she had learned the cure for cancer in a vision from God: "substance from a blue spruce cedar tree." Another correspondent claimed that God recommended "one part of honey to four parts of milk, thoroughly mixed. Eat little else . . . avoid drinking excess of milk beyond that in the mixture." He urged Murphy to give the potion a test. "*If it proves out, give God the credit.* Just remember that for every disease there is a cure and God placed these cures in reach of all."[64]

Others of the hundreds who wrote Murphy during these years did not call upon religion but dissented from orthodox medical views in other ways. The fervor of such people—surely a small minority, but a vocal one, of the population—was as varied as it was deep. People blamed cancer on the "gradual accretion of filth in the soil," on "starch, sugar, and worrying," and on "electricity and frustration." Cures included "vinegar injections," "shots of chlorophyl," "anti-metallic tablets," and "radioactive sperm cells." One writer extolled the potential of "salt, seaweed, and nitrate," which he said cleaned out worms from horses. For sure, it would kill cancer.[65]

A larger number of people continued to think that emotional stress and frustrations led to the disease. One woman told Murphy that cancer most often struck immature people whose "psychological problems were never straightened out in their minds, whose inner yearnings and desires were frustrated . . . people who have never grown up and found their true self." To this woman, who wrote several times, Murphy was at first polite, but finally firm. "Cancer," he explained, "occurs widely among animals and plants. I find it hard to believe that mice or chickens suffer frustration in youth."[66]

Popular notions such as these, however inspired, seemed conservative compared to some of the better-advertised unorthodoxies of the time. One was "orgone therapy," the idea of the psychiatrist Wilhelm Reich. Cancer patients, Reich said, should sit in "orgone accumulators" of sheet iron and cardboard to regain lost "orgones" (sexual forces) and to restore the "distorted sexconomy of the organism." Another was the cure of Mrs. Ruth Drown of Hollywood, California, who advertised a Radio Therapeutic Instrument that, upon payment of a fee, would "tune in" on patients—by remote control if necessary—and make them whole again.[67] The most awe-inspiring of the many diet cures of the era was Max Gerson's regimen of hourly drinks of vegetable and calf's liver juice, combined with coffee enemas given four to six times a day. Gerson, a German-born doctor with his own well-publicized hospital in Nanuet, New York, temporarily persuaded the Gunthers to turn their dying son over to his care.[68]

Many other unorthodox practitioners (and some well-intentioned physicians) paid special homage to the virtues of Glyoxilide, a liquid substance first introduced in the 1930s by a Dr. William Koch of Detroit. While some practitioners dispensed the substance directly to patients, many quacks advertised by mail, offering both Glyoxilide and a syringe with which to inject it. Government investigators finally determined that it was essentially distilled water. Their prosecution of Koch, which began in 1942, made him into something of a martyr and had no visible success in curbing sales of the stuff.[69]

Popular support for the two most widely publicized unorthodox remedies at the time testified clearly to the persistence of quackery among the cancer counterculture in America. The first of these cures were the various arsenic-based potions still being used on patients by Hoxsey, dean of American cancer entrepreneurs since the 1930s. One independent estimate in 1950 figured that Hoxsey was earning $200,000 a year from his Cancer Sanatorium in Dallas.[70] Though repeatedly harassed and investigated by the government, Hoxsey not only managed to keep in business—the wife of a judge before whom he was tried in a lower court had used and believed in his treatments—but to use that harassment to rally fierce loyalty and activism among his many followers.

The letters of Hoxsey's admirers, preserved at the NCI, show that people loved him not only because he promised a painless cure, but also because he was a symbol of the "little man" fighting against Big Government and the "conspiracy" of the doctors. A few believers were conservative, middle-class ideologues who hotly resented federal "meddling" in the daily lives of people. A larger number were relatively poor and ill-educated. Most were bitter and vitriolic. "You need Hoxsey worse than he needs you," one supporter wrote the NCI. "You show me one dead patient of Hoxseys and I can show you 15 dead from your treatment!" Another wrote, "Let us forget the shackles of the AMA . . . and start giving the mothers and fathers and loved ones back to their families." A third, referring to a pending federal action against Hoxsey, added, "it is this case and hundreds more, that has given me courage to carry on the fight against organized medicine."[71] As these letters show, a mixture of ideological passion and class antagonism fueled this segment of the diffuse, volatile cancer counterculture in America.

The other unorthodox remedy that attracted great popular support was new to the late 1940s and 1950s: Krebiozen. This substance was first introduced to America in 1949 by Stevan Durovic,

WE EARNESTLY INVITE ALL DOCTORS OF THE HEALING ART

to investigate our clinic, inspect our records and check our pathological reports and hospital records. A day or a week spent with us will convince the most skeptical minded, *laymen* as well as *physicians* and *surgeons*, that the *Hoxsey* Method of Treatment for the alleviation of those suffering from cancer *is superior to any other treatment afforded sufferers throughout the world.*

The Hoxsey Institution is staffed by competent medical doctors, registered nurses fully experienced in administering the Hoxsey Treatment. Its laboratory is headed by a former teacher of Serology.

Here, their own KLINE tests are made as double check against the patient's record brought from other sources and all forms of blood work required of a competent laboratory are made.

"That Cancer Sufferers May Live To Enjoy A Healthful Life"

Harry M. Hoxsey

The above quotation is from a dedication to Dr. John C. Hoxsey, who devoted his life to the research of the Hoxsey treatment. The Hoxsey treatment is being continually extended in spite of the tremendous difficulties and obstacles which have faced his son, Mr. Harry M. Hoxsey, who is now chief technician. For over twenty years, Mr. Hoxsey has worked with leading biological and pathological laboratories. Today, the Hoxsey Clinic is *administering successfully* the Hoxsey Method of Treatment, after pathological findings showing the patient afflicted with Cancer.

Learn The Truth About Harry M. Hoxsey, America's Independent Fighter For The Truth About Cancer

THE HOXSEY CANCER CLINIC, 4-P, 4507 GASTON AVE., DALLAS 4, TEXAS

THE HOXSEY CANCER CLINIC, PC-4
4507 GASTON AVENUE
DALLAS 4, TEXAS

Gentlemen:

Please send booklet immediately on your HOXSEY CANCER TREATMENT and the astounding Photographic Proofs of successful cancer cures of persons now living through the Hoxsey Method. This places me under no obligation. Thank you.

NAME..........

ADDRESS..........

CITY.......... STATE..........

From the Historical Health Fraud Collection at the American Medical Association, Chicago.

a Yugoslavian doctor, and his brother. That same year the Durovics came to the United States, refugees by way of Argentina, where they claimed to have extracted their "cure" for cancer from the blood of horses. By 1951 they had secured open encouragement from Dr. Andrew Ivy, a stubborn, immensely prolific scientist who was not only a distinguished professor of physiology at the University of Illinois, but also a former chairman of the NCI's National Advisory Council on Cancer. In 1952 Paul Douglas of Illinois, a former professor of economics who was then a liberal Senator, sponsored legislation that gave the Durovics permanent residency (and later citizenship) in the United States. Douglas also began demanding that the government give Krebiozen a fair and full trial.

By then the NCI and the AMA had joined against their common enemies, the quacks. Orthodox scientists complained that Durovic refused to explain how he had made the original substance, which he had long since changed by diluting it (at a rate of 100,000 to 1) in mineral oil. When investigators analyzed such concoctions, they concluded that they were mixtures of horsemeat and pure mineral oil. The AMA branded the remedy as "one of the greatest frauds of the 20th century."[72]

During much of the time from 1949 to 1963 Krebiozen was distributed internationally as a drug to scientific investigators. But the government's refusal to approve it for sale in interstate commerce outraged advocates of the substance and deeply upset thousands of cancer patients and their loved ones. Reading of this wonderful cure, they flooded the Chicago office of the cancer society with appeals for the concoction and begged government officials to relent. One Massachusetts woman told *Newsweek* she was going to hitchhike to Illinois, if necessary, to procure the substance for her dying daughter. Another woman telegraphed a key congressman to insist that Krebiozen was the only thing keeping a dear friend alive. "My friend no longer wants to live because the U.S. Government doesn't care enough about American Cancer victims to give Krebiozen a fair test in the name of humanity."[73]

These pleas did not change the minds of government officials or the AMA. Indeed, the authorities gathered for a mounting attack on quackery in general. In 1959 California responded to this campaign by approving tougher regulations against unorthodox practitioners. Congress approved legislation in 1962 requiring drug producers to prove that their products were efficacious as well as safe. Federal officials drew the noose on the Durovics and Ivy, prosecuting them for violating the food and drug laws. That effort dragged on until early 1966, when they were acquitted. Stevan Durovic was then prosecuted for evasion of some $900,000 in income taxes, whereupon he left to live in Switzerland.

The running battles over Krebiozen and other unorthodox remedies revealed the continuing relevance of class identification in the modern social history of cancer in America. Many of those who sympathized with Durovic—or Hoxsey—were people of modest means. They had scant contact with fee-for-service practitioners, whose wealth they often resented, let alone with the high-powered specialists who catered to celebrities like Taft and Dulles. Medicine, they thought bitterly, came in two forms: for "them" and for "us." People such as these never dreamed of buying health insurance. When they fell seriously ill, they faced terrifying economic burdens. Cancer, which frequently took a long time to "waste" its victims, was especially frightening on economic grounds alone. It would not only kill; it would also bankrupt the family of the victim. The continuing appeal of unorthodox practitioners, who appeared to offer quick and inexpensive cures, depended considerably on the fears and resentments of economically disadvantaged people who were all but excluded from the modern medical culture.

The involvement of eminent figures such as Ivy and Douglas, however, indicates that it is misleading to see such battles only in terms of social class. The polarities in this and other controversies over cancer treatment also exposed political, regional, and religious divisions. Many of those who backed Krebiozen did so out of sympathy for the underdog—the same feeling that created support for Hoxsey. Others were conservatives of wealth and position who perceived the FDA as part of a wider liberal plot against individual freedom, or liberals who resented the power of the AMA and the "priesthood" of fee-for-service practitioners. Still others were simply desperate for help. The anger and energy which activated this amorphous anti-establishment coalition signified the hostility of substantial minorities of Americans to the dictates of the government and the AMA, as well as their stubborn confidence in painless and wondrous cures. As in the past faith in quackery, class resentments, religious fervor, and political feeling combined to give heart to America's socially diffuse but vociferous cancer counterculture.

THE FOLLOWERS of unorthodox healers at least retained some hope. Numerous other Americans, however, displayed the anxiety, fatalism, and shame that had long attended the disease. That was especially true, of course, of many patients, who displayed what one victim called a "gnawing, self-consumptive fear of recurrence."[74] Surveys of patients, in Britain as well as in the United States, showed that most people—especially in the lower classes—still thought that the disease was uniquely painful, disfiguring, and incurable. Many, especially women, persisted in believing that it was an illness born of sin or contagion. "Cancer is a dirty disease," one woman told an interviewer, "that people got who were dirty or who had done something wrong."[75]

For these and other reasons, surveys showed, many cancer patients continued to put off going to a physician until long after they suspected that they had the disease. Some deluded themselves into thinking they could deny death. "I never thought it was anything I couldn't cure myself with lint and ointment," one woman explained. Most other procrastinators knew better, but were afraid to hear the bad news and were terrified of the knife. Surgery, one said, "makes it spread." Another patient added, "I don't believe in cutting, and I was expecting this if I went to a doctor." Perhaps most common was the view of a woman who refused to have an operation. "I always feel," she said, "that if you're cut there it just goes on and you have to have more done—the beginning of a long process leading to the end."[76]

Large numbers of doctors and other professionals close to the cancer scene shared much of this fear and fatalism. They, too, quietly resisted the official Message of Hope. One poll of physicians in the late 1950s showed that 90 percent still preferred not to tell cancer patients the truth. "Feelings of pessimism and futility about cancer," the interviewer concluded, motivated habitual obfuscation of the truth.[77]

Attitudes such as these left thousands of patients feeling alone and depressed. An extreme manifestation of such emotions devastated John Guy Gilpatric, a well-known short story writer. Learning in 1950 that his wife had a malignant tumor of the breast, Gilpatric shot her to death and then killed himself. Others castigated themselves for developing the unmentionable disease and endured their pain and shame alone. A nutritionist, who knew better, confessed later, "I was ashamed to tell anyone I had cancer. The word itself was difficult for me to say. I believed at that time that we are responsible for our bodies, for our health, and our illness. I blamed myself, thinking I had done something wrong . . . I had made a mess of my life."[78]

Families of cancer patients suffered from some of the same emotions. Victims of slowly spreading or recurring forms of the disease lived in limbo. Feeling betrayed by their bodies, they were prone to sharp swings in mood, ranging from almost euphoric elation to rage to profound depression. "Why me?" they demanded again and again. Some insisted angrily that they be given the latest, most expensive therapy, even if that meant selling the house and ruining the family finances. Others, paralyzed by shame, refused to admit that they were ill. The emotional and behavioral extremes evoked by many forms of cancer—in families as well as in patients—made day-to-day existence a protracted misery for thousands of households.

An especially expressive patient, Edna Kaehele, captured many of these feelings in a book that she published on her experiences in 1952. Hearing the diagnosis from her doctor, she felt shattered:

> . . . cancer. It is an unclean word to our minds. A horror beyond which there is no reasoning . . . *Cancer*! The word filled the universe. I could feel it start from some place too deep for conscious thought, whirring to slow life, swelling to immense proportions, bursting at last with the force of an atomic explosion somewhere in the top of my head. Cancer! CANCER! *CANCER*!

From the beginning, Kaehele recalled, the malady gave her no peace of mind. "Everyone who suffers from cancer," she said, "has also suffered from the racking mental torture of wondering just when it started. How? Why?" She imagined that she could feel the alien intruder. "The taste of it," she added awkwardly, "stayed in my mouth for many weeks—a dark, brackish taste unlike anything I had ever known. It was not imagination; it was a literal and actual dark-brown flavor, as though I had eaten a mildewed bath towel."

Kaehele felt helpless before the patient relentlessness of the tumor. Cancer victims, she said, always had to *wait*—to get the diagnosis that was already suspected; to hear the doctor's halting recommendations; above all, to discover if (or when) the tumors would turn up again. Like many others who developed the disease, she thought of the Crab as an ugly, malicious, living entity inside her. "It is not a thing apart," she said. "It is here, there, and everywhere . . . Pin it down at one spot, and it escapes you to attack from another one more vulnerable. Dare to relax your vigilance for one moment, and it separates spirit from body, mind from heart, even mortal from God. Sleeping or waking, in speech or in silence, cancer is the overwhelming shadow distorting the life that has been touched by it."[79]

Few patients, of course, were able to express, as Kaehele did, the disgust, rage, and fear that had overcome millions of cancer victims throughout history. Many were resigned to their fate. Moreover, most people (a large majority never got the disease), though anxious at times, continued to see cancer as a remote fact of life rather than as an immediate threat to their health. They denied that it could happen to them. Little that occurred in the world of cancer in the postwar era—not the expanding faith in science, not the exaggerated (and often commercially motivated) stories about research and treatment—much changed these enduring realities.

The playwright, Tennessee Williams dramatized the fear and denial of cancer in *Cat on a Hot Tin Roof,* first staged in 1955. The hero, Big Daddy, had cancer—a dreadful development whispered among his sons and daughters-in-law but concealed from him and Big Mama, his wife. When Big Mama finally hears the truth, she reacts with terror and rage:

BIG MAMA: Cancer?! Cancer?!
[Dr. Baugh nods gravely. Big Mama gives a long gasping cry.]

MAE and GOOPER: Now, now, now, Big Mama, you had to know . . .

BIG MAMA: WHY DIDN'T THEY CUT IT OUT OF HIM? HANH? HANH?
DR. BAUGH: Involved too much, Big Mama, too many organs affected.
MAE: Big Mama, the liver's affected and so's the kidneys, both! It's gone way past what they call a—
GOOPER: A surgical risk.
MAE: Uh-huh . . .
[Big Mama draws a breath like a dying gasp.]
REVEREND TOOKER: Tch, tch, tch, tch, tch!
DR. BAUGH: Yes it's gone past the knife.
MAE: *That's why he's turned yellow, Mommy!*
BIG MAMA: *Git away from me, git away from me, Mae!*[80]

Eloquent though Williams was on the subject, no one more clearly described these complex emotions than George Crile, Jr., a Cleveland surgeon who grew angry at the way that they crippled the sensitivity and plain common sense of the friends and relations of victims. He told a story from his clinical experience involving a seventy-five-year-old woman who suddenly could not speak. Her family doctor was baffled, but thought she might be suffering from a thyroid cancer that had spread to the brain. There followed a battery of tests, which her children monitored anxiously.

When the results came in, Crile assembled the family and told them the news. It was far worse than cancer, which he might have been able to treat. "There is nothing that can be done," he said. "Your mother has suffered a stroke from a broken blood vessel; the brain is irreparably damaged. There is no operation or treatment that can help." Crile described the scene:

> The oldest daughter leaned forward, tense, and with a quaver in her voice, asked "Did you find cancer?"
> "There was no cancer," I replied.
> "Thank God!" the family exclaimed.[81]

7

The Research Explosion

THE WAR YEARS were discouraging ones for the alliance against cancer. Though the Women's Field Army flourished, securing 350,000 volunteers at its peak in 1943, the American Society for the Control of Cancer continued to struggle. In that year it had an annual budget of only $102,000 and but 1,000 members.[1] By contrast the March of Dimes campaign took in $15 million to combat polio, which afflicted far fewer people but evoked special terror until distribution of the vaccine in the mid-1950s.

The National Cancer Institute fared little better than the ASCC during the war. Its budget for the fiscal year ending June 1945 was $500,000, only slightly more than the 1937–38 budget, and somewhat less in real dollars. Worse, perhaps, it had difficulty spending the money usefully. Many of its in-house staff entered war work, some in the exciting field of radiation. The *Journal of the National Cancer Institute,* founded in 1940, had trouble filling its issues. In 1944 Surgeon General Parran complained that "there is a shortage of talent rather than of money." Kenneth Endicott, director of the NCI in the 1960s, recalled that "the cancer research program was pretty dead all during the war years," the NIH "a nice quiet place out here in the country."[2]

Within a few years this pastoral scene changed dramatically. In 1944–46 a new group of business people eased out the medical elite at the ASCC and renamed it the American Cancer Society. Employing aggressive methods of fund-raising, they collected an astounding $14 million by 1948.[3] For the first time the ACS turned over funds to research. The NCI, too, expanded exponentially. Its budget increased to $1.75 million in fiscal 1946 and to more than $14 million in 1947. By 1961 its funding had leapt to $110 million.[4]

This explosion of financial resources underwrote a new growth industry of cancer research in the late 1940s and 1950s. Then—at last—the alliance against cancer achieved visibililty and political power in American life. While that power rested most broadly on the strength of contemporary cultural values—faith in medical science and expectations about good health—it was distinctively American in its assurance, which grew stronger during the affluent postwar decades, that infusions of money and improvements in medical technology could conquer anything. The alliance depended, finally, on the expert political activity of individual actors who determined to support research against the disease and worked out a systematic arrangement with key congressmen. Together these cultural, economic, and political forces vastly increased support for cancer research and created a solid institutional base which no other nation in the world came close to matching. Nobody in 1940 or 1945 could have imagined such growth.

THE KEY FIGURE in transforming the ASCC was Mary Lasker. She was the wife of Albert Lasker, an advertising tycoon, who for the Lucky Strike account had pioneered in urging women to smoke in the 1920s and 1930s. "Reach for a Lucky instead of a Sweet," his ads proclaimed. In 1942 he set up the Albert and Mary Lasker Foundation in support of medical research. His wife, an intelligent, concerned, and energetic woman, gradually took charge of the foundation.[5] At about the same time, Mary Lasker recalled, her cook fell ill, but hesitated to specify the diagnosis of her troubles. "Cancer," she added, "was a word that you simply could not say out loud." Worse, the doctor sent her cook to a place named something like "Home for the Incurables." Furious, Lasker resolved to take action. In late 1943 she paid a call on Clarence Little at the cancer society in New York.[6]

Lasker was shaken by what she found. Accustomed to a world of big business and big spending, she was surprised by the small scale of the society's operations and stunned to learn that it spent no money on research. With her husband she set out to challenge the doctors' domination of the society and to bring it into the modern world of salesmanship and fund-raising. Briefly securing Little's co-operation, she managed to add leading businessmen to the board in 1944, including Emerson Foote, an advertising expert who had lost both parents to cancer, Lewis Douglas, head of Mutual Life, Elmer Bobst, a wealthy drug company executive, and Thomas Braniff of Braniff Airways. The society raised $832,000 in 1944.

In late 1944 Lasker and her business associates really took charge. Through personal contacts she placed articles on the need for early detection of cancer in the widely read *Reader's Digest*. Tag lines urged readers to send contributions to the newly christened American Cancer Society.[7] These articles alone raised $120,000, more than the ASCC's entire budget two years earlier. In 1945 Eric Johnston, a businessman of national stature who headed the U.S. Chamber of Commerce, directed the society's drive for funds. Making use of radio and appealing aggressively to philanthropists and corporations, Johnston, Lasker, and their friends raised the staggering sum of $4.29 million in 1945.

So powerful an invasion of business people quickly polarized the society. Lasker and her friends could scarcely conceal their impatience with the conservative doctors who had long dominated the organization. The doctors and scientists, in danger of losing control, reacted with predictable alarm and outrage. James Murphy of the Rockefeller Institute complained privately in January 1946 that the "situation of the last six months has been so discouraging that it is difficult for me to keep up any interest in the Society." Little, too, became disenchanted. "The businessmen," he wrote Murphy, "established their reputations outside the field of cancer and have taken up cancer control as a civic interest which is in no way comparable to the relationship of the professional men in the field." He objected especially to the "unjustifiable, troublesome, and aggressive attitude of 'knowing it all' which that group at present . . . is developing."[8]

Little, however, could not withstand the drive of Lasker and her friends, who had shown that they could bring in money—which the doctors had never tried hard to do. He returned to Maine and the Jackson Laboratory, and the lay alliance gained a firm hold on the executive committee. The committee proceeded to turn over a quarter of the society's funds to grants for outside research, thereby broadening its role in the fight against cancer. It also moved to disband the Women's Field Army, which it considered a "Ladies Garden Club style" operation composed of "do-good amateurs."[9] The WFA soon disappeared.

The reconstituted society recognized its dependence on very wealthy contributors. Its appeals stressed that the disease hit everyone—the rich as well as the poor, children as well as old people.[10] As generalizations these were true enough—cancer did afflict some children and young people, and it was not a disease of the slums or of rural poverty. But in fact it remained overwhelmingly an older person's illness. Moreover, the disease caused great suffering among needy people whose general health was more likely to be poor, who were slow to deal with symptoms, and who had relatively little access to high-quality medical care. Cancers recognized as related to industrial work, notably in the asbestos and dye industries, exacted their toll mainly among blue-collar workers.[11] While the society did not totally obscure the important role of social class in mortality from cancer, neither did it play it up. Lasker and her friends were not epidemiologists; they were politically astute and well-connected fund-raisers who knew how to reach people with money.

The new leaders of the society were equally careful not to antagonize private practitioners. Like the ASCC in the past, the ACS waged an unrelenting war against quackery and called on people who suspected cancer to secure qualified medical treatment at the earliest possible opportunity. For a while the Laskers, who enjoyed personal ties with the Truman administration and with the Democratic party, committed the heresy of supporting national health insurance. But few other influential people in the society—business leaders as well as doctors—shared these "socialistic" notions. While approving of federal aid for medical research, the ACS strongly opposed substantial governmental interference with the principle of fee-for-service private practice. Its literature consistently emphasized one slogan: "Every Doctor's Office a Cancer Detection Center."

In recognition of the enduring mystique about cancer, the society continued to emphasize public education. It distributed a new pamphlet, "What People Don't Know About Cancer," which like many other educational materials prepared by the society highlighted the need for self-detection of "Cancer's Seven Danger Signals." These were "Any Sore That Does Not Heal," "A Lump or Thickening in the Breast or Elsewhere," "Unusual Bleeding or Discharge," "Any Change in Wart or Mole," "Persistent Indigestion or Difficulty in Swallowing," "Persistent Hoareseness or Cough," and "Any Change in Normal Bowel Habits."

Many of the society's early publications outlined the frightful ramifications of the disease. Cancer, they explained, cost $2 billion a year in medical treatment and loss of work and productivity. Worse, the disease, still the number-two killer, took more than 160,000 lives per year in the mid-1940s, 200,000 by 1950. Cancer could be expected, they said, to kill 17 million Americans then living.[12] Bobst, a regular speaker for the society, began his addresses with the message, "One in five of us here—every fifth person in this audience—will die of cancer."[13] The society's poster for 1947 proclaimed, "Every Three Minutes Someone Dies of Cancer. Guard Those You Love. Give to Conquer Cancer." This emphasis on the deadliness of the disease resembled the tactics employed throughout American history by many crusaders—including those directing the nascent movement to ban the bomb—who hoped that scare tactics would arouse the masses.[14]

Distressed by this approach, a few people began to criticize the society for fanning cancerphobia. In 1948 the medical director of the American Psychiatric Association complained that "propaganda" about cancer was inspiring fear of death and fomenting popular panic. He pointed to the widely used symbol of the ACS, a naked (and sometimes flaming) sword with two snakes wrapped about the hilt, which highlighted the message of danger. He suggested instead "something less frightening and more cheerful, like a helping hand."[15] Within a few years others joined in the denunciation. Edna Kaehele, although echoing the ACS message of self-examination and early detection, complained bitterly about its arousal of terror. "The public handling of the cancer situation," she wrote in 1952, "has been extraordinarily inept. 'CANCER, OUR

NUMBER TWO KILLER.' Great posters blaze this unfortunate—equally unhelpful—truth across the countryside. Shocking the Sunday afternoon reading public into action? No, into hiding."[16]

No one made this criticism more cogently than George Crile, Jr., in a widely discussed and controversial *Life* magazine article in 1955, "A Plea against Blind Fear of Cancer," and in his book of the same year, *Cancer and Common Sense*. Crile complained that the appeal to fear induced people to demand unnecessarily thorough examinations and to accede to dangerous and radical surgery. "People who never had cancer," he wrote, "have died of operations done in cancer's name. This is the hidden cost of cancer. It is the price we pay for fear." Crile's strong words marked the rise of a campaign, which he helped to lead, against excessive reliance on radical mastectomies for treating breast cancer.[17]

His primary target in 1955, however, was the "weapon of fear" used by the ACS.

> They have portrayed cancer as an insidious, dreadful, relentless invader. With religious fervor they have fashioned a devil out of cancer. They have bred in a sensitive public a fear that is approaching hysteria. They have created a new disease, cancer phobia, a contagious disease that spreads from mouth to ear. It is possible that cancer phobia causes more suffering than cancer itself.[18]

Crile argued also that this phobia of cancer reflected a wider, neurotic dread of death that had captured American culture. "The length of a life," he said, "is not a measure of its value. Jesus died at the age of 33. So did Alexander the Great. The young men of Britain's Air Force in World War II were exposed to a greater risk of instant death than are many patients of cancer. These men knew their fate but they did not live in fear. They had not been taught to fear." He concluded: "The lives that have meaning are those that are lived gallantly, in the joy of living, and with gladness to share that joy. We should build our monuments to the miracle of life, not to the fear of death."[19]

In challenging the surgeons, the ACS, and fears of death Crile chose to ignore the pervasive optimism about research that contemporary magazines and newspapers were also offering: persistent positive thinking counterbalanced the appeal to fear. Nor could he prove that scare stories deeply affected many people: frightened families of cancer victims found little in such accounts that they did not already believe. Still, Crile was an eloquent and perceptive critic of the scare tactics of his day. If letters about his article in *Life* are to be believed, he struck a sympathetic nerve among some readers. The ACS gradually toned down its prophecies of disaster, emphasizing instead in the late 1950s the Message of Hope.

Blessed with unprecedented wealth, the ACS distributed an ever bigger stream of pamphlets, radio scripts, and advertising materials to magazines and newspapers. It also started a scholarly journal, *Cancer,* in 1948, and a magazine, *Ca,* which went to physicians and medical students. In the early 1950s it arranged with the AFL-CIO and corporations to distribute its materials to an estimated 3.5 million American workers.[20]

The society made especially expert use of contacts with writers and publishers. From the beginning it received enthusiastic backing from the *Reader's Digest* and from Henry Luce's *Time* and *Life,* all of which not only carried stories supporting ACS goals but also included calls for contributions during the society's annual fund drive in April, National Cancer Control Month.[21] Especially innovative were the society's "cancer seminars," beginning in 1947, which brought leading science writers (a relatively new and unorganized group) on tours of ACS-funded research operations. Impressed, many writers responded by publishing stories on the need for more money to fight cancer.

When these tours proved popular, the ACS expanded the operation in the 1950s by sponsoring meetings for large numbers of reporters and magazine writers. Many of these took place in March in well-appointed facilities or warm southern resorts, where the writers were treated to reports of the latest research. Scientific peer responses—standard at regular meetings of researchers—were uncommon at these programs. Optimistic stories about cancer research then appeared in America's magazines and newspapers on the eve of the annual April drives for funds.[22]

The society also secured help from prominent personalities in entertainment and politics. In April 1949 the comedian Milton Berle ran a sixteen-hour television "marathon" to raise money for cancer research.[23] President Dwight Eisenhower and his wife Mamie posed

Reprinted with permission from *Cancer News*, 7, no. 2 (1953), 10; © 1953 American Cancer Society.

for widely circulated photographs showing them turning over checks to the society. So did Vice-President Richard Nixon and the Brooklyn Dodgers baseball team.

In developing such publicity leaders of the society wondered from time to time how they might stand in relation to other foes of cancer, notably the major partner in that effort, the NCI. For some this wonder led to worry, especially when the NCI, too, began to boom in the late 1940s. Charles Cameron, scientific director of the ACS, remembered saying, "we're going to be skunked. People are going to say, 'if we're giving all this money in taxes, why do we have to give it out of our philanthropy?' Mary Lasker had no patience with that argument. She said, 'There will never be enough.'"[24]

Lasker was right. Not only did the two organizations manage to coexist; they grew enormously at the same time, with no sign that philanthropists felt the strain. Moreover, the two pillars of the anti-cancer alliance worked harmoniously from the beginning, with the ACS acting by prearrangement as a lobby for NCI appropriations. The two organizations joined in sponsoring quadrennial National Cancer conferences, the first in 1949. Administrators of both establishments consulted regularly, sometimes moving from the employ of one to the other.[25]

The two powers recognized above all that they must divide responsibilities: the ACS would concentrate on public education, the NCI on research. If that meant that the ACS received more publicity, so be it, because both sides would do better in the all-important quest for funds. As Kenneth Endicott put it, "a secret of really effective working relationships between the Society and the NCI is to let them take the lion's share of the credit and don't get uptight about it. Because they reciprocate by pushing for a big budget for NCI. Okay, let them get the headlines, what the hell."[26]

THE NCI, unlike the ACS, did not owe its great growth after 1945 to the purposeful planning of new leaders. On the contrary, the NCI remained but a part of the larger Public Health Service, whose directors—including Surgeon General Parran—were painfully aware of the low level of scientific interest in cancer research during the war.[27] Those researchers who persisted, including the skeleton staff at the NCI, sometimes engaged in divisive controversies. Rhoads of Memorial conceded privately in 1942 that there was "lots of jealousy in the cancer field," in large part because "none of us have really accomplished anything to alter the course of cancer in men. Hence, to justify our existence at all, we must deprecate the work of all others in the field."[28]

Many people simply doubted the wisdom of large-scale federal support for biological research. Conservatives feared that public involvement would threaten the freedom of physicians. Others thought federal aid might destroy the incentive and independence of voluntary organizations and universities. Still others questioned the competence of biological researchers. Dr. Frank Jowett, president of the National Academy of Sciences, explained that "a large infusion of funds would dilute the quality of American science." He measured the potential of science mainly by the number of first-class minds engaged in an endeavor, not by the millions of public dollars given to researchers.[29]

A number of political developments quickly swept such attitudes aside. The Public Health Service Act of 1944 authorized federal grants to individual researchers and private institutions. In the same year the Laskers induced Florida Senator Claude Pepper to conduct well-publicized hearings on behalf of greater spending for medical research. Many who testified argued that the amounts appropriated to fight a given disease ought to bear some relationship to the mortality from that disease.[30] This hard-headed idea gave a quantitative rationale for expending large sums to fight cancer. Then and later Mary Lasker used her friendship with important Democratic politicians to promote her campaign for federal support.

The cause of federal aid for cancer research received a special boost in 1945, when Vannevar Bush, head of the well-funded Office of Scientific Research and Development, came to Parran and told him, "now that the war is over, I think we should go out of business." He suggested that unspent OSRD funds earmarked for medical research go to the Public Health Service.[31] Parran gratefully secured the transfer of OSRD funds, which—together with authorization from the Public Health Act of 1944—gave the NIH much more money for research. Grants increased from $180,000 in fiscal 1945 to $4 million in fiscal 1947.[32]

At that time Parran did not expect the PHS to become the main beneficiary of federal funding for scientific research. On the contrary, many scientists and politicians were then lobbying to establish a National Science Foundation to oversee such appropriations. But the NSF bill became mired in protracted controversy and did not pass until 1950. Meanwhile, the Truman administration failed to secure passage of national health legislation. By default, the Public Health Service—with its satellites the NIH and NCI—remained the most visible federal agency to which health-conscious congressmen could appropriate money.

Broader forces also aided the NCI in the postwar years, some of which seemed especially strong in America. As June Goodfield noted, Europeans showed relatively little enthusiasm for governmental support of cancer research, much of which therefore relied on private donors. The French considered cancer "just one disease among others, being as little moved by appeals for financial support as they would be for new bridges across the Seine."[33] The English, too, seemed unhurried. Although no single cause accounted for these differences, America's determination rested in part on its unparallelled postwar affluence, which gave added weight to demands for good health and to fears of premature death. Cancer, many Americans were ready to believe, was the ultimate sentence of death.

Affluence also facilitated American willingness to spend public funds on medical research, especially in light of Congress's relatively small allotments to social welfare programs. Most European countries, by contrast, had suffered appalling losses of life and property during the war. Less sure of the inevitability of progress, Europeans were sadly accustomed to early death. Reconstruction and social welfare remained their highest domestic priorities. Thus an irony—America, land of historically powerful doubts about the role of the state, erected the most highly centralized and publicly financed apparatus against cancer in the world.

Support for the NCI owed much also to an optimistic, goal-oriented faith in social engineering that struck Goodfield, like other European observers, as a distinctively American approach to scientific and technological problems. In the United States, she suggested, science had become "larger than life."[34] Though Americans had often lionized individual scientists—Benjamin Franklin was a cultural hero—they also showed in practice a readiness to organize large laboratories and other bureaucratic structures to further specific goals, such as the Manhattan Project and the space program (which generated amazing, indeed absurd, media attention).[35] To Goodfield America's "General Motors approach to science" led to a certain loss of serendipity, a bureaucratic conservatism that favored feats of engineering and technological wizardry over basic science. To self-confident Americans, however, a well-financed institute seemed the most efficient avenue toward the conquest of cancer.

The rise of the NCI depended finally on the activity of individuals who knew how to exploit these aspects of the American character. Surgeon General Parran learned that he had to ask Congress for large sums of money or risk losing momentum. Mary Lasker worked effectively to increase funding for cancer research. With Mike Gorman, a knowledgeable lobbyist, doing much of her legwork, she established a working relationship in 1947–48 with key congressional figures, notably Republican Rep. Frank Keefe of Wisconsin, chairman of the House subcommittee on health appropriations, and especially with Democratic Rep. John Fogarty of Rhode Island, Keefe's successor in 1949. her contacts were broadly bipartisan. She grew close to Senator Lister Hill of Alabama, chairman of the committee on labor and public welfare and head of the appropriations subcommittee for health. The son of a physician, Hill was named after Joseph Lister, the pioneering English surgeon who crusaded for antiseptic procedures in the nineteenth century. Hill was a willing, effective advocate of aid for medical research. From the late 1940s to the late 1960s Fogarty and Hill exercised great power over medical research legislation.

Lasker and her allies also relied on James Shannon, the strong-minded head of the NIH from 1955 to 1968, and on the eloquent testimony of leading cancer researchers such as Farber of Boston, Clark of Houston, and other nationally known physicians, like Paul Dudley White of Boston and Michael DeBakey of Houston. Never lacking in money to advance her purposes, Lasker further depended on the financial resources and contacts of a personal friend, Florence Mahoney, whose husband had inherited an interest in the Cox family newspaper chain, the largest network of Democratic papers in the country. Mrs. Mahoney moved to Washington in 1950 and acted as unofficial hostess for the health lobby.[36]

"Mary and her Little Lambs," as opponents came to call them, focused first on cancer, but soon branched far afield to support research on other major diseases. Her approach made excellent political sense. Congressmen found it much more appealing to back research into cancer or heart disease than into "biological investigation." Their constituents, after all, were dying of these illnesses. Playing on these perceptions, Lasker and her allies secured enactment of bills establishing a host of disease-specific institutes, beginning with the Heart Institute in 1948. The proliferation of research centers, which sprang up alongside the NCI in Bethesda, necessitated renaming the National Institute of Health the National Institutes of Health.[37]

Lasker and her friends recognized a key fact of politics: the desire of congressmen to be seen by constituents as warriors against killer diseases. Building on such feelings, Fogarty and Hill in the 1950s coolly awaited budget requests from the fiscally prudent Eisenhower administration and then demanded to know of friendly witnesses—such as Shannon at the NIH—why they had not asked for more. As rehearsed, the witnesses explained that the NCI could use all that Congress could provide. Anxious not to oppose funding of good health, other congressmen chimed in behind Fogarty and Hill. As one fiscally conservative Republican explained during a hearing, "I do not think we should worry about a few million dollars when it comes to finding the cause and cure of these dread diseases."[38] Funding for the NCI increased during the Eisenhower years from $18 to $110 million.

These were indeed encouraging years for medical researchers. Lewis Thomas, a distinguished physician, virologist, and pathologist who was then a member of the National Advisory Health Council reporting to the Surgeon General, remembered that "we had the time of our lives. Everything seemed possible." Gorman said of Lasker's network that it was "probably unparalleled in the influence that a small group of private citizens has over such a major area of national policy." He ascribed her success to a "high class kind of subversion, very high class. We're not second story burglars. We go right in the front door."[39]

Thanks to this "subversion," the NCI flourished, not only in the 1940s and 1950s but also for many years afterward. Between 1948 and 1956 it distributed nearly $100 million in federal money to extramural researchers. Some of this money went for educational programs, field demonstrations, and state cancer control efforts, but the largest single part of it aided laboratory research into the causes and cures of cancer, much of it at large, well-connected institutions such as Memorial Sloan-Kettering. The NCI also received money for additional research facilities of its own and steadily increasing sums for its intramural staff. Other appropriations financed construction of a hospital at Bethesda, postgraduate training fellowships for physicians, and research fellowships for young scientists to work at the NIH. The NCI, ever the biggest of the NIH institutes, was by the mid-1950s the star attraction of what Thomas called the "greatest research institution in the world."[40]

Even then, not everyone shared this favorable view of the NCI. One doctor angrily complained that the NCI was merely a "tool of the American Cancer Society, making a propaganda pitch for that organization. . . . They subsidize and perpetuate ignorance and fraud in the mistaken belief that they are benefiting humanity." Other critics objected that the immensity of funding for cancer enticed grant-hungry researchers into placing a "cancer angle" in their requests for money, thereby distorting the nature of their work and putting "uncomfortable pressures on the independence of scientific institutions." Thomas worried that the sums appropriated were so large that they drew universities, research institutions, and individual scientists into a subservient relationship to Washington.[41]

Other skeptics, including some who worked at the NCI itself, bemoaned the bureaucratic apparatus. There was "more tight control, less freedom . . . it was never quite the same" as in the old days, one complained. Some researchers privately admitted that Congress was throwing more money at the problem—especially at chemotherapy—than the scientists could use wisely. One scientist who went public with these concerns in 1956 said that cancer research "is entering on an era of dollar diplomacy as inordinately large sums are poured into developmental activities that rest on an extremely tenuous premise."[42]

A few scientists began to complain that the NCI devoted far too much of its money to "narrow" laboratory work, thereby neglecting efforts on behalf of cancer control. By control they meant various things, including epidemiological studies, investigations into environmental and occupational exposures, subsidies for the training of cancer clinicians and public-health workers, and financing of public cancer clinics. Much cancer could be prevented, they emphasized, if the NCI would lead campaigns against smoking and finance Pap tests. Instead, they complained, the NCI continued to defer to laboratory researchers and to well-placed surgeons, radiologists, and chemotherapists.

These complaints, muted in the 1940s and early 1950s—there were few widely agreed-upon means of cancer prevention at that time—swelled in later years. One such writer offered an analogy with atomic research.

> One might not expect the scientists who developed the atomic bomb to expand on the thesis that more money should properly be spent on the social sciences—studies that would address the problem of how to address wars, rather than win them once they had begun. In the same way, postwar medical research scientists busily pursued their own interests which invariably led them into smaller and smaller corners of the biomedical research universe. As long as the research establishment recommended the money necessary to pursue the complexities of life itself, they could not be troubled with questions of prevention and health promotion.[43]

FOR MANY OBSERVERS the best test of this research explosion was results. The research effort grew to near-staggering size by the mid-1950s. Cameron, as scientific director of the ACS, observed in 1956 that the society library had recently counted 9,015 original articles about cancer published in one year alone. He added that cancer researchers assembled in hundreds of meetings each year.[44] Now that institutionalized cancer research was coming of age, it was appropriate to ask whether official (as opposed to popular) ideas about causes and cures were changing very much.

Many of the same theories of causation that had been offered before remained in circulation. A handful of serious writers persisted in arguing that cancer was a "disease of civilization" and in claiming (wrongly) that white, middle-class people were more prone than blacks or the poor to the disease.[45] Others added to the age-old literature that blamed cancer on tense personalities or emotional stress.[46] Reflecting the contemporary flowering of psychoanalysis, many of these arguments came from psychiatrists who studied the behavior of patients. As often as not the analysts blamed the victims.

One ingenious psychoanalyst in 1956 claimed to have identified the "major behavioral characteristics of cancer patients." These were "masochistic character structure," "inhibited sexuality," "inhibited motherhood," "the inability to discharge or deal appropriately with anger, aggressiveness, or hostility, covered over by a facade of pleasantness," "unresolved hostile conflict with the mother," and "delay in securing treatment." These affected the pituitary, which overproduced certain hormones, thereby upsetting the balance of the body and creating "cellular chaos" culminating in cancer. Among those who supposedly died in this way were Napoleon, who suffered from afflictions of the pituitary gland; Grant, who grew tense after being swindled; Eva Peron, who had an inordinate drive for power; George Gershwin, who was overambitious; Senator Taft, whose cancer stemmed from political frustration; and Ruth, who had desperately wanted to manage the Yankees.[47]

Correctly dismissing such theories as insubstantial, most researchers turned to the laboratory. Many began looking for viral causes of cancer. Thanks to discoveries of leukemia viruses in mice—and more broadly to excitement over identification of the polio virus—this work gained official respectability by the mid-1950s. The first issue of the new journal, *Virology,* in 1955, appropriately carried an article on Rous's work on chicken sarcoma. Rous himself was still active and attracted attention by suggesting that cancer might be a multistage process, with viruses perhaps acting as initiating causes of cell disorder that is then transformed into malignant growth by chemical carcinogens.[48] By 1960 the search for human cancer viruses had yet to succeed, but it was both promising and intense, with the NCI spending $3.9 million on virus research and the ACS adding $1.8 million more. Both Jonas Salk and Albert Sabin, the polio pioneers, were engaged in the effort.[49]

Other researchers focused on the effects of carcinogens, of which none was more frightening than radiation from atomic and hydrogen bombs. As early as 1946 NCI researchers conducted studies on the effects of atomic radiation on mice.[50] These made it clear not only that the radiation caused cancers of the skin, but that it also afflicted internal organs and that damage could be transmitted to children. Though secret at first, research such as this—as well as the suspicions of citizens—slowly brought the issue of radiation into the open. By the late 1950s it was no secret that atomic testing caused leukemia or that fallout of strontium 90 could pose a threat to millions of Americans. In 1956 Democratic presidential candidate Adlai Stevenson made nuclear testing a major concern of his campaign.

Researchers in the 1950s claimed to be able to identify many other sources of carcinogens, including cigarettes, air pollution, asbestos, X-rays, food additives, aniline dyes, and sunlight. As these concerns aroused attention in magazines and newspapers, Congress grew alarmed and in 1958 approved a number of anticancer measures. Among these was the Delaney amendment, which called on the Food and Drug Administration to refuse approval of food additives if they were found to cause cancer in human beings or animals.[51] Though lacking an adequate data base (and indifferently enforced), the amendment remained on the books, resulting in the banning of cyclamate in 1969 and serving as a beacon of hope to a generation of environmentalists in the 1970s.

No one was more active in the war against occupational exposures than Wilhelm Hueper, a German-born researcher who had come to the United States in the 1920s and had worked for the DuPont Corporation in the 1930s. Studying the causes of bladder cancer among dye workers—already a well-developed line of research in Europe—Hueper told corporate officials in 1938 that the compound beta-naphthylamine caused the tumors. When he tried to publish his findings, however, the company refused permission and then fired him. It was not the corporation's responsibility, DuPont argued, to warn workers of such dangers.[52]

Far from discouraging Hueper, this experience made him all the more determined to sound the alarm about carcinogens in the workplace. In 1942 he published his 896-page *Occupational Tumors and Allied Diseases*. Though hardly a best seller—it had the further misfortune of appearing in the immediate aftermath of the attack on Pearl Harbor—it became a Bible of sorts over the next two decades for a handful of environmentalists, including Rachel Carson. Confirming Hueper's stature, the NCI in 1948 appointed him head of a newly created Environmental Cancer Section within its Cancer Control branch, where he remained until 1964.[53] The NCI began to test compounds for carcinogenic effects on animals, identifying 322 (of 1,329 tested) as early as 1951.[54] Hueper insisted that carcinogens had to be "eliminated from industrial, military, and civilian use . . . that the community be protected by the prevention of the discharge of carcinogenic wastes; that factories be licensed and inspected; that workers be provided with protective clothing, equipment and medical supervision."[55]

The number and variety of proposed theories of causation—"civilization," viruses, various kinds of carcinogens—are an indication that researchers were still groping to comprehend the basic biological processes of the disease. As one investigator admitted in 1949, "looking for the cause of cancer is like looking in a dark room for a black cat that isn't there."[56] To many of the top leaders in the alliance against cancer, moreover, none of the theories was altogether satisfactory. Cancer, they believed, did not stem primarily from civilization, poor diets, viruses, or external agents—important though such carcinogens might be in activating cellular change. While they no longer resorted to the word "irritation" to account for the disease—that, they recognized, was not a very precise way to explain things—they continued to believe that cancer stemmed mainly from inherent imperfections of cells. It followed that laboratory research into cellular behavior, not strategies of prevention or control, must be the front line of defense against the disease.

There were many reasons for the coolness of the ACS and the NCI to environmental explanations. The danger of atomic radiation, for example, was played down by a combination of wishful thinking, Cold War patriotism, and deliberate misrepresentation of existing knowledge. High-ranking governmental officials, including Lewis Strauss of the Atomic Energy Commission, repeatedly minimized the effects—as known to many top researchers—of radioactive fallout.[57] Rhoads publicly asserted as late as 1956 that open-air atomic tests were harmless.[58] While other scientists disputed such assertions—the evidence from Hiroshima (and from the Pacific and the American Southwest) showed otherwise—they attracted little interest during the Cold War years. Many radiologists, indeed, received their training and research money from the defense establishment, especially from the AEC. Only in the late 1950s did a substantial number of physicians rouse themselves to confront the dangers of atomic radiation.

Environmental theories suffered also from the personality and style of Hueper himself. Thanks in part to the many rebuffs he endured, Hueper had an extraordinarily aggressive and abrasive manner. NCI head John Heller said that "Bill could get more people mad in a short time than most any man I have ever encountered." Endicott, who succeeded Heller, added that Hueper so thoroughly distrusted industrial leaders that he scattered accusations wildly. "He would go after them with a meat ax. He was ready to lower the boom on them before others would concede that the evidence was there."[59] Never a strong influence at the NCI, Hueper was tolerated grudgingly and given meager resources for his work. In 1952 the NCI ordered him to cease doing field studies. Support for research into occupational exposures at the NCI totaled only $675,000 as late as fiscal 1958.[60]

Leading figures in cancer research had other, broader reasons for favoring basic laboratory studies over cancer control and prevention. Most cultural and environmental theories, they pointed out, were conjectural as applied to human beings. Alarm concerning chemical carcinogens, for instance, arose mainly from evidence from research on animals. Who was to say that human beings responded in the same way as mice, rats, or dogs? Yet who could make a persuasive ethical case for testing suspected substances on human beings, even on terminal patients? Furthermore, most cancers afflicted older people after apparently long periods of latent bodily change, during which many forces—genetic as well as environmental—might have acted singly or together to produce cancers. How could one factor, such as diet or smoke or industrial pollution, be singled out for blame? This argument against environmental theories was the more powerful because only a small minority of people regularly and demonstrably exposed to suspected carcinogens, such as tobacco, developed cancer. Whatever the role of environmental forces or life styles, it was clear to many experts that a root cause of cancer was what Cameron labeled "individual susceptibility" to the disease.[61] It followed that most preventive measures offered only limited hope.

Orthodox approaches to the search for causes prevailed, finally, because they coalesced comfortably with dominant values in the culture. Two such values were especially relevant. One was the unprecedented prestige of science and of medical researchers. If leading scientists said that cancer was fundamentally an aspect of an individual's cellular physiology, so be it. If they were slow to elaborate the biological mechanisms involved—well, give them some time. In this context dissidents such as Hueper, who had the effrontery to assault the titans of industrial capitalism during the politically conservative 1950s, understandably found it difficult to receive much of a hearing.

The second was the conservative temper of the postwar years. Cameron hit on this point when he recalled why environmental notions had little popular appeal: "I don't think we realized then that the problem was as widespread as it was."[62] He was correct, for America in the 1940s and 1950s was not only unprecedentedly affluent but also apparently free from social conflict, at least in comparison with the depression-ridden 1930s and the war-torn early 1940s. Grateful for this reprieve, many Americans, especially in the ever more numerous middle classes, celebrated capitalism and corporate leadership. Tired of social reform, they showed little interest in erecting elaborate federal regulation of alleged polluters or in pointing accusatory fingers at industrial "statesmen."

Not until the culturally tumultuous late 1960s and the economically unsettled 1970s—decades of growing doubts about American institutions—were environmentalists able to get much of a hearing. Only then did well-entrenched biomedical approaches to cancer—ascendant since the days of Grant—undergo probing questions from a broad range of critics.

As was true regarding theories of causation, familiar orthodoxies on cancer therapies remained in force. The ACS-NCI alliance clung to its faith in early detection and, if possible, early and radical surgery. The ACS, with primary responsibility for education about the disease, continued to sound this message above all others. It gave special publicity to testimonials from members of its "Cured Cancer Club," sensible people who had gone to a qualified physician at the first hint of the "Seven Danger Signals" of cancer.[63] Cameron explained that "over the past two generations the progress of medical science has made it possible to transfer one kind of cancer after another from the category of 'incurable disease' to that of 'curable'"—but *only if* people practiced early detection. He estimated that one-half of cancer patients could be saved if they caught the ailment in time.[64]

Cameron's faith in early detection rested in part on what the ACS and NCI considered to be dramatic advances in surgery in the 1940s and 1950s. These were truly considerable. Surgeons developed much improved methods of minimizing shock and of replacing blood lost during operations and, most important, they used antibiotics to combat infection. These advances strongly attracted medical students to surgical practice. In 1931, 10 percent of doctors identified themselves as specialists in surgery; by 1960 the percentage had jumped to 26 percent. Surgery was a more prestigious and lucrative business in the United States than anywhere else in the world.[65]

Because of surgical advances, increasing percentages of cancer patients survived major operations, and a greater number was cured. For this reason—and because more patients were diagnosed earlier—five-year "cure rates" increased considerably, from around one patient in five in the 1930s to one in three by 1960.[66] This was the most dramatic therapeutic advance in the modern history of cancer.

By then surgeons no longer feared to operate on a number of internal organs. On the contrary, they extolled the magic of the knife. "If you have a nice apple with a rotten spot in it," one patient agreed, "you can still cut out the spot and enjoy the apple. That's how it is with cancer."[67] Another enthusiast added, "Today the patient who has a chest tumor can go to the operating table with no more fear than the patient with gall stones."[68] So self-assured were specialists about the benefits of radical surgery that they told women facing mastectomies to purchase artificial breasts to overcome, they said confidently, the emotional problems associated with loss of a breast.[69]

The enthusiasm for early detection *cum* radical surgery probably peaked around 1955, when one dauntless doctor performed a hemicorporectomy, amputating the legs and pelvis of a cancer patient. Thereafter Crile and others mounted a counterattack. Much radical surgery, they said, was not only unnecessary; it might even hasten metastasis. Studies in the late 1950s of breast cancer surgery suggested that women who underwent simple removal of the breast followed by radiation fared as well as women who endured radical mastectomies that also cut away underlying muscles and axillary tissue.[70]

This counterattack stemmed the tide of heroic surgery, but only slightly and slowly. One physician even argued that radical surgery had to be practiced if student doctors were to learn the tricks of the trade. Crile and others succeeded mainly in raising doubts, not in reversing the increase in the number of surgeons, the number of operations, or the belief—as assured among many doctors as ever—that the knife was the best way of curing most forms of cancer.

Though the allies against cancer believed above all in early detection and surgery, scientific researchers also evinced growing interest in radiotherapy, and later in chemotherapy, during the postwar years. This interest stemmed in part from popular and congressional pressures for quick solutions—pressures that many researchers, perceiving the availability of funding, proved willing to accept.

Radiotherapy had long commanded great attention in Europe, where surgeons were not so dominant as they were in the United States. It appealed to the NCI from the beginning: the first National Advisory Cancer Council had earmarked precious funds to investigate the therapeutic possibilities arising from the cyclotron at Berkeley. In the 1940s and 1950s popular enthusiasm for radiation swelled, and grant-seeking researchers promised that cancer could be defeated with technological "guns" and omnipotent rays. One book aimed at a popular audience in 1943 lauded the cyclotron, operated by a "raypilot" who sat at a remote control panel fifty feet from an eighty-five-ton magnet, from which the ray streamed out "like a flame from an open jet." "There is no doubt," the author concluded, "that the cyclotron will soon become a very important addition to the arsenal of weapons used against cancer."[71] A writer for *Reader's Digest* in 1944 followed in this vein with a breathless account of radiation therapy at the Chicago Tumor Institute. The work, he wrote, was "not so much medical as it is super-precise biological engineering." "Marksmen" at the institute were "finding the bull's-eye of the cancer. Their rays are now a high-powered rifle against the choking death." The use of radiation, he asserted, was "one of the most fantastic events in human history." "If there were tumor institutes like Chicago's in every American city, the fight against cancer would soon be nearly one third won."[72]

After the bombing of Hiroshima and Nagasaki there was no stopping this kind of enthusiasm. *Life* exclaimed in 1946 that "great quantities of all kinds of artificial radioactives can be made in the same piles which produce plutonium for the atomic bomb." Rhoads at Memorial Sloan-Kettering asserted that radioactive isotopes would become the best means of treating cancer in the future.[73] CBS ran a documentary in 1947 entitled "The Sunny Side of the Atom," which cheerfully described the medical wonders to be expected from bomb research. The AMA's health magazine, *Hygeia,* exclaimed in 1947 that "medically applied atomic science has already saved more lives than were lost in the explosions at Hiroshima and Nagasaki."[74]

As if atoning for support of weapons research, scientists, bureaucrats, and journalists continued in the next decade to emphasize the medical blessings of atomic energy. Strauss, who became a trustee of Sloan-Kettering, grew especially enthusiastic about radioactive isotopes.[75] In 1949 the AEC claimed to give away $500,000 worth of "tracers," or radioactive chemicals, to be used only in the war against cancer. Among these were iodine, employed against thyroid cancer; phosphorus, possibly good against tumors of the breast and stomach; and cobalt. Some radioactive materials could be neatly and painlessly injected. Iodine and phosphorus could be swallowed in "Hiroshima cocktails." One self-proclaimed "human guinea pig" at Memorial Hospital in 1946, the writer and lecturer Henry Noble Hall, raised a toast with his "cocktail" of radioactive iodine, "Well, here's to science and to success." He stayed with this treatment for 90 days, imbibing large quantities of the stuff, and emerged to write a personal account, "How I Was Cured of Cancer by Radioactivity."[76]

When Hall died of cancer in March 1949, Americans might well have wondered how much punch the cocktails packed. But the power of positive thinking remained strong among high officials. Strauss, Rhoads, and others continued to celebrate the medical potential of radioactivity, and many scientific writers chimed in. A reporter for *Harper's* in 1949 quoted Chancellor Robert Hutchins of Chicago as predicting that the great new supplies of radioactive materials unleashed as a result of work on the bomb would help solve the riddle of cancer within seven years. The reporter concluded, "we can be sure that atomic energy in its various forms will contribute heavily to the final victory" against cancer.[77]

Journalists, it seemed, never tired of promoting the technological marvels of radiation. In 1951 *Collier's* published a lavishly illustrated article showing a woman lying, helpless and alone, in a huge vault at Brookhaven laboratories in New York. She was being "blasted" by atoms of boron, which were "exploding" the tumor in her brain. The writer explained that this therapy, being used for the first time and with no known results, was a "spectacularly promising phase of atomic research." A year later *Reader's Digest* sang the praises of cobalt, the "poor man's radium," which could be surgically implanted, as the "greatest, most beneficial dividend from the A-bomb."[78]

Life periodically brought its skilled photojournalists to cancer centers and graphically illustrated the blessings of medical technology. In 1952 it featured a story under the heading NEW U.S. CANCER WEAPON describing with appropriate military metaphors a "million dollar mass" of radium which could be shot in twenty-five separate beams at tumors and which would destroy "deep-lying cancers that the surgeon cannot remove." Two years later it ran two feature stories within a month. A GAT FOR KILLING CANCER described a pistol that doctors were using to pump radioactive gold pellets into tumors. The second article, also promoting radiotherapy, featured a cartoon showing a livid cancer cell disappearing under a mushroom cloud. No illustration better symbolized the postwar marriage of the bomb and cancer technology.[79]

Upset at the expectations aroused by such hyperbole, some critics warned that radiation therapy was at best an inexact science, at worst highly dangerous to patients.[80] Quietly sharing some of these doubts, ACS and NCI leaders continued to emphasize the virtues of early detection and surgery and to recommend radiotherapy mainly as an adjunct treatment. But they, too, were intrigued by the possibilities and far from immune to the hope that technological improvements might result in cures. They steadily provided researchers and clinicians with generous financial support for radiotherapy.

Their reaction to the growing vogue for chemotherapy was similar: at times cautious and skeptical, never wholly enthusiastic, but ultimately—because of popular and congressional pressures—supportive in a very large way.[81] Research interest in "chemo" grew in part as a result of the explosion in December 1943 of an Allied ship carrying mustard gas in the harbor of Bari, Italy.[82] Some of the soldiers on ship absorbed the liquefied gas and died from its toxic effects. Autopsies revealed that the gas had inhibited reproduction of white blood cells and therefore led to speculation that it might be useful in treating leukemia, Hodgkin's disease, or cancers of the lymphatic system. The OSRD sponsored secret research into this possibility at Yale and other places during the war.[83]

After the war the research came out into the open and was a main line of investigation at Sloan-Kettering, where Rhoads, who had served as chief medical officer of the Army's Chemical Warfare Division, emerged as an evangelist for chemotherapy. Scientists there tested some 1,500 forms of nitrogen mustard gas and other "alkalyting agents" between 1946 and 1950, occasionally on patients. By then chemotherapeutic research seemed to be paying off. Sidney Farber's experiments with antimetabolites unveiled the wonders of anti–folic acid compounds, which produced constant remissions in cases of acute leukemia among children. No such remissions had ever been produced before. Other promising drugs were ACTH, a pituitary hormone, and cortisone, produced by the adrenal cortex. As one scientist recalled, researchers in the field thought they were entering a "'golden age' of chemotherapy."[84]

The interest in cancer chemotherapy was part of a broader postwar fascination with chemical marvels. The United States, indeed, was in many ways becoming a "drug culture."[85] Streptomycin, tested against tuberculosis in 1943, was shown in clinical trials in 1945 to be the first agent ever discovered to have much effect against the disease. Penicillin, the greatest "wonder drug" of all, was already clearing out the pediatric wards of hospitals, freeing doctors to experiment with drugs on leukemia victims. Doctors were turning enthusiastically to the pharmacy for cures of all kinds of ailments, including mental illness.[86] It seemed possible, indeed plausible, to expect that researchers could somehow find a wonder drug against cancer. In 1953 Rhoads came out and said so: "Inevitably, as I see it, we can look forward to something like a penicillin for cancer, and I hope within the next decade."[87]

The exciting discoveries by well-connected scientists like Farber helped persuade Congress to invest heavily in chemotherapy during the 1950s. In 1954 it gave the NCI $3 million for such work. A year later the NCI established a Cancer Chemotherapy National Service Center and negotiated contracts with private laboratories to produce the drugs. The Veterans Administration, the AEC, and the Food and Drug Administration also participated. By 1957 the chemotherapy program was intense, absorbing almost half of the NCI's budget and testing thousands of chemicals a year.[88]

Endicott, the NCI official who ran the program in its early years, brought mixed emotions to the work. Like many scientists, he resisted highly targeted research, believing instead in providing scientists with utmost freedom to pursue basic biological inquiries. And he doubted that much would come of the effort. "I thought it was inopportune," he recalled, "that we really didn't have the necessary information to engineer a program, that it was premature, and well, it just had no intellectual appeal to me whatever."[89]

Other scientists shared some of Endicott's reservations. Many of them continued to believe that no magic bullet could be found, either in radioactive bombs or pharmaceutical wonders. But other scientists were rhapsodic. Farber hailed chemotherapy as "the greatest mobilization of resources—man, mineral, animal, and money—ever undertaken to conquer a single disease." Rhoads added, "it is no longer a question *if* cancer will be controlled, but *when* and *how soon.*" ACS scientific director Cameron traveled to meetings with two once cancerous hamsters given him by Farber.

The hamsters, he explained to audiences, had received chemotherapy and lived, whereas their untreated litter mates had died of cancer. Endicott, too, became enthusiastic, predicting in 1956 that "chemo" would ultimately make a "tremendously worthwhile contribution. The next step—the complete cure—is almost sure to follow."[90]

Though no "complete cure" followed, the evangelists for chemotherapy in the 1940s and 1950s did not preach entirely in vain. Testing over the next two decades found around thirty drugs for the treatment of human cancer, especially in children. These attacked some ten tumor types, mainly leukemias, Hodgkin's disease, and histiocytic lymphomas which were systemic and therefore untreatable by surgery or radiation. By the early 1980s cancer drugs saved approximately 3,000 patients a year under the age of thirty. One expert concluded that these were "very real gains and they are a fitting memorial to the many thousands of patients who took part in the early trials of various possible forms of chemotherapy."[91]

Despite these achievements, many physicians as well as scientists remained skeptical about chemotherapy. Some objected to the enormous costs of testing (by 1970 the potential of some 400,000 drugs had been explored).[92] "Take the national chemotherapy center," the NCI's chief pathologist complained, "It cost thirty million dollars for quite a number of years, and what is the product?—zero."[93] Another critic scoffed that the search for drugs was driven by the "frantic thought that somewhere in some South American jungle was the answer."[94] Some insiders dubbed the effort the "nothing-is-too-stupid-to-test" program, observing correctly that chemical testing enriched pharmaceutical companies that patented the drugs. The NCI, they charged, was the "Wall Street of Cancer Research."[95]

Other critics stressed the harmful side effects of cancer drugs. The highly toxic drugs damaged normal cells. Many caused vomiting, loss of hair, fatigue and depression. Some writers contended—accurately, as it turned out—that a few of the drugs were themselves carcinogenic. All emphasized what they saw as the dangerously hit-or-miss nature of "chemo." "To find a chemical that will make cancer disappear and leave normal tissues unharmed," one expert observed, "would be like finding a drug that you can take by mouth that will make one ear disappear and not the other."[96]

Critics stressed above all that chemotherapy was of little or no use against many common cancers, including tumors that invaded the gastrointestinal and respiratory tracts of adults. To save 3,000 young lives a year was unquestionably a good thing, but that was a tiny fraction of the more than 400,000 who died annually of cancer by the early 1980s. Although most observers remained ambivalent, they lamented the continuing attraction of Americans to magical cures. As Crile put it, the "trial-and-error attempt to find a poison that will selectively destroy all cancer cells may prove to be a mid-century version of the overemphasis placed earlier in the empiric development of surgical and radiologic techniques."[97]

Some observers offered a rising cry against the entire slant of American cancer research as supported by the ACS and NCI. They reiterated two main points. The first was the same that Ewing and other authorities had emphasized in the 1920s and 1930s: the biology of cancer remained a mystery. The NCI, they said, ought to focus on supporting basic biological science, not highly targeted cancer research. Behind this argument was a fundamental assumption: the key to control of a disease was the slow and demanding business of unraveling its complex biological nature.[98]

The second objection was rooted in a different premise—that it was possible to curb mortality from a disease without knowing everything about its basic biological causes. That had been done, critics pointed out, with cholera, smallpox, pellagra, and other epidemic diseases, and it could be accomplished with cancer. A more productive approach, they said, was to finance public cancer centers whose mission was to find and treat the disease in time to control it. They complained bitterly that the NCI spent billions on "narrow" laboratory researches—and on expensive technologies of limited effectiveness, like radio- and chemotherapy—and little on preventive approaches. They thought the major villains of the drama were private practitioners, many of whom resisted public cancer clinics, and regarded the ACS slogan, "Every Doctor's Office a Cancer Detection Center," as advertising for private practitioners.[99]

Critics pointed with special urgency to advances in preventive measures that, if given proper emphasis, could do much to control the disease. The most useful of these in the 1940s and early 1950s was the test for cervical cancer fashioned by Dr. George Papanicolaou and others in the late 1930s and early 1940s. The Pap smear enabled trained clinicians to find carcinoma-*in-situ*, a precancerous stage that could be eradicated before it became serious.[100] If Pap smears could be made widely and freely available, the critics said, they would halve mortality from cervical cancer, an ailment which especially afflicted poor people who could not afford to see private practitioners.

These critics were on target in lamenting the dearth of public clinics to provide for Pap smears. Cancer medicine, like medicine generally in the United States, continued to reflect the ideology, political power, and economic interests of fee-for-service practitioners and to discriminate against lower-income groups. But those who perceived some sort of conspiracy of private practitioners overlooked other important reasons for the emphasis on biological research over prevention.[101] To begin with, the few existing private clinics did not seem especially cost-effective. Contemporary studies suggested that only one in 125 people tested at the clinics was diagnosed as having cancer. This was a higher percentage of people than of those in the population at large who had cancer at any given time—people who went to the clinics, after all, had reasons for going—but it was nonetheless a small percentage. The cost per cancer patient, one estimate concluded, was between $7,000 and $10,000. From this perspective the slogan, "Every Doctor's Office a Cancer Detection Center," made some sense, especially to the tax- and fee-paying middle classes.[102]

Arguments for preventive measures encountered an even more formidable obstacle: the continuing mysteriousness of cancer. Unlike many infectious diseases (or heart ailments), most forms of cancer could not be prevented. Besides Pap smears, there were no other proven preventive methods in the 1950s. Nor could physicians detect most cancers early enough to help people. They could not even predict very well which members of an at-risk group (such as women in families with a history of breast cancer) might develop the disease.[103]

Aware of these problems, Americans showed little faith in those few clinics which existed. They continued to believe that cancer was a chronic ailment which for the most part could neither be prevented nor cured. As one doctor pointed out to the NACC in 1945, "diagnosis of cancer nowadays is miserable and the treatment is poor. You select detection services and get them going, broadcast to the public; still the people come and you find cancer, eight times out of ten you can do nothing about it. The other times it means extensive radiation or surgery."[104] The head of the NCI's cancer control branch in the 1950s agreed. "We really didn't have the diagnostics of any sort that would tell if a person really had cancer in his body someplace," he recalled. A leading epidemiologist added in 1967, "some fifteen years ago a professor of surgery told me that it was not only a waste of time but faintly immoral to try to prevent cancer."[105]

By contrast to preventive approaches, laboratory research seeking underlying biological causes and cures seemed exciting and heroic, especially in America, where people had ever been fascinated with new scientific and technological frontiers and sure of their ability at problem-solving. In this cultural context middle-class taxpayers accepted the expenditure of millions of dollars to find a cure. If those millions had thus far failed to find one, that was because the scientists needed more time. During the hopeful 1940s and 1950s most Americans showed little impatience about this delay. Though they were growing alarmed about the scourge in their midst, they expected that the experts would someday find a magic cure for the dread disease.

8

Smoking and Cancer

No pleasure can exceed the smoking of the weed," proclaimed an advertisement from the nineteenth century. Millions of Americans agreed—among them Mark Twain, who said, "It's easy to stop smoking. I know because I've done it thousands of times." A hundred years later, Americans are bombarded with reasons for giving up the pleasure of "the smoking of the weed":

> Country-western songwriter and entertainer Sollie "Tex" Williams, a heavy smoker best known for his tune, "Smoke, Smoke, Smoke That Cigarette," died after a year-long battle with cancer, his daughter said . . . her father, who was diagnosed a year ago as having cancer, smoked two packs of cigarettes a day, dropping to about a pack a day before he died. "He tried to quit, but he couldn't," she said.[1]

> Smoking causes lung cancer, heart disease, emphysema and may complicate pregnancy.
>
> Quitting smoking now greatly reduces serious risks to your health.
>
> Smoking by pregnant women may result in fetal injury, premature birth and low birth weight.
>
> Cigarette smoke contains carbon monoxide.[2]

> Cigarette smoking is clearly identified as the chief, single, avoidable cause of death in our society and the most important public health issue of our time.[3]

Cigarette consumption per person over age eighteen rose from 151 per year in 1910 to 1,485 in 1930 to a high of 4,286 in 1963; since then it has decreased, mainly after 1975, to 3,378 in

1985. Between 1935 and 1980 more than one million Americans died of lung cancer caused by smoking.[4] Lung cancer, one medical historian commented, is "the most remarkable epidemic of the twentieth century."[5] Government officials say that cigarette-induced ailments cost $65 billion a year by the mid-1980s, more than $22 billion for medical expenses and the rest attributed to losses of wages, productivity, and taxes.[6] Lung cancer deaths—at least 80 percent caused by smoking—were estimated to total 126,000 in 1985, as opposed to but 2,300 in 1930 and 7,100 in 1940. These 126,000 deaths were 23 percent of cancer mortality in the United States.[7] (Mortality from cancers of the rectum and colon, estimated at 60,000 in 1985, ranked second.) An additional 22,000 Americans died in 1985 from tobacco-induced cancers elsewhere in the body, 20,000 from pulmonary disease, and 225,000 from tobacco-related cardiovascular ailments. The grand total of nearly 400,000 represented more than 1,000 premature deaths linked to smoking a day. As one cancer researcher has commented, "it is almost as if Western societies had set out to conduct a vast and fairly well controlled experiment in carcinogenesis bringing about several million deaths and using their own people as experimental animals."[8]

Without the increase in lung cancer, epidemiologists pointed out, age-adjusted mortality rates from malignant tumors would have declined slightly since the 1930s. But lung cancers caused aggregate age-adjusted rates in the United States to climb slowly. The villain, almost all experts agreed, was tobacco—described by John Cairns as a "fifth column in our midst."[9] Surgeon General C. Everett Koop said in 1986 that people who smoked two packs a day had a rate of lung cancer that was as much as twenty-five times greater than the rate for nonsmokers.[10]

If there were any promising statistics to be found in these numbers, they had to do with the tobacco habits of men. For years men had been the main consumers of cigarettes: from the mid-1920s through the early 1960s more than 50 percent of adult American males smoked. In 1985, 87,000 of the estimated 126,000 lung cancer deaths afflicted men. After the mid-1960s the percentage of adult males who smoked declined considerably—to around 33 percent in 1985—and mortality from lung cancer among white males began in 1984 to decrease for the first time. But women, who had entered the tobacco culture later, were smoking more by this time. In the mid-1930s fewer than 20 percent of adult females smoked in the United States, but during and after World War Two they, too, took up the habit in large numbers. The percentage of adult women who smoked peaked at approximately 33 percent between 1955 and 1975 and declined only to around 28 percent by 1985. By then lung cancer (at more than 38,000) for the first time seemed about to replace breast tumors as the leading source of cancer mortality among women. The American Cancer Society, drawing on evidence that had accumulated since the 1950s, reported that women who smoked while pregnant were more likely to have miscarriages, stillbirths, and premature deliveries, and to give birth to infants with serious mental and physical ailments.[11]

These dramatic developments in smoking, and the consequent rise in mortality from lung cancer, can be traced to profound social, economic, and cultural forces in twentieth-century American life: the rise of large tobacco corporations, the flowering of mass cigarette advertising, the anxieties of world wars, the quest for masculinity, the pressure of peers, the addictive power of nicotine, the spread of female employment, the gospel of women's liberation, sheer pleasure. These and other forces helped to explain why nearly one-third of adult Americans, more than 50 million people, in the mid-1980s persisted in maintaining a habit that substantially increased their risk of premature death.

The persistence of the smoking habit is remarkable. It flourished, after all, during the very years that most Americans expressed great concern for good health, fear of death, and dread of cancer. The tobacco habit, a known risk, clashed sharply with these values. But the contradiction is not altogether surprising. Some who continued to smoke had no choice—they were addicted. Many others simultaneously celebrated competing values, such as the pursuit of personal pleasure and the quest for good health. Quitting, an investment in future gains, was a renunciation of immediate gratification. To some the sacrifice was not worth it.

The clash of values over smoking also revealed—as reactions to diseases often had—significant differences in the attitudes of America's social classes toward health, illness, and the medical profes-

Did you smoke during your pregnancy?

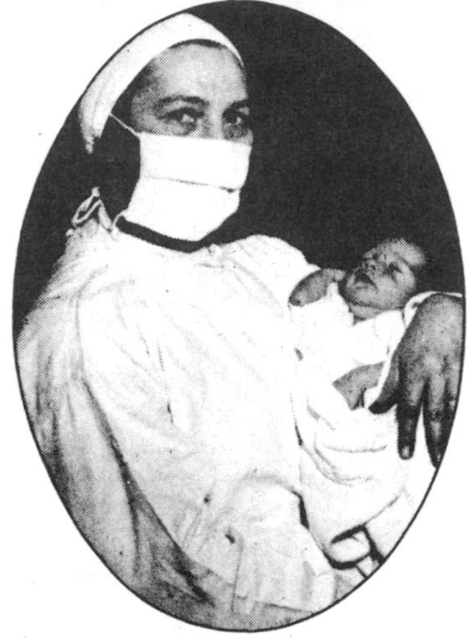

After smoking cigarettes during your pregnancy, did you deliver a premature or small baby who has permanent injuries?

The tobacco industry has known for years that smoking during pregnancy increases the frequency of premature and low birth weight babies, but kept the facts from the public. Premature and low birth weight babies have a much higher frequency of:

- cerebral palsy
- severe retardation
- lung problems
- RLF blindness

To determine whether your child may be legally entitled to collect money from the tobacco company for present and future needs, call today for a free consultation.

Attorney Jerrold C. Katz

KATZ & HARRISON
ATTORNEYS AT LAW

In Denver: 756-3940
Outside Denver: 1-800-826-8674

We are a law firm that concentrates in cases involving permanent injuries to children.

Personal Injury
Medical Malpractice **Defective Products**

Reprinted with permission from Katz and Harrison, Attorneys at Law, 1986.

sion. Since the 1950s the clash has featured on one level a noisy battle between two well-organized interest groups—tobacco companies and health professionals. But on another level it has been a struggle between a mainly middle-class and professional alliance against smoking and a rearguard action especially strong among blue-collar and lower-class people, many of whom continue to have scant access to or faith in scientific medicine. With characteristically American independence of mind, millions of people have felt they ought to be allowed to do as they pleased, even if experts said otherwise.

IN THE 1920s and early 1930s, the wilderness years of cancer control, various researchers cited tobacco as a carcinogen.[12] Their reports reinforced a popular opinion, widespread since before Grant's time, that smoking was unhealthy. Grant's death, indeed, was often used (by Frederick Hoffman, among others) as proof enough of the argument. But the main concern was cancer of the mouth or throat; lung cancer was very rare.

Only in the early 1930s did many doctors begin to encounter the ailment. And only then did surgeons and pathologists start to make the connection between smoking and lung cancer. One of the first was Dr. William McNally of Rush Medical College, who stated in 1932 that "cigarette smoking is an important factor in the increase of cancer of the lungs." In 1938 Dr. Raymond Pearl, a distinguished professor of biometry, claimed in *Science* that smoking was "statistically associated with an impairment of life duration." In the same year the *Science News Letter* carried an article by Drs. Alton Ochsner and Michael DeBakey of New Orleans that asserted, "more persons are dying of cancer of the lung than ever before, probably because more persons are smoking and inhaling tobacco smoke than ever before."[13]

Not everyone, however, agreed. James Tobey, in his popular, sensible book on cancer in 1932, spoke for many who distrusted the "rabid anti-tobacco literature" and the "fanatical reform bodies" who lobbied against smoking just as they had done—with such controversial results—against drinking. "An example of the banal attacks on tobacco," he said, "is the frequent assertion that President Grant suffered from cancer of the throat merely because he smoked to excess." "There is no scientific evidence," he concluded, "to show that My Lady Nicotine has any deleterious effect."[14]

Many doctors in the 1930s agreed with Tobey. Some asserted that the incidence of lung cancer only seemed to be increasing—the result of better diagnoses from X-rays and bronchoscopies. Others thought the increases real, but blamed them on atmospheric pollution or from delayed reactions to the great flu epidemic of 1918–19. Still others believed that lung cancer, which seemed mainly to afflict men, could not be caused by cigarettes, because women also smoked. And many, articulating the contemporary emphasis on "irritation," maintained that tobacco could provoke cancer only among those who overindulged and who were genetically predisposed. If there was a common denominator to these varied views, it was that cigarettes did not do too much harm if smoked in moderation. Clarence Little, summing up the evidence in 1939, concluded on behalf of the cancer society that "the more common use of tobacco is blamed by some for the frequency of lung cancer . . . It is impossible to say how accurate these opinions are."[15]

While the experts debated, the way remained open for proponents of tobacco to push their products. In 1933 Congress approved legislation guaranteeing price supports—and long-range economic security—for tobacco farmers. This step advanced a powerful network of tobacco interests that joined the producers and marketers with governments—federal, state, and local—which derived substantial income from taxes on tobacco products.

Paramount among the tobacco lobby were the cigarette manufacturers, who spent ever increasing amounts on advertising—an estimated $50 million by 1940—to sell their wares. The new mass-circulation magazines such as *Time* and *Newsweek* became heavily dependent on cigarette advertising for revenue. The *Journal of the American Medical Association* carried cigarette ads as late as the 1950s. The battle over smoking in modern America involved considerably more than skirmishes over scientific findings; important economic interests were also at stake.

Beginning in the late 1920s, many ads broke with the past by appealing directly to women. Cigarettes, the ads said in raising the banner of female emancipation, were "torches of freedom." Albert

Lasker's "Reach for a Lucky Instead of a Sweet," aimed at women's weight-consciousness. Many ads dwelt on romance and sex: "Blow Some My Way," a woman purred as she looked longingly at her man puff on a cigarette. As early as 1934 Eleanor Roosevelt showed her independence by smoking publicly. In the late 1930s women's handbags and compacts were routinely designed to hold cigarette packs. By then prominent women gladly posed for full-page color cigarette ads in the magazines. Alice Roosevelt Longworth, Theodore's daughter, praised the virtues of Luckies. "They're a light smoke," kind to the throat, she said. The syndicated columnist Dorothy Kilgallen promoted Camels. The actress Carole Lombard favored Luckies—"they're easier on the throat."[16]

The ads, moreover, tried to make smoking look attractive: cigarettes made women sexually alluring, young men tough and masculine. The American Tobacco Company pushed a brand named "Stud," and John Wayne (who later died of lung cancer) promoted Camels. A cigarette dangled from the lips of Humphrey Bogart playing Sam Spade in "The Maltese Falcon" (1941). A sultry Lauren Bacall made her entrance in "To Have or Have Not" (1944) with the line, "Anybody got a match?" Betty Grable, the ultimate pin-up girl of the forties, posed alluringly for tobacco ads. "With the boys," she said, "it's Chesterfields." Promotions for Luckies used the acronym "LSMFT" to make the sexual connection more explicit. Lucky Strike, the ads said, "Means Fine Tobacco—so round, so firm, so fully packed."[17]

Cigarette consumption jumped enormously during World War Two and in the late 1940s—from 1,976 to 3,552 annually per adult American during the decade. Though some of this increase reflected the growing consumption by women, many of whom broke with traditional roles to enter the labor market, much of it was accounted for by men in the armed services. Young, far from home, often afraid, soldiers turned to cigarettes—which came with C rations—for solace amidst the pressures of war and military discipline.

So taken for granted were cigarettes to American culture in these years that the rapidly rising incidence of lung cancer, which caused 15 percent of cancer deaths by 1950, received relatively little public attention. Neither did the warnings by Ochsner and others.[18] Many doctors, on the contrary, continued to smoke and to dismiss such warnings. As late as 1948 the *Journal of the American Medical Association* stated that "more can be said in behalf of smoking as a form of escape from tension than against it . . . there does not seem to be any preponderance of evidence that would indicate the abolition of the use of tobacco as a substance contrary to the public health."[19]

While the AMA remained reluctant to confront the tobacco lobby for many years thereafter, others jumped in during the 1950s to forge an increasingly aggressive alliance against tobacco. Leaders in this struggle were physicians and epidemiologists who began to publish statistics connecting cigarette smoking and cancer.

One of the earliest to show concern over lung cancer was Dr. Evarts Graham, a surgeon and professor at Washington University in St. Louis. Observing great increases in lung cancers in the mid-1930s, he and his students—including Ochsner—feared a virtual epidemic of carcinoma of the lung. But Graham, a smoker himself, was slow to blame tobacco. "Yes," he told Ochsner, "there is a parallel between the sale of cigarettes and the incidence of cancer of the lung, but there is also a parallel between the sale of nylon stockings and cancer of the lung."[20] Graham's skepticism mirrored contemporary bewilderment about the causes of lung cancer.

But Ernst Wynder, another of Graham's students, was not to be put off. He strongly suspected that tobacco was the villain, and in the 1940s he and Graham launched an epidemiological study of the subject. At the same time a group of British doctors and statisticians embarked on similar research. Both studies were "retrospective," selecting cancer patients (and others without cancer) and then asking both groups about their habits. When these studies were published in 1950, they documented significant statistical correlations between cigarette smoking and lung cancer. "Extensive and prolonged use of tobacco, especially cigarettes," Wynder and Graham concluded, "seems to be an important factor in the inducement of bronchiogenic carcinoma." The British researchers added that "smoking is a factor and an important factor, in the production of carcinoma of the lung."[21]

Because these were careful studies, each involving hundreds of cases of lung cancer, they attracted a fair amount of attention in medical circles. But the researchers tended to stop short of asserting a causal connection between smoking and lung cancer. Other factors, they noted, might also cause the disease. Moreover, Graham and others admitted that they did not know what was carcinogenic about tobacco. Some people wondered if the carcinogenic effect came from insecticides, not from the tobacco itself. The researchers also faced criticism of their methods, for retrospective studies depend heavily on the recollections of patients. For all these reasons the early studies fell short of persuading the doubters.[22]

But the studies were too alarming to be ignored, and over the next few years laboratory researchers showed that tars from tobacco were carcinogenic in animals. Epidemiologists, meanwhile, began conducting "prospective" studies, one of which was funded by the American Cancer Society starting in 1951. These studies used volunteers to locate hundreds of thousands of smokers and nonsmokers and to track their health over time. As early as 1952 the researchers were shocked by the incidence of lung cancer among the smokers, and in 1954 they published the first of many reports.[23] They found that age-adjusted death rates from lung cancer were at least three times higher among male smokers than among nonsmokers, and at least five times higher among heavy smokers.

These researchers, too, conceded that other carcinogens, such as soot or automobile fumes, might also be causing lung cancer. But they were convinced by the study that cigarettes were the major cause of the disease. E. Cuyler Hammond and Daniel Horn, the ACS researchers, had both been cigarette smokers, but they quickly dropped the habit, taking up pipes, when the statistics started coming in. "We believe," they said in 1954, "the associations found between regular cigarette smoking and diseases of the coronary arteries, and between smoking and cancer, reflect cause-and-effect relationships."[24] The ACS joined in by urging smokers to cut consumption. By 1957 Hammond was still more certain. He asserted that people who persisted in smoking two packs a day or more died seven years earlier on the average than nonsmokers and that cigarette smoking increased the chance of fatal coronary attack by 50 percent.[25] In that same year Evarts Graham—though he cut back in 1953 to a pack a day—died from lung cancer.

By this time a few federal officials began to join the slowly developing alliance against smoking. Among these were members of the House Committee on Governmental Operations, which conducted an investigation in 1957 of tobacco advertising, especially ads proclaiming the supposed benefits of newly marketed filter cigarettes. Led by Congressman John Blatnik of Minnesota (who was a smoker), the committee reported in 1958 that "cigarette manufacturers have deceived the American public through their advertising of cigarettes." This kind of pressure encouraged the Federal Trade Commission (which in 1955 had taken steps against ads that implied medical endorsement of smoking) to negotiate a voluntary agreement with the tobacco companies in 1960. The FTC attempted to put an end to exaggerated claims for filter cigarettes.[26]

Perhaps more important to the antitobacco alliance was the gradual participation of the Public Health Service. Under the cautious stewardship of Surgeon General Leroy Burney, the PHS in 1956 established a scientific study group involving the NCI, the National Heart Institute, the ACS, and the American Heart Association. In 1957 the group announced that "there is an increasing and consistent body of evidence that excessive cigarette smoking is one of the causative factors in lung cancer."[27] Venturing further in 1959, Burney singled out cigarettes as the major cause of lung cancer. The cooperation of the PHS—and under it of the NCI—with the ACS suggested that the long-standing professional alliance against cancer was gradually lining up against cigarettes.

To some extent popular magazines lined up, too. As early as 1952 *Reader's Digest,* which refused to carry tobacco ads, ran a scare story entitled "Cancer by the Carton." When laboratory scientists demonstrated the carcinogenic nature of tobacco tars in 1953, *Time* stated that they had proved "beyond any doubt" that smoking caused cancer. A month later *Life* carried a story headed SMOKE GETS IN THE NEWS. It cautioned that the findings of Graham and Wynder, whose research on cigarette tars involved animals, should not induce people to "promptly quit smoking, for this might create nervous ailments." But the article also made it clear that tar from tobacco had caused cancer in mice. It added that statistics on tobacco consumption correlated with significant increases in lung cancer among human beings. Other magazines—*Nation, New Republic, U.S. News and World Report*—also refused to take cigarette advertisements. *Time, Life,* and *Newsweek,* while profiting from big ads, reported the damaging findings of the epidemiologists and the warnings of government officials.[28]

Through thcsc various outlets the alliance succeeded in conveying their arguments to the public. Opinion polls as early as 1954 revealed that 90 percent of respondents had read news stories linking smoking and cancer. Polls also showed ever increasing pluralities of people agreeing that "cigarette smoking is one of the causes of lung cancer." As early as 1954 a lung cancer patient sued the tobacco companies, and the store where he bought his cigarettes, claiming that they had advertised death-dealing products. Though he lost the case, his effort received a fair amount of publicity. Suits like this one signified the rise of hostility already being directed at tobacco companies.

Perhaps the most striking insight into popular attitudes came from opinion polls taken after publication of Hammond's findings in 1957. Of those polled 77 percent claimed to have heard about them. Half of these respondents said that smoking caused cancer, a quarter that it did not, and the rest that they did not know. At that time, 42 percent of the adult population (52 percent of men, 34 percent of women) were smokers. Even this group (by a margin of 38 percent to 36 percent, with 26 percent undecided) thought smoking caused cancer.[29]

These polls made two important things unmistakably clear: first, that smokers were more likely than nonsmokers to reject the warnings about cancer; second, that substantial majorities of the population as a whole recognized that cigarettes were unhealthy. Those who smoked, then and later, did not always know the full extent of the dangers of tobacco. Smokers who were not addicted, however, were making a conscious choice to ignore the expert advice of the alliance against cancer. Their behavior says much about conflicting values in American society.

THE OPPONENTS of the antismoking campaign included first of all some determined and well-financed economic interests. In 1954, following the damaging publicity surrounding the prospective studies (which temporarily depressed cigarette sales), the tobacco companies banded together to establish the Tobacco Industry Research Committee (later renamed the Council for Tobacco Research—U.S.A.). Founders of the committee recognized that they had to fight expertise with expertise, and they contacted Clarence Little, who had been running the Jackson Laboratory in Maine since leaving the ACS. Little agreed to serve (for an annual salary of $20,000) as scientific director.

Why Little joined the committee was never entirely clear—probably it was because his scientific training in genetics led him to associate cancer with genetic predisposition. Whatever the reasons, Little, who stayed at this post until his retirement in 1971, tried to give the committee scientific respectability.[30] He received very considerable resources. Under his direction the tobacco lobby spent an estimated $7 million on research between 1954 and 1964. Most of this work, whose findings had little to do with the effect of cigarettes on health, evoked contempt from independent scientists.

In 1958 the cigarette lobby also formed the Tobacco Institute, Inc., headed by George Allen, former director of the United States Information Agency. Relying on the skill of Hill and Knowlton, a leading public-relations firm, the institute issued a steady stream of releases refuting claims that smoking caused cancer.[31] "We are not on a crusade either for or against tobacco," it announced. "If we have a crusade, it is a crusade for research."[32] Allen elevated tobacco to the status of national symbol. "Through the years," he said,

> tobacco is poetry and plays, novels, and essays. Tobacco is painting and sculpture for great artists. Tobacco has been comfort for the combat soldier, from Valley Forge to Korea. Tobacco is the ambassador of good will around the world. Tobacco is millions of men and women on the farms, in the factories, in stores and offices. Tobacco is a moment of relaxation from today's stress . . . For Franklin Roosevelt, it was a cigarette in a jaunty holder, for Churchill a long cigar, for Einstein, a heavy curved pipe.[33]

Meanwhile, the tobacco companies stepped up their advertising campaigns, the costs of which rose to an estimated $148 million in 1959 (and to $314 million by 1970). Huge as these expenditures were, they were worth it to an industry whose sales were $7 billion in 1960. By then much of the advertising extolled the virtues of filter cigarettes, which the tobacco companies began emphasizing in the 1950s. The tobacco companies sponsored many of the most expensive prime-time TV shows of the 1950s and 1960s—"Arthur Godfrey and His Friends," "The Chesterfield Supper Club," "Stop the Music," and "Your Lucky Strike Theatre." "It was just like wiring the slot machine to keep paying out a perpetual jackpot," one happy advertiser exulted. "My boy, it was like *printing money.*"[34]

Allen, an experienced Washington insider, developed an effective political coalition to counter the enemies of smoking. This coalition included many advertising executives, magazine and newspaper publishers, and the National Association of Broadcasters, who depended heavily on cigarette ads and whose good will was valued by politicians. Some advertisers were on the board of the ACS and resisted the efforts of Hammond and others to involve the society in the crusade against smoking.[35]

Many doctors, too, abetted the tobacco coalition. Some were heavy smokers who could not bring themselves to believe the epidemiological evidence. Others attributed the rise in lung cancer to better diagnosis. Although the AMA journal opened its pages to Hammond and other researchers, top officials of the association refused to accept the causal relationship between smoking and lung cancer or heart disease. Critics charged that the association's refusal arose from its consuming fear of national health insurance: if the AMA had opposed the tobacco interests, it would have antagonized well-placed congressmen who were needed in the fight against "socialized medicine."[36]

The "Smoke Ring," as enemies of the coalition called it, was especially strong in Congress. Its core consisted of politicians from the tobacco-producing and -manufacturing states. Their allies on the Hill included most southerners, who joined the coalition to demonstrate their regional solidarity; Republicans, who had long worked harmoniously with southern Democrats; and conservatives, who were fearful on principle of governmental regulation. Against this formidable combination, the alliance against smoking made little political headway in the 1950s.[37]

Furthermore, some respected researchers continued to doubt the conclusions of the epidemiological studies. Wilhelm Hueper, who still headed the environmental cancer section of the NCI, considered smoking an "unhealthy habit" but concentrated his efforts on the chemical and automobile companies. He thought the air pollution caused by these companies and their products was correlated with the rise in lung cancer. Many laboratory scientists, like Harold Stewart, chief pathologist of the NCI, refused to accept the epidemiological data until it was thoroughly confirmed by experimental research.[38] They accepted the fact that tars from cigarettes, when rubbed into the skin of animals, were carcinogenic. But they insisted that no experiments had yet connected cigarette smoke (as opposed to tars) to cancer in animals, let alone in human beings.[39] Doubts within the NCI itself led Surgeon General Burney and John Heller, director of the institute, to move cautiously until the late 1950s.

Another prominent cancer expert who moved cautiously was Charles Cameron, medical and scientific director of the ACS. Though he accepted the epidemiological data, he resisted the argument that cigarette smoking by itself caused cancer. Like many others at the time, he was troubled by the fact that the vast majority of smokers did not seem to develop the disease—and that a few who did not smoke also were afflicted by it. He wondered if the root cause of lung cancer lay in some predisposing factor, such as genetic makeup. Perhaps the same predisposition led many people to the habit of smoking and—independently—to a susceptibility to cancer.[40]

The defenders of tobacco seized quickly on these and other doubts about the epidemiological case. Again and again they emphasized several points: that only a small minority of smokers ever developed lung cancer (experts later estimated that consistent smokers had between a one in four and a one in ten chance of developing it);[41] that tobacco-induced tumors in animals differed from lung cancer in human beings; that the evidence (such as it was) connecting smoking and lung cancer rested mainly on statistical associations, not on laboratory science; and that the increased incidence of lung cancer stemmed from the aging of the population, not from tobacco. Epidemiological studies pointing a finger at cigarettes, they insisted, were flawed, in part because their findings did not fully consider the health histories or places of residence of their subjects. Little explained in 1954, "I do not feel that a definite cause-and-effect relationship between smoking and human lung cancer has been established on a basis that meets the requirements of definiteness, extent, and specificity of data, which the seriousness and implications of the problem deserve."[42]

While Little ordinarily assumed the high road of scientific proof, he was prepared to join Allen and others in appealing to popular feelings. The scare over cigarettes, they said, was but one of many—over packaged foods, pollution, even Coca-Cola—aroused by meddlesome reformers who had nothing better to do with their time and who resorted, Little charged, to "expensive and pressure propaganda" and "personal misrepresentations and attacks." Cigarettes, tobacco spokesmen added, calmed the nerves. If people were prevented from smoking, they would fall victim to tics, or even beat their wives. Why pick on cigarettes? they asked—after all, many things kill people!

The spokesmen for tobacco devoted special emphasis to the importance of preserving personal freedom. Smokers, they pointed out, were well aware of the "propaganda" against tobacco, yet they continued to enjoy the habit. That was not because smokers were ignorant of warnings; the polls clearly showed otherwise. Nor was it because cigarettes were addictive—this was an argument that tobacco spokesmen dismissed out of hand. Rather, it was because cigarettes gave people pleasure.[43] Millions of Americans concurred. They stressed that they loved the taste, that cigarettes set off their meals, that smoking helped them relax. Their passion for the habit sometimes recognized no bounds. One smoker exclaimed, "they can outlaw cigarettes, label 'em poison, raise the tax, jail everyone that smokes and hang everyone that raises tobacco; but people are gonna smoke."[44]

Indeed, the tobacco lobby implied, smokers knew better than the arrogant, patronizing "experts" who were trying to run people's lives. This was a nicely calculated, populist appeal to the enduring skepticism of many Americans about professional claims for expertise. The defenders of tobacco, like many others who had resisted the medical alliance against cancer in the past, portrayed themselves as embattled Americans resisting dictation from above. The "experts," the tobacco forces said, were obstructing the right of people to do as they pleased.[45]

As arguments like these show, the controversy over smoking involved more than a strictly medical debate over theories and therapies, more than a struggle between well-organized interest groups. It was in a way a debate over culturally ingrained life styles and cherished values. Just as the battle against cancer in America had long been characterized by social and ideological conflict, so too were the postwar arguments over smoking and health.

THE DEBATE intensified greatly following publication in January 1964 of *Smoking and Health: Report of the Advisory Committee to the Surgeon General of the Public Health Service*.[46] This landmark document, ordinarily known as the surgeon general's report on smoking, placed the federal government unambiguously in the camp of the alliance against smoking and prompted increasingly vocal counterattacks by the tobacco coalition in the next two decades.

Luther Terry, the surgeon general in 1964, was hardly a crusader.[47] Until 1962 he had shown little desire to combat the tobacco interests. But he faced increasing pressure for action from a number of organizations, including the ACS, the American Heart Association, the National Tuberculosis Association, and the American Public Health Association. In response he agreed to set up an advisory committee on smoking and health. In doing so Terry acted with political sagacity. To ensure that the committee would have broad support he gave the Tobacco Institute the chance to veto prospective appointees. The ten experts finally named to the committee were chosen from a list of some 150 nominees sent in by health organizations, government agencies, and tobacco interests. None of the ten had taken a public stand on the issue. Three smoked cigarettes, two others smoked pipes and cigars.[48]

The committee, aided by hundreds of consultants, worked diligently and secretly for a year and a half. When it was ready to issue its findings, Terry staged a televised press conference behind closed doors in the State Department auditorium. The thoroughness that went into preparation of the report, together with the theatrics surrounding its publication, assured that the document would attract wide attention in the media.

The committee members were acutely aware of the need to speak with scientific precision and carefully noted the problems involved in talking about a "cause" or "major cause" of fatal diseases. Ailments such as cancer or heart disease, they acknowledged, exhibit the "multiple etiology of biological processes." But this was practically the only sop thrown to the tobacco interests, whose contentions the committee forcefully struck down. Cigarette smoking, the report said, "contributed substantially to mortality from certain specific diseases and to the overall death rate." Cigarette smoking was "causally related to lung cancer in men; the magnitude of the effect of cigarettes far outweighs all other factors. The data for women, though less extensive, point in the same direction." The committee concluded that cigarettes were a "health hazard of sufficient import in the United States to warrant appropriate remedial action."[49]

The committee's conclusions inevitably received wide coverage in the press. *Newsweek,* speaking for most of the magazines and newspapers, called the report "monumental."[50] Alarmed consumers cut back sharply (though temporarily) on cigarette consumption. Other organizations, moreover, demanded governmental action against tobacco. The World Health Organization called for "restriction of advertisements for cigarettes" and "regulations to curb smoking in all places of public entertainment." The ACS, able at last to pinpoint a specific cause of a major cancer, said that "the reduction of cigarette smoking offers greater possibilities than any other available medical or public health measure for the prevention of cancer, of serious illness, of physical disability, of suffering and of premature death in this country—an astounding statement, but true."[51]

The Federal Trade Commission, which had cooperated with the surgeon general's office in preparing the report, showed special zeal for regulating tobacco. Within a week of the report's appearance the FTC requested public hearings on a proposed trade regulation requiring warnings on cigarette ads and packages. It proposed two possible wordings. One read, "CAUTION—CIGARETTE SMOKING IS A HEALTH HAZARD: The Surgeon General's Advisory Committee on Smoking and Health has found that 'cigarette smoking contributes substantially to mortality from certain diseases and to the overall death rate.'" The other said, "CAUTION: Cigarette smoking is dangerous to health. It may cause death from cancer and other diseases." The FTC recommended a ban on "words, pictures, symbols, devices or demonstrations, or any combination thereof that would lead the public to believe that cigarette smoking promotes good health or physical well-being."[52]

In pressing its case the FTC had the support of many in the anticancer alliance, but some influential groups either fought the FTC or stood by on the sidelines. The Agriculture Department not only refused to oppose supports for tobacco farmers but also asserted that it would need much more evidence about the role of tobacco smoke before it would think about recommending health warnings on cigarette packages. The Advertising Federation of America and the American Newspaper Publishers Association joined the cigarette companies in opposing the proposed regulations. The AMA, which accepted a $10 million research grant from the Tobacco Institute to study the health effects of cigarettes, declined to endorse either the report or the FTC's ambitious plans for regulating advertising.

The Tobacco Institute protected its flanks in other ways, too. It hired the prestigious Washington law firm of Arnold, Porter, and Fortas to defend its interests and named as its chief strategist Earle Clements, a former senator from Kentucky. Clements had been campaign coordinator for Lyndon Johnson's presidential bid in 1960. His daughter was press secretary to the first lady. As a former solon Clements had floor privileges in the Senate. He was shrewd, conciliatory, and very influential on the Hill.

Clements played for time. Matters of such import, he explained, ought to be decided by popular representatives in Congress, not by faceless bureaucrats in the FTC. Meanwhile, the Tobacco Institute announced, the cigarette companies would undertake to police themselves. Henceforth cigarette ads would not be aimed at people under twenty-one years of age or placed in college or school media. The companies' new advertising code emphasized that commercials would not "represent that cigarette smoking is essential to social prominence, distinction, success, or sexual attraction."

Accepting such assurances, Congress contented itself with passage of the Federal Cigarette Labelling and Advertising Act of 1965. This legislation authorized federal spending on a National Clear-

Oliphant, © 1985 Universal Press Syndicate. Reprinted with permission. All rights reserved.

inghouse on Smoking and Health, which later proved helpful to foes of cigarettes. The law also required cigarette manufacturers to place a health warning on packages. But it was a watered-down warning: "Caution: Cigarette Smoking May Be Hazardous to Your Health." As critics pointed out, it had little if any impact on per capita cigarette sales, which were higher in 1965–66 than they had been in 1964. If anything, the warnings on packages might protect cigarette manufacturers against law suits by cancer victims and their families. (As of early 1987 the companies had won all these suits.)

Advocates of regulation especially deplored Congress's response to the contentious issue of cigarette advertising. The act not only failed to police such advertising; it also forbade governmental agencies to require any health warnings in cigarette ads for the next four years, during which time—it was hoped—the advertising code of the companies would have stilled the controversy. To the foes of tobacco, who thoroughly distrusted the companies, this was a bitter pill. The journalist Elizabeth Drew expressed this bitterness in an article entitled "The Quiet Victory of the Cigarette Lobby—How It Found Its Best Filter Yet—Congress." She called the legislation an "unabashed act to protect private industry from government regulation."[53]

To no one's surprise the tobacco companies' advertising code had little impact on the nature of cigarette commercials. The enemies of smoking thereby intensified their efforts after 1965. A young New York lawyer, John Banzhaf 3d, was instrumental in getting the Federal Communications Commission to apply the so-called Fairness Doctrine to cigarette commercials. Though many opponents of smoking showed little enthusiasm for this effort—even the ACS, which relied on broadcasters for free air time, was cool to his plans—Banzhaf and the antismoking lobby persevered. After extended legal maneuvering, the FCC agreed in 1967 to act. Henceforth, the commission ruled, radio and television stations would have to run one anticigarette message for every three aired by the tobacco companies.

At first Banzhaf and his newly formed lobby, Action on Smoking and Health (ASH), found that broadcasters simply evaded the rule. The FCC, with only a small staff, could not begin to monitor the stations. ASH therefore concentrated on monitoring one station, WNBC-TV of New York, whose messages ran closer to ten to one on behalf of cigarettes; the antismoking spots mainly appeared between 2 and 6:30 A.M. When ASH shared its findings with the FCC in 1968, the agency stepped up its pressure. Forewarned, WNBC and other stations made a better effort, especially after courts affirmed the Fairness Doctrine in late 1968.

For the next two years the FCC ruling greatly heartened the foes of tobacco. The ACS and other health organizations created anticigarette messages, which were broadcast in what was estimated to be more than $40 million in free air time. The ads were meant to be hard-hitting. One ran a caption, "This is life," next to a group of people having fun. Then someone lit up a cigarette. The fun ended abruptly, and a new caption read, "This cuts it short." Another depicted a tough Marlboro man coughing uncontrollably as he stood at the bar of a saloon. A clean-cut, nonsmoking cowboy then pushed him aside. The word CANCER appeared on the screen, accompanied by the voice-over, "Cigarettes—they're killers." Perhaps the most moving of these messages came from the actor William Talman, the gravel-voiced district attorney on the Perry Mason television show. In a prerecorded message Talman introduced his family to television viewers, revealed that he had lung cancer, and warned people not to smoke. "If you haven't smoked," he said, "don't start. If you do smoke, quit! Don't be a loser."[54] By the time the message appeared on the air, Talman had died, one of many prominent Americans—Nat King Cole, Edward R. Murrow, and Walt Disney were three others—to succumb to lung cancer between 1964 and 1970.

To the tobacco lobby these antismoking spots were extraordinarily threatening. For the first time in modern history the annual per-capita cigarette consumption of American adults moved downward for an extended period of time—from 4,197 in 1966 to 3,969 in 1970. The foes of tobacco then set out to toughen the 1965 law by changing the message on cigarette packs from "Caution: Cigarette Smoking May Be Hazardous to Your Health" to "Warning: The Surgeon General Has Determined That Cigarette Smoking Is Dangerous to Your Health and May Cause Cancer and Other Diseases."

The foes of smoking also took steps to include in new legislation a ban on radio and television cigarette advertising. As in 1965, however, they underestimated the Tobacco Institute. Deeply worried by the anticigarette messages on radio and television, the tobacco forces resolved to compromise. It was better, they thought, to surrender their radio and television commercials than to allow continued airing of the opposing point of view. They recognized that such a ban would not affect their appeals on billboards or in the print media, which happily anticipated much increased advertising revenue. Though the broadcasters fought the proposed ban, their allies deserted them, and the ban passed the Congress in 1970. It went into effect on January 2, 1971, a date established so as to permit cigarette advertising—for the last time—during broadcasts of the football games on New Year's Day.

The legislation also required the companies to relabel their packages. The new message was slightly more explicit than the caution which had been required since 1965, but less alarming than the one desired by the antitobacco forces. It read: "Warning: The Surgeon General Has Determined That Cigarette Smoking Is Dangerous to

Your Health." The companies had managed to prevent mention in the warning of the dread word "cancer"—or of any other smoking-related diseases.

This hotly contested legislation, the Public Health Cigarette Smoking Act of 1970, clearly indicated the political and economic power of the tobacco lobby. The cigarette companies were now free from worry about antismoking messages on radio and television. Relieved, they increased their advertising on billboards and in magazines and newspapers. *Life*'s first three issues in 1971 carried 22 pages of cigarette advertising, all in color. The companies also employed slightly more sophisticated and subtle appeals, such as promoting Virginia Slims tennis tournaments. Perhaps because of these changes, cigarette consumption moved upward again after the decline in the Fairness Doctrine years. Between 1971 and 1976 annual consumption averaged nearly 4,100 per adult, compared to the low of 3,969 in 1970. Total sales increased from 534 billion cigarettes in 1970 to 610 million in 1976.[55]

IN THE YEARS following passage of the Public Health Cigarette Smoking Act, both sides of the controversy continued to fire away at each other. But while the foes of smoking maintained the high ground and won some battles, the tobacco lobby gave nothing away. For the most part, stalemate lasted until 1980.

During these years the anticigarette forces added new arguments to their arsenal. They emphasized that cigarette smoking was becoming an especially serious problem for women in general and for pregnant women in particular.[56] They added that cigarette smoke contained more than forty chemicals known to cause cancer in animals; that tobacco when combined with asbestos and other harmful substances acted as a co-carcinogen in human beings; that there was no such thing as a "safe" cigarette or a "safe" level of cigarette consumption; that exhaled cigarette smoke might be dangerous for nearby nonsmokers; that "smokeless tobacco," such as chewing tobacco or snuff, was also harmful; and that for millions of people nicotine was as addictive as heroin and morphine. One estimate showed that 66 percent of Americans who ever smoked still smoked daily. The average American smoker consumed thirty cigarettes a day.[57]

Many opponents of smoking grew angry with the government, which they said was doing far too little to stop the greatest source of preventable death in the nation. Critics estimated that the NCI used only $10 million of its $900 million budget in 1980 for research and public education concerning the hazards of smoking. Meanwhile, the federal government spent $60 million on subsidies to tobacco growers and permitted tax deductions of $100 million per year to cigarette companies claiming advertising costs as business expenses.[58]

Critics of the government complained that public officials seemed more interested in protecting smokers than in confronting the tobacco lobby. Thus the Federal Aviation Authority ordered the separation of smokers and nonsmokers on planes, and the Interstate Commerce Commission limited smoking on interstate buses. Both actions, foes of tobacco said, had the effect of sanctioning the right of smoking in public places. The critics were especially angry with the Department of Agriculture, which in the mid-1980s was spending more than $5 million a year to develop tobacco for a "safe" cigarette, even though the Department of Health and Human Services had long insisted that there could be no such thing. An Agriculture official responded, "it's a wise investment to make. If a person is going to smoke, let's provide safe tobacco."[59]

Some enemies of smoking wondered whether the government could ever bring itself to harm the tobacco industry. They lamented the economic importance of tobacco in American life. Taxes on tobacco brought in more than $6 billion a year to federal, state, and local treasuries. Preventing smoking, moreover, would enable millions of Americans to live longer, thereby increasing corporate and governmental obligations for pensions and social security benefits. Prevention further threatened a network of economic interests—not only growers, manufacturers, and the print media but also the livelihoods of half a million workers directly employed by the industry and the well-being of corporations owned by the huge conglomerates that the companies had become by the 1980s. By this kind of accounting, the political and economic costs of moving firmly against tobacco were formidable.[60]

Most critics, however, tried to ignore cost accounting, instead calling loudly for reforms. Few demanded prohibition of smoking, which they thought could not be enforced. But some recommended criminalization of the tobacco industry, and many people brought damage suits against the companies. Among the other reforms suggested were the outlawing of cigarette ads; the imposition of maximum tar and nicotine levels in cigarettes; the banning of smoking in public places; the abolition of cigarette vending machines; prohibition of sales to people under the age of twenty-one; ending tax deductions for cigarette ads; the gradual withdrawal of supports to growers, who should be helped to find new employment; and much increased cigarette taxes, especially on "cancer sticks" of high tar and nicotine content. Responding to rising popular alarm about smoking, the AMA finally supported many of these measures in 1986, including a ban on the advertising and promotion of all tobacco products. The association, a spokesman said, "is absolutely committed to producing a smoke-free society by the year 2000. There are no redeeming features to tobacco. We believe people are being manipulated into becoming addicted to it."[61]

If a ban on ads could not be passed, the foes of tobacco argued, Congress should at least appropriate money for antismoking messages on billboards and in the media. The government should also insist that adds carry a much more explicit message, such as: "WARNING: Cigarette smoking is dangerous to health, and may cause death from cancer, coronary heart disease, chronic bronchitis, pulmonary emphysema, and other diseases."[62] In 1985 advertisers were required to include one of four warnings similar in wording to this one in cigarette ads.

As the disputes over health warnings revealed, the opponents of smoking resented most of all the ubiquity and presumed power of cigarette advertising. The cost of such ads in newspapers and magazines soared to more than $500 million by 1980. Other commercials—on highway billboards, transit systems, points of sale in retail outlets—brought the total to more than $2 billion by 1985. In 1981 *Time, Newsweek, TV Guide,* and *Sports Illustrated* ran a total of 1,777 pages of cigarette ads worth $125 million in revenue.[63] Cigarettes were the most advertised product in America and far and away the most important source of advertising revenue for many publications.

Critics complained bitterly that many ads continued to emphasize the sexual appeal and glamor of smoking, thereby entrapping impressionable young readers. They were sure that the ads accounted for the success of the tobacco companies. Fondly recalling the years of anticigarette messages, and pointing to advertising bans in Norway and Finland, the critics maintained that either the abolition of ads or financial support for counteracting messages would substantially reduce sales.

The foes of tobacco also asserted that cigarette advertisements severely compromised editorial objectivity. Magazines that refused to carry ads, they noted, ran many more antismoking stories than those that did. A *Newsweek* cover story of 1976, "What Causes Cancer?" blamed food, drink, drugs, radiation, and dangers from the workplace, but was quiet about tobacco. *Ms.*, which accepted cigarette advertising, did not carry feature stories about smoking and health in its first thirteen years of existence. Other publications, including *Psychology Today* and *Cosmopolitan,* exercised self-censorship, admitting frankly that they did not run antismoking stories for fear of losing revenue not only from cigarette advertisements but also from ads for the many corporations owned by the tobacco conglomerates. The R. J. Reynolds Company, for instance, owned Canada Dry, Del Monte, and Nabisco, and Philip Morris owned Maxwell House Coffee, Minute Rice, Birds Eye, and Kool-Aid.[64]

To many smokers the antitobacco crusaders seemed rabid as well as puritanical—characteristically American clones of the prohibitionists in the 1920s. Perhaps so; indeed, it is interesting to note that antitobacco movements attracted comparably little support in many other Western countries, where the quest for vital good health seemed less urgent than in affluent America. But it was easy to see why the critics of smoking grew so furious during the 1970s and 1980s. Sure of their case—after all, it rested on the findings of Science—they found themselves confronted by an extraordinarily well-organized, politically well-connected, economically powerful lobby for tobacco, which continued to be centered in the Tobacco Institute.[65]

The tobacco interests focused on two points during these years. First, they continued to dismiss epidemiology as nonscientific and to reject the evidence linking smoking and poor health. Instead, they evaded the health issue and emphasized the employment and economic activity that the tobacco industry made possible. Nothing made this approach more evident than the reaction of the Tobacco Institute when it was asked in 1985 about the Department of Agriculture's efforts to develop a "safe" tobacco. "That assumes that cigarettes are unsafe," a public-relations officer of the Institute responded. "We don't know that for sure. We don't know that cigarettes are harmful." A spokesman for the R. J. Reynolds Tobacco Company added, "I don't know anything about it. We don't know of anything that makes a cigarette unsafe, so how could we be working toward a safer cigarette?"[66]

Second, the tobacco interests fought efforts to ban their advertisements. They had a constitutional right, they said, to advertise any product which it was legal to sell. The American Civil Liberties Union, citing freedom of speech, endorsed this argument. The tobacco lobby contended that ads did not induce nonsmokers to take up the habit; they merely made buyers more familiar with brand names and new products. Spokesmen for the industry argued correctly that considerable numbers of American women had taken up smoking well before ads were aimed at them, and they pointed out that smoking was growing very rapidly in many nations where such advertising scarcely existed.[67] A few experts on advertising recognized the logic of these arguments. Advertisements, they said, helped to legitimize smoking, but probably did not induce nonsmokers to take up the habit. A ban on ads, they suggested, would save the tobacco companies huge sums of money and hurt the magazines and newspapers that depended on the ads for revenue.[68]

The foes of tobacco, however, angrily rejected all these arguments. Behind their fury was the same fundamental faith that had animated the progressives, the medical professionals, and the largely middle-class alliance against cancer since the turn of century: tell the people the facts and they would soon take care of themselves. As always, that meant checking for the "danger signals" of cancer and seeing qualified physicians at the earliest possible opportunity. With regard to smoking it meant listening to the scientific evidence—after all, and at last, it was overwhelming and unassailable—and giving up the habit.

The power of advertising, the allies against cancer believed, subverted this process of rational behavior. Ads were as insidious as cancer itself. Americans, they said, were not so foolish as to be unaware of the dangers of smoking—polls had shown otherwise since the 1950s. But thanks to the blitz of commercials, people did not understand the full extent of those dangers. They did not realize that smoking was by far the major cause of lung cancer, that lung cancers threatened to become the leading cause of cancer mortality among women, or that without the spread of lung cancer, age-adjusted mortality rates from cancer were slowly decreasing in the United States. Conned by ads about smoking, almost one-third of the adult population refused to give up the fatal habit.

The critics of cigarette advertising probably had a point. Polls that questioned people about their health and safety strongly indicated that cigarette smoking was not perceived as especially hazardous. One survey placed smoking tenth among health and safety concerns, well behind such matters as putting smoke detectors in the home.[69] This poll suggested that millions of Americans had not listened carefully to the anticancer, antismoking professionals over the years. The foes of tobacco concluded that people would have responded differently had they not been deluged with billions of dollars of cigarette ads in the course of their lifetimes.

But there are two other ways of looking at the always ambiguous evidence about public opinion, advertising, and smoking. One is to recognize that the "Nonsmokers Rights Movement," which became organized in the late 1970s, was finally making progress. Increasingly powerful at the grass roots, it was stronger in health-conscious America than anywhere else in the world. In the 1980s the movement won passage of a wide variety of antismoking ordinances at the local and corporate level. It also helped to modify personal behavior, especially in the middle classes. Beginning in 1976–77 per capita adult consumption of cigarettes underwent the longest sustained decline in American history—from 4,095 in 1975 to 3,378 in 1985.[70] This was the lowest per capita consumption since World War Two. And in 1984 the incidence of lung cancer among white men in America decreased for the first time in at least fifty years.[71] Notable in itself, the decline in smoking was especially striking in contrast to the mostly increasing sales of cigarettes between 1960 and 1975. Coincident with unprecedented spending for tobacco advertising, the trend suggested that millions of Americans were not the mindless lemmings that the foes of advertising sometimes made them out to be.

Another way of understanding public perceptions of the hazards of tobacco is to consider differences in smoking behavior of America's social classes. In the 1940s, 1950s, and 1960s, blue-collar and black Americans were more likely to be smokers than were members of the middle and upper-middle classes. By the 1980s these class differences became pronounced. Accepting the antismoking arguments of the ACS and other health organizations, millions of well-educated, middle-class Americans took greater personal responsibility for their health. At last, they embraced prevention by giving up smoking. But working-class Americans resisted the experts. Some 43 percent of men and 38 percent of women in the working class smoked in 1983, as opposed to 28 percent of men and 30 percent of women in the middle class.[72] Members of the blue-collar classes started smoking earlier in their lives and consumed more cigarettes per day than did middle-class smokers. One survey found that only 15 percent of women with graduate degrees smoked, compared with 45 percent of women who did not finish high school.[73] The death rate from lung cancer was 40 percent higher among black men than among white men. Americans with incomes below the poverty line had a 60 percent higher chance than other people of developing lung cancer.[74] Smoking had become more and more a manifestation of social class: the higher one's socioeconomic standing, the less likely one is to smoke.

From the perspective of many professionals in the antismoking alliance, this dangerous behavior was proof of their argument: ill-educated Americans found it hard to resist the allure of the ads. But this is probably a very limited perspective, for the polls indicated that poorer Americans knew a good deal (though perhaps not all they needed to know) about the perils of tobacco. Given the publicity accorded a series of reports from the surgeon general's office, not to mention television, newspaper, and magazine features about the dangers of tobacco, they could hardly have been acting out of ignorance. It is unlikely that many people started smoking primarily because they were seduced by ads. Rather, they smoked (as did many middle-class Americans) for more complicated reasons, including the pressure of peers. Many kept on smoking simply because nicotine was addictive or too pleasurable to give up.

Many blue-collar Americans smoked, finally, because they did not respond readily to the experts—epidemiologists, researchers, government bureaucrats, middle-class health professionals, do-gooders—who presumed to tell them how to take care of themselves. Like other Americans in the postwar era, they respected scientists and researchers. Though less expansive than middle-class people in their expectations about good health and long life, they, too, greatly feared cancer. But their faith in the medical profession was often ambivalent, and their quest for good health did not always involve thinking far ahead to future consequences of current behavior. Some of them, including many with religious commitments, continued to take a somewhat fatalistic attitude toward matters of life and death. Others chose to enjoy pleasures in the present—what futures, after all, could many poor people anticipate? Still others, members of only slowly changing ethnic, regional, or occupational subcultures, embraced the life styles (including smoking) of their parents, peers, and co-workers. Some, perhaps, saw smoking, however unconsciously, as a way of demonstrating their social distance from the often domineering middle and upper-middle classes. To smoke was to assert the right to be free, to be an American. And millions could not drop the habit: no amount of health "propaganda" could induce them to quit.

The struggle over smoking in postwar America was indeed a test of scientific expertise against the wealth and power of modern advertising. It featured a particularly fierce conflict between health professionals and well-organized special interests. At the same time, however, the struggle was also a conflict of cultural values, a conflict between the urgent pursuit of good health and the desire to pursue that goal on one's own terms, enjoying the daily pleasures of life in the process.

In this struggle, as in others involving the alliance against cancer over the years, many Americans showed that they would cling to habits offering short-run personal satisfaction, the experts notwithstanding. While people feared cancer, they sought to deny the possibility that death would strike them. Moreover, most smokers never developed cancer—why not take a chance? People put abstract mortality statistics out of mind and went about their lives in ways that accorded most comfortably with their past habits, cultural traditions, and personal predilections. For millions in the mid-1980s that meant clinging to a cigarette habit even in the face of clear and present dangers.

9

Popular Fears, Official Dreams

THE CONTROVERSIES over smoking during the 1960s and early 1970s reproduced in microcosm broader differences in American attitudes toward cancer. On the one hand, manifestations of cancerphobia mounted in the United States. The variety of fearful expressions—from healthy people, patients, and quacks—attested to the endurance of highly emotional perceptions of the dread disease. On the other hand, the well-established alliance against cancer was more hopeful than ever. Indeed, the debates over smoking heartened the ACS and others who preached the Message of Hope. At last they could not only preach; they could also claim to know how to prevent a major form of malignant disease! Given a new lease on life, they argued confidently that science could conquer other cancers as well. Collaborators of the alliance, including activist government officials, shared this professional optimism and lobbied hard for the means to eradicate the scourge. The result, a landmark in the American experience of the disease, was the "war on cancer" started by the National Cancer Act of 1971.

This contrast between popular fears and official dreams was nothing new. Millions of people, especially in the less favored classes, had always been skeptical about, not to say hostile to, professional expertise. During Grant's time folk perceptions of cancer differed profoundly from medical orthodoxies. By the twentieth century, the continuing appeal of unorthodox practitioners, and of widely held popular notions, alarmed leaders of the AMA and the cancer society. Even in the 1940s and 1950s a substantial minority of Americans clung to ideas ridiculed by hopeful physicians and researchers.

Still, this contrast never seemed sharper than in the 1960s and early 1970s. That was not because members of the ever diffuse cancer counterculture grew more numerous. Though some foes of orthodoxy were organizing more efficiently, they did not attract much attention at the time. Rather, the contrast grew because of the aggressiveness of the anticancer alliance, which aroused unprecedented optimism about the potential of science and the beneficence of government. The appeal of positive thinking, especially to the politically influential middle classes, was at its peak in the heady, hopeful days of the 1960s, years of unparalleled prosperity, confident governmental activism, and high expectations for social change. The optimism lasted, insofar as official responses to cancer were concerned, into the early 1970s, when the scientists, publicists, lobbyists, and bureaucrats who had long dominated the alliance succeeded in attracting substantial sums of money to assist their cause. Never before—or since—did they enjoy such politically firm command.

FIRST, the fears. As in the past these rested on perceptions of the insidious and indiscriminate spread of the disease. During the 1960s cancer took the lives of more than two million Americans. Among them were such well-known figures as House Speaker Sam Rayburn (1961), environmentalist Rachel Carson (1964), and tennis star Maureen Connolly (1969). Victims in the early 1970s included the football player Brian Piccolo (1970), coach Vince Lombardi (1970), Adam Clayton Powell, Jr., Walter Winchell, and Edward, Duke of Windsor (all 1972); the film star Betty Grable (1973); and newscaster Chet Huntley, jazzman Duke Ellington, comedian Jack Benny, and Charles Lindbergh, all in 1974. Prominent women—Marvella Bayh, wife of Indiana Senator Birch Bayh, the actress Shirley Temple Black, and (within a month of each other in 1974) Betty Ford and Happy Rockefeller—underwent well-publicized surgery for breast cancers. Many of these people were young or middle-aged when afflicted.

Reading about the ordeals of these cancer patients, sensitive Americans could be excused for thinking that the disease was spreading rapidly. In fact, however, alarmist perceptions exaggerated the dangers. As some writers were beginning to emphasize, five-year survival rates (measured from the time of diagnosis) had improved, from perhaps one out of five patients in the 1930s to one out of three by 1960. This did not mean that science had found a magic bullet; the improvement took place mainly in the 1940s and 1950s, the result of earlier diagnoses and especially of surgical advances, which lengthened the lives of many patients. After 1960 survival rates did not change much, if at all. Still, the improvement by 1960 offered grounds for modest hope, not public despair.[1]

Apocalyptic perceptions of cancer mortality were similarly exaggerated. Though lung cancer was reaching epidemic proportions by the 1960s, mortality from some other cancers, notably of the stomach and cervix, continued to decrease. Aggregating all sites, most epidemiologists continued to report slight increases (almost a half of one percent per year) in age-adjusted cancer mortality. By 1970 the rate was 130 per 100,000 people, as opposed to 120 in 1940 and 125 in 1960.[2] Similarly small increases were occurring in most other industrialized nations that kept accurate statistics. Some countries, including the United Kingdom and West Germany, seemed to have slightly higher age-adjusted death rates from cancer than did the United States. From this statistical perspective cancer was not becoming a significantly greater threat to the health of Americans.[3]

Still, the worries of many people in the 1960s were understandable. Amid the increasingly contentious debates over cancer statistics, a consensus emerged among experts that for most forms of cancer survival rates were lower and death rates higher for black males, blue-collar workers, and the poor than they were for middle-class whites, who were better informed about methods of self-detection, smoked less, were generally healthier, and had better access to medical care.[4] These facts clearly refuted the idea that cancer was a disease of the favored classes or of "civilization." The high incidence of cancer among poor people confirmed the pessimism, fear, and superstitions that they had long felt about the disease.

It was equally clear that the number of cancer deaths was continuing to increase, mainly because the population contained ever larger numbers of elderly people. By 1970 cancer killed 330,000 Americans a year, or nearly twice as many as in 1950.[5] Still the second leading cause of mortality, it accounted for 18 percent of total deaths and afflicted one in four people during their lifetimes. While many other serious ailments had come under control—even heart diseases were becoming more manageable—cancer seemed as incurable as ever. Emphasizing these grim facts, popular magazines aroused public concern. Typical was a *Newsweek* cover story in 1971:

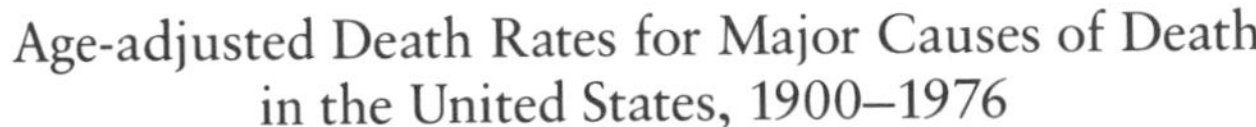

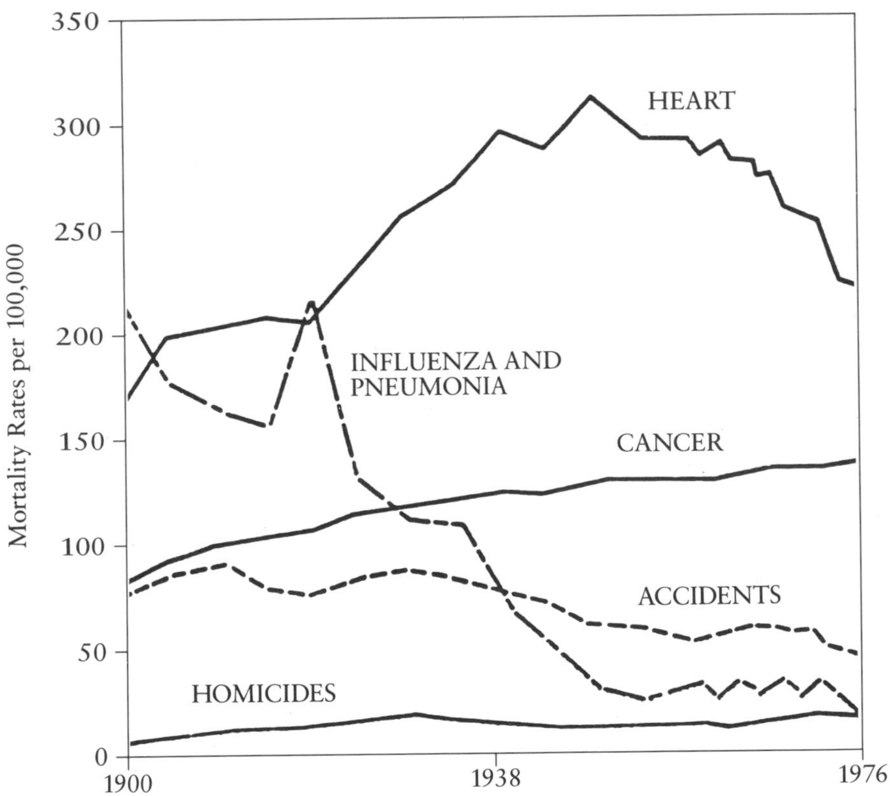

From Marvin Schneiderman, "The Uncertain Risk We Run: Hazardous Materials," in P. C. Schwin and W. A. Albers, eds., *Societal Risk Assessment* (New York, 1980), 19–41.
Reprinted with permission from Marvin Schneiderman.

> This year alone some 330,000 Americans will die of cancer. Of the 200-odd million Americans now alive and well, fully 25 per cent, or some 50 million, will one day hear their doctors pronounce the dread diagnosis. Of these, about 34 million will die, and even some of those who are saved may not consider themselves lucky. Thousands will be disfigured by the therapists' attempts to excise or burn away the malignancy. Other thousands will linger on, for months, for years, some for quite a few years. Perhaps the cruelest truth of all is that of those doomed to die this year of cancer, 4,000 are children.[6]

Not all cancer patients were terrified by the stories. Like Babe Didrikson Zaharias, some had absorbed the Message of Hope pressed by the ACS. Steeped in the culture of modern medicine, they faced the disease by checking themselves for the "Seven Danger Signals," having regular medical examinations, and seeking the most advanced therapy. Arthur Godfrey, having recovered from lung cancer surgery, told people, "I had cancer. I had a good surgeon who did a courageous job. As a result, I got cured. It's as simple as that, nothing to weep over." Fred Hutchinson, manager of the Cincinnati Reds, echoed Godfrey's message. After undergoing radiation for cancer of the thymus gland, he said, "So many people have the wrong attitude—they treat it in a hush-hush manner. After all, cancer is a disease, but it's not a social disease. It's something that happens." Upbeat messages such as these found a place in a book entitled *The Climate Is Hope: How They Triumphed over Cancer* (1965). It was dedicated to the "1,300,000 living Americans who have been cured of cancer because their disease was diagnosed early and treated promptly and properly."[7]

The vast majority of cancer patients had neither the prominence nor the desire to publicize their ordeals. But they too, like Grant and thousands of others since his time, faced cancer with fortitude. They did all they could to find qualified medical aid and submitted to recommended treatments, even if doing so meant prolonged suffering. A Wisconsin woman characterized this stoic approach in a letter to her sister in 1963:

> I have two drainage tubes that go to the suction machine. The tubes go right into the small intestine and of course I drain constantly. The pressure is gone and I have not had a hypo for three days. As very little gets to where it belongs, I just drink—liquid diet—and it goes

> into the jar—I am still on I.V.s and shall continue to be. All the tube does is to relieve the pressure and keeps me from vomiting and intense pain. I'm a regular sieve.[8]

But thousands of Americans showed neither the public confidence of Godfrey nor the grimmer hope of those who accepted modern therapeutics. Many, like President Lyndon Johnson, who had a skin cancer removed from his ankle in 1967, concealed their situation from friends. (Disclosure of Johnson's treatment came only in 1977, four years after his death; even then his family and physicians issued denials.)[9] For the majority of less favored patients scary magazine and newspaper articles chipped away at the old conspiracy of silence but at the same time confirmed the anguish and dread already in their hearts. These emotions, and the superstitions that often accompanied them, remained widespread in the 1960s and early 1970s—a half century after the alliance against cancer began proclaiming its Message of Hope.

Among the many sources that revealed these emotions are polls and interviews by social workers and psychologists. These show not only that cancer remained by far the most feared of illnesses, but also that many people still dreaded to hear the word. "I don't want to know if it's cancer," a patient explained. "I don't want to know I'm doomed." Many patients who were told the truth hugged it to themselves, enduring alone the panic, terror, rage, suspicion, self-pity, acquiescence, and surrender that often afflicted the dying. Others did not want to know the whole truth and turned themselves over to the care of others. One patient, laughing nervously, explained, "I'm content to let them do what they want because I'd only worry if I knew the details."[10]

Many patients who surrendered their fate to medical professionals found little to restore their confidence. Studies of the attitudes of doctors and nurses—in England as well as in the United States—revealed that they, too, continued to hold deeply pessimistic views of the disease. As in the past they were as afraid as their patients to use the word "cancer" or to face the whole truth. They talked of cancer in hushed tones and with drawn faces. Their apprehension conveyed itself to the sick, many of whom grew all the more lonely, confused, and afraid.[11]

Studies also showed that a minority of patients, especially those who were poor and ill-educated, still felt deeply ashamed of getting cancer, as did their families. One-fifth of a sample of lower-class women in England thought the disease was heritable, "catching" like the flu, or caused by immorality. Surveys of American patients revealed comparable feelings of guilt or shame. Many patients in the secular culture of postwar America lacked consolation from religious faith. Unable to explain their cancer as a punishment imposed by a retaliatory God or to foresee their deliverance in heaven, they blamed themselves for their suffering and awaited death.[12]

These studies, useful as they are, scarcely convey the panic, dread, and superstition of many people, including some who did not have the disease themselves. Letters written to doctors better expose the power of complex and shifting emotions, particularly among Americans who read stories about "cures" in magazines and newspapers. One such article, which appeared as a *Life* cover story in 1962, focused on the promising viral research of Peyton Rous.[13] CANCER MAY BE INFECTIOUS, it asserted carelessly. Rous was then inundated with letters, many of them ungrammatical, from people who worried that "germs" caused cancer. "Despite the warning against alarm," one woman wrote, "I am scared. Intellectually I realize fear is unwarranted but emotionally it is with me." Explaining that she lived in "close contact" with a lung cancer patient who coughed a lot, she wondered if she, too, might succumb to the cancer "germ." Another woman asked Rous's pardon for writing, but lamented, "I am so troubled that I just can't sleep." Three people in her apartment building had died of the disease. "Is there anything I can do to kill the germ . . . Can the rooms be fumigated, or what can one do to make it safe to live in these rooms? . . . Should I give up my lease and move out? Please help, I am so desperate I just don't know what I can do."[14]

Other correspondents were almost as desperate. An Illinois woman explained to Rous that she was "much concerned about catching cancer from items in our home where my sister passed away two years ago with cancer." Could commercial cleaners rid the place of germs, she asked, "or should all items—books and pens used by the victim be destroyed?" A Canadian man told Rous that his first and second wives, his daughter, and his wife's parents had all died of cancer. "Do you think," he asked, "the cancer causing virus can be transmitted from husband to wife in normal sexual intercourse? In other words, am I a Cancer Carrier?"[15]

Five years later another article, this one in *Reader's Digest,* evoked a somewhat different but equally anguished spate of letters. These came to Sloan-Kettering, where doctors were extolling the potential of cryosurgery, involving rapid deep freezing and slow thawing of malignant tissue, which thereupon might die without need of the knife. As described the method appeared to be virtually bloodless and painless, and desperate people wrote for help. "Doctor," one man wrote, "if you can try this method on me I'd be gratefull the rest of my life. I don't want to let this linger on and on when there is a chance for me to live . . . I'm in desperation trying to find a doctor who would try the cryosurgery method." A woman wrote that she had a tumor "the size of a grape fruit, and Angina Pectoris and Artersilrois, and my Doctor says I can't have an operation . . . I read about you in the papers, and this cynosurgery [*sic*] sounds wonderful."[16]

Other people begged for assistance to relatives. A woman explained that her sixty-five-year-old brother had thyroid cancer. "He dreads the surgeon's scalpel, but says he is sure he would not fear cryosurgery." Another woman (most writers were women—men, perhaps, were reluctant to show fear) wrote that her husband had "30 or 40 tumors all over his body, I hope to God you help him. He is a very sick man suffer so much. I have 11 children and I hope and pray you can do something. This poor man can't not live like this." A third correspondent pleaded on behalf of his mother, who had just had a mass removed from her breast. "Doctor, will you please take her case? Try to save my mother's life for me. How much would you cost? . . . Please answer soon."[17]

Many writers—there were hundreds—saw cryosurgery as a magic deliverance. "This article is like a God sent light in the darkness of our sorrow," one woman wrote. Another correspondent explained that his eleven-year-old son had lost a leg to cancer and now had spots on his lung. "I have been praying for a miracle," he said. "I hope and pray that one day medical science will discover the cause and cure of this dread disease."[18]

Frightened people cannot be neatly categorized. A few expressed folk superstitions more common in the 1860s than in the 1960s. A larger number indicated doubt or distrust of orthodox medical practices, especially surgery. By contrast many other letters offered detailed and medically literate descriptions of tumors. These came from desperate people who believed so strongly in the potential of science that they were ready to try the latest "cure" that experts could supply.

In general, however, the letter writers had in common two prevalent feelings. The first was that cancer was mysterious and insidious. Whether positive, negative, or ambivalent about doctors, these correspondents had little faith in existing therapies. They disbelieved optimistic predictions, and they feared the worst. The second emotion was especially strong among patients and their relatives: desperation. Also distrustful of official optimism, these people nonetheless responded to new technological possibilities when the disease struck close to home. The spontaneous expression of these emotions—fear, distrust, and desperation—betrayed the continuing dread of the disease in postwar America.

While most of these people were at least on the fringe of the modern medical culture in America, a smaller number of others denounced regular practitioners and asserted the virtues of unorthodox remedies. As in the past some of these people made a business of such cures. Among the books that Americans could buy in the 1960s were *Has Dr. Max Gerson a True Cancer Cure?* (1962), *The Incredible Story of Krebiozen: A Matter of Life or Death* (1962), *Laetrile: Control for Cancer* (1963), *Cancer Cures* (1965), and *People's Cancer Handbook* (1967). In these same years, the ACS estimated, more than 10,000 Americans joined such antiestablishment organizations as the National Health Federation and the International Organization of Cancer Victims and Friends, Inc.[19]

Though these commercial operators offered a range of therapies, most did not differ greatly from the unorthodox practitioners who had long infuriated the ACS and the AMA. Walter Stearns, who ran the Stearns Chiropractic Sanitarium and Hospital in Denver, circulated a large newpaper (featuring pictures of pretty women at his hospital) in which he promised to cure almost everything from polio to cerebral palsy.[20] Many other healers relied on pamphlets or word of mouth and testimonials from "cured" patients to demonstrate their successes. All were united in two key respects: they demanded "freedom of choice" in cancer medicine, and they excoriated the "monopoly" of the AMA, government regulators, and drug companies. Many nurtured a bitter, conspiratorial view of the world that aligned them with ideologues of the right.

As in earlier years, commercial practitioners were but a few of the many people who claimed personal cures for cancer. Some were sure that God, not doctors, had the final answer. One woman told NCI chief Kenneth Endicott that she had had a dream in which she had prayed to God and "cried out to him to help find a cure for cancer. I heard a *beautiful clear voice* say 'herein lies the answer.' I looked in the palm of my hand and saw a *potato*. It was a large potato with moist earth. As I looked at it, I awoke." Another explained to President Johnson that she had had a "revelation" that decoded the enigma of cancer. Like many of her persuasion, she denounced "scientists who deliberately hide discoveries when they cannot themselves profit" and concluded, "At some point it *must* be revealed. GOD will punish us for allowing good people to die of this disease, after HE has shown us what to do. HE will also expect us to give HIM credit and not to reveal these findings as medical discoveries."[21]

Most of the hundreds who wrote the NCI, however, did not seem especially religious. Many stressed the virtues of diet or of various ointments and salves.[22] Others thought the cause of cancer was loss of water in the body. "When the cells lose this amount of liquid," a woman wrote, "irritation begins, just as a oil is used as a lubricant, the same applys to water." Another correspondent insisted that all cancer victims exude a "powerful, permeating, and offensive odor." The cure was "frequent soaking, bathing, or syringing cancer tissue with lard to remove cancer odor, or gas." Still others, repeating old notions about the role of stress, blamed poor relationships between patients and their parents. "Somehow or other," one man wrote, "the body or an organ has been 'shocked' by some action of the father—an abruptness, divorce, aloofness, any of a number of things."[23]

Some of these people were more defensive than unorthodox theorists had been in the past. They stressed that they did not want to be thought of as "quacks." One wrote, "I sincerely hope very much that you don't think I'm cracked or off my rocker." Their self-consciousness may have reflected the spread of mass communications, especially television, which slowly altered the world of quackery. Though believers in unorthodox methods continued to flourish in the South and West and in special subcultures, other Americans were not so cut off from mainstream urban culture as they had been twenty-five or fifty years earlier. And many rural people once attracted to unorthodox healers had moved away to the cities and the suburbs. Some of these, sharing in postwar prosperity, moved upward educationally and economically and discarded the folk beliefs of their parents and former neighbors. Just as technological and social changes made inroads against provincial subcultures, so they slowly invaded the insularity that had long helped to sustain America's unorthodox practitioners and folk healers.

Still, neither the healers nor their followers were easily cowed by the prestige of orthodox medicine or the research establishments of postwar America. On the contrary, some rebels were more assertive than ever. Feeling threatened by modern ways, they fiercely defended their ideas and raged at orthodox practices, especially surgery and radiation. They grew more vocal in denouncing government regulators, whose reach had expanded over the years. The counterculture flourished in fact *because* the various and unorganized critics of the "Cancer Establishment" offered resistance—often bitter, harsh, and ideologically reactionary—to the pressures of modernity, liberalism, governmental intrusion, laboratory science, and secular thought.

During the politically tumultuous 1960s some of these angry foes of medical orthodoxy found themselves in partial though highly uneasy agreement with rebels of a very different sort: political liberals. Few of these liberals had much interest in the nostrums of the healers, but they had equally serious doubts about the power of the AMA and about the priorities of the alliance against cancer. These doubts contrasted sharply with the official dreams of the Cancer Establishment.

Some critics directed their fire mainly at the AMA, not at cancer scientists in particular. They were angry at the opposition of the association to national health insurance and at what they perceived as the greed of American physicians. Attempting to demythologize medicine and science, they emphasized the human failings and blunders of doctors. By the late 1960s liberal medical students were staging protests outside AMA meetings and demanding reforms to bring medical care within reach of the poor.[24] Other critics took aim at the ACS-NCI network that had solidified, with ever increasing funding, by 1960. As in the 1940s and 1950s they complained that the alliance against cancer focused heavily on laboratory research, enriching well-connected institutions like Sloan-Kettering while spending only a pittance on cancer clinics for the poor or on promoting preventive measures such as Pap smears. The NCI, they added, moved gingerly on the smoking issue and suppressed Hueper and other investigators of workplace carcinogens.

These denunciations were harsh. The ACS, for example, devoted much of its time and money to campaigning for Pap smears and self-examination for breast cancer and to warning about smoking. Moreover, it was still unclear whether cancer clinics were very cost-effective in lowering mortality rates. Earlier, admittedly limited efforts along these lines had not accomplished much. Even Pap smears, some doctors pointed out, were not the main reason for the heartening decline in the incidence of cervical cancer, which had begun—in part because of improved hygiene among the poor—before the tests had become widely available in the 1950s.

Defenders of federal efforts replied also that the NCI was making a good-faith effort to promote cancer control. Thanks in part to financial support and direction from the NCI, all fifty states had cancer control measures in place by the mid-1960s, as compared to but eighteen in 1945. In the late 1960s the NCI's Cancer Control Branch hired commercially successful writers—James Michener, Jacqueline Susann, Neil Simon—to put together widely distributed films pushing early detection and prevention. In contrast to the 1930s, when the Women's Field Army had pioneered in this effort, cancer control programs had expanded considerably.

But the critics persisted nonetheless, for they correctly noted the continuing low priority of preventive efforts by the anticancer alliance. At no time in the 1960s did the NCI allot more than a small fraction of its funds for cancer control.[25] Under NIH Director James Shannon and a series of NCI directors from the 1940s through the 1960s, the federal campaign against cancer remained heavily oriented toward biological and chemotherapeutic research. Preventive efforts received between $10 and $30 million per year during the late 1960s, of a total NCI budget that rose from $110 million in 1961 to around $200 million by 1969.

Other foes of the alliance against cancer complained more angrily than before about the way in which the research money was used. A few raised the most basic question: why throw so much taxpayers' money at cancer (far more than amounts available for any other disease) when America's infant mortality rate was higher than that of fourteen other countries in the world? The government, they said, should spend less on fighting chronic problems such as heart disease and cancer—some of them perhaps incurable—and more on diseases afflicting children, the handicapped, and the mentally ill. Higher funding, they said, should go to preventive campaigns for auto safety or against smoking. Above all, they said, the poor still received inferior medical attention; the government should tend to their pressing needs.[26]

Another group of critics questioned the priorities of the NCI in spending its research money. Shannon was an articulate, domineering spokesman for basic biological research, but Lasker and her allies, while approving of such investigations, lobbied hard for more applied research as well.[27] No one, they said, knew the precise biological mechanisms by which aspirin relieved pain, or how tranquilizers really worked, yet these remedies reduced human suffering. Although Shannon generally had his way until the mid-1960s, the Lasker group used contacts with President Johnson and key congressmen to demand greater emphasis on applied research. This controversy flared openly in the early 1970s during acrimonious debates over the National Cancer Act.[28]

It is intriguing to speculate about what might have happened if these varied critics of the AMA and NCI had joined forces with the two amorphous groups of people in America who had traditionally doubted the claims of the anticancer alliance. These were the fearful patients and their relatives who impatiently sought cures for what they considered—positive thinkers notwithstanding—a mysterious and deadly disease, and the healers and others—members of the diffuse cancer counterculture—who distrusted the orthodox professional establishment. Had these very different kinds of people organized to forge a working coalition, they might have challenged the funding for the NCI or pushed it to reorder its priorities.

To a limited extent the NCI was forced to change in the iconoclastic late 1970s, but not before then. Though the Vietnamese war aroused antiestablishment feelings, scientific researchers and orthodox practitioners temporarily maintained their cultural authority in the 1960s and early 1970s. Angry patients, doubting relatives, and resentful healers, after all, were scattered. Save for a few wealthy quacks, they were mostly poor and enjoyed little political influence. Many expressed an uninformed conglomeration of opinions about cancer and its cure. What they shared was a mood, not a passion for organization or coalition. For all these reasons no united movement against the anticancer alliance developed in the 1960s. The confident claims of science and biomedical expertise continued to resonate loudly among the middle-class leaders whose opinions remained central in American culture.

FROM THE LEADERS came the dreams. These rested first on developments in basic biological research following the elucidation in 1953 of the structure of DNA. By the early 1960s, with a general understanding of the genetic code, scientists knew much more about the way that viruses were constructed, as well as about the biochemical mechanisms that enable them to multiply and to form copies within cells. They began to understand the structure of biologically important molecules (such as proteins), how they were coded, how they functioned in the metabolism of the cell, and how they carried specific biological information from one generation to another. These developments rejuvenated the life sciences, which seemed on the verge of answering the great question, "What is Life?"[29]

Though most scientists attracted to molecular biology were more interested in basic biological exploration than in applied cancer research, many of their contemporaries were certain that the understanding of DNA would soon work wonders in the cancer field, and vice versa. As early as 1961 Isidor Ravdin, past president of the American College of Surgeons, predicted, "it is now certain that cancer will come under control, just as diabetes has." Congressman John Fogarty, at the peak of his political influence, affirmed that "basic research in the biochemistry of cancer and knowledge of cell nutrition over the past few years represents progress that is greater than any produced by research during the past 50 years." James Watson, who won a Nobel prize for his explication of DNA, added later that "the essential biochemistry of cells can be worked out within the next decade or two."[30]

A second reason for optimism came from the federal government, which fell into the hands of activists during the Kennedy-Johnson years. Rejecting the cautious approach of the fiscally conservative Eisenhower administration, leading officials lobbied to expand the federal role, especially in health care. Eisenhower's lukewarm backing of the NIH, they argued, had created something of a "medical Sputnik." President Kennedy's Special Conference on Heart Disease and Cancer demanded a "vast expansion of medical research."[31] Assisted by Fogarty, Senator Lister Hill, and the Lasker network, these activists worked successfully for medicare and medicaid, passed in 1965. They greatly increased federal spending on medical research. By 1970 the NCI alone had more than $200 million to work with, twice as much as it had commanded ten years earlier.[32]

Careful observers again warned that researchers still had much to learn about the basic biology of cells. Much of the NCI's money, they added, went to scientists who included a cancer angle in grant proposals—how else to get funded?—but whose work had little direct clinical relevance. For these and many more fundamental reasons it was hardly surprising that no dramatic "breakthroughs" occurred in these years. Cancer researchers made useful contributions to molecular biology and by the 1970s undertook promising work in immunology, but they did not succeed in unraveling the arcane workings of the dread disease.[33]

The researchers gave renewed attention to virology, which many considered the hope for the future. "There isn't the slightest doubt in our minds," said the chief of the laboratory of infectious diseases at the NIH, "that human cancers are caused by viruses. To this extent, they are simply infectious diseases."[34] The dream of identifying these viruses and manufacturing a vaccine captivated many scientists, some of whom did important studies that later led to

Reprinted with permission from *Cancer News,* 24, no. 1 (1970), 1; © 1970 American Cancer Society.

discoveries of viruses associated with human cancer and with AIDS.[35] In the 1960s and early 1970s, however, they were repeatedly frustrated. A few became so hotly competitive to break the news of discovery that they came out with premature, inaccurate, and even dishonest announcements.[36]

Despite such discouragements, many newspapers and popular magazines continued to accentuate the positive. As previously, they showed special fascination with applied research and with technological developments, such as body scanners and lasers, which *Life* said could "blast tiny tumors into oblivion—instantly, accurately, with little pain or bleeding." In 1961 *Newsweek* lauded the outlook of the head of the AMA, who said that "to save human lives, medical technology put extraordinary machines and instruments to work at an unprecedented rate during 1960. And the future of automation in medicine looks bright."[37]

Statements like these demonstrated that the "search for optimism," as one skeptical observer called it, still predominated. Headlines and captions emphasized the promise. "A Cancer Breakthrough / Virus Discovery a Medical First," and "Cancer: Has the Tide Finally Turned?" were characteristic examples. Experts tirelessly stressed the necessity of spending more money on cancer research. "The next ten years," Sidney Farber explained in 1971, "will be wonderful ones for cancer therapy." *Newsweek* columnist Stewart Alsop, himself a leukemia patient, added, "the time could come quite soon when the beast will be tamed . . . Surely it is worth a major national effort to speed the coming of that time."[38]

These arguments became part of extraordinary pressure that built up during the late 1960s for a federal "war on cancer." Enthusiasts for this war, led by Lasker and her allies, opened their campaign by complaining that cancer researchers did not have enough money. The war in Vietnam, they said, had killed some 41,000 Americans in four years, whereas cancer had killed 320,000 in one. Conceding that dollar amounts for cancer research were increasing, they pointed to the more rapidly escalating cost of scientific equipment. Thanks in part to the war, they said, the money available for research was decreasing as a percentage of federal spending and of the GNP. One writer noted that in one year America spent $410 per capita on defense, $125 on the war, and only 89 cents on cancer. "We have only this little David of a one-dollar-per-person per-year national budget to slay this Goliath of an enemy." Another enthusiast emphasized, "if the American people can accept the placing of a man on the moon and similar projects as important national goals, surely finding a cure or control for cancer is a reasonable and worthwhile national goal."[39]

Those who supported this goal asserted optimistically that cancer was not a hopeless puzzle. On the contrary, the ACS argued in a pamphlet published in 1971, "cancer is one of the most curable of the major diseases in this country." It proceeded by stressing the improvement in survival rates (without making it clear that there had been little if any progress since the 1950s). A leading cancer researcher added, "we are on the verge of important advances. Therefore, we must affirm the sense of excitement with which new resources will be greeted." R. Lee Clark, the influential head of the M. D. Anderson Hospital in Houston, stated simply, "with a billion dollars a year for ten years we could lick cancer."[40]

Advocates of cancer funding, whether liberal or conservative politically, appealed to patriotism. The United States, they said with characteristically American self-assurance, must be first in the fight against cancer—just as it was in the fight for freedom. The Lasker forces were so sure of this premise that in December 1969 they placed a full-page ad in the *New York Times* reading MR. NIXON, YOU CAN CURE CANCER. Their faith in government showed how far this idea had advanced since the creation of the NCI in 1937. Liberals hailed the accomplishments of the New Frontier and the Great Society and pointed to the "war" already being fought against poverty in America. Other advocates, including the columnist Ann Landers, emphasized what government could accomplish when spurred to action by recalling its triumph of placing of a man on the moon. A Landers column to this effect in April 1971 unleashed such an avalanche of mail on Capitol Hill (Senator Alan Cranston of California said he received 60,000 letters) that congressional secretaries placed signs on their desks to "Impeach Ann Landers."[41]

Others who joined the war resurrected the idea that beating cancer was like smashing the atom. President Nixon, who converted to the cancer war in 1971, took this approach. Nixon's reasons were mainly political: he was anxious to outflank Senator Ted Kennedy, a potential presidential candidate who was then leading the Lasker forces. In his State of the Union message of January 1971 Nixon proclaimed that "the time has come when the same kind of concentrated effort that split the atom and took man to the moon should be turned toward conquering this dread disease. Let us make a total commitment to achieve this goal."[42]

Nixon's support helped make cancer a major issue of the 1971 congressional session. As pressure for action mounted it revealed cracks in the anticancer alliance. Some, like Shannon (by then retired but vocal), favored greatly increased appropriations but wanted them earmarked primarily for basic research and controlled by the NIH itself. Others, including many in the Lasker-ACS network, thought that this approach had mired the NCI in bureaucracy. They lobbied hard for a bill to give the NCI the kind of independent access to the White House enjoyed by such agencies as the AEC and NASA. Direct access, they thought, would help the institute win the war more rapidly.

After hard infighting a compromise satisfied most of the contenders. The final bill stipulated that the NCI director was to be appointed directly by the president and to submit NCI financial requests to the budget office. These measures gave the NCI special status among the institutes of the NIH, but it otherwise remained under the overall management of the NIH. This was an awkward arrangement, but both houses finally approved it. Nixon signed the bill into law two days before Christmas, 1971.[43] He added, "I hope in the years ahead we will be able to look back and see that this action has been the most important action taken by this administration."

These divisions within the anticancer alliance, however, were relatively unimportant in the broader context of the debates over the act. More striking was the consensus among almost all involved—Democrats as well as Republicans, liberals as well as conservatives—that the federal government must be the source of action against cancer, and that much more money was needed. Few people seriously questioned these premises or argued that other national health needs were more deserving of support. To oppose big spending against cancer was—as one observer noted—to oppose Mom, apple pie, and the flag.[44] All who backed the bill agreed to increase

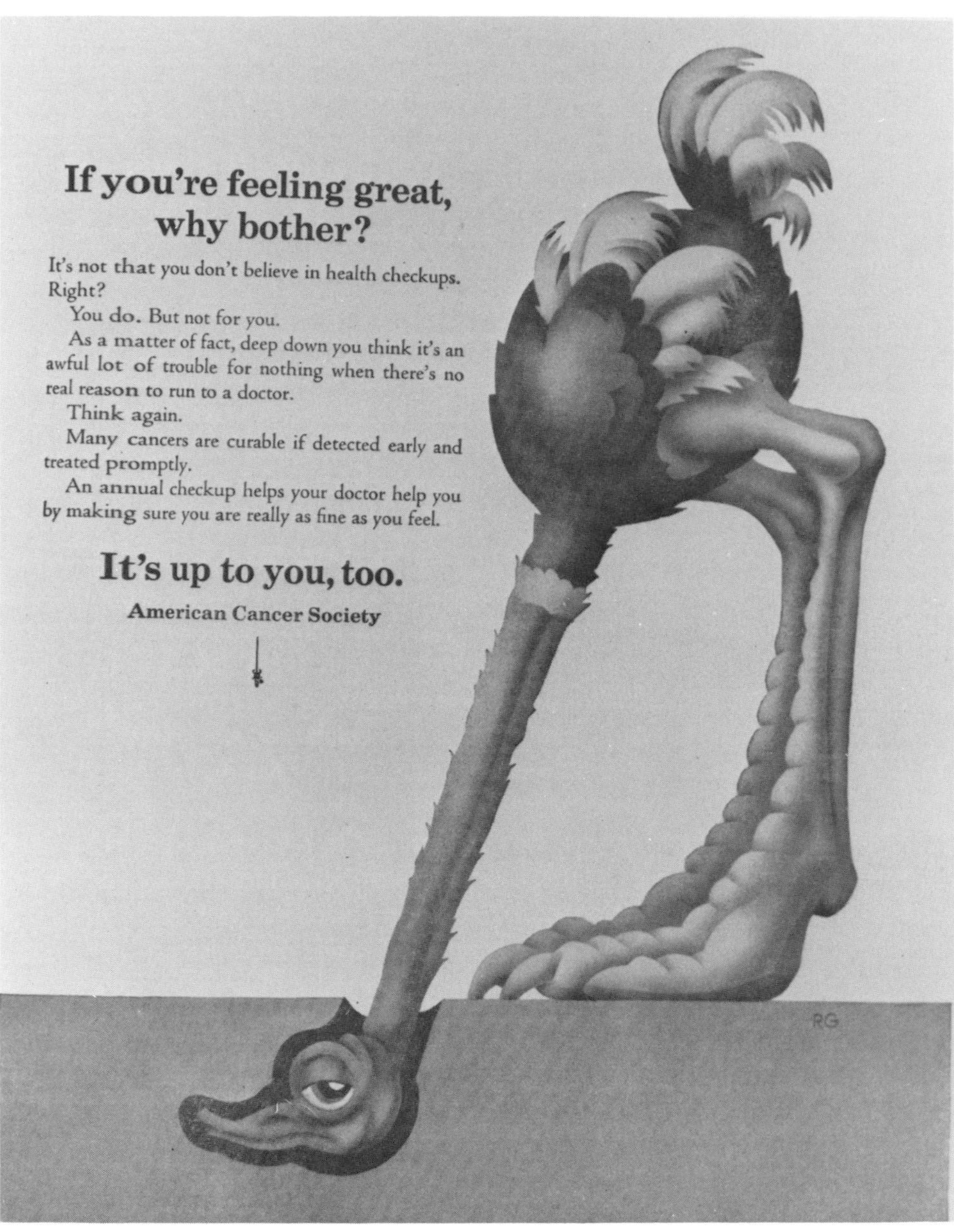

Reprinted with permission from *Cancer News,* 23, no. 2 (1970), 23; © 1970 American Cancer Society.

appropriations for the NCI to more than $400 million in fiscal 1973, to nearly $1 billion by the end of the decade. Since the start of the war on cancer, the NCI has been the major source of support for research on cancer in America.[45]

THE WAR ON CANCER of 1971 was the high-water mark for the decades-old alliance against cancer in America. Approval of the law showed that Congress saw cancer as the dread disease of the age and federal money as the means of stemming its advance. The utopian dreams of the alliance had triumphed, at least temporarily, over the fears, doubts, and fatalism that traditionally had challenged the optimism of the elites.

In the next few years the allies who had lobbied for the act vociferously defended the wisdom of their actions. The increases in funding, they said correctly, invigorated basic research in virology and immunology. In 1978 NCI researchers at last discovered a virus associated with human cancer.[46] The money hastened promising work on DNA recombination and on therapeutic possibilities such as monoclonal antibodies, a major hope of cancer scientists by the mid-1980s. Centralization of the cancer effort (which the professionally oriented allies against cancer had always wanted) facilitated further cooperation between the NCI and the ACS and private research empires like Memorial Sloan-Kettering. Even critics were pleased when some of the new money supported seventeen "comprehensive cancer centers," which treated patients and disseminated information about the illness.[47]

But opponents of the war on cancer counterattacked with a directness that would have been virtually unthinkable in the 1940s and 1950s. Demanding more emphasis on basic biological research, Watson exclaimed that supporters of the act had sold the American public a "nasty bill of goods about cancer." The whole enterprise, he said, was "a bunch of shit." Others denounced the "Cancer Establishment," the "Cancer Rip-off," and "Mrs. Lasker's War." Congress, one opponent said, had been "bewitched by words" and "whipped into a rhetorical frenzy with talk of 'universal anguish and suffering.'" The cancer act, still another concluded, "flushed out the worst instincts of Washington's health bureaucrats, sullied the unblemished record of the American Cancer Society lobby, and turned medical brother against brother. Malignancy makes for strange bedfellows."[48]

Many critics resented what they considered the hype that had accompanied lobbying for the bill. From the beginning they were sure that the results could never come close to matching the rhetoric. They wrote, moreover, in an ever more sullen cultural climate. One blow after another—disaster in Vietnam, backlash against the Great Society, Watergate, the oil crisis, inflation—divided American society and called into question the integrity of its institutions. When the NCI failed to produce immediate results, some people readily compared its "fumbling" to the country's involvement in Southeast Asia. Both, like the war on poverty, were battles that had "failed." "It's like Vietnam," one cancer researcher said in 1975. "Only when the public realized that things were going badly did pressure build to get out."[49] "By comparison with the fight against polio," another expert added, "the war in cancer is a medical Vietnam."[50]

It would be wrong, however, to see these complaints as mere reflections of cultural malaise, great though that was. The critics were correct in deploring the misleading analogies of the atomic bomb and space exploration with cancer research. Sol Spiegelman, director of Columbia University's Institute of Cancer Research, was one of several eminent researchers who decried that distortion during debates on the bill. "An all-out effort at this time," he said, "would be like trying to land a man on the moon without knowing Newton's laws of gravity."[51] Like Shannon and others who were part of the NIH-university research network, they insisted correctly that vast amounts of basic biological work remained to be done, that some of the money for highly targeted research against cancer was wasted, and that overcentralized direction inhibited creative minds.[52]

Some critics went further, maintaining that the NCI-ACS network was little more than a high-powered lobby representing private practitioners and its own special interests. "More people were making a living off cancer," they charged, "than ever died of it." The Cancer Establishment, the critics added, relied on money, not scientific expertise, to seduce investigators into unsavory forms of competitive grantsmanship. "I have some advice for young researchers in biology," one angry scientist exploded. "Stay out of cancer research because it's full of money and just about out of science." The NCI, Watson added, was "very weak in strong people. Its situation is completely different from the Manhattan Project, which was full of scientists with strong academic careers behind them. The people in NCI, however, are not the best people in American science. They spend all their time putting out big books."[53]

Other critics complained that the NCI was almost as deaf as ever to preventive approaches. Though the NCI created comprehensive cancer centers, it continued to emphasize research into virology, immunology, chemotherapy, and radiation. Of $581 million at its disposal in fiscal 1974 the NCI spent but $2.7 million on investigating the role of nutrition. The NCI's emphasis reflected the priorities of American medical research in general—it was neither new nor unique to the field of cancer research. But that was small consolation to critics. An angry scientist complained:

> it doesn't serve to rock the boat. Look, when you've got 10,000 radiologists and millions of dollars worth of equipment, you give radiation treatments, even if study after study shows that a lot of it does more harm than good. What else are they going to do? They're doing what they've been trained to do. Like the surgeons. They're trained to cut, so they cut.[54]

Another foe of the NCI summed up in 1979 the disillusion that many top scientists felt after eight years' experience with the war. NCI research, he said,

> continues to yield a great many details relevant only to the sub-sub-specialist. It also yields erroneously premature announcements popularized in the dailies as "great discoveries." In reality, an awesome heap of rocks has been gathered and is still growing, but the old edifice has not sufficiently been repaired nor has a new building been erected. The era of lavish spending, born out of the affluence of a society overconfident of its economic power and spurred by the sheer desperation and fear of losing political, military, and medical world leadership, has been an era bare of rational thinking and planning in matters of human cancer.[55]

CRITICISM of the Cancer Establishment was both a predictable reaction against the enthusiastic rhetoric of 1971 as well as an expression of a broader cultural malaise. The criticism was slightly exaggerated, for the spending, while greatly increased, hardly kept pace with inflation and was far from lavish in comparison with federal outlays for defense, agricultural price supports, and other well-protected special interests. All of the money received by the NCI from 1937 through 1973 was about equal to the amount spent to launch one big space lab.[56] Moreover, NCI money enhanced basic biological knowledge. On a more immediately practical level it gave major financial support to the testing of chemicals for carcinogenic effects—a laborious and expensive process useful to scientists throughout the world. Some of those who denounced the Cancer Establishment were scientific know-nothings who foolishly expected breakthroughs. These are rare indeed in the history of science.

Still, it is fair to say that the advocates of the war on cancer had been unwise to promise so much. The cancer act was their greatest triumph, but it aroused great popular expectations. The war also slighted preventive approaches, some of which had already demonstrated promise.[57] Though the anticancer alliance rejected the fears and fatalism of the people, many of whom were grossly misinformed, it promised considerably more than it could deliver—at least in a relatively short time.

In so doing the allies against cancer damaged some of their dreams. The contrast between their optimistic predictions and the continuing deadliness of most forms of the disease suggested to disillusioned, impatient observers that the dreamers might have no better answers than the skeptics. By the late 1970s this counteroffensive affected bigger targets than the NCI, and the war on cancer floundered. Increasing numbers of people began to criticize the establishment of science and of modern medicine as a whole, to question what for many decades had been central elements in the culture of most middle-class Americans.

10

The Alliance under Siege

"I LOOK for the end of cancer before this century is over . . . Indeed, I now believe it could begin to fall into place at almost any time, starting next year or even next week, depending on the intensity, quality, and luck of basic research."[1] By 1983, when Lewis Thomas made this optimistic prediction, the official dreams of the 1960s and 1970s were beginning to look more and more like realities to many in the anticancer alliance. Expenditures for medical care had leaped from $12 billion in 1950 to $230 billion in 1980, or from 5 percent to almost 10 percent of the GNP. No other nation spent so high a percentage of its income on health. The spending, moreover, seemed worthwhile. Infant mortality was decreasing, life expectancy rising every year. The gap between the mortality of blacks and whites, and the rich and the poor, seemed to be narrowing. The biomedical revolution of the twentieth century appeared poised for its final triumphs.[2]

At the same time, however, popular fears of cancer still gripped a significant number of Americans. As a leading medical writer pointed out:

> When it comes to cancer, American society is far from rational. We are possessed with fear . . . cancerphobia has expanded into a demonism in which the evil spirit is ever present, but furtively viewed and spoken of obliquely. American cancerphobia, in brief, is a disease as serious to society as cancer is to the individual—and morally more devastating.[3]

The 1970s, moreover, were years of especially sharp cultural tension in the United States. Disoriented by Vietnam and Watergate, distressed by inflation and rising unemployment, many Americans came to question the nation's institutions, including the profession of medicine in general and the alliance against cancer in particular. Having developed enormous expectations in the affluent postwar years—for good health and the good life—they became acutely aware of the gap separating these expectations from reality. As one perceptive scholar noted, people were "doing better and feeling worse." The war on cancer, many thought, had stalled, and utopian predictions of the experts seemed hollow. Furthermore, critics charged, the "medicalization" of American society had resulted in an impersonal, callous, and technologically frightening system of care.[4]

In this turbulent and increasingly iconoclastic cultural climate the well-financed alliance against cancer determined to stand its ground. Much criticism of the medical profession, after all, was aimed at the wealth and alleged incompetence of individual physicians or at the impersonal care received at hospitals, not at the activities of medical researchers. The ACS, the Lasker network, and the NCI continued to attract considerable sums of money. Though heart diseases killed more than twice as many people, cancer still pulled open the purse strings of politicians and philanthropists. During the 1970s twice as much federal money (almost a billion dollars a year by 1980) went to conquer the "Big C," as cancer victim John Wayne called it, as to fight any other disease.[5]

Yet by the late 1970s the alliance against cancer had lost some of the glow that had illuminated it from the 1950s through the debates over the war on cancer in 1971. More than at any time since its days of groping in the 1920s and 1930s it was besieged by criticisms. The seventies witnessed an unprecedented flowering of popular doubts concerning science, professional expertise, orthodox medicine, and the "priests" of the "Cancer Church." Members of the diverse cancer counterculture, long resentful, burst forth into the open.

Nothing more clearly revealed this popular reaction than the environmentalist crusade. The movement attracted epidemiologists, laboratory scientists, anticorporate liberals, conservationists, and agitators from the right as well as the left of the political spectrum. Never well organized, they spoke out in many voices. Some expressed a romantic primitivism that left them open to criticism. But they were united in their belief that man-made chemicals—in pesticides, food additives, industrial processes—were destroying the environment and bringing on a virtual epidemic of cancer. The environmentalist movement, as much as any development of the twentieth century, reflected popular doubts about the Cancer Establishment.

The crusaders for environmental purification played effectively on the fear of cancer. They portrayed cancer not only as a disastrous disease but also as the ultimate result of runaway industrial growth. This linkage of cancer with urbanization and industrialization was hardly new in the United States, but by the late 1970s it had so much popular appeal that it placed the alliance against cancer on the defensive. No, the NCI felt obliged to rebut in the title of a 1979 pamphlet, "Everything Doesn't Cause Cancer."

IN DEFENDING themselves medical spokesmen correctly emphasized the extraordinarily impressive improvements in the health of the American people during the twentieth century. A wealthy nation such as the United States, they added, could and should support an elite of specialists and researchers. Advanced technology, Thomas said, was both necessary and proper. "The mechanization of medicine," he said, "is here to stay. The new medicine works." He explained that "the major diseases of human beings have become approachable biological puzzles, ultimately solveable. It follows from this that is is now possible to begin thinking about a human society relatively free of disease."[6]

Enthusiasts of this point of view received support of a sort from an unexpected source: reformers eager to demystify death. A key article, "Who's Afraid of Death on a Leukemia Ward" (1965), initiated a movement for greater honesty with terminally ill children. Following Elisabeth Kübler-Ross, whose book *On Death and Dying* (1969) attracted considerable attention, many other writers assailed the "denial of death" as a major source of cancerphobia. As Thomas himself complained, "death has been made to seem unnatural, an outrage; when people die—at whatever age—we speak of them as having been 'struck down,' 'felled.' It is as though in a better world we would all go on forever." Though it is doubtful that these new-style "thanatologists" did much to domesticate death in the minds of people—popular fears seemed as profound as ever—they did try to counteract exaggerated expectations about physicians. They also aided in the broader effort to promote franker, less authoritarian relations between doctors and patients.[7]

The allies relied further on formidable weapons against cancer, including advanced chemotherapy and radiotherapy, more sophisticated surgical procedures,[8] additional comprehensive cancer centers. They also emphasized that cancer physicians were now being prepared in a newly approved subspecialty of internal medicine—medical oncology. By 1983 some 5,000 doctors were certified in this growing field.[9] Some new developments, such as immunotherapy, aroused especially favorable attention, particularly from the always enthusiastic popular magazines. *Time* devoted cover stories to Sloan-Kettering's immunological research and to the promise of the "natural drug" interferon. Other stories lauded the potential of BCG (Bacillus-Calmette-Guerin), a strain of tuberculosis bacteria said to be "100 per cent effective" against cancer in animals.[10] By the early 1980s this sort of incautious and—for many patients and their families—cruelly misleading journalism provoked angry indictments of science writers, publishers, and cancer "propagandists."[11] Still, the stories persisted, fueled by hopeful researchers and competitive grant applicants who carried the Message of Hope.

Magazines and newspapers emphasized this message in stories about newsworthy cancer patients in the 1970s, as they had since the 1950s. Betty Ford was candid about her breast surgery in 1974 and advised other women, "Once it's done, put it behind you and go on with your life." She added, "I've heard women say they'd rather lose an arm, and I can't imagine such talk. It's so stupid." A *New York Times* editorial reminded readers that "the First Lady's ordeal should underscore once again the crucial need for constant vigilance against the spread of malignancies."[12]

Cancer patients by this time were appearing in television and movie melodramas, such as *Love Story* (1970), *Brian's Song* (1971), about Chicago Bears' star Brian Piccolo, and *Babe* (1975), which told the story of Zaharias. These films were sentimental. One critic uncharitably (but accurately) called *Love Story* "high-gloss histrionics." Another observed that Ali McGraw, playing the heroine

Reprinted with permission from *Time,* March 31, 1980.

with leukemia, "went out with apple-cheeked spunk." In real life Piccolo had raged, "Can you believe this shit?" and had to be sedated. At death he was fifty pounds underweight, unconscious, and connected by tubes to hospital machinery. In *Brian's Song*, however, he passed away peacefully, his wife proclaiming her love for him. Defending the movie, a cancer society spokesman explained that "if you portray cancer on that screen with all its degradation and pain, you haven't got a prayer. If they ever walked into a ward, they'd run away so fast. And we want them to stop running away from this goddam disease."[13]

Critics pointed out that official optimism was sometimes transparently unpersuasive. The allies against cancer were especially fortunate, therefore, in being able to fall back on a major development in the field of cancer research in the late 1970s. That was the growing importance that many of the allies assigned to the role of diet and nutrition in controlling the disease.

Some of the evidence for this development came from laboratory tests for identifying carcinogenic agents, both natural and man-made, in food additives. More important was epidemiological research, which attracted greater attention in the 1970s than before.[14] Epidemiologists showed that migrants to other countries (such as Japanese to America or Americans to Israel) tended in time to show patterns of cancer incidence similar to those of natives in their new environments. The incidence of stomach tumors among Japanese, who consumed large amounts of smoked fish, was perhaps the highest in the world; among Japanese-Americans who adapted to American habits it approximated the much lower rate in the United States.[15] Epidemiologists added that Mormons, who neither smoked nor drank and who ate lots of grains, fruits, and vegetables, had low rates of colon and stomach cancer, and that Seventh-Day Adventists, who adhered to lacto-vegetarian diets, were less prone to colon cancer than were other groups in American society.[16]

This evidence was far from conclusive, and it remained subject to differing interpretations. Experts cautioned that it was extraordinarily difficult to single out the role of specific foods among all the environmental and genetic elements that may cause cancer. Doubters also pointed out apparently complicating findings. Colon cancer in the Netherlands, for instance, was twice as common as in Finland, even though per capita fat intake was roughly the same in both countries. The same cancers were low both among Mormons, who ate meat, and among Seventh-Day Adventists, who did not. Fat intake alone, it seemed, could hardly account for varying rates of cancer incidence.[17]

The doubters, noting the long, sad history of claims for dietary panaceas, also cautioned that there were no thoroughly controlled studies of the effects of diet over the life spans of individuals and that it was therefore premature to leap to conclusions. One governmental study agreed that there was an overall association of cancer and diet, but "no reliable indication of exactly what dietary changes would be of major importance in reducing cancer incidence and mortality."[18] Another official study, which recommended reductions of 25 percent in fat intake, conceded that the contribution of diet to the reduction of risk could not be quantified: "It is not now possible, and may never be possible, to specify a diet that protects all people against all forms of cancer."[19]

Though admitting these uncertainties, many experts were nonetheless intrigued by the possibilities. Their interest rested not only on the accumulation of epidemiological evidence but also on other considerations. They had long recognized that diets were associated with a number of chronic diseases, including heart ailments; it was plausible to suspect that nutrition had an important role in cancer as well. Reducing fat intake, moreover, hardly seemed likely to harm many people. The allies against cancer, finally, felt pressure from advocates of preventive strategies. For all these reasons they were more receptive than in the past to the general view that dietary habits were associated with a number of lethal tumors, especially of the gastrointestinal tract.

The epidemiological evidence about nutrition was attractive above all because it suggested that people could do something (besides giving up smoking) to prevent certain common forms of cancer. Reflecting this belief, a high-level scientific study concluded in 1982 that "the United States will eventually have the option of adopting a diet that reduces its incidence of cancer by approximately one-third." Such a change would be "equivalent to the reduction in mortality from the infectious diseases" in the nineteenth century.[20] Richard Doll and Richard Peto, perhaps the most respected epidemiologists of cancer, estimated that dietary habits (especially excessive consumption of fats) could be associated with approximately 35 percent of cancer mortality.[21] These experts were among a growing chorus of spokesmen, including leaders of the NCI and American Cancer Society, who began to stress the desirability of more fiber, fruit and green vegetables, and less fat, in diets.

The new respectability of dietary theories, which had often been the preserve of zealots, was a dramatic turn of events in the history of American thinking about cancer. Those who had lashed out against "civilization" and "luxurious living," it seemed, may have stumbled on a few truths. The growing interest in dietary remedies showed that the allies against cancer, with the wonderfully persuasive example of smoking at hand, were far more willing than they had ever been to look to life styles as key causes of cancer, and to preventive approaches as curbs of mortality. Epidemiological evidence about tobacco and food, they thought, suggested environmental causes for as much as two-thirds of cancer mortality in the world.

EVEN WITH THIS SHIFT in emphasis the dreamers and the optimists lost ground to the doubters. During the late 1970s and early 1980s various critics assailed the official line with unprecedented forcefulness. Many people seemed to agree that the anticancer alliance could claim credit for but a few good ideas and that, yes, everything *did* cause cancer.[22]

A sign of this mood was the downpour of discontent that followed a "Meet the Press" television show on American medical practices in 1978. A similar program in 1961 had evoked a modest amount of mail, most of which had been deeply respectful of doctors. Not so in 1978, when hundreds of listeners rejected positive views of physicians. Some wrote to complain about various forms of medical malfeasance or to demand the freedom to tend to their health as they pleased. Others, joining a letter-writing campaign engineered by special interests, insisted on their right to take laetrile, the latest unorthodox remedy for cancer. Like most of the correspondents, they expressed outrage at governmental regulation of unorthodox practitioners.[23]

Underlying these complaints were two main themes, which energized critics from the left as well as from the far right. The first was that doctors were paid a great deal for knowing very little. The medical profession, one writer asserted, "comes off as mostly a pack of charlatans, making money off cancer who do not know a damn thing . . . Just keep the money coming and we'll keep talking through our hats." The second common complaint was that health care had become impersonal. "The medical system of treatment," one man wrote, "has been taken over to a large extent by electronic gadgets and chemical compounds . . . Since the Societies (Cancer, Heart, etc.) and the government have injected themselves into the health field, the love that was once in the practice of medicine no longer seems to be there."[24]

Other critics of orthodox medicine in the 1970s elaborated on these objections: the health care system continued to underemphasize public-health reforms and to discriminate against minority groups and the poor; physicians abandoned primary care in favor of high-paying specializations; male doctors were callous and sexist in treating women; specialists were in the thrall of expensive machinery; physicians regularly misdiagnosed and mistreated illness. To judge from alarming statistics about relatively high rates of infant mortality in the United States, especially among blacks, some of these complaints were justified. Studies also appeared to document the frequency of misdiagnosis. More than half of 272 death certificates sampled in Connecticut inaccurately or imprecisely listed the cause of death.[25]

Many people concluded that they would be better off to depend less on doctors and more on themselves. Embracing timeless holistic ideas, they asserted that health required more than the absence of disease. It meant "feeling whole," personally controlling one's body, being in tune with nature. For some critics it followed that people should keep doctors at arm's length—especially surgeons and other high-tech specialists. Other holists doubted that there was much to be gained from elaborate and expensive medical checkups, which seemed to symbolize the excessive medicalization of American culture.

Important to many of these critics was self-care: no smoking, only moderate drinking, adequate sleep and exercise, three balanced meals at regular times. While many physicians retorted that this emphasis "blamed the victim," others responded that self-care made more sense than turning to doctors for answers to all sorts of problems. Contemporary cultural phenomena—the extraordinary vogue for jogging, the sale of vitamins and health foods, growing drives to restrict smoking—suggested that millions of citizens tended to agree.[26]

A number of those who practiced self-reliance were well-educated, middle-class people who consulted physicians in a crisis. Far from rejecting the culture of modern medicine, they still felt that science and medicine could improve the quality of life. But they were more ambivalent about what experts could do for them. And millions of other Americans continued to voice still deeper suspicions of doctors. Among them were large numbers of mostly poorer, not so well educated people who still turned to charismatic faith healers—one estimate placed their number at five million in the mid-1970s. During these years, when evangelists like Oral Roberts made highly effective use of television and other methods of merchandising, believers openly expressed class and religious resentments against the modern, secular world.

Many of these true believers had never subscribed to medically orthodox explanations of disease. Only God, they thought, could really cure people. "Doctors cannot heal," one evangelist explained. "They can keep you alive and I thank God for them. I wouldn't want to be without them. I believe in them. But I don't believe they can heal." Another evangelist told the faithful, "a cancer came upon my leg, and it looked as if the enemy was going to get me . . . But I prayed unto the Lord and He healed me."[27] It was a sign of the cultural turbulence of the period that religiously motivated people such as these could find common cause—deep doubts about orthodox medicine—with ardent vitamin users, health food advocates, and others who relied chiefly on themselves for good health.

Other critics of American medicine in the 1970s took a different tack. Instead of relying on themselves—or on God—they demanded reforms to widen access to better treatment. These critics included articulate, well-educated liberals as well as growing numbers of working-class and poor people who had developed a larger sense of entitlement in the more prosperous postwar years. Expecting to live happier, healthier lives than their parents, they asserted their right to decent services of all kinds. They hotly resented a system of medical care that provided well for "them," badly for "us." Some of these poor people, as well as many in the middle classes, were influenced by the civil rights and women's liberation movements and were more acutely aware of their rights, including the right to control their own bodies. "Our Bodies, Ourselves," feminists proclaimed. Many women objected especially to radical mastectomies; other people demanded the legalization of euthanasia. Reflecting these varied views, philosophers, lawyers, and others rejuvenated the study of medical ethics and scrutinized every move of physicians. Contentious patients launched medical malpractice suits, which seemed to proliferate in the late 1970s.[28]

It is easy to exaggerate the numbers and strength of the people who subscribed to one or more of these critical views of the medical profession in the late 1970s. Judging from the continuing reliance on physicians—as indicated by the steadily high number of visits that Americans made to doctors' offices—the great majority of people continued to have faith in the ability of practitioners. This, too, was a constant amid social and cultural change. Moreover, many critics of the medical profession were highly ambivalent, denigrating doctors on the one hand but demanding answers from them on the other. Other critics recognized that many physicians seemed to be listening to the complaints and making a greater effort to reform past practices: the profession was far from monolithic. Finally, the critics of the medical profession did not form a cohesive movement; they were united, if at all, mainly in mood, and they had few organizational skills. Then as earlier they were not much of a match for the politically well-connected professionals in the alliance against cancer.

Close observers of American medicine also agreed that many critics exaggerated their case by seizing on a relatively small number of flagrant medical blunders. Many clinical problems, moreover, simply had no easy answers—a fact that most physicians readily admitted. Balanced studies of contemporary medicine emphasized above all that societies are likely to receive the medical systems that they deserve. Americans lived in a competitive, bureaucratic, and capitalistic culture and should not have expected the profession of medicine to be much different from, or much more sensitive than, other national institutions.[29]

Still, the critics of American medicine were increasingly vociferous by 1980. Their very variety suggested the quandary in which the medical profession found itself. Good health, Americans believed, was a preeminent national goal, yet progress in health care fed ever greater expectations that the profession could not satisfy. The millions of Americans who grew frustrated by this gap between hopes and realities posed a threat to the authority of doctors by the early 1980s. It was by then a very different cultural climate from the optimistic one which had nourished the war on cancer in 1971.

BECAUSE ALARM about the "Big C" remained a central concern in American culture it was virtually axiomatic that doubts about the profession of medicine would also affect the so-called Cancer Establishment. Critics questioned the ACS, the NCI, and satellite empires such as Memorial Sloan-Kettering, which together had received billions of dollars in funds during the postwar years.

Some emphatically refuted the optimism of writers such as Thomas. Like Ewing in the prewar era, they emphasized the frustrating gaps in knowledge about the disease. What was the exact definition of cancer? Was it one disease or hundreds? What was the nature of precancerous lesions? When and why did a growth become a malignant tumor? Were cancers, as most experts had insisted since the time of Virchow, mainly local in origin, or were they (like leukemia and many breast cancers) also multifocal? Did cancers stem primarily from life styles, from environmental exposures, or from some genetically transmitted imperfections of the cells? For all the progress that had been made over the years, experts in the 1970s could not arrive at a consensus on these very old questions.[30]

Aware of the need for greater knowledge, well-informed writers in the 1970s aired profound doubts about the prospects for magic bullets. "It is unlikely," one wrote, "that there will be any sudden breakthrough in the near future. There will be no universal cure, no single vaccine against cancer. Certainly not in this decade. Probably not in this century. And possibly never." Another added that "so little is known about the control of cell growth that there is no way of guessing when we will arrive at the necessary understanding—it could be in the next 10 or 20 years, or not for another century."[31]

For some people his caution extended even to strategies of cancer control. Although they continued to stress the importance of some preventive measures, such as not smoking, they were more doubtful about other measures, such as early detection. For example, they estimated that at least two-thirds of cancers had already begun to metastasize by the time patients were diagnosed as having the disease. With this depressing fact in mind, they continued to question the cost-effectiveness of screening programs for breast cancer.[32] Mammography, one study later concluded, facilitated earlier detection, but it remained unclear whether the result was truly a decline in mortality from breast cancer or merely a prolongation of the interval between diagnosis and death.[33]

One thoughtful writer on cancer, John Cairns, attempted in 1978 to estimate the cost and utility of screening programs. He compared the results of a New York City program that annually screened 31,000 women, aged forty to sixty-four, for breast cancer with those for a control group of 31,000 who were not tested. After nine years there were 91 deaths from breast cancer among those tested and 128 among the controls. The cost per life "saved" (if the cost could be lowered to twenty-five dollars per test) was approximately $50,000. If screening programs were developed for each of ten forms of cancer thought to be detectable early, the total bill (for tests of twenty-five dollars on all Americans over forty-five) would be $15 billion per year. Cairns's conservative estimate of the annual cost of treating all cancer cases at the time of his study (there were 350,000 cancer deaths in 1977) was in the neighborhood of $3.5 billion.

Cairns agreed that the cost of cancer screening would be lower if tests were confined to certain high-risk groups in the population, for instance heavy smokers or women with a family history of breast cancer. But he noted that people had never shown much faith in such programs and would be unlikely to use them. Moreover, many high-risk groups were not so easy to identify, and they were numerous. "Until there is some . . . technological breakthrough," he concluded sadly, "it is hard to view screening programs as anything other than an interim measure, which could produce a slight drop in mortality and would give the impression of activity at a time when the public has been led to expect great advances."[34]

Cairns was especially pessimistic about popular reactions to prevention campaigns. Like many experts, he was persuaded that the surest ways to avoid the disease were to stop smoking and to eat more balanced diets. But millions of people refused to heed such advice. Their behavior demonstrated a constant feature of the modern social history of cancer: the durability of personal habits. Most people clung to established life styles, especially those which gave them great pleasure. With so much to enjoy in the affluent society, they were often more intent on gratifying themselves in the here and now than on worrying about the long-range costs of self-indulgent behavior. That was probably especially so among poorer people, who had less to look forward to in old age. Given the power of life styles and the pervasiveness of the consumer ethic, the possibilities for widespread citizen support of cancer prevention were distinctly limited.

Cancer's "establishment," too, came in for special criticism during the late 1970s and early 1980s. The cancer authority Michael Shimkin, while supportive of research, noted in 1983 that the research effort resembled the Strategic Air Command. "One-third of the force is always in the air, coming and going to site visits, reviews, conferences, and meetings to which the same people talk on the same subjects to the same audience." Objecting to the "profusion of centers, comprehensive, specialized, and what-have-you," he called for "longer investments in smaller laboratories, and leave them alone to reach for the brass ring." His criticism was well-taken. Other critics were harsher, perceiving the billions for cancer research as fundamentally corrupting. "All cancer-related activities," a critic complained, "ultimately become malignant themselves."[35]

As a visible part of the research network the American Cancer Society became a focus of such criticisms. Its wealth was envied; by the late 1970s the society had become a huge fund-raising operation which bore little resemblance to the medically dominated organization that Clarence Little had headed in the early 1940s. Relying on some 2.5 million volunteers (more than 1 percent of the population), the ACS raised $85 million in 1979, plus an additional $35 million from legacies. One contemporary writer considered it "possibly the most powerful and persuasive voluntary health agency in the world."[36]

Most dispassionate observers of the ACS agreed that its support of research and ts continuing educational work made it a useful friend of the NCI. Advocates of prevention admitted that it devoted considerable effort to campaigns against smoking and, by the early 1980s, for proper nutrition. But critics nonetheless were tiring of its cheerful positive thinking. The society, they thought, could not be relied on to bring fresh perspectives to the fight on cancer. "The institutional stake of the American Cancer Society," one careful scholar wrote in 1977, "appears to be in maintaining an image that 'we're-always-making-progress,' rather than in supporting a critical review of the National Cancer Program."[37]

Other critics lambasted the ACS as a power elite composed mainly of white male corporate executives, wealthy philanthropists, and conservative doctors. For this reason, they added, the society proved reluctant to confront special interests, especially large industrial and chemical companies spewing carcinogens into the environment. Samuel Epstein, a cancer researcher who focused on environmental problems, asserted that "by emphasizing individual responsibility for early detection, without providing information on environmental or occupational carcinogens other than tobacco, the American Cancer Society has implicitly created an impression that it endorses industry's 'blaming the victim' perspective." Hypercritical, Epstein concluded that the society had "exercised an essentially negative if not detrimental influence on cancer prevention."[38]

Underlying much of this disenchantment in the late 1970s were continuing popular fears that the Cancer Establishment had no good answers—that the disease remained a virtual sentence of death. Doctors and nurses, who saw more cancer than did anybody else, displayed almost as much dread as ever. Physicians called it "torture," "Buchenwald," "a death sentence," a "date of execution." Medical students were equally uneasy. "Cancer is different," one said. "It conjures up ideas of suffering . . . and sort of being like leprosy." Another added, "I think of cancer as a monolith . . . cancer is a terminal illness and cancer is a failure." A third said that "other serious illnesses are similar to a machine breaking down, whereas cancer is macabre."[39]

Though most physicians were more open than in the past, some still feared to tell patients what they knew. To do so, one physician said, was "the cruelest thing in the world." Instead, they continued to resort to euphemism and evasion. "You've got a bit of thickening there," one doctor informed a woman with breast cancer. "We'll take a bit of it out and have a look at it under the microscope, and if there are any suspicious cells there, we'll have to do a more radical procedure." Another told a lung cancer patient, "the X-rays showed that you have some inflammation on your lung. Now, this has to be treated, or it could turn nasty. So we've decided to give you some radiotherapy to get rid of it for you." A nurse defended such evasions by stressing that too many people think cancer "is a killer and that's it . . . They would just break down. Some would shut up and go into a shell. They won't speak, won't eat, and won't drink and just lose the will to live generally."[40]

It was easy to denounce physicians who concealed the whole truth from their patients, and many observers in the 1970s, reflecting the movement for patients' rights, did so. Most people, they said, wanted to be fully informed if they had cancer and were intelligent and strong enough to accept the facts; some patients angrily demanded to know everything about the course of their disease and their treatment.[41] If health care personnel were more forthright, critics said, they could help patients and their families to deal with the ailment.

It nonetheless remained true that some patients did not wish to hear the whole truth. It was also obvious that most patients and their relatives still found cancer an extraordinarily fearful experience. Upon her sister's illness the writer Jessamyn West, remembering both her grandmothers "dying screaming," pondered the "loneliness of death by cancer. The slow, certain, measured tread." When her sister's suffering grew unbearable, West gave her suicide pills. One patient on being diagnosed foresaw "horrible, lonely weeks leading up to an inexorable death." Another remembered that "the gloom of death hung over me like a poisonous cloud. The suddenness of it all still had me reeling. It was as if reality had not caught up with me." After being operated on, he awoke "convinced that they would find me riddled with cancer. My life was now completely out of my own hands. I wanted to slow time down, but the opposite seemed to be happening. I was hurtling toward the unknown."[42]

Other Americans continued to imagine that cancer was somehow "dirty" and contagious. As in the past they feared to confront their symptoms, especially when they affected sexual organs, and blamed themselves for developing a stigmatizing sickness. Healthy people, too, sometimes shunned contact with the malady. News stories asserted that a minority of interns shied away from shaking hands with cancer patients. Taxi passengers in New York were reputed to order drivers to skirt the area of Memorial Sloan-Kettering. Recovered patients returning to their jobs were sometimes asked not to use communal coffee cups. A student told her professor that she had cancer and heard him cry, "Oh, my God, Jesus Christ," whereupon he fled the room. "Cancer," she concluded, "is the modern day leprosy . . . people have the idea that if you use the same telephone you're going to get it."[43]

For some recovered patients the return to work presented a special shock. Co-workers occasionally shunned them or asked to be moved from their presence. A later poll reported that more than half of recovered cancer patients in white-collar employment, and more than 80 percent of those in blue-collar work, encountered problems on returning to the job. A few were dismissed; others were denied promotion and pay hikes; larger numbers were forced to give up group health and life insurance. A forty-two-year-old bookkeeper who had had a colostomy explained, "I received a death sentence twice: once when my doctor told me I have cancer, then when my boss asked me to quit because the cancer would upset my fellow workers. Except for my wife, that job was my whole world."[44]

All these developments of the late 1970s and early 1980s—doubts about science and medicine, pessimism about cancer and its prevention, criticisms of the Cancer Establishment, enduring popular fears and superstitions—were evidence of the cultural disarray of the period. They also resulted in a renewed flowering of unorthodox ideas about the disease. Members of the diverse cancer counterculture, having been ridiculed by the experts after World War Two, reemerged more boldly to denounce their enemies. Their activities highlighted two largely unchanging components of antiestablishment ideas: a profound ambivalence about modern industrial civilization and a demand that people be allowed to do whatever they wished—professional expertise notwithstanding—to take care of themselves.

Ambivalence about civilization assumed varied guises. A few people echoed the very old and erroneous idea that cancer scarcely existed in nonindustrial or "primitive" cultures. Anthropologists, they claimed, had found little trace of malignant diseases in Africa or other economically underdeveloped areas of the world. Their arguments revealed the continuing belief of Americans in the blessings of the countryside and the evils of the city, the factory, and the tensions of modern commercial life.[45] These critics of industrialism were part of an alternative America which had always resisted social change.[46]

A larger number of people pursued a similar theme by arguing that civilization wrenched people from their "natural" settings. Many who took this view were part of what the writer Norman Cousins called the "holistic health explosion" of the era. They distrusted many orthodox explanations of disease, and particularly the rigid distinction often made between physical and mental causes of sickness. Cancer and other ailments, they said, might stem from the lack of "natural foods" or exercise. Books such as *High Level Wellness* and *The Whole Person* and magazines such as *Organic Gardening and Farming* represented such thinking.[47] Anti-"establishment" in varied ways, the advocates of holistic medicine drew heavily on historically durable beliefs about the need to sustain a healthful balance between the body and the environment. They felt people should rely mainly on themselves, not on the intrusive intervention of high-tech, impersonal medicine.[48] They grew more vocal, if not more numerous, in the 1970s and early 1980s.

Assertive psychologists, also adapting holistic explanations, persisted in blaming "stress" for a range of human ills, including cancer. A few singled out bottle feeding and other sources of "infantile trauma" as the root of cancer. Mothers who were tense, one wrote, channeled their unease to their babies, who stored it as a "translocated gene ready to be activated in the face of additional subsequent irritation. Cancer is thus stored as a land mine implanted in the individual."[49] Other analysts reiterated arguments—so little seemed to change—to the effect that cancer patients were passive, tense, "bottled up," and emotionally deprived as a result of "bleak" and "lonely" childhoods. One study concluded that cervical cancer often hit women with a "helplessness-prone-personality." Another found that cancer victims were likely to have "experienced life as a series of alienating, depriving, depressing, and destructive episodes." A third wrote that cancer struck people who were "lonely, emotionally isolated, and who have difficulty forming deep relationships with other people."[50]

Most of these psychologically oriented writers causally connected the evils of modern civilization, the intensification of stress, and the rise of cancer mortality. A small minority were physicians and biological researchers who cited laboratory studies showing that animals under stress were especially likely to develop cancer (and many other diseases). Stress, they said, set off changes in hormonal activity which in turn damaged the body's immune defenses.[51] Other writers used epidemiological evidence of low rates of certain cancers among nuns, Mormons, and Christian Scientists—groups thought to have minimized the stresses associated with modern life.

No one was more persistent in emphasizing the role of stress than Lawrence LeShan, whose *You Can Fight for Your Life: Emotional Factors in the Causation of Cancer* (1977) became a key text in this antiestablishment movement. LeShan was a New York psychologist whose work was based on psychological tests and structured personal interviews with patients and their relatives. He concluded that emotional weaknesses promoted a "cancer personality." "Any situation that tends to disrupt the formation of strong, meaningful relationships," he wrote, "can be predicted to result in higher cancer mortality rates." He singled out as causes the "loss of sense of purpose in life," the "inability to express anger or resentment," "self-alienation," or the "inability to become aggressive in [one's] own defense."[52] As the title of his book made clear, LeShan wanted people to stand up and fight for their lives.

Other well-known proponents of this general point of view were O. Carl Simonton, a radiotherapist, and his wife Stephanie, a psychologist. They, too, believed that cancer stemmed from stress and consequent defeatism. As therapy they recommended "visualization," by which emotionally scarred cancer patients were taught to relax and to visualize healthy cells moving out to battle against the cancer cells. Sick people, having reassumed control over their emotions, could ultimately heal their bodies.[53]

By the late 1970s many other holistically oriented writers were also exploring the presumed relationships among civilization, stress, emotions, and disease, especially cancer. The literature, indeed, was so vast that the NCI commissioned a review of the subject.[54] Other writers took the subject seriously enough to try to evaluate the findings.[55] That scientists braved the thicket of this literature attested to the volume of assaults on the orthodox medical consensus.

Most of these reviewers quickly dismissed LeShan and the Simontons, but some conceded that theories about stress might be valid in a few limited respects. Many diseases, they pointed out—peptic ulcers, rheumatoid arthritis, hypertension, ulcerative colitis—seemed related to stress. Moreover, studies suggested that patients with a "fighting spirit" contended with tumors better than did those who were hopeless, and that cancer patients who received psychotherapy along with chemotherapy lived longer than those who received chemo alone. Writers like Norman Cousins and other well-known figures, including Senator Hubert Humphrey and the paleontologist Stephen Jay Gould (both cancer patients), emphasized the importance of the human spirit in contending with serious illness. When Gould asked Nobel laureate Sir Peter Medawar for the best prescription against cancer, Medawar answered, "a sanguine personality."[56]

Reviewers of the literature on stress were also intrigued by immunological research, which together with work on nutrition was the latest "cutting edge" in the field. They agreed that psychological forces might influence hormones, which could control the rate of growth of certain tumors. They thought that there might be a connection between emotions (however caused), the body's immune defenses, and the course of a number of serious ailments, including mononucleosis, flu, and genital herpes.[57]

These were the cautiously favorable responses to the psychological theories. Most orthodox scientists, however, simply ignored or dismissed stress theories. Some asserted that "quacks" like LeShan and the Simontons appealed only because they capitalized on continuing popular fears of the knife. A spokesman for Memorial Sloan-Kettering branded the Simontons' work—which to be sure was on the fringe—a "cruel hoax." An editorial in the *New England Journal of Medicine* later concluded, after studying 359 people with advanced cancer, that "belief in disease as a direct reflection of mental state is largely folklore."[58]

The writer Susan Sontag was equally devastating. She devoted much of her widely noted *Illness as Metaphor* (1977) to a refutation of the idea that cancer (from which she had recovered) sought out the emotionally depressed. The notion that there was a "forlorn, self-hating, emotionally inert creature, the contemporary cancer personality," she said, succeeded only in blaming the victim. Like other critics, she recognized that the flowering of psychological perspectives reflected the inadequacy of most medical explanations of cancer. That was one reason why the disease had long been a metaphor for the evils of society. Ailments that could not be explained inspired a spate of theories ranging from the imaginative to the bizarre.[59]

Other critics tore apart the methods of the stress theorists. They showed that interviews with patients were unreliable, that stress in patients was more likely the result than the cause of the disease, and that the long latency period of most tumors made it hard to measure the role of recognizable traumatic experiences, let alone of stress in general or of "personalities." Those who blamed emotions, critics added, tended to ignore other more probable causes (including smoking) and to offer few controls to test their data. It was true, Medawar pointed out, that some stressful people (as measured by psychological tests) developed cancer, but how many of them developed some other disease, or no disease at all?

Criticisms such as these had always characterized orthodox medical thought on the subject. The vast majority of experts recognized the formidable problems associated with testing arguments that civilization causes stress and stress causes cancer. Given the large gaps in those arguments, the experts had an easy target. The belief in the emotional causation of cancer still did not stand up well under scrutiny. But scientific debates, of course, are conducted in the context of the culture. Those who worried about the role of stress (and of civilization) had never had much faith in the experts and simply dismissed their critics. "Countless scientific studies," one wrote "Meet the Press" in 1978, "show that many cancers are a result of STRESS and other emotional problems. How long will the American Cancer Society continue to ignore this?"[60] A few years later the *New England Journal of Medicine* heard from equally vociferous adherents of the theory of stress, among them well-funded university researchers, usually in the field of psychology. Surprised, the deputy editor for the journal—who had branded such ideas "folklore"—admitted that she was "astonished by the intensity of the debate." "It's as if I had attacked motherhood and happiness."[61]

In the late 1970s holistic and psychological explanations flourished in concert with a second source of hostility to medical orthodoxy: the growing determination of many in the cancer counterculture to be rid of dictation from self-styled experts who for so long had preached the gospels of early detection, expensive medical care, and painful treatments such as surgery, radiation, and chemotherapy. Many people showed this determination by proclaiming the virtues of alternative therapies. One historian estimated in 1980 that Americans spent more than $500 million a year on unorthodox cancer remedies.[62]

Worried physicians recognized that the advocates of therapies not approved by the medical profession were applying modern techniques of organization, publicity, and self-advertising. No longer were the proponents of unorthodoxy just scattered groups under the sway of charismatic entrepreneurs; now they joined in organizations such as the International Association of Cancer Victims and Friends (1966) and the Committee for Freedom of Choice in Cancer Therapy (1972). This group, formed by John Birch Society sympathizers, furiously opposed governmental regulation. Well-funded and politically active, it claimed 500 chapters with 35,000 members in 1977.[63]

Laetrile, which had circulated underground at least since the early 1920s under the name amygdalin, became the cause célèbre of these groups in the 1970s. Derived from the pits of apricots, it could be taken orally but was usually given by injection. It did not attract widespread attention until the early 1960s, when a combination of circumstances—the closing of Hoxsey's clinic in Dallas, promotion of laetrile by an aggressive manufacturer in Canada, timely publicity in *The American Weekly*—made it better known. When California prosecuted a physician who was prescribing it, the Committee for Freedom of Choice aggressively took up his cause.[64]

For all these reasons laetrile emerged by the mid-1970s as the unorthodox cancer remedy *extraordinaire*. One contemporary opponent of the substance called it "the greatest episode of quackery in our history." So great was popular interest in the substance during its most heralded years—in 1977 and 1978—that *Newsweek* carried a cover story on it and "60 Minutes," the television series, devoted a program to it. Polls suggested that a majority of people favored legalization of laetrile in interstate commerce. It was estimated that 70,000 Americans took the substance in 1978, roughly one-fifth of the number of Americans who died of cancer in that year.[65]

Defenders of medical orthodoxy, led by agencies of the federal government, persistently harassed the producers and marketers of laetrile. They argued that it was ineffective (a clinical trial confirmed this in 1982) and that in its oral form it was dangerous.[66] At least one person died of cyanide poisoning from an overdose of laetrile pills. Opponents of laetrile added angrily that the substance was big business: a year's supply of it could cost a user thousands of dollars. These determined opponents managed to keep the situation partly under control. The Food and Drug Administration refused to make it legal in interstate commerce. Thanks to these efforts, and to the inability of laetrile enthusiasts to offer credible evidence for their claims, the uproar over the substance subsided slightly by the early 1980s.

Meanwhile, however, the advocates of laetrile managed to raise

Reprinted with permission from *Newsweek*, June 27, 1977.

some embarrassing questions. Why, they asked, did the federal government ban commerce in laetrile when it permitted cigarettes, a known killer, to be traded? And they used heart-stirring pleas of the sick to win public sympathy. Twenty-seven states legalized laetrile within their borders, and courts allowed shipment across state lines if a physician requested it for a terminally ill patient. The *New York Times* editorialized that dying people ought to have access to it–in such cases it could hardly do any harm.

The opponents of laetrile found it especially frustrating that so many Americans seemed deaf to their reasoned, scientific arguments. That deafness, however, was not confined to the laetrile problem: millions of people refused to acknowledge the dangers of smoking. One scholar lamented this fact by entitling an article on laetrile "Science and Technology in the Pits." Lewis Thomas added unhappily, "These are bad times for reason, all around. Suddenly all the major ills are being coped with by acupuncture. If not acupuncture, it is apricot pits."[67]

Because of the excitement over laetrile, scholars made an effort to find out what kinds of people favored it. They discovered that many of its most active lobbyists were right-wing ideologues opposed to all sorts of public interference. Many of these lobbyists, who were well funded and well organized, also fought governmental attempts to fluoridate water, to mandate airbags in automobiles, to require vaccinations against swine flu, and to ban saccharine or controversial food additives. Some were religious fundamentalists who called for the teaching of creationism in the schools. The demand for laetrile was part of a broader right-wing reaction against the liberal, regulatory "excesses" of the 1960s.

Users of laetrile were more diverse. Many, of course, were desperately ill people—the actor Steve McQueen was one—who thought they had exhausted all orthodox remedies for cancer. Thousands of others used the substance because they believed that it was generally good for their health. Producers of laetrile claimed that cancer was a "deficiency disease" controllable through proper nutrition; they insisted that laetrile was not a drug but a vitamin (and therefore should not be regulated).[68] Many Americans who supported this argument already belonged to a medical subculture that attributed healthful benefits to vitamins, chiropractic, and natural foods. They were likely to be female, white, and reasonably well-off. (The expense of laetrile remained considerable.)[69] Their involvement in the crusade for laetrile indicated that the inchoate cancer counterculture, while including many who were poor, still attracted people of means, many of whom regularly visited doctors. Polarities of ideology and of personal predilection cut across those of social class.

The advocates of laetrile hotly denounced the cancer "experts" who presumed to tell people how to take care of themselves. One asked, "how can critics honestly question the monetary motives of the Laetrile movement and not do the same for the American Medical Association and the American Cancer Society?"[70] Another exclaimed, "you people in authority consider all the rest of us a bunch of dummies . . . You set yourself up as God and Jesus Christ all rolled up into one. And we don't have any rights." A third complained bitterly that anyone who challenges the orthodoxies is "likely to be dishonored, denounced, and crucified, unless he is a fair-haired boy of the dominating oligarchy."[71] Complaints such as these revealed a characteristically American resistance to being told how to behave. They expressed a fundamental feeling of many in the antiestablishment culture: the desire to be free to choose what is best for oneself and to escape the centralized authority, medical and otherwise, that had accumulated throughout the twentieth century.

THE UNORTHODOXIES of the 1970s—emphasis on the effects of civilization and stress and defiant defense of remedies such as laetrile—exposed some of the ferment in the cultural world of cancer. Compared with a third development, however, these were relatively unimportant. More than any other phenomenon the burgeoning and much more broadly based environmentalist movement embodied popular disaffection from cancer orthodoxy. As the singer Joe Jackson put it in 1982,

> Everything, everything gives you cancer.
> Everything, everything gives you cancer.
> There's no cure, there's no answer.
> Everything gives you cancer.[72]

Concern about the environment was hardly new to the 1970s. Throughout world history writers had urged moderation and emphasized the sense of well-being which results from living in harmony with nature. Americans had always idealized the countryside and been ambivalent about industrialization and the city.[73] Sanitarians and public-health officials had effectively demonstrated the environmental aspects of infectious diseases, and scientists had long recognized that chemical carcinogens threatened the workplace.

Articulate environmentalists in the 1960s and 1970s reiterated these ideas while drawing additional power from two newer forces. One was the unprecedented and seemingly unending prosperity of the 1960s. Affluence excited already extravagant expectations for good health and long life, but these hopes were threatened by oil spills on the shoreline, the dumping of toxic wastes, pollutants in the atmosphere, and—perhaps the most lasting and widespread environmental danger of all—pesticides that contaminated not only wildlife but also the water and food that people consumed. Pollution offended aesthetic as well as hygienic sensibilities, especially of people in the more affluent middle and upper classes. Environmentalists of earlier years had been much concerned with conservation—with preventing waste and enhancing national resources; in the 1960s and 1970s they were more eager to preserve the environment from rapid change and to promote the public health.

The second force fueling the environmentalist movement was the growing feeling that industrial growth was dangerous in itself. This belief drew heavily on the eloquent arguments of Rachel Carson, whose *Silent Spring* (1962) was the key document of the new environmentalism. Focusing on the dangers from chemical pesticides such as DDT, Carson presented a coherent ecological view of the world. Nature, she argued, was mostly benign, a wonderfully cooperative ecosystem. Its vitally important balance could be preserved—and the public health safeguarded—only if its interdependent pieces were protected from the potentially devastating ravages of man-made change.

This view had deep historical roots, but it resurfaced with special resonance during the late 1960s and early 1970s.[74] Ecologists needed only to underscore the headlines of the day: use of Agent Orange in Vietnam, automobile fumes, acid rain, pesticides. Deeply disturbing news stories appeared about "cancer cities" and "cancer clusters" afflicted by mysterious carcinogens.[75] Cancer, it seemed, was everywhere in the neighborhood, a silent, noxious force that one could almost see and smell and taste.[76] Later events, such as the accident at Three Mile Island nuclear power plant in Pennsylvania and discovery of toxic chemicals dumped in the Love Canal, further awakened the public sense that environmental pollution could lead to terminal disease.

The figurative relevance of these events to cancer was obvious. Cancer, after all, was a kind of uncontrolled, runaway growth. In this sense cancer was an apt metaphor, as well as harsh evidence for everything that the environmentalists dreaded. Unless the "metastasis" of economic growth could be controlled and the ecosystem preserved, cancer might stalk the world in an epidemic of awesome destructiveness. As Hueper put it, "through a continued, unrestrained, needless, avoidable and, in part, reckless increasing human contamination of the human environment with chemical and physical carcinogens . . . the stage is being set for a future occurrence of an acute, catastrophic epidemic."[77]

Hueper's vision greatly influenced Carson, who devoted a chapter of *Silent Spring* to the carcinogenic effects of pesticides, herbicides, and other substances. Its title, "One in Every Four," made it abundantly clear that cancer was a growing menace to human life. The world, Carson said, was a "sea of carcinogens" that would cause cancer in 45 million living Americans (in two-thirds of all families). Some carcinogens, she said, were natural, such as ultraviolet radiation from the sun or arsenic washed out of the soil into food and water supplies. The majority, however, were man-made, some of which damaged germ cells and thus harmed future generations. Though Carson did not call for the abolition of all pesticides, she singled out "five, or possibly six" as definitely carcinogenic in human beings, and she emphasized that there was no such thing as a "safe" dose of a carcinogen.[78]

Drawing explicitly on Hueper's work, Carson likened the contemporary scene to the 1880s and 1890s. At that time, she pointed out, Americans lived in a sea of microorganisms, "just as today's carcinogens pervade our surroundings." The danger from such organisms, she reminded readers, had abated only in part because of the discovery of "magic bullets" and "wonder drugs." More important, she said, had been "measures to eliminate disease organisms from the environment." It followed that the control of cancer, too, would never come from a "magic pill that we shall take each morning before breakfast." On the contrary, people must "identify the environmental causes and eliminate them or reduce their impact." She concluded: "For those in whom cancer is already a hidden or a visible presence, efforts to find cures must of course continue. But for those not yet touched by the disease and certainly for the generations as yet unborn, prevention is the imperative need."[79]

Carson's vision later gripped many people attracted to the causes of environmentalism and cancer prevention. Sure that cancer was a man-made scourge—and therefore preventable—activists politicized the issue. Samuel Epstein blamed industrial pollution for 30 to 40 percent of cancers.[80] Larry Agran, who published a popular book on cancer in 1977, foresaw a "cancer pox" and the "unmistakeable emergence of a national cancer epidemic" which would ultimately kill three of every four Americans.[81] Jane Brody, a science writer for the *New York Times,* explained in the same year that

> the average person in modern societies lives in a veritable sea of carcinogens. The air we breathe, the food we eat, the drugs we take, the water we drink, the clothing we wear, all may contain substances that have been shown to cause cancer in animals or man. We are exposed to carcinogens through the habits we develop and the jobs we hold. Even the natural radiation from sky and earth, as well as the ultraviolet rays of life-giving sunlight, probably contribute to the human burden of cancer.[82]

Except for Hueper and Carson, most leading environmentalist writers published their major works between 1975 and 1980. During these years the media gave dramatic and scary coverage to their concerns. A CBS documentary in 1975, "The American Way of Death," focused on the role of man-made chemical carcinogens and emphasized (incorrectly) that the United States was the most cancer-prone nation in the world. CBS followed in 1976 with a special report, "The Politics of Cancer," denouncing the chemical industry. A *Newsweek* cover story in 1976 also focused on man-made causes of cancer. Citing Epstein, it worried about a "major epidemic" and concluded, "few disagree that the environment and what man has done to it loom increasingly as the major source of the second greatest killer . . . in the nation."[83]

The environmentalists drew upon a variety of sources, including studies, some of them decades old, demonstrating the carcinogenic character of aniline dyes, coal tars, asbestos, solar radiation, and fallout from atomic explosions.[84] Drawing on the relevant research of molecular biologists, they attempted to go beyond talk of "irritation" and to explain the processes by which carcinogens worked. They argued that many chemical carcinogens (and radiations) damaged DNA and that some also acted as mutagens, causing developmental errors that appeared as birth defects.[85] It was therefore vitally important to identify the more potent mutagens in the environment so that they could be controlled or eradicated.

Other ecologists cited frightening data about pesticides, nitrites used to preserve foods, birth-control pills, and estrogen replacement therapy for menopausal women. Especially alarming were reports of the carcinogenic effect of DES (diethylstilbestrol), a synthetic estrogen that caused cancer among mice yet was nonetheless widely used for beef and poultry.[86] Prescribed, uselessly, to prevent women from miscarrying, it led to vaginal cancer among some of their daughters. It was banned in 1976.

Equally useful to environmentalists were data developed from the much accelerated testing of industrial chemicals and products in the 1970s. A review of these tests in 1978 concluded that 26 of 420 suspected carcinogens thus far tested were associated with cancer in human beings, including benzene, benzidine, mustard gas, vinyl chloride, nickel, arsenic, and shale oil.[87] All were shown to be carcinogenic either in epidemiological studies of human beings or in laboratory tests on animals. Other studies suggested that a much larger number of substances—700 to 800 tested so far—offered "reasonably solid evidence of carcinogenicity" in animals.[88]

The environmentalists relied especially on epidemiological studies of cancers in other countries and of migrants to the United States. These works showed significant international variation in the incidence of cancer at different sites in the body. Researchers compared the lowest national incidence for each site with the incidence for that site in the United States and assumed that the differences were attributable to the environment. They concluded that at least 80 percent of cancers in America were associated with environmental forces, defined broadly to include not only chemical carcinogens but also personal habits, such as drinking and smoking, and diet. All the environmentalist writers—and popular media—highlighted this striking percentage. By 1979 it was conventional wisdom that environmental factors were a major cause of cancer.[89]

In helping to conduct such studies the government necessarily became involved in the environmental cause. Legislation, notably the Occupational Safety and Health Act of 1970 and the Toxic Substances Control Act of 1976, empowered the Environmental Protection Agency (EPA), formed in 1969, and other bureaucracies to conduct tests and to regulate the use and production of chemicals.[90] Slow to move in the early 1970s, these agencies grew more aggressive during the presidency of Jimmy Carter. The EPA decided in 1977 that "any evidence of tumorigenic activity in animals is a signal that an agent is a potential human carcinogen." It added that there was no such thing as a measurably "safe level of exposure" to carcinogens.[91] Meanwhile, the Food and Drug Administration became more active in enforcing the Delaney amendment of 1958, which had called for bans on food additives known to cause cancer in animals or human beings.

HEW Secretary Joseph Califano circulated a widely discussed draft document in 1978 on occupational cancer. Based in part on the work of respected NCI researchers, it named substances "related to" cancer in the workplace, singling out asbestos, which it said would kill some two million workers already exposed within the next three decades. Cancer deaths from occupational sources, the draft document estimated, could account for 23 to 38 percent of total mortality from cancer in ensuing decades. Though unpublished—a sign of its scientifically questionable assertions—it was used as evidence by some environmentalist writers. No government document of the 1970s more assertively highlighted the occupational dangers from cancer.[92]

Federal efforts in this area, however, fell far short of satisfying the leading environmentalists. Agran and Epstein, as major critics, lamented the slow pace of federal activity and the meager public resources available for environmental action. The Occupational Safety and Health Agency, Agran complained in 1977, was "little more than a ragtag bureaucracy" of less than 1,500 health and safety officers. He estimated that the agency needed at least $1 billion per year (as opposed to the $100 million it received) to carry out its job.[93]

Like others, Agran also thought the agency, though housed within the Labor Department, was far too sympathetic to the needs of management. Slighting the serious limitations of measurement technology, these critics complained that OSHA refused to set exposure for known human carcinogens at the zero level—a refusal that they said endorsed the idea of "safe" levels of exposure. The agency waited until 1974 to move gingerly against asbestos manufacturers, acting only after being petitioned to do so by the AFL-CIO, but even then its regulations affected only a few workers and had little effect.[94]

The environmentalists aimed equally sharp criticism at what they saw as the upper-class Cancer Establishment, including the NCI, the ACS, and large grant receivers such as Memorial Sloan-Kettering. All these groups, the environmentalists said, had dragged their feet for years on cancer control, especially when it threatened major petrochemical corporations. These critics differed only in their explanations for the delay. Some said the alliance against cancer was complacent, while others, citing the presence of corporate leaders on the ACS board, charged that it had deliberately shielded a gang of irresponsible polluters.[95] The critics singled out the NCI for special condemnation. Having muzzled Hueper until he retired in 1964, they said, it continued to slight environmental concerns during the 1960s and early 1970s. In 1976 the institute's chief of chemical testing resigned, complaining bitterly that he had been given insufficient resources.[96] NCI leaders countered that it was doing all it could given the dearth of scientific talent in the area. It also reminded critics that it had no regulatory powers in any event.

Environmentalists nonetheless intensified their complaints about the NCI, charging it with failing to sound the alarm against industries pouring thousands of untested, unmonitored chemicals into the environment every month.[97] They complained that the institute had only slowly changed its internal budgetary priorities. Epstein estimated in 1978 that the NCI, with a budget of around $900 million, allocated only around 12 percent of it (virological work

From *Herblock on All Fronts* (New American Library, 1980).
Reprinted with permission from Herblock Cartoons.

excluded) to environmental research—at a time when many people were asserting that 80 percent or more of cancers in the United States stemmed at least in part from environmental causes.[98]

Fueling the frustration of Epstein and other environmentalist crusaders was the certitude that most cancers were preventable. To this extent they agreed with the antitobacco activists and those who were concentrating on the effects of diet. For all their sometimes apocalyptic warnings, these preventionists were optimistic. They were sure that cancer was not so mysterious after all, that it could be blamed in part on an identifiable number of man-made carcinogens and on personal habits. Much of it could be prevented if the government would act and people would only listen.

But the enemies of smoking had developed their positions with care and with considerable epidemiological evidence. To a lesser extent, so had the proponents of better nutrition. A number of these advocates had become allies of established biological researchers, some of whom estimated cautiously that as much as two-thirds of cancer mortality could be prevented if people would stop smoking and eat different foods. The more outspoken environmentalists, by contrast, had taken their cues from rebels like Hueper. They attacked not only corporate America but also the ACS and the NCI. Like those who saw stress as a cause of cancer and laetrile as a cure, with whom they otherwise had little in common, they resented the cancer alliance. The attention these critics received, and the unprecedented consternation they aroused among the public, articulated and deepened the cultural disarray of post-Vietnam, post-Watergate America.

READING the anguished cries of the environmentalists, one skeptical observer in 1978 commented that "some people are likely to end up feeling that cancer is everywhere, that society is doing nothing but poisoning the environment, that it is not safe to trust anything or anybody, and that the products of technology are poison and disease."[99] Similar skepticism led the NCI to put out its pamphlet, "Everything Doesn't Cause Cancer" in 1979. These were signs that many people were having second thoughts about the environmentalist world view, which began to weaken.

Part of the reaction against environmentalist arguments was the still lingering belief that cancer was a mysterious, indiscriminate, and relentless killer which no one, including government regulators, could really do very much about. Some of the people who felt this way were political conservatives who resented what one called the "environmental Windmill-tilting" of the liberals; after all, "we all must die from something."[100] In the early 1980s, at the peak of reactions against liberal crusades, these feelings were widespread, but not restricted to political conservatives. Environmentalists, many others seemed to agree, were as tiresome and puritanical as the various regulatory "experts" who presumed to indoctrinate the public.

Doubters also emphasized that cancer, like other diseases, was complex, caused neither by environmental nor genetic forces alone. Environmental carcinogens, they added, most likely afflicted people who were genetically predisposed to cancer. Those without that predisposition—the majority of smokers, for example—did not develop the disease. It followed, these writers concluded, that environmentalist views of cancer needed careful, thoughtful presentation and understanding, not sensationalist reporting that oversimplified the etiology of disease.[101]

Meanwhile, others raised doubts about the scientific evidence for the environmentalist case. Until researchers could learn more about the nature of cellular transformation, they said, it would be impossible to prove that cancer was abetted, let alone caused, primarily by man-made carcinogens. Edith Efron, whose book *The Apocalyptics: Cancer and the Big Lie* (1984) was easily the most withering assault on the environmentalist world view, scorned what she called the "one molecule theory" which linked the minutest concentration of a chemical in the human cell to the spread of cancer. Lewis Thomas said bluntly, "the plain fact of the matter is that we do not know enough about the facts of the matter, and we should be more open about our ignorance."[102]

Efron accused some environmentalists of oversimplification in implying that all external carcinogens were man-made. On the contrary, she pointed out, many cancer-causing agents—solar radiation was the best example—were natural to the world. "Carcinogens," she said, "are not just single entities; they are aspects of the earth, they are preconditions for birth, reproduction, and survival, they are augurs of life and death, they are an attribute of existence itself." She concluded that many environmentalists were either anticorporate zealots or romantics who set forth the tired, one-sided view that "natural" is good. The circumstances of cancer were much more complex.[103]

Critics of environmentalism (Efron included) granted that scientists had identified some dangerous chemical and physical carcinogens afflicting human beings and agreed that the leading killers, tobacco and asbestos, must be controlled. Most writers also continued to worry about chemical pesticides, use of which in the United States expanded from 200 million pounds per year in the 1950s to 1.1 billion pounds per year by the mid-1980s. Many of these pesticides were highly toxic and water soluble, thereby capable of contaminating the groundwater, plants, and food. Even DDT, though banned, still lingered in the environment.[104]

But the doubters wondered about many other substances which were said to have a "probable" or "substantial"—what, really, was that?—potential for causing cancers in human beings. They stressed that not all substances that provoked cancers in often heavily dosed laboratory animals necessarily caused them in human beings as well. Most cancers, they insisted, developed only slowly in human beings. To assert that man-made chemicals were major sources of cancer was to leap to premature conclusions.[105] Scientific evidence, they added, was not solid enough to justify the heavy hand of federal regulation.

Some writers asked environmentalists to count the costs of regulation and purification. Suppose it were true, they said, that a hundred man-made substances could be proved to provoke cancers among human beings. What would it cost to ban them? Their answer was that the bill might be so astronomical as to be politically unacceptable. Medawar noted thoughtfully that there were some technological developments, such as the automobile, which were known to kill hundreds of thousands of people but which no one would dare to banish. He used this example to demonstrate the often conflicting values of public health and technological advance.[106]

In the same vein another writer reminded his readers that "safety was a luxury good" which only the upper-middle classes (the heart of the environmentalist movement) in very affluent societies would think of paying for. For the Occupational Safety and Health Agency to take a rigid stand against carcinogen-spewing coke ovens would cost about $1 million for each life saved. By contrast, mandatory use of automobile seat belts—which many states were unwilling to impose—would have cost almost nothing while preventing perhaps 20,000 deaths a year. His most powerful example, of course, was smoking. "A country," he wrote, "which accepts 200,000 deaths a year from smoking . . . will not—and to be consistent should not—go further and pursue environmental contaminants to extremes."[107]

Other critics convincingly refuted the claim that between 23 and 38 percent of forthcoming cancer mortality would come from carcinogens in the workplace. These percentages, they showed, were based on the assumption that all workers in the industries covered, irrespective of the length of time that they had been employed or the degree of their exposure to harmful substances, had the same risk of getting cancer as did the relatively small number of workers who had been heavily exposed for many years. This sort of statistical overkill, critics said, was common among environmentalist zealots.

Many of these critics correctly stressed the relationship between cancer and mortality and social class. A number of tumors attributed to occupation, they said, could be explained by habits of diet, smoking, or personal hygiene. Mortality from most cancers, they added, was higher among poor people than among the upper-middle classes, in part because poor people were generally less healthy, in part because they were more likely to have unhealthful habits (such as smoking), in part because they had a relatively low awareness of symptoms, and in part because they could not afford to go to doctors for help.[108] Similar social differences, experts added, accounted for some of the differences in cancer mortality by city, state, or region on which epidemiological studies that supported environmentalist arguments had relied.[109]

The most careful critics of apocalyptic environmentalism, Doll and Peto, concluded in 1981 that "we do not, ourselves, consider particularly reliable any explicit numerical estimates of the proportion of cancers currently ascribable to occupation." They went on to say that the number of American cancer deaths traceable mainly to the workplace was probably around 17,000 a year, of which 11,000 or so were caused by lung cancers partly due to smoking. Deploring such numbers, they called for more effective safeguards. But they concluded that the environmentalist crusaders against occupational cancer had exaggerated grossly. Cancer deaths from such causes amounted to less than 4 percent of total mortality from the disease.[110]

Epidemiologists also found fault with other statistics employed by the environmentalists. Some tumors in industrialized nations such as the United States were just as common in mostly rural countries such as New Zealand, Iceland, and Finland. Furthermore, age-adjusted mortality rates from many common cancers in America (tobacco-induced lung cancers excepted) were no greater in the 1970s than they had been fifty years earlier—before the rapid growth of the petrochemical industries. While it was true that the use of some controversial substances—notably pesticides—had greatly expanded only since 1950 and might yet prove to be important causes of cancer among human beings, most experts doubted that would happen. "Most of the types of cancer that are common today in the United States," Doll and Peto concluded, "must be due mainly to factors that have been present for a long time."[111]

These critiques, though effective, did not demolish all the arguments of environmentalists, let alone popular fears about environmental causes of cancer, which remained intense. Doll and Peto, among other critics, agreed that man-made chemical carcinogens posed a problem too serious too be ignored, that many industrialists unconscionably obscured the dangers, and that until more was known about controversial chemicals it would ordinarily be prudent to opt for strict regulation. The NCI's pamphlet, "Everything Doesn't Cause Cancer," also urged prudence. "There is no adequate evidence," it noted, "for the existence of a safe threshold for any carcinogen . . . Human cancers have occasionally followed very low exposures." The NCI added that about thirty substances were carcinogenic in human beings and that "several hundred" more provoked cancer in animals. "We must heed the warnings provided by laboratory animal experiments and reduce or eliminate human exposure to probable cancer-causing agents."[112] This response from the NCI, the heart of the anticancer alliance, showed that environmentalist arguments could not be ignored. Henceforth the dangers from pesticides, food additives, pollution, and workplace exposures were to be taken more seriously.

Still, it became clear by the mid-1980s that the more sweeping environmentalist views of cancer attracted less top-level official attention than they had in the late 1970s. Though continuing to arouse popular fears—stories about "cancer clusters" regularly awakened alarm—these forms of environmentalism lost force among most leading experts, who accepted the powerful evidence about tobacco and grew more seriously concerned about diets but rejected sensational findings about cancer-causing chemicals. The decline of apocalyptic versions of environmentalism owed something to the politically conservative mood of the 1980s, but much also to the trenchant criticisms they received. Like many explanations of cancer, some of the environmental claims suffered from exaggeration, oversimplification, and gaps in scientific understanding.

In historical perspective the environmentalist crusades that peaked in the late 1970s were interesting as much for what they revealed about American culture as for what they explained—or did not explain—about cancer. Many advocates of environmentalist explanations, while disagreeing with alarmists who singled out the "stress" of modern civilization, shared with them a profound unease about technology, industrialization, and urbanization. Articulate and numerous, they intensified the deep-rooted cancerphobia that was if anything more pronounced than ever. They were in fact a major source of the diffuse yet unprecedentedly vocal antiestablishment rebellion, one in which otherwise very different groups, such as defenders of laetrile, participated at the same time.

These opponents of the Cancer Establishment, while impossible to count, were surely a minority even at their peak of agitation. They disagreed, often sharply, in their political views; they came from a wide range of social backgrounds; they never formed a cohesive or self-conscious coalition. But they were numerous, and they were united in their skepticism about many once unquestioned

American values and institutions. More than ever before they appealed to a wide audience of people, including many in the middle classes, who shared related doubts: about progress, growth, expertise, professional direction, the claims of physicians and researchers, the medicalization of society. The experts be damned, they said, everything *did* cause cancer.

Such popular doubts led people to varied conclusions. Some followed Carson and demanded greater attention to preventive measures, while others grew despairing—if cancer was everywhere, what was the point of throwing money at the NCI? Both points of view spread in the 1970s and endowed the heterogeneous cancer counterculture with greater visibility than at any time since Grant's illness became public knowledge a hundred years earlier. It remained to be seen how well the nation's medical institutions could summon again the vitality and the cultural authority that they had displayed throughout much of the twentieth century.

11

More Promises, More Fears

IN DECEMBER 1985 the National Cancer Institute announced a new treatment, adoptive immunotherapy, that was producing dramatic results. The therapy involved removing white blood cells from patients and then culturing them with interleukin-2, an immune system activator. When returned to the bloodstream, the new "killer cells" attacked the cancer. Tumors in 11 of 25 seriously ill patients, the NCI said, decreased in size by 50 percent or more after the treatments. NCI Director Dr. Vincent DeVita, Jr., exclaimed that it was the "most interesting and exciting biological therapy we've seen so far."[1]

As usual in the modern history of the disease the popular media gave enthusiastic coverage to these promising claims. *Fortune* called the news a "Cancer Breakthrough," and *Newsweek* highlighted a cover story, "The Search for a Cure." NBC and ABC evening news led off with reports on the discovery. Cancer patients besieged hospitals and cancer centers with pleas for help. The NCI Hotline received 2,000 calls within two days and temporarily had to discontinue the service. Some people offered large sums of money to be guinea pigs. "What the callers are saying," an NCI spokesman explained, "is, 'Our mother, our brother, our sister is dying at this very moment. We have nothing to lose. We want to be a candidate.'"[2]

Had these callers carefully read the full story, they might not have been so hopeful. Underneath the optimistic lead paragraphs were some sobering facts: the results, stemming from only eight months' experience with the therapy, were preliminary; the treatment required costly, extensive hospitalization; the method had unpleasant and dangerous side effects, such as significant retention of fluids, anemia, chills, fever, digestive upsets, jaundice, confusion, and problems in breathing. Anemia, diarrhea, or fever afflicted 18 of the 25 subjects.

Three days later the researchers disclosed that one patient treated with the new method had died. The head of the research team, Dr. Steven Rosenberg, who earlier in 1985 had helped to remove cancer from President Reagan's colon, explained that the dead patient had not been one of the 25 described in their report, but he admitted that he could not be sure if the patient had died because of the treatment or because of the advanced form of the cancer. "It's a complicated medical situation," he emphasized, "because you start with a lot of toxicity due to cancer and it's pretty hard to distinguish what is due to treatment and what is due to the cancer."[3]

THE FUROR generated by the NCI's announcement was yet another example of official optimism about the imminent discovery of a cure. Immunotherapy, moreover, had excited researchers since the late 1970s, when the ACS announced a $2 million grant for work on interferon, which was thought to have antiviral and antitumor properties. But the media coverage of interleukin-2 in late 1985 was remarkably prominent and the popular excitement perhaps greater than usual. The episode repeated with special clarity a very old pattern: implied claims for a cure, exaggerated coverage in the media, desperate hope among fearful people, cruel disappointment when the predictions proved to be premature. The more things changed, the more they seemed to stay the same.

Or had they stayed the same? Compared with the culturally unsettled years of the late 1970s, they had changed slightly. By the mid-1980s the cancer counterculture had lost a little ground. The holists and psychologists, though still attracting a popular following, had failed to convince most experts; laetrile had cured no one; the environmentalists, while continuing to arouse great public apprehension, commanded slightly less official attention. To many Americans the cultural malaise associated with Vietnam, Watergate, and stagflation had receded into history. Until late 1986 a self-assured Ronald Reagan exuded confidence in American institutions, including the profession of medicine, and he publicly placed himself in the care of specialists when he became ill.

For all these reasons the anticancer alliance recovered much of its self-assurance. The cancer society continued to flourish, enlisting more than two million volunteers and raising well over $200 million a year.[4] The National Cancer Institute, while less of a political power than it had been during the early 1970s, remained the biggest and best-funded institute at the NIH. In 1986 it supported 2,100 full-time employees and oversaw a budget of almost $1.3 billion a year, more than half of the roughly $2.2 billion spent nationally on cancer research. Though NCI funding did not satisfy the thousands of scientists clamoring for support—the field was more competitive than ever—it was generous by contrast to other areas of federally supported health research. Total federal funding in 1985 for the heart institute was $850 million; for research into problems of drug abuse and alcohol it was $130 million; for AIDS research (in 1986) it was $244 million.[5] About half of the NCI's funding went to cancer centers and to university researchers and technicians, and $200 million to in-house scientists; as in the past, much smaller sums financed preventive efforts.[6] Seeking more centralized control, the NCI developed PDQ (Physician's Data Query), a computerized data base on clinical trials. In 1986 the PDQ listed 1,000 institutions accepting patients for new and highly experimental forms of treatment.[7]

Reflecting this recovered sense of security, the official allies against cancer reasserted their positive thinking. "The next few decades," the cancer society said in 1984, "will probably see continued advances in the prevention and earlier detection of cancer . . . until most, if not all, cancers are either highly preventable or curable." Lewis Thomas added in 1986, "we're beginning to understand what a cancer cell is and how it works. These are things we didn't know when we declared our ambitious war on cancer . . . We're in a new world."[8]

The messengers of hope in the ACS and the NCI, though disputed by objective experts, reiterated optimistically that five-year survival rates were continuing to improve, rising to almost one of two patients by 1985.[9] The NCI claimed further that America could cut its age-adjusted mortality from the disease in half by the year

2000.[10] *Newsweek* observed that cancer was perhaps the "first and only 'chronic' disease that IS curable." It quoted Dr. Samuel Hellman, physician-in-chief at Memorial Sloan-Kettering, who asked, "Did you ever hear of anybody being cured of cardiovascular disease?"[11]

The allies against cancer were particularly pleased by the management of President Reagan's illness in the summer of 1985. When his malignancy was detected, neither the president nor his doctors seriously attempted to hide the diagnosis. What a contrast, experts said, to the euphemisms offered to Grant, to the furtive behavior of Cleveland, or to the secrecy surrounding the deaths of Ruth and Taft! Surgeons described the operation in clinical detail for the mass media. For the allies against cancer the case was a high point in their long campaign for early detection, surgery, and public discussion of the disease. Their campaign against the conspiracy of silence, they were sure, had curbed cancerphobia.

The cancer alliance in the mid-1980s concentrated on three main lines of attack on the malady. First, the allies highlighted accumulating (though still incomplete) epidemiological evidence about the role that improved nutrition could play in preventing tumors, especially of the colon. Better diets, many experts continued to think, could cut cancer mortality by as much as 35 percent. As of 1984 the ACS and NCI began actively to promote this view, urging people to reduce their intake of fats, smoked and salt-cured foods, and alcohol and to increase their consumption of fibers, cruciferous vegetables, and foods rich in vitamins A and C.[12]

The second line of attack relied on findings from virological research, on which the NCI spent some $135 million in 1985. After almost a century of disappointments this work seemed at last to be bearing some fruit. Linking at least four viruses to cancer in human beings, researchers managed to identify a virus that was associated with a rare form of human leukemia. Papilloma viruses—the same that more commonly caused genital warts—seemed when sexually transmitted to be associated with cervical cancer.[13]

The third and most exciting avenue of attack was the investigation of "oncogenes," or cancer-causing genes. Molecular biologists said that oncogenes appear to be activated after intricate and often slowly developing biological processes initiated by other genes, viruses, or exogenous and endogenous carcinogens. The oncogenes then excite cellular behavior, which is normally regulated, thereby producing uncontrolled growth. If scientists could figure out ways to "switch off" these oncogenes, they would be at what the ACS called the "threshold of a kind of 'golden age' of medicine."[14]

Researchers in the mid-1980s placed special long-range hopes on the therapeutic potential of biological response modifiers, or "biologicals"—bodily substances such as interleukin, interferon, and monoclonal antibodies that "honed in" on foreign cells and marked them as targets for other cells from the immune system. Generally much less toxic than chemotherapies, biological modifiers could be produced in large quantities through genetic engineering, which an aggressive biotechnology industry promoted excitedly in the mid-1980s. Some optimists in 1985 anticipated that the biologicals (together with vaccines and other improvements in therapy) could cut cancer mortality by as much as 25 percent in the year 2000.[15]

The advocates of prevention also grew more aggressive in the 1980s. Drawing on the consensus of epidemiologists, they estimated that the powerful evidence about cigarettes, together with softer data about nutrition, explained as much as two-thirds of cancer mortality. They urged people to change a number of habits associated with cancer, not only smoking and fat-filled diets but also excessive drinking, promiscuous sex, and prolonged exposure to radiation from the sun.[16] The conservative Reagan administration, advocates of prevention added, should do more to clean up the environment and to regulate and tax the producers of known carcinogens, such as asbestos and tobacco. (In 1986 the Defense Department first refused to discontinue generous discounts on purchases of cigarettes by military personnel, but then forbade Army personnel to use tobacco save in specially designated areas.)[17] Society, preventionists added, should devote greater resources to screening of high-risk people. Mammograms every one to three years for all women over fifty, John Cairns said, could cut deaths from breast cancer (38,400 in 1985) by as much as a fourth.[18]

Though the advocates of prevention were more vocal in the 1980s than earlier, and though they had important and concrete answers to offer, they still failed to get the priority in federal funding that they thought they deserved. Moreover, they continued to encounter popular resistance. Many Americans quit smoking, but millions of others ignored their advice. Some preventive steps required people to battle against addictions. Others necessitated giving up some of the pleasures of the consumer culture. And still others cost money: mammograms, for instance, called for outlays of between $100 and $250, which helped to explain why 80 percent of American women older than forty did not have the recommended exams in 1986. For these and other reasons Congress and the NCI continued to emphasize funding for laboratory research. The hope for cure without disruption of life styles was yet another of the many unchanging features of America's twentieth-century experience with cancer.

JUST AS UNCHANGING was the most culturally revealing feature of the modern history of cancer in America: stubborn popular skepticism about the pretensions of physicians in general and the Cancer Establishment in particular. This skepticism, not to say resentment, had long affected substantial minorities of poorer, less educated people, as well as believers in self-help or unorthodox approaches to disease. It reflected the endurance of traditional beliefs and behavior—of powerful subcultural continuities—in the face of otherwise rapid social change. By the 1980s it had also spread to many Americans—how many it is impossible to say—in the middle classes. This widening skepticism was a major legacy of the reaction during the 1970s against exaggerated claims for science and technological medicine.

Some people, having great expectations about the possibilities of the good life, were more than skeptical—they were angry. Scientists, they agreed, had gained greater control over the physical world, and doctors could do much more for some cancers, especially leukemias affecting children, than they could a few decades earlier. But human nature, alas, had not seemed to change. From the hucksterism of the Gilded Age to the claims for interleukin-2 and the commercialization of genetic engineering a hundred years later, some experts promised more than they could deliver, leaving patients and their families emotionally drained and destitute.

Cancer patients and their families also grew angry at the ever escalating costs of treatment. In 1986 some 37 million Americans, one in six, had no health insurance, and millions more had only limited coverage against the high costs of cancer therapy. One careful study calculated that total medical costs of cancer approximated $13 billion in 1980 (plus some $37 billion in lost wages). It further estimated that treatment of cancer absorbed about one-ninth of total health expenditures in the United States (third behind heart diseases and accidents) and that payments from insurance companies and government agencies covered only two-thirds of these expenditures. Average first-year costs for treatment of lung cancer, experts said, came to around $4,380 in 1980, for breast cancer around $5,800. The cost of treatment for terminal cancer patients in their last year of life then averaged $15,000. It was no wonder that the cancer survival rate of people below the poverty line was 10 to 15 percent lower than the average rate for all cancer patients, or that many Americans deeply resented the Cancer Establishment.[19]

Though some of these angry Americans were quacks and ideological zealots, many were temperate, once hopeful people who sensed that government-supported cancer research had been oversold and that the much-trumpeted war against cancer had failed. Given the historically persistent gap between the highly publicized promises of some of the allies against cancer and the often discouraging reality of cancer medicine, their impatience, if often extreme, was understandable.

In challenging the optimists disillusioned Americans did not need to look very far for evidence. Despite efforts at prevention, the incidence of cancer appeared to be increasing steadily—by around 1 percent per year—in the 1970s and early 1980s.[20] Cancer also continued to kill more people each year. The ACS estimated that some 462,000 Americans, more than ever before, died of various forms of the disease in 1985.[21] That was one death every 68 seconds. Another 910,000 people in 1985 were newly diagnosed (plus 400,000 cases, like Reagan and Richard Nixon, of nonserious forms of skin cancer). Students of the problem estimated that more than 5 million Americans suffered from the disease in 1985, that 66 million Americans then living—almost a third of the population—would eventually develop the illness, and that more than one-fifth would die of it.[22] Other experts observed gloomily that cancer was the only major disease for which age-adjusted mortality was still increasing.[23] By the year 2000, a few authorities prophesied, the many forms of cancer would surpass heart diseases (which were coming under better control) to become the leading cause of death in the United States.[24]

Epidemiologists reminded people that the aging of the population continued to account for some of these trends. Age-adjusted mortality from all forms of cancer, they reiterated, was still rising only slowly—at the rate of about 0.5 percent per year.[25] Without lung cancer, which stemmed mainly from smoking, age-adjusted cancer mortality was decreasing at a rate of slightly less than 1 percent per year.[26] But these demographic reminders continued to be small consolation to the millions of Americans who had watched loved ones perish from cancer, to the growing numbers of elderly people who were most susceptible to the disease, or to the many others whose family histories or personal habits stamped them as high risks.

Optimistic statements about improved survival rates, moreover, were highly questionable: most objective observers emphasized that historical statistics on survival rates rested on changing standards of diagnosis and reporting and were therefore unreliable. Five-year survival-rates for most major forms of cancer, they said, had changed little, if at all, since the 1950s—closer to one in three than to one in two.[27] And many of the survivors remained ill or could expect to develop other malignancies later in their lives. Some died of other diseases that became fatal following complications hastened by cancer.[28] Objective observers noted also that one unchanging area of uncertainty was the inability of physicians to know when most cancer patients were cured, or whether to continue painful, toxic therapies. Confronted with these realities, Americans could be excused for doubting the positive thinking of the allies and for continuing to dread the disease.

People could also be excused for continuing to wonder about the claims for basic scientific understanding of cancer. As many writers pointed out, cancer was probably not a single ailment but 200 or so different illnesses, many of them rare and each with its distinctive origins and development. Knowledge of cancers, they added, remained mainly empirical. Despite the gains in scientific understanding of oncogenes and genetic engineering, researchers still had much to learn about the multiplication and territorial restraints of most cells and tissues.[29] For all the progress in basic research since World War Two—and it had been exciting in the area of molecular biology—scientists still knew considerably more about the natural world outside the human body than they did about the biology of human development.

Breast cancer, a special fear of many women (119,000 were diagnosed as having it in 1985, and 38,400 died of it), served as an alarming case in point of these gaps in knowledge. Researchers estimated that approximately one-fourth of breast cancer patients had a mother or a sister who had also developed (or would develop) the disease. Among this minority, genetic forces appeared to be at work. Researchers added that most breast cancers seemed to be hormonal in nature—not provoked primarily by chemical carcinogens or by tobacco. They urged women to secure periodic checkups, to exercise regularly, and to reduce their consumption of fats or calories. But researchers and doctors also admitted that their understanding of breast cancers was incomplete. Not sure what caused the hormonal changes, they suspected that many breast cancers, perhaps constitutional rather than local in origin, might already have metastasized by the time they were large enough to detect. They further disagreed over the value of exercise and diet. "It's really very depressing," an epidemiologist for the ACS remarked in 1986. "After all this work we don't know much more about the causes of breast cancer than we did twenty years ago."[30]

Careful writers conceded these gaps in understanding and added that gains in basic research did not always improve clinical management of the disease, at least in the short run. "Unfortunately," one noted, "although present knowledge may point research in the direction of potential cures, major advances, with some exceptions, are still years away."[31] Another added, "neither the intrinsic nature nor the true cause of cancer is properly known, and the modest therapeutic successes of the 1940s and 1950s have not been significantly improved on."[32] Two thoughtful epidemiologists, sadly reviewing mortality statistics in 1986, were even more blunt. Urging more attention to preventive measures, they concluded, "thirty-five

Mammography can detect breast cancers even smaller than the hand can feel.

For too many years breast cancers that could have been cured could not be found. The only means available was the human hand. When mammography (low-dose x-ray examination) proved it could detect lumps infinitely smaller than fingers could feel, at minimal risk, a great breakthrough was achieved. Now there is hope that the leading cause of cancer deaths in women will lose its place in our lives.

Women, without symptoms of breast cancer, ages 35 to 39, should have one mammogram for the record; women 40 to 49 should have a mammogram every one to two years, and women 50 and over, once a year. All women are advised that monthly breast self-examination is an important health habit. Ask your local Cancer Society for free information on mammography and breast self-examination.

The American Cancer Society wants you to know.

AMERICAN CANCER SOCIETY

Reprinted with permission from *Cancer News*, 38, no. 1 (1984), 24; © 1984 American Cancer Society.

years of intense effort focusing largely on improved treatment must be judged a qualified failure."[33] Though disputed by the messengers of hope, these were probably accurate assessments of the state of knowledge about cancer in the mid-1980s.

Objective observers further recognized that physicians were still struggling to find effective ways of detecting most cancers in their early stages. This historically controversial matter continued to pose very complicated problems of research, medical education, and implementation. Doctors and health officials had comparable trouble in developing satisfactory screening programs. While Pap smears helped to control cervical cancer, screens for breast cancer did not seem to be reducing deaths—mortality from it remained stable from 1970 to 1983, then rose mysteriously for white women under fifty.[34] The utility of screens for lung and colon cancers, the leading killers, were unsubstantiated.[35] Given these persistent problems, many practitioners remained skeptical about claims for the value of early detection and for the efficacy of screening.

While informed writers conceded the complicated nature of these issues, many people grew increasingly impatient with doctors. Even Reagan's specialists, they said, could have discovered his cancer earlier. Many other doctors, they complained, were simply careless or lazy. Surveys showed that only one-tenth of doctors followed ACS guidelines for detecting breast cancer. Twenty-five percent did not bother with Pap smears. "I guess a lot of physicians," one unhappy critic said, "figure that if they check the breast and feel the belly they're doing a good enough job."[36]

Some doctors remained ill-educated about the guidelines, while others resisted the task of testing "private" organs or hesitated to perform frequent, time-consuming examinations. Patients, too, avoided such tests, not only out of fear or embarassment but also because some of the tests were expensive and uncovered by insurance. Many simply denied that they might have the dread disease. The hopeful refrain, "it won't happen to me," continued to be almost as widespread in the 1980s as it had been throughout the century.

Other critics of medical practice persisted in questioning standard treatments of the disease, consequently failing to recognize improvements in diagnosis, surgery, and chemotherapy since World

War Two. Knowledgeable doctors were able to relieve considerable pain and suffering, extending and bettering the quality of life for many thousands of people every year. They were also able to curb mortality from a number of cancers. Several rare forms of the disease, notably leukemias affecting children, were being treated with heartening success. And psychiatrists, social workers, and counselors were doing more than in the past to ease the emotional pain of patients and their families. It was wrong-headed to argue, as some critics did, that professionals in the health field had done nothing to stem the scourge of cancer in modern America. Some things, after all, had changed.

Many people nonetheless continued to denounce practitioners. Some deplored the continuing emphasis on surgery, especially on women. While surgeons less often resorted to radical, disfiguring operations in dealing with breast or colon cancer, they were unable significantly to improve survival rates.[37] When they said, "we got out all we could see," patients were skeptical, believing that the cancer—ever "lurking" in the body—would come back, that the paternalistic and optimistic doctors knew less than they claimed.

Skepticism of expert advice was probably as great in the 1980s as in the culturally turbulent 1970s. To judge from the frequency of complaints about the medical profession, many patients were tired of the Message of Hope and were ready to let nature take its course. A small number found solace from the growing hospice movement; others refused to submit to heroic medical intervention; many insisted on taking primary responsibility for their own health. Like Grant a hundred years earlier, they turned to physicians mainly for relief of suffering, not to extend their lives of misery. After all, everyone died of something.[38]

The growing emphasis of oncologists on chemotherapy, which was given to some 200,000 patients in 1985, provoked especially loud complaints. Perhaps 10,000 of these patients were cured, many of them children and young people with leukemia or Hodgkin's disease. Although this was a sizable figure, it was far smaller than the number of Americans who might have been saved through the widespread adoption of preventive approaches: more than 100,000 Americans died annually from lung cancer caused by tobacco.[39] Many of the toxic drugs, moreover, continued to have awful effects, including vomiting and the loss of hair in clumps. Michael Shimkin complained in 1985, "we have gone on a binge of giving every cancer patient every possible chemotherapy, usually toxic cocktails made by mixing three or four different drugs . . . Chemotherapy is one of many areas where modern medicine has gone overboard."[40]

Along with these complaints about treatment, people continued to express powerful fears of the disease. One sign of such fears was the sheer quantity of newspaper and magazine articles about cancer. These proliferated as never before—almost 1,500 during one 40-day period charted by the NCI in 1981.[41] The stories attested to the greater openness about cancer—this was one notable change that helped any number of patients deal better with the disease. It is not so clear, however, that the stories lessened public apprehension. Many articles raised the specter of "cancer towns" and of widespread environmental dangers. Television dramas and films, while less obsessed with cancer than the press, often wallowed in mawkishness and awe.[42]

Another manifestation of popular fears was the persistence of old notions, misperceptions, and general unease. Though most people had learned to use the word "cancer," a few still could not bear to do so. One woman exemplified this reticence by insisting on referring to her breast tumor as "Buster." A small number of Americans still thought that all cancers were either hereditary or contagious: hospice workers at a dinner party were stunned to note that a recently diagnosed cancer patient was asked to use plastic eating utensils and to take her food on paper plates. Physicians, too, used language which exposed their horror of the disease. One surgeon told the family of a man on whom he had just operated that the patient was "rotten clear through." Accounting for such expressions, another doctor observed that "cancer is associated not only with death, but with death in its worst form—a lingering, slow, miserable death . . . every time a cancer patient gets a cold, or wakes up feeling weak or has an unexplained fever or unexplained pain, no matter how many years they've been in remission, they think, 'it's back.'"[43]

Many people, indeed, still used cancer as a metaphor for all sorts of things that frightened them. The military bureaucracy, one re-

Beware: cancer can 'run in the family'

Dear Ann Landers:

I'm a 52-year-old woman who worries a lot about cancer. Although I get an annual checkup and have never had any symptoms, the reason I am so terrified is because my mother, two aunts and a sister, as well as two cousins, have had cancer.

Is cancer hereditary? Some say it is, others say no. I live in a small town in Nebraska and although I like my doctor very much I have the feeling he is not very well informed about this disease. He is in his late 60s and I think perhaps he has not kept up with the latest.

What can you say to quiet my fears and make me feel better about the medical care I am receiving? I'm sure there are many people in small towns across the country

who share this problem. Please don't give away the city. My doctor would recognize me at once.
— Anonymous Reader In Mid-America

Dear Anonymous:

Cancer is not hereditary in the same way that blue eyes or skin color are, but the experts say family history is indeed a factor. When cancer seems to "run in the family," checkups should be a must on a regular basis.

Reprinted with permission from Ann Landers, News America Syndicate, August 29, 1985.

porter wrote, was a "cancerous growth" in American life. Another described the "spreading cancer of red ink" in the federal budget. The columnist William Safire called a legal dispute a "cancer of hate," and a headline writer referred to THE ECONOMIC CANCER THAT BELIES GORBACHEV'S PUBLIC CONFIDENCE.[44] The omnipresence of such expressions, appearing as spontaneously in the 1980s as they had for a hundred years, attested to the continuing cancer-consciousness of American culture.[45]

Only one development in the 1980s seemed to have the power to eclipse fears of cancer in America. That was the eruption of Acquired Immune Deficiency Syndrome, or AIDS. Compared with cancer (to which it was related in some ways), AIDS was a blip on the medical landscape. Between 1981 and 1986 it killed only 15,000 Americans. But many characteristics of AIDS aroused terror. It was a "dirty thing" that especially hit promiscuous homosexuals and intravenous drug addicts and, like cancer, it slowly ravaged its victims. It was regarded as always fatal.

Most frightening, AIDS was infectious. Most experts at first believed that it could be transmitted only in a few ways, through contaminated needles or homosexual union.[46] But by 1986 scientists came to recognize that heterosexual union, too, could spread the syndrome. They also anticipated frightening increases in the number of victims. One researcher exclaimed that AIDS would "probably prove to be the plague of the millenium."[47] The head of the World Health Organization added, "we stand nakedly in front of a very serious pandemic as mortal as any pandemic there ever has been."[48] Federal officials calculated in 1986 that at least 1,500,000 Americans were already infected by AIDS, and predicted that five to ten million Americans would be infected by the end of 1991, at which time a cumulative total of at least 180,000 people would have been killed by the syndrome.[49]

The response to such warnings was severe. Workmen refused to service facilities frequented by homosexuals; hospital aides feared to approach AIDS patients; community leaders prevented AIDS-afflicted children from going to school. A CBS poll found that 47 percent of people thought it was possible to become infected by drinking from a glass used by an AIDS victim.[50] Though reacting slowly at first to fears ("Afr-AIDS") such as these, Health and Human Services Secretary Margaret Heckler declared in early 1985 that AIDS was America's number-one health priority. Some of the money taken to meet this priority—$60 million at that time—came from funds intended for cancer research. Nothing like that had ever happened to the once sacrosanct NCI. And in late 1986 a panel of experts from the Institute of the National Academy of Sciences urged a quadrupling in federal funding for AIDS research by 1990—or $1 billion per year.[51]

If AIDS were to become epidemic in the United States, it was certain that cancer would lose some of its hold on the fears and imaginations of the American people. By 1987, however, no such epidemic had occurred. The terror that attacked people at high risk, moreover, seemed a little less intense among the general population. While popular fears were spreading rapidly, they were not yet out of control as of mid-1987. Indeed, neither AIDS nor any other threat to health as yet displaced the tenacious grip that cancer had on the American popular imagination. As ever cancer loomed as an alien, surreptitious, and voracious invader that seemed to attack anybody, anywhere, and to advance relentlessly until it killed its victims and impoverished their families. This dreadful vision of the disease, like so much else in the modern cultural history of the malady, continued to be confirmed by the personal experiences of millions of families. Medical advances notwithstanding, popular fear has remained one of many enduring realities that have highlighted the story of cancer in American culture since the 1880s. Despite the rapid pace of change in the past century, this fundamental concern has indeed stayed much the same.

That did not mean that cancerphobia profoundly affected the day-to-day thinking and behavior of most people. Save for those who developed the disease, it ordinarily did not. Though Americans cared greatly about good health, which was essential to the good life, the great majority had pressing concerns that overrode premonitions of serious sickness. Though they dreaded early death—especially the "wasting away" associated with many forms of cancer—they denied, often nervously, that it could happen to them. They also cherished other values central to the culture: the freedom to do as they liked and to enjoy the pleasurable habits, such as smoking, drinking, and meat eating, of the consumer society. More than 50 million Americans still smoked in 1987.

The continuing dread of cancer also did not mean that people despaired of improvements in the future. Many knowledgeable writers, while deploring the exaggerated claims for cancer research, still anticipated gradual progress. They welcomed the headway that crusades against tobacco were making and were encouraged by continuing epidemiological research into the effects of nutrition. Other writers looked forward to a reordering of priorities that would shift attention from chemotherapy to preventive approaches. Scientists especially awaited possible benefits of basic research in molecular biology—what Michael Shimkin called the "quiet, intense exploration of cells."[52] These quiet explorations were not always the stuff of dramatic newspaper headlines, but they held out some promise for the future.

All the same, the mystery and power of cancer were steady reminders of mortality. No other malady held cancer's unique capacity to serve as metaphor and mirror for a range of social concerns or as a manifestation of social, economic, and ideological divisions. In a society that feared death above all things, no other illness was dreaded so much. As Shimkin explained in 1980,

> Cancer is now the most feared of human diseases . . . For most of the fortunate citizens of the United States, the pale rider of pestilence is now retired, and the cadaverous rider of hunger is too obese to maintain his seat. We must now face different riders, one in the shape of a mushroom cloud, and one in the shape of a crab.[53]

Bibliographic Note

In this topically organized bibliography I list those books and archival collections which proved most useful to me. I mention here but a few of the many articles and documents relevant to the cultural history of cancer in modern America; the notes provide references to numerous others.

History of Health and Health Care in Modern America

Among the most helpful sources are Anita Clair Fellman and Michael Fellman, *Making Sense of Self: Medical Advice Literature in Late Nineteenth Century America* (Philadelphia, 1981); Thomas McKeown, *The Role of Medicine: Dream, Mirage, or Nemesis?* (Princeton, N.J., 1979), which critically examines the healing claims of medicine; George Rosen, *From Medical Police to Social Medicine; Essays on the History of Health Care* (New York, 1974), *Preventive Medicine in the United States* (New York, 1975), and *The Structure of American Medical Practice, 1875–1941* (Philadelphia, 1983). Charles Rosenberg offers a collection of insightful essays in *No Other Gods: On Science and American Social Thought* (Baltimore, 1976). The most recent major overview of medicine in American society is Paul Starr, *The Social Transformation of Medicine* (New York, 1982).

Other important commentaries on the role of medicine in American society include the essays of Lewis Thomas, especially *The Medusa and the Snail: More Notes of a Biology Watcher* (New York, 1979) and *The Youngest Science: Notes of a Medicine-Watcher* (New York, 1983). Sophisticated articles by historians and social scientists are collected in Judith Leavitt and Ronald Numbers, eds., *Sickness and Health in America* (Madison, Wis., 1978); Susan Reverby and David Rosner, eds., *Health Care in America: Essays in Social History* (Philadelphia, 1979); and Morris Vogel and Charles Rosenberg, eds., *The Therapeutic Revolution: Essays in the Social History of Medicine* (Philadelphia, 1979). Useful articles include John C. Burnham, "American Medicine's Golden Age: What Happened to It?" *Science,* 215 (March 19, 1982), 1474–1479; and Leon R. Kass, "Regarding the End of Medicine and the Pursuit of Health," *Public Interest,* 40 (Summer 1975), 11–42.

For more specialized studies see James Burrow, *AMA: Voice of American Medicine* (Baltimore, 1963), and *Organized Medicine in the Progressive Era: The Move toward Monopoly* (Baltimore, 1977); Kenneth Ludmerer, *Learning to Heal: The Development of American Medical Education* (New York, 1985); A. McGehee Harvey, *Science at the Bedside: Clinical Research in American Medicine, 1905–1945* (Baltimore, 1981); and Robert Kohler, *From Medical Chemistry to Biochemistry: The Making of a Biomedical Discipline* (Cambridge, England,

1982). See also John Duffy, *The Healers: A History of American Medicine* (Urbana, Ill., 1976); James H. Cassedy, *Charles V. Chapin and the Public Health Movement* (Cambridge, Mass., 1962); Donald Fleming, *William H. Welch and the Rise of Modern Medicine* (Boston, 1954); Stanley Reiser, *Medicine and the Reign of Technology* (Cambridge, England, 1978); Gerald Grob, *Mental Illness and American Society, 1875–1940* (Princeton, N.J., 1983); and Victoria Harden, *Inventing the NIH: Federal Biomedical Research Policy, 1887–1937* (Baltimore, 1986).

Also helpful for special purposes are Michael S. Pernick, *A Calculus of Pain and Suffering: Pain, Professionalism, and Anesthesia in Nineteenth Century America* (New York, 1985); Barbara Gutmann Rosenkrantz, *Public Health and the State: Changing Views in Massachusetts, 1842–1936* (Cambridge, Mass., 1972); Regina Markell Morantz-Sanchez, *Sympathy and Science: Women Physicians in American Medicine* (New York, 1985); John and Robin Haller, *The Physician and Sexuality in Victorian America* (New York, 1977); and William Rothstein, *American Physicians in the Nineteenth Century: From Sects to Science* (Baltimore, 1972). Social histories of hospitals include David Rosner, *A Once Charitable Enterprise: Hospitals and Health Care in Brooklyn and New York, 1885–1915* (Cambridge, Mass., 1982); and Morris Vogel, *The Invention of the Modern Hospital: Boston, 1870–1930* (Chicago, 1980).

Richard Harrison Shryock, *The Development of Modern Medicine: An Interpretation of the Social and Scientific Factors Involved* (Madison, Wis., 1947), is still useful. Rosemary Stevens, *American Medicine and the Public Interest* (New Haven, 1971), contains much information on twentieth-century developments. The most withering (and one-sided) indictment of contemporary American medical practice is Ivan Illich, *Medical Nemesis: The Expropriation of Health* (New York, 1976).

Important books on the history of biological thinking include Garland Allen, *Life Science in the Twentieth Century* (New York, 1975); William Coleman, *Biology in the Nineteenth Century* (New York, 1971); Mark Haller, *Eugenics: Hereditarian Attitudes in American Thought* (New Brunswick, N.J., 1963); Kenneth Ludmerer, *Genetics and American Society: A Historical Appraisal* (Baltimore, 1972); Ernst Mayr, *The Growth of Biological Thought: Diversity, Evolution, and Inheritance* (Cambridge, Mass., 1982); and Daniel Kevles, *In the Name of Eugenics* (New York, 1985).

The Social History of Health and Diseases in America

The starting point for this genre of historical writing is Rene Dubos, *Mirage of Health: Utopias, Progress, and Biological Change* (New York, 1959), which places the history of ideas about health in a broad context. See also Rene and Jean Dubos, *The White Plague: Tuberculosis, Man, and Society* (Boston, 1952). Other excellent studies of individual diseases in their social settings include James H. Jones, *Bad Blood: The Tuskegee Syphilis Experiment—A Tragedy of Race and Medicine* (New York, 1981); Allan Brandt, *No Magic Bullet: A Social History of Venereal Disease in the United States since 1880* (New York, 1985); and Charles Rosenberg, *The Cholera Years: The United States in 1832, 1849, and 1866* (Chicago, 1962).

See also David Courtwright, *Dark Paradise: Opiate Addiction in America before 1940* (Cambridge, Mass., 1982); Richard H. Shryock, *National Tuberculosis Association, 1904–1954: A Study of the Voluntary Health Movement in the United States* (New York, 1957); and John Paul, *A History of Poliomyelitis* (New Haven, 1971). William McNeill, *Plagues and Peoples* (New York, 1976), is a sweeping account of epidemic diseases in world history. Relevant articles include Gerald Grob, "The Social History of Medicine and Diseases in America: Problems and Possibilities," *Journal of Social History,* 10 (June 1977), 391–409; and Guenter B. Risse, "Epidemics and Medicine: The Influence of Disease on Medical Thought and Practice," *Bulletin of the History of Medicine,* 53 (Winter 1979), 505–519.

Key historical sources dealing broadly with health in America are Harvey Green, *Fit for America: Health, Fitness, Sport, and American Society* (New York, 1986); and James Whorton, *Crusaders for Fitness: The History of American Health Reformers* (Princeton, N.J., 1982).

The sociology of medicine has attracted some able writers, especially Eliot Freidson, *Profession of Medicine: A Study of the Sociology of Applied Knowledge* (New York, 1970); Talcott Parsons, "Definitions of Health and Illness in the Light of American Values and Social Structure," in E. Gartly Jaco, ed., *Patients, Physicians, and Illness* (New York, 1972), 165–187; Henry Sigerist, "The Special Position of the Sick," in David Landy, ed., *Culture, Disease, and Healing: Studies in Medical Anthropology* (New York, 1977), 388–394; and Renee Fox, "The Medicalization and Demedicalization of American Society," in John Knowles, ed., *Doing Better and Feeling Worse: Health in the United States* (New York, 1977), 9–22. Knowles's volume contains many good essays on American health and medicine in the 1970s.

Other sources concerned with medicine, society, and values include Peter Conrad and Joseph W. Schneider, *Deviance and Medicalization: From Badness to Sickness* (St. Louis, Mo., 1980); Joseph R. Gusfield, *The Culture of Public Problems: Drinking, Driving and the Symbolic Order* (Chicago, 1981); Elliot A. Krause, *Power and Illness: The Political Sociology of Health and Medical Care* (New York, 1977); and David Mechanic, ed., *Readings in Medical Sociology* (New York, 1980).

Recent Commentaries on Cancer in America

A handful of books is indispensable to an understanding of cancer in America since the 1960s. A good place to begin is Michael Shimkin, *Science and Cancer* (Washington, 3d rev. ed., 1980), a solid authoritative treatment of various aspects of the disease. Two fine overviews—equally strong in handling scientific matters—are John Cairns, *Cancer: Science and Society* (San Francisco, 1978), and June Goodfield, *The Siege of Cancer* (New York, 1975). A fourth "must" is Richard Doll and Richard Peto, *The Causes of Cancer* (Oxford, 1981), which meticulously reviews epidemiological trends.

Equally necessary is the four-volume *History of Cancer Control in the United States, 1946–1971* (Washington, D.C., 1978), a collection of interviews and other documents and data. It strongly urges more attention to prevention and control of the disease. The materials were put together by the History of Cancer Control Project, UCLA School of Public Health, under the sponsorship of the National Cancer Institute's Division of Cancer Control and Rehabilitation.

I add to this short list of essential sources the provocative essays by Susan Sontag, *Illness as Metaphor* (New York, 1977). As the title suggests, these reflect on the social and cultural meaning of diseases, notably tuberculosis and cancer.

Important assessments of the state of research and prevention in the 1980s are Robert Weinberg, "The Secrets of Cancer Cells," *Atlantic,* 252 (Aug. 1983), 82–88; and "The Molecules of Life," *Scientific American,* 253 (Oct. 1985), 48–56; John Bailar III and Elaine Smith, "Progress against Cancer?" *New England Journal of Medicine,* 314 (May 8, 1986), 1226–1232; and John Cairns, "The Treatment of Diseases and the War against Cancer," *Scientific American,* 253 (Nov. 1985), 51–59. Particularly clear and authoritative are John Langone, "Cancer: Cautious Optimism," Daniel Greenberg, "What Ever Happened to the War on Cancer?" and Lewis Thomas, "Getting at the Roots of a Deep Puzzle," in *Discover,* 7 (March 1986), 36–66. Other up-to-date accounts are R. Nery, *Cancer: An Enigma in Biology and Society* (London, 1986); Edward Sylvester, *Target: Cancer* (New York, 1986); and "Cancer" supplement, *Washington Post,* Sept. 30, 1986.

Several writers have criticized aspects of what I call the orthodox medical world of cancer. These include Joseph Hixson, *The Patchwork Mouse* (Garden City, N.Y., 1976), which explores in fascinating depth a case of research falsification; Philip Nobile, *King Cancer: The Good, the Bad, and the Cure of Cancer* (New York, 1975); Ralph Moss, *The Cancer Syndrome* (New York, 1980), a specially hard-hitting critique of the NCI; and Richard Carter, *The Gentle Legions* (New York, 1961), which has a chapter on the American Cancer Society. Two articles by Daniel Greenberg are particularly probing: "'Progress' in Cancer Research—Don't Say It Isn't So," *New England Journal of Medicine,* 292 (March 27, 1975), 707–708; and "A Critical Look at Cancer Coverage," *Columbia Journalism Review* (Jan.–Feb., 1975), 40–44. A thoughtful review of debates about cancer in the 1970s is P. B. Medawar, "The Crab," *New York Review of Books,* 24 (June 9, 1977), 10–15.

Provocative evaluations of preventive approaches include Louise Russell, *Is Prevention Better than Cure?* (Washington, D.C., 1986); and Lenn Goodman and Madeleine Goodman, "Prevention—How Misuse of a Concept Undercuts Its Worth," *Hastings Center Report* (April, 1986), 27–38.

Historical Accounts of Cancer

Several works offer scholarly treatments of aspects of cancer in history. These include L. J. Rather, *The Genesis of Cancer: A Study in the History of Ideas* (Baltimore, 1978), which focuses on scientific ideas about the disease; Michael Shimkin, *Contrary to Nature* (NIH, Washington, D.C., 1979), a wide-ranging, illustrated history of cancer research and researchers; Nathaniel I. Berlin, "The Conquest of Cancer," *Perspectives in Biology and Medicine,* 22 (Summer 1979), 500–518; and Henry E. Sigerist, "The Historical Development of the Pathology and Therapy of Cancer," *Bulletin of the New York Academy of Medicine,* 9 (Nov. 1932), 642–653.

For the American scene key historical treatments are Donald F. Shaughnessy, "The Story of the American Cancer Society," Ph.D. dissertation, Columbia University, New York (1957); Stephen P. Strickland, *Politics, Science, and Dread Disease: A Short History of United States Medical Research Policy* (Cambridge, Mass., 1972), which is excellent on postwar political developments; and Richard A. Rettig, *Cancer Crusade: The Story of the National Cancer Act of 1971* (Princeton, N.J., 1977), an authoritative monograph on the early years of the "war on cancer."

Studies focusing on the NIH and NCI include Donald Swain, "The Rise of a Research Empire: NIH, 1930 to 1950," *Science,* 138 (Dec. 1962), 1233–1237; Wyndham Miles, "Creation of the National Cancer Institute," unpublished manuscript (1973), and "The National Cancer Act of 1971," unpublished manuscript (c. 1972), both in my possession, compliments of Miles; Michael Shimkin, *As Memory Serves: Six Essays on a Personal Involvement with the National Cancer Institute, 1938 to 1978* (NIH Publication no. 83–2217, Sept. 1983); William A. Yaremchuk, "The Origins of the National Cancer Institute," *Journal of the National Cancer Institute,* 59 (Supplement, Aug. 1977), 551–558; and J. R. Heller, "The National Cancer Institute: A Twenty Year Retrospect," ibid., 19 (Aug. 1957), 147–190. These two issues of the *JNCI* are devoted to the historical development of the agency.

For more details on historical episodes in this book see Thomas Pitkin, *The Captain Departs: Ulysses S. Grant's Last Campaign* (Carbondale, Ill., 1973); John J. Brooks et al., "The Final Diagnosis of President Cleveland's Lesion," *Transactions of the College of Physicians of Philadelphia,* 5th ser., vol. 2 (March 1980), 1–25; and Sharon Romm, *The Unwelcome Intruder: Freud's Struggle with Cancer* (New York, 1983).

Contemporary Accounts of Cancer

The following sources, listed in chronological order of their publication, are the most significant expositions of approaches toward cancer in American history since the 1880s: Charles P. Childe, *The Control of a Scourge, or How Cancer Is Curable* (London, 1906), which was widely cited on this side of the Atlantic; James Ewing, *Neoplastic Diseases: A Textbook on Tumors* (Philadelphia, 1919), the authoritative medical text on the subject for the next generation; James Tobey, *Cancer: What Everyone Should Know about It* (New York, 1932), a well-written account for popular consumption; George Crile, *Cancer and Common Sense* (New York, 1955), which warned against cancerphobia and excessively radical therapies; Edward J. Beattie, Jr., with Stuart D. Cowan, *Toward the Conquest of Cancer* (New York, 1980); and NCI, "Everything Doesn't Cause Cancer," (NIH Publication no. 84–2039, rev. ed., Feb. 1984).

Other contemporary studies, also in chronological order, are Percivall Pott, "Chirurgical Observations Relative to the Cataract, the polypus of the nose, the cancer of the scrotum, the different kinds of ruptures, and the mortification of the toes and feet" (London, 1775), available also in NCI Monograph no. 10 (Feb. 1963), 7–13; Samuel Gross, *On the Results of Surgical Operations in Malignant*

Diseases (Philadelphia, 1853); Herbert Snow, *Clinical Notes on Cancer: Its Etiology and Treatment* (London, 1883); Willard Parker, *Cancer: A Study of 397 Cases of Cancer of the Human Breast* (New York, 1885); J. Ellis Barker, *Cancer, How It Is Cured, How It Can Be Prevented* (London, 1924), an unorthodox account; and John Cope, *Cancer: Civilization and Degeneration* (London, 1932), whose argument is obvious from its title.

See also George H. Bigelow and Herbert L. Lombard, *Cancer and Other Chronic Diseases in Massachusetts* (Cambridge, Mass., 1933), an early epidemiological study; Charles Oberling, *The Riddle of Cancer* (New Haven, 1944), which emphasizes the role of viruses; Charles Cameron, *The Truth about Cancer* (Englewood Cliffs, N.J., 1956), by the scientific and medical director of the American Cancer Society; Pat McGrady, *The Savage Cell: A Report on Cancer and Cancer Research* (New York, 1964), a well-written, solid treatment; and Jane E. Brody with Arthur Holleb, *You Can Fight Cancer and Win* (New York, 1977).

Epidemiological Studies

Frederick Hoffman, *The Mortality from Cancer throughout the World* (Newark, 1915), was in its day the most influential discussion of the subject. Much useful information may be found in another early study: J. W. Schereschewsky, "The Course of Cancer Mortality in the 10 Original Registration States for the 21-Year Period, 1900–1920" (United States Public Health *Bulletin* no. 155, Washington, D.C., 1925). For trends since then the most careful treatment is provided in Richard Doll and Richard Peto, *The Causes of Cancer* (Oxford, 1981).

Also useful are James E. Enstrom and Donald F. Austin, "Interpreting Cancer Survival Rates," *Science,* 195 (March 4, 1977), 847–851; NCI and Cancer Research Center, Academy of Medical Services, USSR, *Cancer Epidemiology in the USA and USSR* (Bethesda, Md., 1980); Patricia Butler and Lee Sanderson, "Epidemiology," in Charles Shaw, ed., *Prevention of Occupational Cancer* (Boca Raton, Fla., 1981), 55–107; Committee on Diet, Nutrition, and Cancer, Assembly of Life Sciences, National Research Council, *Diet, Nutrition, and Cancer* (Washington, D.C., 1982); and Joseph F. Fraumeni, Jr., "Epidemiologic Approaches to Cancer Etiology," *Annual Review of Public Health,* 3 (1982), 85–100.

Cancer Patients

It is difficult to generalize about the experiences and feelings of cancer patients, but some interesting studies have been published. These include Barrie R. Cassileth, ed., *The Cancer Patient: Social and Medical Aspects of Care* (Philadelphia, 1979); Jim McIntosh, *Communication and Awareness in a Cancer Ward* (New York, 1977); and Andrew Slaby and Arvin Glicksman, *Adapting to Life-threatening Illness* (New York, 1985). See also Jean Aitken-Swan and Ralston Paterson, "The Cancer Patient: Delay in Seeking Advice," *British Medical Journal* (March 12, 1955), 623–627; and Aitken-Swan and E. C. Easson, "Reactions of Cancer Patients on Being Told Their Diagnosis," ibid. (March 21, 1959), 779–783.

There is also a substantial body of literature by patients and relatives of patients. Some of these, in chronological order, are S. Farwell-Hinckson, *How I Cured My*

Cancer without an Operation (Toronto, 1928), a plea for dietary reforms; John Gunther, *Death Be Not Proud* (1949), a moving narrative of the author's son's death from a brain tumor; Edna Kaehele, *Living with Cancer* (Garden City, N.Y., 1952), one of many inspirational accounts; Walter S. Ross, *The Climate Is Hope: How They Triumphed over Cancer* (Englewood Cliffs, N.J., 1965); and Stewart Alsop, *Stay of Execution: A Sort of Memoir* (Philadelphia, 1973), perhaps the most interesting of all these books.

More recent accounts—reflecting the greater openness about the disease—are Doris Lund, *Eric* (New York, 1974), by the mother of a cancer victim; Jessamyn West, *The Woman Said Yes: Encounters with Life and Death* (New York, 1976), which includes a discussion of the death of the author's sister; Gerda Lerner, *A Death of One's Own* (New York, 1978), concerning the cancer afflicting the author's husband; Morris Abram, *The Day Is Short: An Autobiography* (New York, 1982), a fighting memoir by a man with leukemia; Anthony J. Sattilaro with Tom Monte, *Recalled by Life* (Boston, 1982), another fighting memoir; and Curtis Bill Pepper, *We The Victors* (Garden City, N.Y., 1984), which consists of inspirational accounts by patients.

Tobacco and Other Carcinogens

Many scholars and journalists have written about the tobacco industry, especially since 1960. In order of appearance, useful books include A. Lee Fritschler, *Smoking and Politics: Policymaking and the Federal Bureaucracy* (New York, 1969); Thomas Whiteside, *Selling Death: Cigarette Advertising and Public Health* (New York, 1970); Kenneth M. Friedman, *Public Policy and the Smoking-Health Controversy: A Comparative Study* (Lexington, Mass., 1975), which deals with the United States, Great Britain, and Canada; Ronald Troyer and Gerald Markle, *Cigarettes: The Battle over Smoking* (New Brunswick, N.J., 1983); and Peter Taylor, *The Smoke Ring: Tobacco, Money, and Multinational Politics* (New York, 1984).

Especially helpful is Elizabeth Whelan, *A Smoking Gun: How the Tobacco Industry Gets Away with Murder* (Philadelphia, 1985). Among the many important publications of the surgeon general's office are *Smoking and Health: Report of the Advisory Committee to the Surgeon General of the Public Health Service* (Washington, D.C., 1964); and *The Health Consequences of Smoking for Women: A Report of the Surgeon General* (Washington, D.C., 1980). If there is a persuasive, well-documented defense of smoking, I do not know of it, but I have included the counterclaims of the tobacco forces in the notes to this book.

Several books touch on the relationship between chemical carcinogens, environmental damage, and cancer. Key sources include Rachel Carson, *Silent Spring* (New York, 1962); Wilhelm Hueper and W. D. Conway, *Chemical Carcinogenesis and Cancers* (Springfield, Ill., 1964); Samuel S. Epstein, *The Politics of Cancer* (Garden City, N.Y., 1978), an extreme and critical account; Larry Agran, *The Cancer Connection, and What We Can Do about It* (Boston, 1977); and Frank Graham, Jr., *Since Silent Spring* (Boston, 1970). See also Toxic Substances Strategy Committee, *Toxic Chemicals and Public Protection* (Washington, D.C., 1980). A spirited rebuttal of many environmentalist arguments is Edith Efron, *The Apoca-*

lyptics: Cancer and the Big Lie—How Environmental Politics Controls What We Know about Cancer (New York, 1984).

Unorthodox Views of Cancer

Americans' disenchantment with medical orthodoxy is the subject of a vast literature. Among the recent scholarly books exploring aspects of this disenchantment are Wayland Hand, *Magical Medicine* (Berkeley, 1980); David Edwin Harrell, Jr., *All Things Are Possible: The Healing and Charismatic Revivals in Modern America* (Bloomington, Ind., 1975); and Donald Meyer, *The Positive Thinkers: Religion as Popular Psychology from Mary Baker Eddy to Oral Roberts* (New York, 1980).

For alternative views of cancer, one may begin with works focusing on psychological causes. Some recent examples include Lawrence LeShan, *You Can Fight for Your Life: Emotional Factors in the Causation of Cancer* (New York, 1977); Jerome Cohen, Joseph W. Cullen, and L. Robert Martin, eds., *Psychological Stress and Cancer* (Chichester, England, 1984); Jean Tache, Hans Selye, and Stacy B. Day, eds., *Cancer, Stress, and Death* (New York, 1979); and Frederick B. Levenson, *The Causes and Prevention of Cancer* (New York, 1985). A valuable article is Samuel J. Kowal, "Emotions as a Cause of Cancer: Eighteenth and Nineteenth Century Contributions," *Psychoanalytic Review*, 42 (July 1955), 217–227. Sontag's *Illness and Metaphor* (New York, 1977) is critical of psychological theories. A recent account is David Locke and Douglas Colligan, *The Healer Within: The New Medicine of Mind and Body* (New York, 1986).

For the history of cancer "quackery" the starting points are Samuel Hopkins Adams, *The Great American Fraud* (New York, 1905); AMA, *Nostrums and Quackery: Articles on the Nostrum Evil and Quackery Reprinted from the Journal of the American Medical Association* (Chicago, 1911); and Arthur Cramp, comp., *Nostrums and Quackery* (Chicago, 1921), an updated version. Other relevant sources include Stewart Holbrook, *The Golden Age of Quackery* (New York, 1959); Sarah Stage, *Female Complaints: Lydia Pinkham and the Business of Women's Medicine* (New York, 1979); Morris Fishbein, "History of Cancer Quackery," *Perspectives in Biology and Medicine*, 8 (Winter 1965), 139–166; James Harvey Young, *The Medical Messiahs: A Social History of Health Quackery in Twentieth Century America* (Princeton, N.J., 1967); American Cancer Society, *Unproven Methods of Cancer Management* (New York, 1971); and Gerald Markle and James Petersen, eds., *Politics, Science, and Cancer: The Laetrile Phenomenon* (Boulder, Colo., 1980).

Death and Dying

Attitudes toward death both reflect and influence views of cancer. The major scholarly treatment of such attitudes is Philippe Ariès, *The Hour of our Death* (New York, 1981), and his shorter *Western Attitudes toward Death, from the Middle Ages to the Present* (Baltimore, 1974). An influential book is Elisabeth Kübler-Ross, *On Death and Dying* (New York, 1969). Others include Ernest Becker, *The Denial of Death* (New York, 1973); James J. Farrell, *Inventing the American Way of Death, 1830–1920* (Philadelphia, 1980); David Hendin, *Death as a Fact of Life* (New York, 1984); and David E. Stannard, ed., *Death in America* (Philadelphia, 1975). Relevant articles are Charles O. Jackson, "American Attitudes to Death," *Journal of American Studies,* 11 (Dec. 1977), 297–312; and the irreverent piece by Leslie H. Farber, "O Death, Where Is Thy Sting-a-Ling-a-Ling?" *Commentary,* 63 (June 1977), 35–43.

Archives

Letters, pamphlets, and other primary documents in archives proved to be unexpectedly rich sources of material for this book. In particular they provided first-hand popular reactions to cancer. I list here the collections I found helpful.

American Cancer Society, New York City. The society (known as the American Society for the Control of Cancer until 1945) made available to me some of its in-house material, including its publications, *Campaign Notes,* (191?–1930), *Bulletin,* (1930–1944), *Cancer News,* and "Cancer Facts and Figures." These give a clear idea of the society's main interests and goals since its founding in 1913.

National Library of Medicine, Bethesda, Maryland. This fine library houses several collections of material relevant to the history of cancer, including the "Papers and Minutes of the American Society for the Control of Cancer," 1913–1916, a four-volume collection of correspondence and minutes; and many transcripts of interviews with leading figures engaged in cancer research and prevention. I used interviews with Carl Baker, William Bryan, Leroy Burney, Rolla Dyer, Kenneth Endicott, John Heller, Thomas Parran, David E. Price, Leonard Scheele, Roscoe Spencer, Harold Stewart, and C. J. Van Slyke. I also found considerable material in the collections of Frederick Hoffman, Ernest Daland, Harold Stewart, Frank Horsfall, Louis Dublin, and Wilhelm Hueper and in the folders on Ulysses S. Grant and John Hancock Douglas.

Library of Congress, Manuscript Division, Washington, D.C. Useful collections here included the John Hancock Douglas papers, which contain much information on Grant's illness and death; and the Lawrence Spivak papers concerning television specials on cancer in the 1960s and 1970s.

National Archives, Washington, D.C. The National Archives houses the papers of the Public Health Service (Record Group 90) and the National Institutes of Health (Record Group 443). The NIH papers include many documents relating to the National Cancer Institute. The notes to the text attest to my great debt to these vast collections of letters, pamphlets, and documents.

College of Physicians of Philadelphia. This is a rich repository of medical materials. Among those I found most useful were the papers of W. W. Keen, one of President Cleveland's doctors; the papers of E. B. Krumbhaar; and clippings collected by Frederick Hoffman.

National Cancer Institute, Bethesda, Maryland. I am indebted to Kenneth Thibodeau of the NCI for making available to me the fascinating files labeled "Treatment and Cures," 1959–66, which in 1986 were to be sent to the National Archives to become part of Record Group 90. They contain materials documenting a broad range of popular attitudes toward cancer.

American Philosophical Society, Philadelphia. Two very extensive collections here are the James B. Murphy and Peyton Rous papers. Both scientists were greatly involved in cancer research; the collections include many fascinating letters from patients and their relatives.

Rockefeller Archives, Pocantico Hills, New York. Among the relevant collections here are many notebooks of clippings on the Memorial Sloan-Kettering Cancer Center in New York; the papers of Hayes Martin, full of information on quackery; the papers of William Cahan, which contain letters from patients; and the papers of the Office of the Messrs. Rockefeller, Medical Interests, which include correspondence and documents relating to the American Society for the Control of Cancer.

Columbia University, Oral History Project, New York City. This center houses transcripts of many interviews with leading cancer researchers. I consulted the interviews of John Heller, Kenneth Endicott, Thomas Parran, Leonard Scheele, James Shannon, Rolla Dyer, Harold Stewart, Joseph Aub, and Howard Andervont.

New York Academy of Medicine, New York City. The collections I found useful here are the papers of Fordyce Barker and of Willard Parker, as well as scrapbooks, clippings, and letters relating to President Cleveland's surgery in 1893. I also consulted the papers of the Public Health Archives, 1911–1968, from the files of the Committee on Public Health of New York.

Duke University, Durham, North Carolina. The papers of George Allen of the Tobacco Institute are housed in the university's archives.

Providence College, Providence, Rhode Island. The papers of Representative John Fogarty of Rhode Island, a key supporter of legislation against cancer, contain information on political developments in the 1950s and 1960s.

State Historical Society of Wisconsin, Madison. The society xeroxed for me correspondence from the James family papers detailing the private reactions of a family member who had cancer.

University of Maine, Orono. The archives of the university house the papers of Clarence C. Little, long-time head of the American Society for the Control of Cancer and later scientific director for the Tobacco Institute. They are disappointingly thin.

University of Pittsburgh, Hillman Library. The library has the papers of Thomas Parran, surgeon general from 1936 to 1948, which I occasionally found very helpful.

Countway Library, Harvard Medical School, Boston, Massachusetts. Among the important collections at this fine library are the records of the Cancer Commission of Harvard University, 1905–1940; and an unpublished manuscript by cancer epidemiologist Herbert Lombard, "The Massachusetts Cancer Program: An Autobiographical Record" (1959).

Notes

Prologue: The Travail of General Grant

1. Justin Kaplan, *Mr. Clemens and Mark Twain: A Biography* (New York, 1966), 261–262, 271–278.

2. Cited in Thomas Pitkin, *The Captain Departs: Ulysses S. Grant's Last Campaign* (Carbondale, Ill., 1973), 25. See also the excellent account by William McFeely, *Grant: A Biography* (New York, 1981), 495–517.

3. Pitkin, *The Captain Departs,* 26.

4. Robert Steckler and Donald Shedd, "General Grant: His Physicians and His Cancer," *American Journal of Surgery,* 132 (Oct. 1976), 508–514; Karl Wold, "Ulysses S. Grant—His Last Battle," *Tic,* 34 (July 1975), 10–12; Francelia Butler, *Cancer through the Ages: The Evolution of Hope* (Fairfax, Va., 1955), 67–68; Rodney Nelson, "The Final Victory of General U. S. Grant," *Cancer,* 47 (Feb. 1981), 433–436; George Elliott, "The Microscopial Examination of Specimens Removed from General Grant's Throat," *Medical Record,* 27 (March 14, 1885), 289–290. Sharon Romm, *The Unwelcome Intruder: Freud's Struggle with Cancer* (New York, 1983), 33–34, describes a similar tumor. See also George de Schweinitz, "An Essay on Painful Tumors," 1881, College of Physicians of Philadelphia.

5. Kaplan, *Mr. Clemens,* 273.

6. *New York Times,* March 1, 1885.

7. Pitkin, *The Captain Departs,* 28–30.

8. *New York Times,* Sept. 9, 1884; *New York Tribune,* April 8, 1885.

9. *New York Tribune,* April 8, 1885.

10. Besides the excellent account by Pitkin, see George Shrady, "General Grant's Last Days," *Century,* 76 (May–June 1908), 102–113, 275–285; Nelson, "Final Victory"; and Horace Green, "General Grant's Last Stand," *Harper's Magazine* (April 1935), 533–539.

11. *New York Times,* March 29–April 2, 1885.

12. David Courtwright, *Dark Paradise: Opiate Addiction in America before 1940* (Cambridge, Mass., 1982), 173, indicates that opiates were widely prescribed at the time, addicting thousands of patients a year.

13. *New York Times,* April 1–4, 1885.

14. *New York Times,* April 2, 1885.

15. Dr. Fordyce Barker to Dr. John Rogers, May 6, 1885, New York Academy of Medicine, New York City.

16. *New York Times,* April 4, 1885.

17. See Kaplan, *Mr. Clemens,* 277–278; McFeely, *Grant,* 501; Stefan Lorant, "The Baptism of U. S. Grant," *Life,* 30 (March 26, 1951), 91–102.

18. *New York Tribune,* June 16, 17, 1885.

19. *New York Tribune,* June 17, 1885.

20. *New York Tribune,* June 21, 1885.

21. Pitkin, *The Captain Departs,* 66.

22. *New York Tribune,* June 19, 1885.

23. Shrady, "Last Days," 102–113.

24. Grant notes to Douglas, box 1, John Hancock Douglas papers, Library of Congress, Manuscript Division.

25. Grant notes, June 17, 1885, Box 1, Douglas papers.

26. *New York Tribune,* July 23, 1885.

27. Douglas diary, 282–283, Douglas papers.

28. *New York Tribune,* July 24, 1885.

29. *New York Tribune,* July 23, 1885.

1. Cancerphobia in the Late Nineteenth Century

1. L. J. Rather, *The Genesis of Cancer: A Study in the History of Ideas* (Baltimore, 1978); Henry Sigerist, "The Historical Development of the Pathology and Therapy of Cancer," *Bulletin of the New York Academy of Medicine,* 8 (Nov. 1932), 642–653; James Tobey, *Cancer: What Everyone Should Know about It* (New York, 1932), 23–40; Charles Oberling, *The Riddle of Cancer* (New York, 1944), 9–14; A. McGehee Harvey, "Early Contributions to the Surgery of Cancer," *Johns Hopkins Medical Journal,* 135 (Dec. 1974), 399–417.

2. Hippocrates cited in Samuel Gross, *On the Results of Surgical Operations in Malignant Diseases* (Philadelphia, 1853), 161; Celsus in Tobey, *Cancer,* 27.

3. Cited in Michael Shimkin, *Contrary to Nature* (Washington, D.C., 1979), 92.

4. Cited in Patricia Butler and Lee Sanderson, "Epidemiology," in Charles Shaw, ed., *Prevention of Occupational Cancer* (Boca Raton, Fla., 1981), 55–107.

5. Joseph Fraumeni, Jr., "Epidemiologic Approaches to Cancer Etiology," *Annual Review of Public Health,* 3 (1982), 85–100; Oliver Hayward, "The History of Oncology," *Surgery,* 58 (Aug., Sept., Oct., 1965), 460–468, 586–599, 745–757.

6. See J. Hill, *Cautions against the Immoderate Use of Snuff* (London, 1781).

7. Shimkin, *Contrary to Nature,* 161. See also Cushman Haagensen, "An Exhibit of Important Books, Papers, and Memorabilia Illustrating the Evolution of the Knowledge of Cancer," *American Journal of Cancer,* 18 (May, 1933), 42–126.

8. Rather, *Genesis of Cancer,* 3–41.

9. Stanley Reiser, *Medicine and the Reign of Technology* (Cambridge, England, 1978), 77–79.

10. Rather, *Genesis of Cancer,* 3–14; Erwin Ackerknecht, *Rudolf Virchow: Doctor, Statesman, Anthropologist* (Madison, Wis., 1953); William Coleman, *Biology in the Nineteenth Century* (New York, 1971), 16–20, 32–33; James Ewing, *Neoplastic Diseases: A Textbook on Tumors* (Philadelphia, 1919), 21–22; E. B. Krumbhaar, "Experimental Cancer, An Historical Retrospect," *Annals of*

Medical History, 7 (June 1925), 132–140; Thelma Brumfield Dunn, *The Unseen Fight against Cancer* (Charlottesville, Va., 1975), 158; R. Nery, *Cancer: An Enigma in Biology and Society* (London, 1986), 62–82.

11. Wilson Onuigbo, "The Paradox of Virchow's Views on Cancer Metastases," *Bulletin of the History of Medicine,* 36 (Sept.–Oct. 1962), 444–449; Shimkin, *Contrary to Nature,* 129–130; Nery, *Cancer,* 319–320.

12. Reiser, *Medicine,* 77–79.

13. Paul Starr, *The Social Transformation of American Medicine* (New York, 1982), 135–138; Charles Rosenberg, "What It Was Like to Be Sick in 1884," *American Heritage* (Oct./Nov. 1984), 23–31; A. Scott Earle, "The Germ Theory in America: Antisepsis and Asepsis (1867–1900)," *Surgery,* 65 (March 1969), 508–522.

14. Some surgical procedures advanced independently of knowledge about germs. The first successful appendectomies took place in the late 1880s. See Stewart Brooks and Natalie Brooks, "Appendicitis at 100," *American Heritage,* 37 (April/May 1986), 35–37.

15. Charles Rosenberg, "And Heal the Sick: The Hospital and the Patient in Nineteenth Century America," *Journal of Social History,* 10 (June 1977), 428–447; Rosenberg, "The Therapeutic Revolution: Medicine, Meaning, and Social Change in Nineteenth Century America," in Morris Vogel and Charles Rosenberg, eds., *The Therapeutic Revolution* (Philadelphia, 1979), 3–25; Edmund Pellegrino, "The Sociocultural Impact of Twentieth Century Therapeutics," ibid., 245–266.

16. Rene Dubos, *Mirage of Health: Utopias, Progress, and Biological Change* (New York, 1959); Lewis Thomas, "On the Science and Technology of Medicine," *Daedalus,* 106 (Winter 1977), 34–46; Oliver Sacks, *Awakenings* (New York, 1983), 205–206. Many breast cancers, later experts were to suggest, may well be systemic, not local. See Edward Sylvester, *Target: Cancer* (New York, 1986), 218–228.

17. Starr, *Social Transformation,* 55–57; William Bennett, "The Genealogy of Mass. General," *American Heritage* (Oct./Nov. 1984), 41–52; Thomas McKeown, *The Role of Medicine: Dream, Mirage, or Nemesis?* (Princeton, N.J., 1979), 177. But see also John Warner, "Science in Medicine," *Osiris,* 1 (1985), 37–58.

18. Kenneth Ludmerer, *Learning to Heal: The Development of American Medical Education* (New York, 1985); Robert Hudson, *Disease and Its Control* (Westport, Conn., 1983), 141; Anita Clair Fellman and Michael Fellman, *Making Sense of Self: Medical Advice Literature in Late Nineteenth Century America* (Philadelphia, 1981), 4–9.

19. D'Arcy Power, "The History of Amputation of the Breast," *Liverpool Medico-Chirurgical Journal,* 42 (1934), 1–28; Sigismund Peller, *Cancer Research since 1900* (New York, 1979), 203; John Duffy, *The Healers: A History of American Medicine* (Urbana, Ill., 1976), 249.

20. Charles Rosenberg, *The Trial of the Assassin Guiteau* (Chicago, 1968), 3–10.

21. Duffy, *The Healers,* 231–233; David Courtwright, *Dark Paradise: Opiate Addiction in America before 1940* (Cambridge, Mass., 1982), 173.

22. James Harvey Young, "The Persistence of Medical Quackery in America,"

American Scientist, 60 (May–June 1972), 318–326; Young, "The Regulation of Health Quackery," *Pharmacy in History,* 26 (1984), 3–12; Stewart Holbrook, *The Golden Age of Quackery* (New York, 1959), 33–40.

23. *New York Tribune,* August 8, 1885. Also Rosenberg, "To Be Sick in 1884."

24. Tobey, *Cancer,* 30–32; Francelia Butler, *Cancer through the Ages: The Evolution of Hope* (Fairfax, Va., 1955), 126.

25. Wayland Hand, *Magical Medicine* (Berkeley, 1980), 1–14, 73, 192, 203.

26. James Harvey Young, *Medical Messiahs: A Social History of Health Quackery in Twentieth Century America* (Princeton, N.J., 1967), 15; Butler, *Cancer through the Ages,* 22–26; Francelia Butler, "Cancer in Colonial Times," in American Society for the Control of Cancer, *Bulletin* (Aug. 8, 1933); Morris Fishbein, "History of Cancer Quackery," *Perspectives in Biology and Medicine,* 8 (Winter 1965), 139–166.

27. William Stone, "A Review of the History of Chemical Therapy in Cancer," *Medical Record* (Oct. 7, 1916); Donald Shaughnessy, "The Story of the American Cancer Society," Ph.D. diss., Columbia University, New York, 1957, 73–76; Peter Collier and David Horowitz, *The Rockefellers: An American Dynasty* (New York, 1976), 8.

28. *New York Times,* April 8, July 24, 1885. The remedy was more widely advertised as "S.S.S.," Swift's Syphilitic Specific.

29. Gross, *Surgical Operations,* 13–14. See also Dr. Benjamin Rush to Elisha Hall, July 6, 1789, College of Physicians of Philadelphia. Rush confessed that he had nothing to offer Mary Washington, George's mother, who had breast cancer.

30. *Boston Medical and Surgical Journal* (March 23, 1982), 281, (Jan. 3, 1884), 20.

31. Shimkin, *Contrary to Nature,* 176; Reiser, *Medicine,* 89–90, 141–142.

32. Butler, *Cancer through the Ages,* 46–50, 79–91; Seale Harris, *Women's Surgeon: The Life Story of J. Marion Sims* (New York, 1950), 377–381; Bob Consodine, *That Many May Live* (New York, 1959), 18–27; *New York Times,* March 8, 17, 1884; "A Century of Commitment," pamphlet put out by the Archives Committee, Memorial Sloan-Kettering, 1984.

33. See Willard Parker, *Cancer: A Study of 397 Cases of Cancer of the Human Breast* (New York, 1885), 34–35; Herbert Snow, *Clinical Notes on Cancer: Its Etiology and Treatment* (London, 1883), 19.

34. Later, of course, researchers recognized that certain cancers (of the breast, stomach, and large intestine) are more common among relatives of those who have had the disease than in the general population. But physicians and epidemiologists in the late nineteenth century had no solid evidence for their cruder hereditarian notions. See John Cairns, *Cancer: Science and Society* (San Francisco, 1978), 52–53.

35. Parker, *397 Cases,* 52–58.

36. Paul Rosch, "Stress and Cancer," in Gary Cooper, ed., *Psychosocial Stress and Cancer* (Chichester, 1984), 3–19. See also *New York Times,* April 6, 1885; and for a critique, Susan Sontag, *Illness as Metaphor* (New York, 1977).

37. Harold Simmons, *The Psychosomatic Aspects of Cancer* (Washington, D.C., 1956), 105–106; Paul Rosch, "Stress and Cancer," in Jean Tache et al., eds., *Cancer, Stress, and Death* (New York, 1979), 187–212; Samuel Kowal, "Emo-

tions as a Cause of Cancer: Eighteenth and Nineteenth Century Contributions," *Psychoanalytic Review,* 42 (July 1955), 217–227.

38. Dubos, *Mirage of Health,* 197–199; Charles Rosenberg, *The Cholera Years: The United States in 1832, 1849, and 1866* (Chicago, 1962), 16–17; Richard Shryock, *National Tuberculosis Association, 1904–1954: A Study of the Voluntary Health Movement in the United States* (New York, 1957), 33; George Rosen, "Disease, Debility, and Death," in H. Dyos and Michael Wolff, eds., *The Victorian City: Images and Realities* (London, 1973), vol. 2, 625–668.

39. Fellman and Fellman, *Making Sense of Self,* 14–70; Gerald Grob, "The Origins of American Psychiatric Epidemiology," *American Journal of Public Health,* 75 (March 1985), 229–236; Donald Meyer, *The Positive Thinkers: Religion as Popular Psychology from Mary Baker Eddy to Oral Roberts* (New York, 1980), 25–26; Charles Rosenberg, "George M. Beard and American Nervousness," in Rosenberg, *No Other Gods: On Science and American Social Thought* (Baltimore, 1976), 98–108; J. J. Caldwell, "The Connection Between Excessive Nerve and Brain Worry and Bodily Disease, with Pathology and Treatment of Cancer" (Baltimore, 1874?), College of Physicians of Philadelphia.

40. Parker, *397 Cases,* 11, 25–26, 58.

41. Snow, *Clinical Notes,* 25–31.

42. Rosenberg, "Therapeutic Revolution."

43. See Steven Locke and Douglas Colligan, *The Healer Within: The New Medicine of Mind and Body* (New York, 1985), 133–154; and H. J. Mattern, "The Psycho-Social Care of Cancer Patients," in E. Grundman and J. W. Cole, eds., *Cancer Centers* (New York, 1979), 275–278.

44. Sontag, *Illness as Metaphor.*

45. Parker, *397 Cases,* 11.

46. Snow, *Clinical Notes,* 14–24.

47. Elizabeth Whelan, *A Smoking Gun: How the Tobacco Industry Gets Away with Murder* (Philadelphia, 1985), 38–46; Richard Tennant, *The American Cigarette Industry* (New Haven, 1950), 15–50.

48. Whelan, *Smoking Gun,* 37.

49. *New York Tribune,* March 1, 1885.

50. Cited in Karl Wold, "Ulysses S. Grant—His Last Battle," *Tic,* 34 (July 1975), 10–12.

51. *New York Tribune,* July 31, 1885. Also George Shrady, "General Grant's Last Days," *Century,* 76 (May–June, 1908), 102–113, 275–285; Robert Steckler and Donald Shedd, "General Grant, His Physicians and His Cancer," *American Journal of Surgery,* 132 (Oct. 1976), 508–514; F. B. Smith, *The People's Health, 1830–1910* (New York, 1979), 329.

52. Mrs. Ormsby to Parker, June 14, 25, 1881, Parker papers, New York Academy of Medicine, New York City.

53. F. B. Smith, *People's Health,* 326–328.

54. Snow, *Clinical Notes,* 45. See also Joan Austoker, "The 'Treatment of Choice': Breast Cancer Surgery, 1860–1965," paper presented at American Association for the History of Medicine, Rochester, N.Y., May, 1986.

55. Cited in Nick Salvatore, *Eugene V. Debs: Citizen and Socialist* (Urbana, Ill., 1982), 83.

56. Shimkin, *Contrary to Nature,* 151–152. Haagensen, "Exhibit of Books,"

85–86; Parker, *397 Cases,* 10; Charles Childe, *The Control of a Scourge, or How Cancer Is Curable* (London, 1906), 101–102; Gross, *Surgical Operations,* 6–23.

57. Childe, *Control of a Scourge,* 69–70, 272.

58. *New York Tribune,* March 19, 1885.

59. Butler, *Cancer through the Ages,* 66–67. "Bullet-cysts" were much discussed during Garfield's ordeal in 1881.

60. John Hancock Douglas, "Three Years in the Sanitary Commission . . . and Attendance for Nine Months upon General Grant," 28, box 1, Douglas papers, Library of Congress, Manuscript Collection; *New York Tribune,* Jan. 12, 1885.

61. Michael Shimkin, "Neoplasia," in John Bowers and Elizabeth Purcell, eds., *Advances in American Medicine* (New York, 1976), 210–250; Gross, *Surgical Operations,* 10.

62. Guy Howe, *How to Prevent Sickness* (New York, 1918), 189. Kipling cited in Shimkin, *Contrary to Nature,* 79.

63. Frederick Hoffman, in American Society for the Control of Cancer, *Bulletin* (Aug. 1933); *Boston Medical and Surgical Journal* (Nov. 14, 1884), 474–475; *New York Times,* Aug. 8, 1885; "The Increase of Cancer," *Current Literature* (Sept. 1900); Robert Grove and Alice Hetzel, *Vital Statistics Rates in the United States, 1940–1960* (Washington, D.C., 1968), 87.

64. Philippe Ariès, *The Hour of Our Death* (New York, 1981), 568–582; Charles Jackson, "American Attitudes to Death," *Journal of American Studies,* 11 (Dec. 1977), 297–312; Lewis Saum, "Death in the Popular Mind of Pre–Civil War America," in David Stannard, ed., *Death in America* (Philadelphia, 1975), 30–48; Martin Pernick, *A Calculus of Suffering: Pain, Professionalism, and Anesthesia in Nineteenth Century America* (New York, 1985).

65. See Saul Brody, *The Disease of the Soul: Leprosy in Medieval Literature* (Ithaca, 1974), 54–66; Allan Brandt, *No Magic Bullet: A Social History of Venereal Disease in the United States since 1880* (New York, 1985), 186; Henry Sigerist, "The Special Position of the Sick," in David Landy, ed., *Culture, Disease, and Healing: Studies in Medical Anthropology* (New York, 1977), 388–394.

66. Quotes in Shryock, *National Tuberculosis Association,* 87, and in John Burnham, "Medical Specialists and Movements toward Social Control in the Progressive Era: Three Examples," in Jerry Israel, ed., *Building the Organizational Society* (New York, 1972), 19–30. See also Rene and Jean Dubos, *The White Plague: Tuberculosis, Man, and Society* (Boston, 1952), 96–101, 185–186; Sontag, *Illness as Metaphor,* 35–36, 81; William Rothstein, *American Physicians in the Nineteenth Century* (Baltimore, 1972), 267–272.

67. See Fitzhugh Mullan, *Vital Signs: A Young Doctor's Struggle with Cancer* (New York, 1983).

68. Childe, *Control of a Scourge,* 3; Leon Edel, ed., *The Diary of Alice James* (New York, 1964), 207; Alice James, *Alice James: Her Brothers, Her Journal* (New York, 1934), 231.

2. *The Rise of the Doctors*

1. Other presidents have been said to have had cancer, among them George Washington and Franklin D. Roosevelt, but no solid evidence supports such suppositions.

2. W. W. Keen, "The Surgical Operations on President Cleveland in 1893," *Saturday Evening Post* (Sept. 22, 1917), 24ff.; John Stuart Martin, "When the President Disappeared," *American Heritage,* 8 (1957), 10ff.; John Brooks et al., "The Final Diagnosis of President Cleveland's Lesion," *Transactions and Studies of the College of Physicians of Philadelphia,* 2 (March 1–25, 1950). Plastic models of Cleveland's jaw exist in the New York Academy of Medicine, New York City; part of his jaw, as well as some of the surgical instruments used, may be seen at the College of Physicians of Philadelphia.

3. Later analysis classified the tumor as a verrucous carcinoma, a cancer well associated with use of tobacco. Cleveland, like Grant, was a cigar smoker. Such tumors, if removed early (as Cleveland's was), were considered considerably less life-threatening than the form of cancer contracted by Grant. See Brooks et al., "Final Diagnosis."

4. Clippings in scrapbook and letters of Dr. W. W. Keen, College of Physicians of Philadelphia, esp. Dr. J. D. Barker to Thomas Lamont, May 9, 1905; and "Notes" by Dr. R. M. O'Reilly, June–July 1893. Dr. Keen was the surgeon. Emphasis mine.

5. In Brooks et al., "Final Diagnosis," one physician said that a postmortem had found extensive cancer in Cleveland's intestines, but there was no way to verify this statement or to know whether it was related to the tumor in his jaw.

6. James Tobey, *Cancer: What Everyone Should Know about It* (New York, 1932), 42–60.

7. Barrie Cassileth, "The Evolution of Oncology as a Sociomedical Phenomenon," in Cassileth, ed., *The Cancer Patient: Social and Medical Aspects of Care* (Philadelphia, 1979), 3–15; Donald Shaughnessy, "The Story of the American Cancer Society," Ph.D. diss., Columbia University, New York, 1957, 19. My publisher was as worried as Childe's, urging me to drop the word "cancer" from the main title.

8. A key source on broad scientific developments in hereditarianism is William Coleman, "Cell, Nucleus, and Inheritance: An Historical Study," *Proceedings of the American Philosophical Society,* 109 (June 1965), 124–158.

9. Michael Shimkin, *Science and Cancer,* 3d rev. ed. (Washington, D.C., 1980), 75–78; John Cairns, *Cancer: Science and Society* (San Francisco, 1978), 52–53; R. Nery, *Cancer: An Enigma in Biology and Society* (London, 1986), 222–234.

10. Mark Haller, *Eugenics: Hereditarian Attitudes in American Thought* (New Brunswick, N.J., 1963), 42; Daniel Kevles, *In the Name of Eugenics: Genetics and the Uses of Human Heredity* (New York, 1985), 57–69.

11. Sigismund Peller, *Cancer Research since 1900: An Evaluation* (New York, 1979), 162–163; "Why Early Cancer Is Curable," *Scientific American,* 113 (Aug. 1915), 149.

12. Francelia Butler, *Cancer through the Ages: The Evolution of Hope* (Fairfax, Va., 1955), 79–91; Bob Consodine, *That Many May Live* (New York, 1959), 27–42.

13. Clipping from the *New York World,* April 6, 1914, in the Frederick Hoffman scrapbook, Hoffman papers, College of Physicians of Philadelphia.

14. *New York Sun,* June 5, 1913, ibid.

15. James Harvey Young, *The Medical Messiahs: A Social History of Health Quackery in Twentieth Century America* (Princeton, N.J., 1957), 48–50, 129–30; Young, "Self-Dosage Medicine in America, 1906–1981," *South Atlantic Quarterly,* 80 (Autumn 1981), 379–390; Samuel H. Adams, *The Great American Fraud* (New York, 1905); American Medical Association, *Nostrums and Quackery: Articles on the Nostrum Evil and Quackery Reprinted from the Journal of the American Medical Association* (Chicago, 1911), 23–71.

16. Adams, *Collier's Weekly* (Jan. 13, 1906), 48–54; AMA, *Nostrums,* 24–27.

17. Stewart Holbrook, *The Golden Age of Quackery* (New York, 1959), 19. See also Tobey, *Cancer,* 214–219.

18. Holbrook, *Golden Age,* 24; AMA, *Nostrums,* 46–49; Morris Fishbein, "History of Cancer Quackery," *Perspectives in Biology and Medicine,* 8 (Winter 1965), 139–166.

19. Charles Childe, *The Control of a Scourge, or How Cancer Is Curable* (London, 1906), 255–270; *New York Times,* July 25, 1913.

20. *New York Times,* July 19, 1908; for Walker, see ibid., Nov. 19, 1908, and Wyndham Miles, "Creation of the National Cancer Institute," typescript (1973) in my possession. See also Alfred Spring to Rep. Vreeland, April 13, 1910, general file 2236, box 214, Public Health Service papers, Record Group 90, National Archives, Washington, D.C., for evidence of Walker's attempt to interest Congress. The College of Physicians of Philadelphia has an illustrated copy of Walker's *Cancer and Sarcoma* (Buffalo, 1908?).

21. Holbrook, *Golden Age,* 9; AMA, *Nostrums,* 59–60.

22. Guy Livingston Howe, *How to Prevent Sickness* (New York, 1918), 181.

23. Cited in David Shi, *The Simple Life: Plain Living and High Thinking in American Culture* (New York, 1985), 201. See also Harvey Green, *Fit for America: Health, Fitness, Sport, and American Society* (New York, 1986), 219–282.

24. F. B. Smith, *The People's Health, 1830–1910* (New York, 1979), 329–330.

25. Dr. George White, *Campaign Notes* (Oct. 1918). This in-house magazine of the American Society for the Control of Cancer (available at the American Cancer Society, New York City), was unpaginated.

26. John Huber, "Heredity in Cancer," *Collier's,* 55 (June 26, 1915), 32; Howe, *How to Prevent Sickness,* 188.

27. "Increase of Cancer," *Current Literature,* 29 (Sept. 1900), 302–303; Mayo, *Campaign Notes* (Sept. 1918); Frederick Hoffman, *The Mortality from Cancer throughout the World* (Newark, 1915), 150–151, 174–175; Green, *Fit for America,* 283–317.

28. *New York Times,* Sept. 24, 1907; "Cancer and the Meat Eater," *Current Literature,* 43 (Nov. 1907), 560.

29. Childe, *Control of a Scourge,* 26–32.

30. Ibid., 36, 18–22.

31. Ibid., 153–154, 202.

32. Ibid., 276.

33. A. McGehee Harvey, *Science at the Bedside: Clinical Research in American Medicine, 1905–1945* (Baltimore, 1981), 38–129.

34. Barrie Cassileth and Harold Lief, "Cancer: A Biopsychosocial Model," in Cassileth, ed., *Cancer Patient,* 17–31. For studies that employ cultural perspectives of diseases, see Allan Brandt, *No Magic Bullet: A Social History of Venereal Disease in the United States since 1880* (New York, 1985); Renee Fox, "The Medicalization and Demedicalization of American Society," in John Knowles, ed., *Doing Better and Feeling Worse: Health in the United States* (New York, 1977), 9–22; Guenter Risse, "Epidemics and Medicine: The Influence of Disease on Medical Thought and Practice," *Bulletin of the History of Medicine* (Winter 1979), 505–519; and Charles Rosenberg, *The Cholera Years: The United States in 1832, 1849, and 1866* (Chicago, 1962).

35. Kenneth Ludmerer, *Learning to Heal: The Development of American Medical Education* (New York, 1985), 202–204.

36. Cited in Rene Dubos, *Mirage of Health: Utopias, Progress, and Biological Change* (New York, 1959), 143.

37. Cited in Paul Starr, *The Social Transformation of American Medicine* (New York, 1982), 160. See also Charles Rosenberg, "Inward Vision and Outward Glance: The Shaping of the American Hospital, 1880–1914," *Bulletin of the History of Medicine,* 33 (1979), 346–391; David Rosner, *A Once Charitable Enterprise: Hospitals and Health Care in Brooklyn and New York, 1885–1915* (Cambridge, Mass., 1982), 3–8, 50–54; Morris Vogel, *The Invention of the Modern Hospital: Boston, 1870–1930* (Chicago, 1980), 1; Vogel, "The Transformation of the American Hospital, 1850–1920," in Susan Reverby and David Rosner, eds., *Health Care in America: Essays in Social History* (Philadelphia, 1979), 105–116; George Rosen, "The Place of History in Medical Education," in *From Medical Police to Social Medicine: Essays on the History of Health Care* (New York, 1974), 32–33.; Judy Barrett Litoff, *American Midwives: 1860 to the Present* (Westport, Conn., 1978), 135–152; and Gerald Grob, "The Social History of Medicine and Diseases in Medical Thought and Practice," *Journal of Social History,* 10 (June 1977), 391–409.

38. From *Life* magazine, cited in John Burnham, "American Medicine's Golden Age: What Happened to It?" *Science,* 215 (March 19, 1982), 1474–1479.

39. Barbara Gutmann Rosenkrantz, *Public Health and the State: Changing Views in Massachusetts, 1843–1936* (Cambridge, Mass., 1972), 14–15; Thomas McKeown, *The Role of Medicine: Dream, Mirage, or Nemesis?* (Princeton, N.J., 1979), 180; Richard Harrison Shryock, *The Development of Modern Medicine* (Madison, Wis., 1947), 34–36.

40. Chapin cited in Starr, *Social Transformation,* 190–192. See also James Cassedy, *Charles V. Chapin and the Public Health Movement* (Cambridge, Mass., 1962), 59–77, 92–100, 110–125, 140–142; Rosen, "What Is Social Medicine?" in *Medical Police,* 60–119; Rene Dubos, *Mirage of Health,* 133; Barbara Gutmann Rosenkrantz, "Cart before Horse: Theory, Practice, and Professional Image in American Public Health, 1870–1920," *Journal of the History of Medicine,* 29 (Jan. 1974), 55–73; and John Burnham, "Medical Specialists and Movements toward Social Control in the Progressive Era: Three Examples," in Jerry Israel, ed., *Building the Organizational Society* (New York, 1972), 19–30.

41. Eliot Freidson, *Profession of Medicine: A Study of the Sociology of Applied Knowledge* (New York, 1970), 287–288; Rosemary Stevens, *American Med-*

icine and the Public Interest (New Haven, 1971), 55–97; Barbara Ehrenreich and Deirdre English, *For Her Own Good: 150 Years of Experts' Advice to Women* (Garden City, N.Y., 1978), 77–81; Peter Conrad and Joseph Schneider, *Deviance and Medicalization: From Badness to Sickness* (St. Louis, 1980), 14–33; and E. Richard Brown, *Rockefeller Medicine Men: Medicine and Capitalism in America* (Berkeley, 1979), 97.

42. Edwin Post Maynard, Jr., "The Practice of Medicine in 1921," *Bulletin of the New York Academy of Medicine,* 48 (July 1972), 807–817; William McNeill, *Plagues and Peoples* (New York, 1976), 135, 140, 151; Joseph Aub interview, Columbia University, Oral History Project, 52–53.

43. Peter English, *Shock, Physiological Surgery, and George Washington Crile* (Westport, Conn., 1981); Michael Shimkin, *Contrary to Nature* (Washington, D.C., 1979), 261–262.

44. Peter Collier and David Horowitz, *The Rockefellers: An American Dynasty* (New York, 1976), 61; Lewis Thomas, *The Medusa and the Snail: More Notes of a Biology Watcher* (New York, 1979), 160–162.

45. Ludmerer, *Learning to Heal,* 47–138; Harvey, *Science at the Bedside,* 126–129, 183–186; Robert Kohler, *From Medical Chemistry to Biochemistry: The Making of a Biomedical Discipline* (Cambridge, England, 1982), 121–157.

46. Dubos, *Mirage of Health,* 157; James Burrow, *Organized Medicine in the Progressive Era: The Move Toward Monopoly* (Baltimore, 1977), 8–9; Lewis Thomas, "Biomedical Science and Human Health: The Long-Range Prospect," *Daedalus,* 106 (Summer 1977), 163–171; Starr, *Social Transformation,* 139–144; McNeill, *Plagues and Peoples,* 235–257. Quote from Robert Hudson, *Disease and Its Control* (Westport, Conn., 1983), 211–212. This was an exaggeration—Salvarsan was far from a miracle cure.

47. Philip Nobile, *King Cancer: The Good, the Bad, and the Cure of Cancer* (New York, 1975), 37–38; Donald Fleming, *William H. Welch and the Rise of Modern Medicine* (Boston, 1954), 123–124; D'Arcy Power, "The History of Amputation of the Breast," *Liverpool Medico-Chirurgical Journal,* 42 (1934), 1–28; Stevens, *American Medicine,* 49–50, 77–97; Cushman Haagensen, "An Exhibit of Important Books, Papers, and Memorabilia Illustrating the Evolution of the Knowledge of Cancer," *American Journal of Cancer,* 18 (May 1933), 42–126; Gert Brieger, "American Surgery and the Germ Theory of Disease," *Bulletin of the History of Medicine,* 40 (March–April, 1966), 135–145; A McGehee Harvey, "Early Contributions to the Surgery of Cancer: William H. Halsted, Hugh H. Young, and John G. Clark," *Johns Hopkins Medical Journal,* 135 (Dec. 1974), 399–417.

48. McKeown, *Role of Medicine;* John and Sonja McKinlay, "The Questionable Contribution of Medical Measures to the Decline of Mortality in the United States in the Twentieth Century," *Milbank Memorial Fund Quarterly* (Summer 1977), 405–428.

49. Rosenberg, *Cholera Years,* 160–164; Henderson cited in Conrad and Schneider, *Deviance,* 33.

50. Freidson, *Profession of Medicine;* Gerald Markowitz and David Rosner, "Doctors in Crisis: Medical Education and Medical Reform during the Progressive Era, 1895–1915," 185–205, and E. Richard Brown, "He Who Pays the Piper:

Foundations, the Medical Profession, and Medical Education," 132–153, in Reverby and Rosner, eds., *Health Care;* Rosenberg, "Inward Vision"; Michael Pernick, *A Calculus of Pain and Suffering: Pain, Professionalism, and Anesthesia in Nineteenth Century America* (New York, 1985), 241–248.

51. Starr, *Social Transformation,* 110–121; James Burrow, *AMA: Voice of American Medicine* (Baltimore, 1963), 27–66.

52. Osler cited in Ehrenreich and English, *For Her Own Good,* 62–69, 81–84. See also John Ettling, *The Germ of Laziness: Rockefeller Philanthropy and Public Health in the New South* (Cambridge, Mass., 1982), 207–208, 222–223; Charles Rosenberg, *No Other Gods: On Science and American Social Thought* (Baltimore, 1976), 12–13, 123–131; Anita Clair Fellman and Michael Fellman, *Making Sense of Self: Medical Advice Literature in Late Nineteenth Century America* (Philadelphia, 1981), 17–18; Robert Wiebe, *The Search for Order* (New York, 1967).

53. Gerald Grob, *Mental Illness and American Society, 1875–1940* (Princeton, N.J., 1983), 108–111, 142–143; Grob, "The Origins of American Psychiatric Epidemiology," *American Journal of Public Health,* 75 (March 1985), 229–236.

54. Rene and Jean Dubos, *The White Plague: Tuberculosis, Man, and Society* (Boston, 1952), 215; Richard Shryock, *National Tuberculosis Association, 1904–1954: A Study of the Voluntary Health Movement in the United States* (New York, 1957), 159–172.

55. Shryock, *National Tuberculosis Association,* 184–187.

56. Howe, *How to Prevent Sickness,* 1–35; citation in John Burnham, "Change in the Popularization of Health in the United States," *Bulletin of the History of Medicine,* 58 (Summer 1984), 187.

57. For the five "Ds" see Frank Thompson, *Health Policy and the Bureaucracy: Policies and Implementation* (Cambridge, Mass., 1981), 4. Also see James Farrell, *Inventing the American Way of Death, 1830–1920* (Philadelphia, 1980), esp. 217; Donald Meyer, *The Positive Thinkers* (New York, 1980), 40–43; Dubos, *Mirage of Health,* 249–251; and James Whorton, *Crusaders for Fitness: The History of American Health Reformers* (Princeton, N.J., 1982), 9–11. A key article is Talcott Parsons, "Definitions of Health and Illness in the Light of American Values and Social Structure," in E. Gartly Jaco, ed., *Patients, Physicians, and Illness* (New York, 1972), 165–187.

58. Fellman and Fellman, *Making Sense of Self,* 46–49, 126–130; Richard Fox and T. J. Jackson Lears, eds., *The Culture of Consumption* (New York, 1983), 4–16.

3. *The Alliance against Cancer*

1. Carole Haber, *Beyond Sixty-Five: The Dilemma of Old Age in America's Past* (Cambridge, 1983), 50–51, 62–70.

2. There was only a slight increase, however, in the proportion of the aged in the total population—from 4.7 to 5.4 percent.

3. Michael Shimkin, *Science and Cancer* (New York, 1980), 79–80; R. Nery, *Cancer: An Enigma in Biology and Society* (London, 1986), 141–144, 160–163, 173–176.

4. Sigismund Peller, *Cancer Research since 1900: An Evaluation* (New York, 1979), 54–60; Sharon Romm, *The Unwelcome Intruder: Freud's Struggle with Cancer* (New York, 1983), 73–78.

5. June Goodfield, *The Siege of Cancer* (New York, 1975), 91–93.

6. It was later to become the leading cause of death for Americans under fifty-five.

7. J. J. McCoy, *The Cancer Lady: Maud Slye and Her Heredity Studies* (New York, 1977), 119–120, 140–145; Peller, *Cancer Research*, 276–277.

8. *Newsweek,* April 10, 1937, 26–28, a cover story on Slye.

9. Nery, *Cancer,* 184–185, 207–208.

10. E. B. Krumbhaar, "Experimental Cancer: An Historical Retrospect," *Annals of Medical History,* 7 (June 1925), 132–140; C. C. Little, "Evidence That Cancer Is Not a Simple Mendelian Recessive," *Journal of Cancer Research,* 12 (1928), 30–46; John Parascandola, "Maud Cerdine Slye," in Barbara Sicherman and Carol Hurd Green, eds., *Notable American Women, The Modern Period: A Biographical Dictionary* (Cambridge, Mass., 1980), 651–652.

11. American Cancer Society folders, Peyton Rous papers, American Philosophical Society, Philadelphia.

12. Shimkin, *Science and Cancer,* 51; Thelma Brumfield Dunn, *The Unseen Fight against Cancer* (Charlottesville, Va., 1975), 136–137; Peller, *Cancer Research,* 55–56; *New York Times,* Feb. 14, 1912; "Cancer Is a Newly Discovered Animal," *Current Literature* (Feb. 1912), 186.

13. Dr. W. Ray Bryan interview, Oral History on Cancer, National Library of Medicine, Bethesda, Md., 42, 67.

14. Wyndham Miles, "Creation of the National Cancer Institute," typescript (1973) in my possession; H.R. 848, 61st Cong., 2d Sess., *Congressional Record* April 9, 1910, 4458; *New York Times,* April 10, 1910.

15. *New York Times,* April 17, 1910.

16. *New York Times,* Jan. 13, 1914.

17. Charles Childe, *The Control of a Scourge, or How Cancer Is Curable* (London, 1906), 43; Adams, "What Can We Do about Cancer?: The Most Vital and Insistent Question in the Medical World," *Ladies Home Journal* (May 1913), 21–22; Mayo in *New York Times,* April 10, 1914; James Ewing, *Neoplastic Diseases: A Textbook on Tumors* (Philadelphia, 1919), 103.

18. Katsusaburo Yamagiwa and Koichi Ichikawa, "Experimental Study of the Pathogenesis of Cancer," *Journal of Cancer Research,* 3 (1918), 1–29.

19. Elizabeth Whelan, *A Smoking Gun: How the Tobacco Industry Gets Away with Murder* (Philadelphia, 1985), 47–49; "The Cigaret Habit—A New Peril," *Independent* (Feb. 18, 1904), 377–378; Irving Fisher, *Bulletin 30 of the Committee of One Hundred on National Health* (Washington, D.C., 1909), 4; Ronald Troyer and Gerald Markle, *Cigarettes: The Battle over Smoking* (New Brusnwick, N.J., 1983), 33–34.

20. Lin Bonner, "Why Cigarette Makers Don't Advertise to Women," *Advertising and Selling,* 7 (Oct. 20, 1926), 21; Troyer and Markle, *Cigarettes,* 40, (Pershing quote); Richard Tennant, *The American Cigarette Industry: A Study in Economic Analysis and Public Policy* (New Haven, 1950), 75–84; Office of the Surgeon General, *The Health Consequences of Smoking for Women* (Washington, D.C., 1980).

21. Milton Rosenblatt, "Lung Cancer in the Nineteenth Century," *Bulletin of the History of Medicine,* 38 (Sept.–Oct. 1964), 395–425.

22. Ewing, *Neoplastic Diseases,* 11.

23. Childe, *Control of a Scourge,* 280; Frederick Hoffman, *The Mortality from Cancer throughout the World* (Newark, 1915), 185–186; Alice Hamilton, "What We Know about Cancer," *Survey* (Nov. 20, 1915), 188–189.

24. *New York Times,* Oct. 16, Nov. 1, 1907, April 3, 1910; "Electricity for Cancer," *Literary Digest,* 4 (Sept. 26, 1914), 512.

25. *New York Times,* June 27, 1909.

26. See *New York Times,* Oct. 18, 1908, Dec. 22, 1911, March 26, 1912, Feb. 19, 1915; Burton Hendrick, "New Facts on Cancer," *McClure's,* 35 (May 1916), 109–112; "The Autolysin Treatment for Cancer," *Survey,* 35 (Dec. 11, 1915), 284; "Escharotics as the Long-Sought Cure for Cancer," *Current Literature,* 43 (Aug. 1907), 218. For Coley, see Joseph Hixson, *The Patchwork Mouse* (Garden City, N.Y., 1976), 138–142; *New York Times,* Oct. 17, 1895, July 29, 1908.

27. Richard Weil, "Chemotherapy and Cancer," *Huntington Fund* (1916), 1–20; William Stone, "A Review of the History of Chemical Therapy in Cancer," *Medical Record,* Oct. 7, 1916. Allan Brandt, *No Magic Bullet: A Social History of Venereal Disease in the United States since 1880* (New York, 1985), and Rene Dubos, *Mirage of Health: Utopias, Progress, and Biological Change* (New York, 1959), emphasize the American quest for "magic bullets."

28. Cushman Haagensen, "An Exhibit of Important Books, Papers, and Memorabilia Illustrating the Evolution of the Knowledge of Cancer," *American Journal of Cancer,* 18 (May 1933), 42–126; *New York Times,* June 1, 1906; Michael Shimkin, *Contrary to Nature* (Washington, D.C., 1979), 269–270.

29. *New York Herald,* Jan. 9, 1914.

30. "Radium, Cure for Cancer," *Current Literature,* 35 (Sept. 1903), 348; *New York Times,* May 2, 1905; Joseph Aub interview, Columbia University, Oral History Project, 209.

31. *New York Times,* Jan. 8, 1914.

32. *New York Times,* Jan. 12, Feb. 6, 1914; Frederick Hoffman scrapbook, 1913–14, Hoffman papers, College of Physicians of Philadelphia.

33. Ralph Moss, *The Cancer Syndrome* (New York, 1980), 55–56; Harold Rusch, "The Beginnings of Cancer Research Centers in the United States," *Journal of the National Cancer Institute,* 74 (Feb. 1985), 391–403; "Prospectus: The New Memorial Hospital for the Treatment of Cancer and Allied Diseases" (1936), box 1, Sloan-Kettering Cancer Center papers, Rockefeller Archives, Pocantico Hills, N.Y.

34. Gioacchino Filla, "Radium Technique at the Memorial Hospital, N.Y.," *Archives of Radiology and Electrotherapy,* 25 (June 1920), 3–19; Henry Janeway, *Radium Therapy in Cancer at the Memorial Hospital, N.Y.* (New York, 1917).

35. From a statement by the American Society for the Control of Cancer, Dec. 12, 1913, Frederick Hoffman papers, National Library of Medicine; *New York Times,* Jan. 2, 21, 24, 1914, Sept. 30, 1915.

36. *Chicago Tribune,* Dec. 1922, file 2236, box 214, U.S. Public Health Service papers, Record Group 90, National Archives, Washington, D.C.

37. Adams, "What Can We Do?" 21; Guy Howe, *How to Prevent Sickness*

(New York, 1918), 191–193. The Public Health Service chimed in. See its *Cancer: Facts Which Every Adult Should Know* (Washington, D.C., 1919).

38. Morris Manges, "The General Practitioner's Response in the Early Diagnosis of Cancer," *American Journal of Surgery,* 29 (1915), 377–379; American Society for the Control of Cancer, *Campaign Notes* (Nov.–Dec., 1918); James Wright, Jr., "The Development of the Frozen Section Technique, the Evolution of Surgical Biopsy, and the Origins of Surgical Pathology," *Bulletin of the History of Medicine,* 59 (Fall 1985), 285–326.

39. Kenneth Chorley to File, Sept. 15, 1925, box 6, Office of Messrs. Rockefeller, Medical Interests, Rockefeller Archives.

40. Quote in University of California, Los Angeles, *A History of Cancer Control in the United States, 1946–1971* (Washington, D.C., 1976). vol. 1, 12; see also American Society for the Control of Cancer (henceforth identified as ASCC), *Campaign Notes* (Oct. 1918, Nov. 1920), for two of many complaints by cancer scientists about doctors. Also Donald Shaughnessy, "The Story of the American Cancer Society," Ph.D. diss., Columbia University, New York, 1957, 25, 36–39.

41. Dr. Alfred Wood to Frederick Hoffman, July 25, 1916, Hoffman papers, National Library of Medicine.

42. John Cairns, *Cancer: Science and Society* (San Francisco, 1978), 155–159.

43. *New York Times,* July 15, 1914.

44. Kenneth Chorley to Col. Woods, Dec. 22, 1925, Office of Messrs. Rockefeller, box 6, Rockefeller Archives. Rockefeller subsequently became a major benefactor of Memorial Hospital, New York.

45. Dunn, *Unseen Fight,* 18–44; Vincent DeVita, Jr., "The Evolution of Therapeutic Research in Cancer," *New England Journal of Medicine,* 298 (April 4, 1978), 907–910; Michael Shimkin, *As Memory Serves: Six Essays on a Personal Involvement with the National Cancer Institute, 1938 to 1978* (Washington, D.C., 1983), 8–9.

46. Krumbhaar, "Experimental Cancer."

47. A. McGehee Harvey, *Science at the Bedside: Clinical Research in American Medicine, 1905–1945* (Baltimore, 1981), 258–259.

48. Many sources describe the founding of these and subsequent cancer research institutions. See V. A. Triolo and I. L. Riegel, "The American Association for Cancer Research, 1907–1940," *Cancer Research,* 21 (Feb., 1961), 137–167; Rusch, "Research Centers"; and Eleanor MacDonald, "History of the Cancer Program in Massachusetts," in George Bigelow and Herbert Lombard, eds., *Cancer and Other Diseases in Massachusetts* (Cambridge, Mass., 1933), 160–172. Important sources relating to the program at Harvard are the papers of the organization at the Countway Medical Library, Harvard University. See "History of the Harvard Cancer Commission," box 7.

49. *New York Times,* Nov. 17, Dec. 8, 1909, Oct. 8, Nov. 12, 1912, Nov. 22, 1914.

50. Frank Adair, "The Relation of a Cancer Institute to the General Medical Profession," ASCC *Bulletin,* 21 (Nov. 11, 1939), 2–4; "A Century of Commitment," pamphlet put out by the Archives Committee of Memorial Sloan-Kettering Center, 1984.

51. "Cancer Organizations in France, Belgium, England, Germany, and Swe-

den," ASCC *Bulletin* (Nov. 1931), 1–5; Shimkin, *Contrary to Nature* 279–290; Charles Tobey, *Cancer: What Everyone Should Know about It* (New York, 1932), 293–295; Barrie Cassileth, "The Evolution of Oncology as a Sociomedical Phenomenon," in Cassileth, ed., *The Cancer Patient* (Philadelphia, 1979), 3–15; George Rosen, "Patterns of Health Research in the United States, 1900–1960," *Bulletin of the History of Medicine,* 39 (May–June, 1965), 201–221.

52. Key sources on the ASCC include Shaughnessy, "American Cancer Society"; Michael Shimkin, "Neoplasia," in John Bowers and Elizabeth Purcell, eds., *Advances in American Medicine: Essays at the Bicentennial* (New York, 1976), 210–250; Tobey, *Cancer,* 38–40, 277–280; and ASCC, *History of the American Society for the Control of Cancer, 1913–1944* (New York, 1944?). Key primary sources are *Campaign Notes,* house organ of the ASCC (starting in 1918); and the papers of Frederick Hoffman, National Library of Medicine, Bethesda, Md. (hereafter cited as Hoffman papers). For newspaper coverage of the founding, see *New York Times,* May 23, June 10, Nov. 30, 1913.

53. W. W. Richardson to George Soper, April 29, 1926, and George Soper to Thomas Debevoise, June 25, 1927, box 6, Office of Messrs. Rockefeller, Medical Interests, Rockefeller Archives; Raymond Fosdick, *John D. Rockefeller, Jr.: A Portrait* (New York, 1956), 383–386.

54. *New York Times,* April 23, 1913.

55. By 1916 the ASCC had only 700-odd dues-paying members, at 5 dollars each per year. It relied on an executive secretary initially paid $3,500 per year. Its total expenditures in 1915 were $6,997. By contrast, the National Tuberculosis Association oversaw the sale of $3.8 million in Christmas seals in 1919. Its expenses for the first half of that year were $156,000. Shaughnessy, "American Cancer Society," 32–46; Richard Shryock, *National Tuberculosis Association, 1904–1954: A Study of the Voluntary Health Movement in the United States* (New York, 1957), 126–144.

56. Hoffman papers, 1913–14 volumes.

57. ASCC, *History;* Hoffman papers, 1915 volume.

58. ASCC, *History; Campaign Notes* (March, Sept. 1918); pamphlets in Hoffman papers.

59. Curtis Lakeman address, April 15, 1914, Hoffman papers; "Cancer: A Controllable Disease: How the Women's Clubs Can Help," *Campaign Notes* (Sept. 1919).

60. Pamphlets, Hoffman papers; Louis Dublin, *After Eighty Years: The Impact of Life Insurance on the Public Health* (Gainesville, Fla., 1966), 38–40.

61. Hoffman, "The Menace of Cancer," *Transactions of the American Gynecological Society,* 38 (1913), 397–452. Also Hoffman to Curtis Lakeman, April 1, 1914, and to Forrest Dryden, April 23, May 2, and Sept. 12, 1913, Hoffman papers; and *Campaign Notes* (Feb. 1918). For Hoffman, see James Cassedy, "Frederick Hoffman," *Dictionary of American Biography,* suppl. 4 (1974), 384–385. See also Louis Dublin, "The Relation of Cancer to Economic Condition" (1917) and "The Interest of the Community in Cancer" (1916), in Louis Dublin papers, National Library of Medicine, Washington, D.C.

62. Hoffman to E. Atlee, Jan. 28, 1914, Hoffman papers; *Campaign Notes* (Dec. 1919).

63. *Journal of the American Medical Association,* 77 (Oct. 29, 1921), 1425.

64. America's war dead numbered around 116,500 (53,400 in battle). In this same eighteen-month period perhaps 120,000 Americans died from cancer (according to ASCC estimates).

65. ASCC, *History.*

66. *Campaign Notes* (Aug. 1919, Jan. 1920); "Suggestions to Lecturers," Hoffman papers, 1916 volume.

67. *Campaign Notes* (Dec. 1921); *New York Times,* Sept. 27, 1922; "Cancer Weeks," *Hygeia,* 1 (Nov. 1923), 524.

68. W. S. Richardson to John D. Rockefeller, Jr., Feb. 11, 1921, box 6, Rockefeller Medical Interests, Rockefeller Archives; Campaign Notes (Feb. 1921, March 1922); Shaughnessy, "American Cancer Society," 48–55.

69. Peller, *Cancer Research,* 108. See also Richard Doll, *Prevention of Cancer* (London, 1967), 30–31.

70. "Cancer," *Fortnightly Review* (Aug. 1903), 350; census of 1906 described in Tavia Gordon et al., "Cancer Mortality Trends in the United States, 1930–1955," *National Cancer Institute Monograph,* 6 (1961), 133–134; government report was Fisher, *Bulletin 30,* 52–53.

71. Hoffman, *Mortality,* vii, emphasis his. See also Hoffman, "Menace of Cancer," *Survey,* 30 (Aug. 30, 1913), 664–666; *New York Times,* Sept. 13, 1913.

72. Within a few decades statistics revealed that mortality from cancer afflicted American blacks more than whites. It also became clear that northeastern states had slightly higher cancer mortality rates than other areas. These developments probably reflected class differences (blacks and poor people smoked more, were more unhealthy in general, and received inferior medical care), as well as variations in the quality and reporting of diagnoses (weakest in the rural South). See Gordon et al., "Cancer Mortality," 131–350; Fred Burbank, "Patterns in Cancer Mortality in the United States, 1950–1967," *National Cancer Institute Monograph,* 33 (1971); and Cairns, *Cancer,* 46–47.

73. Hoffman, *Mortality,* 13–14, 38–47, 232–263; Hoffman to Forest Dryden, May 2, 1913, Hoffman papers. Because cancer tended to afflict older people, it was of course important to use age-adjusted mortality rates. Unless otherwise indicated, only such figures will be used in this book.

74. Later calculations by the Census Bureau confirmed the gist of Hoffman's argument. The bureau estimated that age-adjusted cancer mortality rates increased from 80 per 100,000 population in 1900 to nearly 100 per 100,000 in 1920. (Age-adjusted rates continued to increase considerably until the 1930s, whereupon they rose more slowly, to 120 per 100,000 in 1940. Still more gradual increases occurred thereafter; the rate was 133 per 100,000 in 1980). See Robert Grove and Alice Hetzel, *Vital Statistics Rates in the United States, 1940–1960* (Washington, D.C., 1968), 87; United States Bureau of the Census, *Statistical Abstract of the United States, 1984,* 78.

75. Childe, *Control of a Scourge,* 16–18. See also Abraham Lilienfeld et al., *Cancer Epidemiology: Methods of Study* (Baltimore, 1967), 52.

76. Walter Willcox, "Statistics of Causes of Death," ASCC *Bulletin* (April 1934), 8–9.

77. United States Bureau of the Census, *Mortality from Cancer and Other Malignant Tumors in the Registration Area of the United States, 1914* (Washing-

ton, D.C., 1916); Gordon et al., "Cancer Mortality"; J. E. Rush, "Cancer Statistics," *Journal of the American Medical Association,* 84 (May 2, 1925), 1376–1377.

78. *Campaign Notes* (Dec. 1922, Aug. 1924).

79. United States Bureau of the Census, *Mortality Statistics, 1920* (Washington, D.C., 1922), 42–43; J. W. Schereschewsky, "The Course of Cancer Mortality in the 10 Original Registration States for the 21-Year Period, 1900–1920," U.S. Public Health *Bulletin,* no. 155 (Washington, D.C., 1925), 1–69 (quote on p. 3); A. M. Stimson to Schereschewsky, Dec. 29, 1922, box 214, file 2236, Public Health Service, Record Group 90, National Archives, Washington, D.C.

80. Bigelow and Lombard, eds., *Cancer and Other Diseases,* 5–6.

81. An exception was coverage of the influenza epidemic of 1918–1919.

82. *New York Times,* March 4, Aug. 13, 14, Dec. 23, 1906; Feb. 18, March 28, July 1, 1907. See also C. W. Saleeby, "Cancer—Can It Be Cured?" *McClure's,* 27 (Aug. 1906), 438–444; and Saleeby, "The Coming Conquest of Cancer," *Harper's Weekly,* 50 (March 3, 1906), 30.

83. *New York Times,* June 16, 1907, Feb. 1, 1909, Feb. 27, 1910.

84. *New York Times,* April 20, 1913.

85. See *New York Times,* June 15, 1902, Feb. 4, 1911, May 15, 1911; "The Relation of Beer to Cancer," *Current Literature,* 35 (Sept. 1903), 347; "A Suspected Connection between Cancer and the Daisy," ibid., 53 (Dec. 1912), 661; "Pigmentation and Cancer," *Nature,* 83 (May 5, 1910), 294–295.

86. Childe, *Control of a Scourge,* 242–243.

87. *New York Times,* Jan. 21, 1914; *New York World,* 1913, Hoffman scrapbook, Hoffman papers, College of Physicians of Philadelphia; "A Great Surgeon's Theory That Cancer Is a Newly Discovered Animal," *Current Literature,* 52 (Feb. 1912), 185–186; I. W. Voorhes, "Scourge of Cancer," *Independent,* 70 (March 23, 1911), 609–613.

88. *New York Times,* Feb. 13, 1914; Barbara Gutmann Rosenkrantz, *Public Health and the State: Changing Views in Massachusetts, 1842–1936* (Cambridge, Mass., 1972), 161.

4. *The Wilderness Years*

1. *Congressional Record,* 1928, 9048–9050. See also William Yaremchuk, "The Origins of the National Cancer Institute," *Journal of the National Cancer Institute,* 59 (Supplement, Aug. 1957), 551–558.

2. In fact, the Public Health Service was then using small amounts of its funds to support research on cancer, but Neely was correct in asserting that Congress had never passed a bill specifying such use.

3. Charles Jackson, *Food and Drug Legislation in the New Deal* (Princeton, N.J., 1970), 19–21; Francis C. Wood, "Latest Cancer Cure," *New Republic,* 62 (April 23, 1930), 264–265.

4. ASCC, *Campaign Notes* (June 1929).

5. *Campaign Notes* (Jan. 1929).

6. Virginia Gardner, "Vanity, Modesty, and Cancer," *Hygeia* 11 (April 1933), 300–302; introduction by Bloodgood to James Tobey, *Cancer: What Everyone Should Know about It* (New York, 1932).

7. *Campaign Notes* (Oct. 1929).

8. Lauren Ackerman and Juan del Regato, *Cancer: Diagnosis, Treatment, and Prognosis* (St. Louis, 1962), 26–28; James Murphy, "The Cancer Control Movement," *Campaign Notes* (July 1944).

9. John Cox, "The Present State of Treatment Facilities in the United States," ASCC *Bulletin* (May 1931); Tobey, *Cancer,* 99–100.

10. Thomas Parran radio speech, April 1, 1941, folder 561, Parran papers, University of Pittsburgh, Hillman Library.

11. Donald Shaughnessy, "The Story of the American Cancer Society," Ph.D. diss., Columbia University, New York, 1957, 111–115, 169–170; file folders 70–75, Parran papers; ASCC folders, Peyton Rous papers, American Philosophical Society, Philadelphia.

12. Hoffman, *New York Times,* July 8, 1926; Hoffman, "The Cancer Record of 1930," ASCC *Bulletin* (Aug. 1931). Statistics used here—slightly different from those given by Hoffman—are from Robert Grove and Alice Hetzel, *Vital Statistics Rates in the United States, 1940–1960* (Washington, D.C., 1968), 87.

13. Richard Shryock, *National Tuberculosis Association, 1904–1954: A Study of the Voluntary Health Movement in the United States* (New York, 1957), 241.

14. ASCC *Bulletin* (May 1939); "Cancer: The Great Darkness," *Fortune,* 15 (March 1937), 112ff.

15. Thomas Parran, "Cancer and Old Age," *Scientific Monthly,* 51 (Oct. 1940), 293–298.

16. "Special Report of the Departments of Public Health and Public Welfare Relating to the Prevention of the Disease of Cancer," Massachusetts House Document No. 1200 (Boston, 1926); Tavia Gordon et al., "Cancer Mortality Trends in the United States, 1930–1955," in *National Cancer Institute Monograph,* 6 (Washington, D.C., 1961), 145–146.

17. "Cheerful Cancer Figures," *Scientific American,* 156 (Feb. 1937), 104; Louis Dublin, "Statistics on Mortality and Morbidity from Cancer in the United States," *American Journal of Cancer,* 29 (April 1937), 736–742.

18. ASCC *Bulletin* (July 1940), 4–6.

19. "The Increase of Cancer of the Lung," ASCC *Bulletin* (Aug. 1932), 5; "Cancer of the Lung," ibid. (Sept. 1938).

20. William Graves, "Achievements in the Campaign against Cancer," ASCC *Bulletin* (May 1932); Tobey, *Cancer,* 191; Dublin, "The Chance of Death from Cancer," *Surgery, Gynecology, and Obstetrics,* 5 (May 1927), 274–280; Dublin, "Programs in Cancer Control," Metropolitan Life Company pamphlet, 1935, box 5, Dublin papers, National Library of Medicine, Bethesda, Md.; Dublin and Alfred Lotka, *Twenty-Five Years of Health Progress* (New York, 1937).

21. My counts of *New York Times Index* and of *Guide to Periodical Literature,* 1925–1937. Comparable estimates may be found in Tobey, *Cancer,* 283; and Herbert Lombard et al., "Evaluation of the Cancer Educational Program in Massachusetts," ASCC *Bulletin,* 26 (Sept. 1944), 98–104.

22. William Woglom, "Cancer—The Common Enemy," *Atlantic Monthly* (June 1928); Joseph Bloodgood, "The Greatest Scourge in the World," *Good Housekeeping* (Feb. 1929).

23. John Morton, "Cancer and Publicity," speech, Dec. 1935, file 70, Parran papers.

24. "Publisher Evaluates Cancer Cure," *Hygeia,* 9 (March 1931), 293.

25. Frank Adair, "Progress of Research in Cancer," ASCC *Bulletin* (July 1934), 1–3. See also Ludvig Hektoen, "Fight Cancer with Knowledge," *Hygeia,* 8 (June 1930), 533–535.

26. W. E. Gye, "The Aetiology of Malignant New Growth," *Lancet* (July 18, 1925).

27. "Cancer Yields a Secret," *New Republic,* 43 (July 29, 1925), 250–252; Rous to Edward Krumbhaar, Aug. 19, 1925, Krumbhaar folder, Rous papers.

28. The Gye folders in the Rous Papers are a mine of information.

29. Wood to Edward Krumbhaar, Aug. 29, 1925, Krumbhaar papers, College of Physicians of Philadelphia.

30. For an assessment of the state of research, see Carl Voegtlin, "Memorandum on Present Day Theories of the Causes of Cancer," July 15, 1925, 1930–1938 files, box 6, NIH papers, Record Group 443, National Archives, Washington, D.C.

31. William Castle et al., "Necrosis of the Jaw in Workers Employed in Applying Paint Containing Radium," *Journal of Industrial Hygiene,* 7 (Aug. 1925), 371–382; "Another New Disease," *Hygeia,* 3 (July 1925), 408; and William Sharpe, "The New Jersey Radium Dial Painters: A Classic in Occupational Carcinogenesis," *Bulletin of the History of Medicine,* 52 (Winter 1978), 560–570. See also Krumbhaar papers, for many letters and materials relating to this tragedy.

32. "The Great Darkness," *Fortune* (Feb. 1937); "Cancer Statistics in Various Trades and Professions," *Monthly Labor Review,* 23 (Aug. 1926), 271–274; "British Study of Mule Spinners' Cancer," ibid. (Nov. 1926), 979–981; "Identify Substance Causing Coal Tar Cancer," *Scientific American,* 148 (March 1933), 186.

33. William H. Donner to Clarence C. Little, Jan. 14, 1933, box 732, Clarence Little papers, University of Maine, Orono; "The Great Darkness."

34. Wood to Peyton Rous, April 17, 1938, Rous papers.

35. Michael Shimkin, *As Memory Serves: Six Essays on a Personal Involvement with the National Cancer Institute, 1938 to 1978* (Washington, D.C., 1983), 35; Joseph Aub, interview, Columbia University, Oral History Project, 217–218; Henry Sigerist, "The Historical Development of the Pathology and Therapy of Cancer," *Bulletin of the New York Academy of Medicine,* 9 (Nov. 1932), 642–653.

36. *Index Catalogue of the Library of the Surgeon General's Office,* fourth series, volume C (Washington, D.C., 1938).

37. *Time* (July 8, 1935, April 20, 1936, May 8, 1939); *Newsweek* (Sept. 1, 1934, Nov. 9, 1935).

38. *Time* (May 29, 1939), 52.

39. Max Cutler, "Cancer," ASCC *Bulletin* (Feb. 1938), 1–4.

40. It was in the 1930s that surgeons began performing lobotomies on mental patients. See Elliot Valentin, *Great and Desperate Cures: The Rise and Decline of Psychosurgery and Other Radical Treatments for Mental Illness* (New York, 1986).

41. Sharon Romm, *The Unwelcome Intruder: Freud's Struggle with Cancer*

(New York, 1983), 107; Harry Salzstein, "The Average Treatment of Cancer," *Journal of the American Medical Association,* 91 (Aug. 18, 1928), 465–470.

42. "Is Cancer Education Effective?" ASCC *Bulletin* (Sept. 1934); Stanley Reimann and Frederick Safford, "The Avoidable Delay in the Treatment of Carcinoma," ibid. (Oct. 1931).

43. Wood, "Meeting of Executive Committee of New York Committee on Public Health," Feb. 2, 1924, Public Health Association papers, New York Academy of Medicine, New York City.

44. Wood, "The Diagnosis of Cancer," ASCC *Bulletin* (Jan. 1931).

45. Herbert Lombard, "The Massachusetts Cancer Program: An Autobiographical Record," typescript, 49, Lombard papers, Countway Library, Harvard University, Cambridge, Mass.

46. Lewis Thomas, *The Youngest Science: Notes of a Medicine Watcher* (New York, 1983), 27–34.

47. Ewing, *Time* (May 6, 1940), 60. See also Ewing, "The Public and the Cancer Problem," *Science,* 87 (May 6, 1938), 403.

48. Thomas Wolfe, *Of Time and the River* (New York, 1935), 240.

49. See Derek Freeman, *Margaret Mead and Samoa: The Making of an Anthropological Myth* (Cambridge, Mass., 1983), 3–50, 95–109.

50. Warren Susman, *Culture as History* (New York, 1984), 113–120.

51. Donald Meyer, *The Positive Thinkers* (New York, 1980), 96–100.

52. See Elida Evans, *A Psychological Study of Cancer* (New York, 1926).

53. Auden, "Miss Gee," (1937), *Collected Shorter Poems* (New York, 1964), 109–112.

54. A. McGehee Harvey, *Science at the Bedside: Clinical Research in American Medicine, 1905–1945* (Baltimore, 1981), 47–50, 163.

55. J. Ellis Barker, *Cancer: How It Is Caused, How It Can Be Prevented* (London, 1924). See also Ben Sussman, *My Fight against Cancer* (New York, 1928); and Percival Masters, *Behind the Cancer Scourge* (London, 1933).

56. Barker, *Cancer,* 143, 306–307, 321–330, 389, 409.

57. Cope, *Cancer: Civilization and Degeneration* (London, 1932), 133–134.

58. C. Louis Leipoldt, "Cancer and the Natural Life," *Fortnightly Review,* 133 (Feb. 1930), 214–220.

59. "The Great Darkness," viii–ix. See also "Studies on Cancer and Diet," *Hygeia,* 5 (Feb. 1927), 99.

60. Herbert Lombard and Carl Doering, "Report," ASCC *Campaign Notes* (June 1929); W. Cramer, "The Prevention of Cancer," *Lancet,* 1 (Jan. 6, 1934), 1–5.

61. Robert and Helen Merrell Lynd, *Middletown: A Study in Modern American Culture* (New York, 1929), 439–442.

62. Lynd and Lynd, *Middletown,* 430–437.

63. Baker to Herbert Hoover, Sept. 29, 1929, Hugh Cumming to Baker, Nov. 11, 1936, Baker to Franklin D. Roosevelt, July 31, 1936, file 0725, box 34, NIH papers, National Archives.

64. Arthur Cramp, "Cancer Is Conquered," *Hygeia* (March 1932), 432–433; Shaughnessy, "American Cancer Society," 79–80.

65. Hoxsey to Rep. Percy Priest (Ill.), Nov. 8, 1945, Hayes Martin papers, Rockefeller Archives, Pocantico Hills, N.Y.

66. Baker, "Where Sick Folks Get Well" (1938?), Hayes Martin papers.

67. Ross Dietrick to Rous, June 16, 1925, Cancer Quacks folder, Rous papers, American Philosophical Society. See also "Cancer Cures," James Murphy papers, American Philosophical Society, for a rich file of letters offering home remedies from the 1920s through 1950.

68. Willie Davis to Rous, July 24, 1925; Mrs. A. M. Collins to Rous, n.d. (1925), Cancer Quacks folder, Rous papers.

69. B. M. Leady to Mr. President, Sept. 13, 1922; P. C. Puckett to Washington Bureau, May 16, 1922, and others in general file 2236, box 14, Public Health Service papers, Record Group 90, National Archives.

70. *New York Times,* Dec. 16, 1926; Shaughnessy, "American Cancer Society," 130–132; ASCC *Campaign Notes* (Dec. 1926).

71. Copeland to Surgeon General Hugh Cumming, June 2, 1927, box 51, PHS papers.

72. Shaughnessy, "American Cancer Society," 131–132; Richard Carter, *The Gentle Legions* (New York, 1961), 148.

73. Soper, "Analysis of the Applications for the Saunders Cancer Awards," in *Bulletin of the American College of Surgeons* (April 1928), reprinted in *Cancer News,* 13 (Spring 1959), 10–14. See also Shaughnessy, "American Cancer Society," 133; ASCC *Campaign Notes* (Jan. and Sept. 1928); *New York Times,* Jan. 22, 1928.

74. Isobel Duguid, ASCC *Bulletin* (March 1937); Ruth Coleman to Gentlemen, n.d. (1940), and Margery Leonard to Gentlemen, Dec. 12, 1934, Harvard Cancer Commission papers, box 9, Countway Library, Harvard University.

75. Lombard, "Massachusetts Cancer Program," 69–75.

76. Traian Leuceutia and Carl Weller, "The Cancer Problem in Michigan," ASCC *Bulletin* (March 1934).

77. George Park, "The Organization of a Tumor Clinic in a General Hospital," ASCC *Bulletin* (May 1934).

78. Letters to *Life* (March 22, 1937), 76.

79. David Riesman, "What You Should Know about Cancer," *Hygeia,* 13 (Dec. 1935), 1091.

80. Max Cutler, "Cancer," ASCC *Bulletin* (Feb. 1938), 1; Emil Novak, "Cancer: Its Cause and Prevalence," *Hygeia,* 17 (Sept. 1939), 819–821.

81. Poll for April 1939 in George Gallup, *The Gallup Poll, 1935–1971* (New York, 1972), vol. 1, 150. See also poll for April 1940, 216.

5. Government Joins the Fight

1. Carl Voegtlin to L. R. Thompson, Oct. 8, 1937, general files, box 96, NIH papers, Record Group 443, National Archives. Voegtlin, soon to head the National Cancer Institute, explained after a tour of European facilities that the NCI offered the United States the opportunity to make a "comprehensive attack on the cancer problem which today does not exist anywhere in the world."

2. *Time* (Aug. 16, 1937), 30; Thomas Parran interview, National Library of Medicine, Bethesda, Md., 118–121.

3. *Congressional Record,* vol. 81 (part 5), 1937, 5411.

4. *Congressional Record,* vol. 81 (part 6), June 21, 1937, 6107. Congress consisted of 96 Senators and 435 Representatives—a total of 531, one-eighth of which is 66.

5. Transcript of National Advisory Cancer Council (NACC), Nov. 27, 1937, box 6, NIH papers; Stephen Strickland, *Politics, Science, and Dread Disease: A Short History of United States Medical Research Policy* (Cambridge, Mass., 1972), 14.

6. Michael Bliss, *The Discovery of Insulin* (Chicago, 1982), 11.

7. Lewis Thomas, "Biomedical Science and Human Health: The Long-Range Prospect," *Daedalus,* 106 (Summer 1977), 163. See also Robert Hudson, *Disease and Its Control* (Westport, Conn., 1983), 212–213. For contemporary sources on sulfa drugs see Perris Long and Eleanor Bliss, "Para-amino-benzene-sulfanomide and Its Derivatives," *Journal of the American Medical Association,* 108 (Jan. 2, 1937), 32–37; and *New York Times,* April 17, 1937.

8. Rosemary Stevens, *American Medicine and the Public Interest* (New Haven, 1971), 132–133; John Burnham, "Change in the Popularization of Health in the United States," *Bulletin of the History of Medicine,* 58 (Summer 1984), 183–197; Warren Susman, *Culture as History* (New York, 1984), xxv–xxvi.

9. James Harvey Young, *Medical Messiahs: A Social History of Health Quackery in Twentieth Century America* (Princeton, N.J., 1967), 147; Richard Fox and T. J. Jackson Lears, eds., *The Culture of Consumption* (New York, 1983), 24–26; Morris Vogel, *The Invention of the Modern Hospital: Boston, 1870–1930* (Chicago, 1980), 75–77; *Boston Globe,* Feb. 23, 1926.

10. Barbara Gutmann Rosenkrantz, "Damaged Goods: Dilemmas of Responsibility for Risk," *Milbank Memorial Fund Quarterly/Health and Society,* 57 (1979), 1–37.

11. *Newsweek* (May 9, 1936), 33; *New York Times,* June 5, 1939.

12. *Time* (July 5, 1937), 37.

13. A. Hunter Dupree, *Science in the Federal Government: A History of Policies and Activities to 1940* (Cambridge, Mass., 1957), 268–270; Strickland, *Politics,* 4–10; G. Burroughs Mider, "The Federal Impact on Biomedical Research," in John Bowers and Elizabeth Purcell, eds., *Advances in American Medicine,* 2 (New York, 1976), 806–872; George Rosen, "Patterns of Health Research in the United States, 1900–1960," *Bulletin of the History of Medicine,* 39 (May–June, 1965), 201–221; and Wyndham Miles, "Creation of the National Cancer Institute," 1973, copy in my possession.

14. Robert and Helen Merrell Lynd, *Middletown: A Study in Modern American Culture* (New York, 1929), 445–446; George Soper, "National Aspects of the Cancer Problem," pamphlet, 1927, Ernest Daland papers, National Library of Medicine.

15. Barbara Gutmann Rosenkrantz, *Public Health and the State: Changing Views in Massachusetts, 1842–1936* (Cambridge, Mass., 1972), 178–182.

16. Miles, "Creation of the NCI"; Rolla Dyer interview, 1962, Columbia University, Oral History Project; Kenneth Endicott interview, 1964, National Library

of Medicine; Elizabeth Drew, "The Health Syndicate—Washington's Noble Conspirators," *Atlantic Monthly,* 220 (Dec. 1967), 75–82.

17. Hoffman, *Campaign Notes* (Nov. 1920).

18. For Soper, see Ralph Moss, *The Cancer Syndrome* (New York, 1980), 261–262; for Ewing, see *Campaign Notes* (March 1928).

19. Eleanor Macdonald, "History of the Cancer Program in Massachusetts," in George Bigelow and Herbert Lombard, *Cancer and Other Chronic Diseases in Massachusetts* (Cambridge, Mass., 1933), 160–172; History of Cancer Control Project, UCLA School of Public Health, *A History of Cancer Control in the United States* (Washington, D.C., 1978), vol. 3, 737–738.

20. Bigelow and Lombard, *Cancer,* vii–ix, 86–94; Bigelow, "The Cancer Program in Massachusetts," pamphlet (Baltimore, 1929), in box 1, Daland papers; James Tobey, *Cancer: What Everyone Should Know about It* (New York, 1932), 288–290; Robert Kelso, "Cancer Education in Massachusetts," *New England Journal of Medicine,* 200 (Jan. 17, 1929), 116–118; "Special Report of the Departments of Public Health and Public Welfare Relative to the Prevention of the Disease of Cancer," Massachusetts House Doc. No. 1200, Dec. 1925; *Boston Globe,* Feb. 23, 1926; Rosenkrantz, *Public Health,* 162–168.

21. Jack Cole, "The Connecticut Tumor Registry," in E. Grundmann and Jack Cole, eds., *Cancer Centers: Interdisciplinary Cancer Care and Cancer Epidemiology* (New York, 1979), 259–262; Michael Shimkin, *Contrary to Nature* (Washington, D.C., 1979), 419.

22. Clifton Read, "State Cancer Programs," ASCC *Bulletin* (Aug. 1938), 8; Thomas Parran radio talk, March 29, 1940, file folder 543, Parran papers, University of Pittsburgh, Hillman Library.

23. Herbert Yaremchuk, "The Origins of the National Cancer Institute," *Journal of the National Cancer Institute,* 59 (Supplement, Aug. 1977), 551–558; Miles, "Creation of the NCI," 9–11; *Congressional Record,* Oct. 24, 1929, 4832–4833, May 23, 1930, 9424–9425.

24. Thomas Parran interview, Columbia University, Oral History Project, 118–120; Rosen, "Patterns of Health Research"; Bess Furman, *A Profile of the United States Public Health Service, 1798–1948* (Washington, D.C., 1973), 374.

25. Victoria Harden, *Inventing the NIH: Federal Biomedical Policy, 1887–1937* (Baltimore, 1986), 148–159; Strickland, *Politics,* 7–10.

26. See box 108, file 1310, Public Health Service papers, Record Group 90, National Archives, for evidence of PHS cancer activities, 1928–1931.

27. Surgeon General Hugh Cumming to Dr. Francis Wood, Dec. 21, 1935, box 51, PHS papers; Michael Shimkin, *As Memory Serves: Six Essays on a Personal Involvement with the National Cancer Institute: 1938 to 1978* (Washington, D.C., 1983), 13–23; Harold Stewart interview, Columbia University, Oral History Project, 15–26.

28. Albert Soiland, "The Social and Economic Aspects of Cancer," ASCC *Bulletin* (May 1935), 1–5.

29. Thomas Parran interview, 1962, National Library of Medicine, 131.

30. Paul Starr, *The Social Transformation of American Medicine* (New York, 1982), 339–340.

31. Richard Shryock, *National Tuberculosis Association, 1904–1954: A*

Study of the Voluntary Health Movement in the United States (New York, 1957), 227–228.

32. Donald Swain, "The Rise of a Research Empire: NIH, 1930 to 1950," *Science,* 138 (Dec. 1962), 1233–1237; Yaremchuk, "Origins of the NCI."

33. *Time* (March 22, 1937), 49.

34. Mark Haller, *Eugenics: Hereditarian Attitudes in American Thought* (New Brunswick, N.J., 1963), 89; Daniel Kevles, *In the Name of Eugenics* (New York, 1985), 69.

35. Box 727, C. C. Little papers, University of Maine, Orono; *Current Biography* (Dec. 12, 1944), 35–38.

36. *Time* (March 22, 1937), 54–56 (cover story on Little).

37. "Reports of the Managing Director of the ASCC," Oct. 1935, March 2, 1936, file folders 72 and 73, Parran papers; ASCC *Bulletin* (Oct. 1937).

38. *Time* (March 22, 1937), 51.

39. ASCC, *History of the American Society for the Control of Cancer, 1913–1944* (New York, 1944?); Donald Shaughnessy, "The Story of the American Cancer Society," Ph.D. diss., Columbia University, New York, 1957, 190–191; Little, "The Conquest of Cancer," *Good Housekeeping* (Dec. 1936), 77ff.

40. "Report of the Managing Director of the ASCC," May 1936, file folder 73, Parran papers.

41. Shaughnessy, "American Cancer Society," 195–198; "Annual Reports by Field Representatives" of ASCC, Oct. 1936, file folder 73, Parran papers.

42. "Report of the Managing Director of the ASCC," Oct. 1937, file folder 74, Parran papers.

43. Shaughnessy, "American Cancer Society," 173, 188; ASCC *National Bulletin* (Oct. 1939), 2–10; Moss, *Cancer Syndrome,* 262–263. See also Richard Carter, *The Gentle Legions* (New York, 1961), 16–18.

44. "Report of Managing Director of ASCC," Aug. 25, 1937, file folder 74, Parran papers.

45. Clifton Read, "Publicity in the Cancer Campaign," ASCC *Bulletin* (July 1938), 8–9; "Reaching the Public," ibid. (July 1939), 7.

46. Read report, March 27, 1937, file folder 75, Parran papers.

47. "Cancer: The Great Darkness," *Fortune,* 15 (March 1937), 112ff.; *Life* (March 1, 1937); *Time* (March 23, 1937).

48. *Newsweek* (April 10, 1937).

49. Elaine MacDonald to Huntington Memorial Hospital, April 15, 1938; Ros Pederson to Hospital, March 24, 1938; Pearl Fisher to Hospital, n.d. (April 1938?), box 6, Harvard Cancer Commission Papers, Countway Library.

50. *Time* (July 5, 1937), 36.

51. *Time* (Aug. 16, 1937), 30; *New York Times,* Aug. 6, 1937.

52. Parran to Little, March 30, 1937, box 6, NIH papers.

53. Yaremchuk, "Origins of the NCI"; Miles, "Creation of the NCI"; Swain, "Rise of a Research Empire."

54. "Remarks by Senator Bone," at laying of cornerstone of the NCI, June 24, 1939, in Parran papers.

55. G. W. McCoy (head of NIH) to Jackson, July 26, 1935, general records, box 86, NIH papers.

56. Maverick to George McCoy, Dec. 16, 1936; Jackson to McCoy, Dec. 15, 1936, general records, box 86, NIH papers.

57. Jackson correspondence, box 51, Public Health Service papers; Transcript of meeting of National Advisory Cancer Council, Nov. 9, 1937, box 6, NIH papers.

58. Miles, "Creation of the NCI."

59. John Heller interview, 1964, National Library of Medicine, 24; Furman, *Profile of the PHS,* 397.

60. C. C. Little to Parran, March 24, 1932, March 8, 1935, Jan. 10, 1936, Jan. 30, 1936, and Parran to Little, Jan. 28, 1936, file folder 70, Parran papers.

61. Parran to Homer Bone, March 18, 1937, 1930–1948 files, box 6, NIH papers.

62. Strickland, *Politics,* 25–26, describes Parran as a reluctant convert to the cause.

63. A. E. Taylor to Parran, July 22, 1937, general file 0725, box 62, NIH papers.

64. Vera Long to FDR, July 27, 1937, general file 0725, box 50, NIH papers. This file, boxes 50–62, contains many other such letters.

65. "Answers to 'Questions on the Cancer Problem,'" March 1937, ASCC folders, James Murphy papers, American Philosophical Society, Philadelphia.

66. Rous to William Gye, June 14, 1937, Peyton Rous papers, American Philosophical Society.

67. Little to Surgeon General Cumming, June 22, 1933, box 732, Little papers.

68. *Journal of the American Medical Association,* 109 (Oct. 16, 1937), 16.

69. *Congressional Record,* July 23, 1937, 7509.

70. J. R. Heller, "The National Cancer Institute: A Twenty Year Retrospect," *Journal of the National Cancer Institute,* 19 (Aug. 1957), 147–190.

71. Parran to Ewing, Sept. 1, 1937, general records, box 41, NIH papers.

72. Little to Parran, Jan. 18, 1939, file folder 71, Parran papers.

73. Transcripts of NACC meetings, Nov. 9, 27, 1937, boxes 6 and 7, NIH papers. Harold Stewart interview, Columbia University, Oral History Project, 32. Contrast the vision, focusing on treatment and prevention, of J. W. Schereschewsky, "The Prevention and Control of Cancer—A Plan for Nationwide Organization," ASCC *Bulletin* (Nov. 1938), 2–6.

74. Minutes of NACC meetings, Nov. 9, 1937, 218; Jan. 3, 1939, 9, box 8, NIH papers; Lawrence to Compton, Oct. 3, 1938, box 6, NIH papers.

75. Heller, "NCI"; *Time* (Nov. 28, 1938), 41.

76. Shimkin, *As Memory Serves,* 24–26; Thelma Dunn, "Intramural Research Pioneers, Personalities, and Programs: The Early Years," *Journal of the National Cancer Institute,* 59 (Supplement 2, 1977), 605–616.

77. Parran interview, Columbia University, Oral History Project, 94–95; minutes of NACC meeting, Nov. 9, 1937, 55–56, 218–242, NIH papers; Ludvig Hektoen, "The National Cancer Institute Act," ASCC *Bulletin* (Nov. 1938), 1–3.

78. Minutes of NACC meeting, Nov. 9, 1937, 131–133, NIH papers.

79. Minutes of NACC meeting, Nov. 9, 1937, 91–92, NIH papers.

80. Yaremchuk, "Origins of the NCI," 556.

81. Strickland, *Politics,* 13.

6. Hymns to Science and Prayers to God

1. Paul Boyer, *By the Bomb's Early Light: American Thought and Culture at the Dawn of the Atomic Age* (New York, 1985), 266.

2. Paul Starr, *The Social Transformation of American Medicine* (New York, 1982), 335–336; Allan Brandt, *No Magic Bullet: A Social History of Venereal Disease in the United States since 1880* (New York, 1985), 171.

3. Edna Kaehele, *Living with Cancer* (Garden City, N.Y., 1952), 96.

4. Leighton Cuff, "America's Romance with Medicine," *Daedalus,* 115 (Spring 1986), 137–159. For polio, see John Paul, *A History of Poliomyelitis* (New Haven, 1971), 426–440; Aaron Klein, *Trial by Fury: The Polio Vaccine Controversy* (New York, 1972), 107; Starr, *Social Transformation,* 346–347. In fact, the Salk vaccine was rushed into production; some of it contained living tumor virus particles, which luckily did not prove to be carcinogenic for humans.

5. Richard Carter, *The Gentle Legions* (New York, 1961), 17–21; Richard Shryock, *National Tuberculosis Association, 1904–1954: A Study of the Voluntary Health Movement in the United States* (New York, 1957), 267–268.

6. Edmund Pellegrino, "The Sociocultural Impact of Twentieth-Century Therapeutics," in Morris Vogel and Charles Rosenberg, eds., *The Therapeutic Revolution* (Philadelphia, 1979), 262.

7. Peter Conrad and Joseph Schneider, *Deviance and Medicalization: From Badness to Sickness* (St. Louis, 1980), 17–34; Aubrey Lewis, "Health as a Social Concept," *British Journal of Sociology,* 2 (1953), 109–124.

8. Philippe Ariès, *The Hour of Our Death* (New York, 1981), 575–582, 613–614; George Crile, *Cancer and Common Sense* (New York, 1955).

9. Renee Fox, "The Medicalization and Demedicalization of American Society," in John Knowles, ed., *Doing Better and Feeling Worse: Health in the United States* (New York, 1977), 9–22.

10. Cited in John Burnham, "American Medicine's Golden Age: What Happened to It?" *Science,* 215 (March 19, 1982), 1475. See also Donald Meyer, *The Positive Thinkers* (New York, 1980), 252–255.

11. History of Cancer Control Project, UCLA School of Public Health, *A History of Cancer Control in the United States, 1946–1971* (Washington, 1976), vol. 3, 526–527 (hereafter cited as *Cancer Control*); Roscoe Spencer, "Communique on Cancer," *Reader's Digest,* 49 (Oct. 1946), 77–81.

12. F. Crowninshield, "At Last We Begin a Determined Crusade against Cancer," *Saturday Evening Post,* 218 (Feb. 2, 1946), 100.

13. John Cairns, *Cancer: Science and Society* (San Francisco, 1978), 165–166.

14. Parran, "USPHS Policy on Cancer," April 30, 1947, file folder 759, Parran papers, University of Pittsburgh, Hillman Library; Samuel Spencer, "Where Are We Now on Cancer?" *Saturday Evening Post,* 220 (June 5, 1948), 30–31.

15. George Gallup, *The Gallup Poll, 1935–1971* (New York, 1972), vol. 2, 875. See also polls of April 1953 (vol. 2, 1138), March 1960 (vol. 3, 1657), Feb. 1965, (vol. 3, 1926).

16. Eliza Patterson and T. R. Talbot, "Early History of the Institute for Cancer Research, 1927–1957, and Recent History, 1957–1976," *Institute for Cancer Research Scientific Report* (1977–1978), no. 23, 15–51.

17. Michael Shimkin, "Neoplasia," in John Bowers and Elizabeth Purcell, eds., *Advances in American Medicine* (New York, 1976), vol. 1, 210–250; Harold Rusch, "The Beginnings of Cancer Research Centers in the United States," *Journal of the National Cancer Institute,* 74 (Feb. 1985), 391–403.

18. Scrapbooks, 1946–1956, Sloan-Kettering Cancer Center papers, Rockefeller Archives, Pocantico Hills, N.Y. (hereafter SKCC papers).

19. *Time* (Aug. 20, 1945), 64; Archives Committee, Memorial Sloan-Kettering Center, "A Center of Commitment" (New York, 1984).

20. *Newsweek* (March 10, 1947), 54; Lawrence Galton, "Cancer, The Child Killer," *Collier's*, 121 (May 15, 1948), 64ff.; Steven Spencer, "Cancer Kills Children, Too," *Saturday Evening Post,* 223 (April 28, 1951), 32–33. See also Margery Darrell, "If I Should Die before I Wake," *Look,* 18 (Nov. 30, 1954), 127–130; and John Gunther, *Death Be Not Proud* (New York, 1949), the moving story of the author's son's battle and death from cancer at age seventeen.

21. Scrapbooks, 1946–1947, SKCC papers.

22. Scrapbook, 1946, clippings Jan. 7, Feb. 6, 7, 1946, SKCC papers.

23. Scrapbooks, 1942–1960, SKCC papers.

24. Steven Spencer, "Can We Check the Rising Toll of Lung Cancer?" *Saturday Evening Post,* 22 (April 8, 1950), 36–37; *U.S. News and World Report* (April 28, 1950), 13; Louis Dublin and M. Castle, "Fewer Women Now Die of Cancer," *Ladies Home Journal,* 68 (Jan. 1951), 41.

25. *Time* (June 27, 1949), 66–73.

26. William Laurence, "Science Is Conquering Polio, Heart Disease, Cancer," *Look,* 17 (Sept. 8, 1953), 24; Evan Wylie, "Twenty-Four Hours in the Fight against Cancer," *Reader's Digest,* 68 (June 1956), 111, emphasis his.

27. Leonard Engel, "Long, Slow Battle with Cancer," *Harper's,* 205 (Aug. 1952), 82–86. See also Henry Schacht, "Cancer and the Atom," ibid., 199 (Aug. 1949), 83–87; and J. Lear, "Food and Cancer," *Saturday Review,* 39 (Oct. 6, 1956), 57–58.

28. *Life* (April 25, 1957), 57; ibid. (May 5, 1958), 102–112; R. and E. Brecher, "They Volunteered for Cancer: Inmates of Ohio State Penitentiary," *Reader's Digest,* 72 (April 1958), 62–66. See also *Newsweek* (June 22, 1959), cover story, 51–52.

29. June Goodfield, *The Siege of Cancer* (New York, 1975), 194–195.

30. Ibid. But see Daniel Fox, *Health Policies, Health Politics: The British and American Experience, 1911–1965* (Princeton, 1986), 171–174, on exaggerations by British media.

31. Helen Kenyon, "'Cured,'" ASCC *Bulletin* (Jan. 1942), 8–9; "I'm Not Afraid of Cancer," *Hygeia,* 16 (Feb. 1938), 138–140.

32. John Brody, "I Lost My Battle with Cancer," *Saturday Evening Post,* 221 (Feb. 5, 1949), 23ff.; James Ball, "My Wife Died of Cancer," ibid., 229 (Nov. 24, 1956), 122.

33. Lael Wertenbaker, "Death of a Man," *Look,* 21 (Mar. 19, 1957), 40–42.

34. Marion Flexner, "Cancer—I've Had It," *Ladies Home Journal,* 64 (May 1947), 57; Gretta Palmer, "I Had Cancer," ibid. (July 1947), 143–148.

35. "Man Who Licked Cancer," *Reader's Digest* (Nov. 1951), 9–12.

36. *Life* (April 18, 1955), 202.

37. Dooley died of cancer in January 1961. Godfrey's surgery was a success; he lived until 1980.

38. *New York Times,* Jan. 6, 7, Feb. 16, April 3, May 9, 1947.

39. *New York Times,* Aug. 11–17, 1948.

40. *New York Times,* Aug. 16–18, 1948.

41. James Patterson, *Mr. Republican: A Biography of Robert A. Taft* (Boston, 1972), 600–602.

42. Patterson, *Mr. Republican,* 602–612.

43. *New York Times,* Aug. 1, 1953.

44. *New York Times,* April 12, 13, 18, 1953.

45. Quentin Reynolds, "Girl Who Lived Again, Babe Didrikson Zaharias," *Reader's Digest,* 65 (Oct. 1954), 50–55.

46. Zaharias, "This Life I've Led," *Saturday Evening Post,* 228 (July 23, 1955), 30; *New York Times,* Aug. 7, Sept. 13, 1955.

47. *New York Times,* Jan. 29, Aug. 15, Sept. 3, 28, 29, 1956.

48. *New York Times,* Sept. 28, 1956.

49. *New York Times,* Feb. 29, March 4, Nov. 27, 1956; Jan. 15, 1957; *Life* (Jan. 28, 1957), 44.

50. *New York Times,* Nov. 4, 7, 1956; Nov. 3, 1957.

51. *Time* (Feb. 23, 1959), 17.

52. *Newsweek* (Feb. 23, March 2, April 20, 1959); *New York Times,* Feb. 21, April 15, 16, 1959.

53. *New York Times,* May 25, 1959; *Time* (June 1, 1959), 12; *Newsweek* (June 8, 1959), 27.

54. Gallup, *Gallup Poll,* poll of Feb. 1949 (vol. 2, 788–789).

55. Gallup, *Gallup Poll,* polls of June 1946 (vol. 1, 583), June 1948 (vol. 1, 741), Feb. 1949 (vol. 2, 788–789), and April 1954 (vol. 2, 1231).

56. William Lammers, *Public Policy and the Aging* (Washington, D.C., 1983), 5.

57. Richard Doll and Richard Peto, *The Causes of Cancer* (Oxford, 1981), 1208, 1211–1212, 1274–1282; James Enstrom and Donald Austin, "Interpreting Cancer Survival Rates," *Science,* 195 (March 4, 1977), 847–851; George Crile, Jr., "The Cancer Problem: A Speculative Review of the Etiology, Natural History, and Treatment of Cancer," *Perspectives in Biology and Medicine,* 3 (Spring 1960), 358–381.

58. Louis Dublin, "The Latest in Cancer," *Women's Home Companion* (March, 1947), box 5, Dublin papers, National Library of Medicine, Bethesda, Md.

59. Edith Greenwald, *Cancer Epidemiology* (New York, 1983), 15; Richard Doll, *Prevention of Cancer* (London, 1967), 130; Crile, *Cancer,* vii, 117–118.

60. Hans Toch et al., "The Public Image of Cancer Etiology," *Public Opinion Quarterly,* 25 (Fall 1961), 411–416.

61. Gallup, *Gallup Poll,* poll of Aug. 1947, (vol. 1, 667); Charles Cameron, *The Truth about Cancer* (Englewood Cliffs, N.J., 1956), 119.

62. Gunther, *Death,* 37, 106; James Harvey Young, *Medical Messiahs: A So-*

cial History of Health Quackery in Twentieth Century America (Princeton, N.J., 1967), 360; Peyton Rous, "Concerning the Cancer Problem," *American Scientist,* 34 (July 1946), 329–357; Bruce Barton, "After a Long Illness," *Reader's Digest,* 60 (April 1952), 1–3.

63. NACC meeting, June 5, 1947, box 10, NIH papers, Record Group 443, National Archives; Bill Fay, "Cancer Quacks," *Collier's,* 127 (May 26, 1951), 24–25; Cameron, *Truth,* 87.

64. Bertha Simon to Rockefeller Institute, Feb. 2, 1950, Ralph Morford to Cancer Foundation, Dec. 30, 1948, Cancer Cures folders, James Murphy papers, American Philosophical Society, Philadelphia.

65. Letters to Murphy, Cancer Cures folders, 1948–49, Murphy papers.

66. Letters to Murphy; Sarah Gutwill to Murphy, Oct. 8, 1949, Murphy to Gutwill, Oct. 29, 1949, Cancer Cures folders, 1948–49, Murphy papers.

67. Young, *Medical Messiahs,* 239–259; Fay, "Cancer Quacks"; Michael Shimkin, "The Market in Nostrums," *Harper's,* 252 (June 1976), 58.

68. ACS, *Unproven Methods of Cancer Management* (New York, 1971), 6; Gerson file, Hayes Martin collection, SKCC papers.

69. Koch file, Hayes Martin collection, SKCC Papers.

70. Fay, "Cancer Quacks."

71. Hellen Thornburg to William Baum, Oct. 19, 1956; C. H. Smith to NCI, June 8, 1947; Clark Shields to NCI, April 25, 1950, in Diseases file, Treatments and Cures, PHS papers, National Cancer Institute, Bethesda, Md.

72. Patricia Spain Ward, "'Who Will Bell the Cat?' Andrew C. Ivy and Krebiozen," *Bulletin of the History of Medicine,* 58 (1984), 28–52; Warren Young, "Whatever Happened to Dr. Ivy?" *Life* (Oct. 9, 1964), 110–126; ACS, *Unproven Methods,* 135–138; *Newsweek* (April 9, 1951), 42; Shimkin, "The Market in Nostrums," 58.

73. *Newsweek* (April 9, 1951), 42; Dorothea Seeber to John Fogarty, May 27, 1958, box 32, Fogarty papers, Providence College, Providence, R.I.; Krebiozen folder, Hayes Martin collection, SKCC papers.

74. Fitzhugh Mullan, *Vital Signs* (New York, 1983), 63.

75. Jean Aitken-Swan and Ralston Paterson, "The Cancer Patient and Delay in Seeking Advice," *British Medical Journal,* 1 (March 12, 1955) 623–627.

76. Ibid.

77. Donald Oken, "What to Tell Cancer Patients: A Study of Medical Attitudes," *Journal of the American Medical Association,* 175 (April 1, 1961), 1120–1128; Jean Aitken-Swan and E. C. Easson, "Reactions of Cancer Patients on Being Told Their Diagnosis," *British Medical Journal,* 1 (March 21, 1959), 779–783; Bettina Schorne-Seifert and James Childress, "How Much Should the Cancer Patient Know?" *Ca,* 36 (March/April, 1986), 85–94.

78. *Time* (July 17, 1950), 50; Elizabeth Rivers, in Melvin Krant, "What Cancer Means to Society," *Proceedings of the ACS* (3d National Conference on Human Values, Washington, D.C., April–May, 1981), 15–19.

79. Kaehele, *Living with Cancer,* 10, 13, 35, 54.

80. Tennessee Williams, *Cat on a Hot Tin Roof* (New York, 1975), 146–147.

81. Crile, *Cancer,* 15–16.

7. The Research Explosion

1. Herman Pitts, "Educational Program of the ASCC," ASCC *Bulletin* (Nov. 1943), 122–126; "Financing Cancer Control," ibid. (Dec. 1943), 134–135; Richard Carter, *The Gentle Legions* (New York, 1961), 153–154.

2. J. R. Heller, "The Origins of the National Cancer Institute," *Journal of the National Cancer Institute,* 59 (Suppl., Aug. 1957), 551–558; Parran to Carl Malmberg, Nov. 20, 1944, general file, box 46, Public Health Service papers, Record Group 90, National Archives, Washington, D.C.; Joseph Aub, "Report of the John Collins Warren Laboratories of the Harvard Cancer Commission," April 1943, box 10, Harvard Cancer Commission papers, Countway Library, Harvard University, Boston, Mass.; Endicott interview, Columbia University, Oral History Project, 12.

3. Carter, *Gentle Legions,* 156–158; Donald Shaughnessy, "The Story of the American Cancer Society," Ph.D. diss., Columbia University, New York, 1957, 257–259.

4. Daniel Greenberg, "What Ever Happened to the War on Cancer?" *Discover,* 7 (March 1986), 47–64; History of Cancer Control Project, UCLA School of Public Health, *A History of Cancer Control in the United States, 1946–1971* (Washington, D.C., 1976), vol. 3, 527 (hereafter cited as *Cancer Control*); Heller, "Origins"; Transcript of National Advisory Cancer Council (NACC) meeting, March 29, 1946, box 10, NIH papers, Record Group 443, National Archives.

5. *New York Times,* May 31, 1952; Samuel Epstein, *The Politics of Cancer* (Garden City, N.Y., 1978), 325; Elmer Bobst, *Bobst: The Autobiography of a Pharmaceutical Pioneer* (New York, 1973), 224–228; Elizabeth Drew, "The Health Syndicate—Washington's Noble Conspirators," *Atlantic Monthly,* 220 (Dec. 1967), 75–82; Stephen Strickland, *Politics, Science, and Dread Disease: A Short History of United States Medical Research Policy* (Cambridge, Mass., 1972), 134.

6. *New York Times,* Nov. 21, 1985.

7. Shaughnessy, "American Cancer Society," 221–227; Carter, *Gentle Legions,* 156–160; Leonard Scheele interview, National Library of Medicine, Bethesda, Md., 27.

8. Murphy to James Ripley, Jan. 22, 1946; Little to Murphy, Dec. 26, 1945, ASCC file, Murphy papers, American Philosophical Society, Philadelphia.

9. Charles Cameron (medical and scientific director of ACS, 1946–56) interview, *Cancer Control,* vol. 3, 792.

10. Eric Johnston to John D. Rockefeller, Jr., April 1, 1945, Office of the Messrs. Rockefeller, Medical Interests, box 6, Rockefeller Archives, Pocantico Hills, N.Y.

11. John Moseley, "The Problem of Cancer in Negroes," ASCC *Bulletin* (July 1944), 77–78; John Cairns, "The Treatment of Diseases and the War Against Cancer," *Scientific American,* 253 (Nov. 1985), 51–59.

12. Charles Kettering to David Rockefeller, March 16, 1949, Office of Messrs. Rockefeller, Medical Interests, box 6, Rockefeller Archives.

13. *Newsweek* (April 9, 1945), 100–103; Carter, *Gentle Legions,* 172.

14. Paul Boyer, "A Historical View of Scare Tactics," *Bulletin of the Atomic Scientists* (Jan. 1986), 17–19.

15. *Time* (Nov. 15, 1948), 88.

16. Edna Kaehele, *Living with Cancer* (Garden City, N.Y., 1952), 54.

17. Crile, "A Plea against Blind Fear of Cancer," *Life* (Oct. 31, 1955), 140.

18. Crile, *Cancer and Common Sense* (New York, 1955), 7–8.

19. Crile, "Plea," 142.

20. *Cancer Control*, vol. 3, 817–821.

21. Lois Mattox Miller, "Small Towns Tackle Cancer," *Reader's Digest*, 50 (April 1947), 119–120; *Life* (April 15, 1946, April 21, 1952); *Time* (April 26, 1948), 76.

22. Joseph Hixson, *The Patchwork Mouse* (Garden City, N.Y., 1976), 29–31; Ralph Moss, *The Cancer Syndrome* (New York, 1980), 264–265.

23. *Life* (April 25, 1949), 112.

24. *Cancer Control*, vol. 3, 856.

25. *Cancer Control*, vol. 3, 553–554.

26. *Cancer Control*, vol. 4, 19.

27. Strickland, *Politics*, 48; Transcript of meetings of NACC, April 7, 1945, box 9, and March 29, 1946, box 10, NIH papers.

28. Rhoads to Edwin Wilson, Jan. 3, 1942, box 11, Harvard Cancer Commission papers.

29. Strickland, *Politics*, 37.

30. Strickland, *Politics*, 36–39; Drew, "Health Syndicate."

31. Donald Swain, "The Rise of a Research Empire, NIH, 1930 to 1950," *Science*, 138 (Dec. 1962), 1233–1237; Thomas Parran interview, National Library of Medicine, 96; John Heller interview, Columbia University, Oral History Project, 40–42.

32. Strickland, *Politics*, 25–30.

33. Goodfield, *The Siege of Cancer* (New York, 1975), 152.

34. Goodfield, *Siege*, 178–179.

35. See Thomas Wolfe, *The Right Stuff* (New York, 1979), esp. 130–133, 190–191, for attention to "hype" about space. Analogies with support for the NCI are not altogether inappropriate.

36. Drew, "Health Syndicate"; Rolla Dyer interview, Columbia University, Oral History Project, 49; Mary Lasker to Fogarty, Aug. 22, 1957, box 28, Fogarty papers, Providence College, Providence, R.I.

37. Natalie Davis Spingarn, *Heartbeat: The Politics of Health Research* (New York, 1976), 24–50; Paul Starr, *The Social Transformation of American Medicine* (New York, 1982), 341–344; Swain, "Rise of a Research Empire"; Leonard Scheele interview, National Library of Medicine, 30–31.

38. Strickland, *Politics*, 97–101, 121–122.

39. Lewis Thomas, *The Youngest Science: Notes of A Medicine Watcher* (New York, 1983), 174; Drew, "Health Syndicate."

40. Heller, "Origins"; Thomas, *Youngest Science*, 174.

41. Mitchel Auerbach to Marion Folsom, March 28, 1957, box 32, Fogarty papers; Don K. Price, "The Scientific Establishment," in Robert Gilpin and Chris-

topher Wright, eds., *Scientists and National Policy-Making* (New York, 1964), 19–40; Thomas, *Youngest Science,* 175.

42. Harold Stewart interview, Columbia University, Oral History Project, 22–24; Thelma Dunn, "Intramural Research Pioneers, Personalities, and Programs: The Early Years," *Journal of the National Cancer Institute,* 59 (Suppl., 1977), 605–617; Strickland, *Politics,* 149.

43. *Cancer Control,* vol. 1, 112.

44. Charles Cameron, *The Truth about Cancer* (Englewood Cliffs, N.J., 1956), 128.

45. Van Potter, "The Role of Nutrition in Cancer Prevention," *Science,* 101 (Feb. 2, 1945), 105–109; Charles Perkins, *What Price Civilization?: The Causes, Prevention, and Cure of Human Cancer* (Washington, D.C., 1946).

46. "Personality and Cancer," *Scientific American,* 186 (June 1952), 34; *Time* (Aug. 30, 1954), 45.

47. Harold Simmons, *The Psychogenic Theory of Disease: A New Approach to Cancer Research* (Sacramento, 1966). See also Samuel Kowal, "Emotions as a Cause of Cancer: Eighteenth and Nineteenth Century Contributions," *Psychoanalytic Review,* 42 (July 1955), 217–227.

48. Michael Shimkin, *Contrary to Nature* (Washington, D.C., 1979), 335; Charles Oberling, *The Riddle of Cancer* (New Haven, 1944); Edward Sylvester, *Target: Cancer* (New York, 1986), 172–173; W. Ray Bryan to Rous, May 5, 1952, and Rous to Harry Weaver, Oct. 9, 1958, ACS folder, Rous papers, American Philosophical Society, Philadelphia.

49. *Wall Street Journal,* May 10, 1960.

50. Transcript of NACC meeting, March 29, 1946, Box 10, NIH papers.

51. *Cancer Control,* vol. 2, 159; Cameron, *Truth,* 66–72.

52. *Cancer Control,* vol. 2, 132–35.

53. Shimkin, *Contrary to Nature,* 229; "Technology and Culture," *Scientific American,* 179 (Dec. 1948), 27.

54. Shimkin, *Contrary to Nature,* 347.

55. Geoff Conklin, "Cancer and the Environment," *Scientific American,* 180 (Jan. 1949), 11–15.

56. Roscoe Spencer, "The Mystery of Cancer Growth," *Hygeia,* 27 (May 1949), 323.

57. Strauss, "The Medical Profession and Atomic Energy," *Journal of the American Medical Association,* 138 (1948), 1225–1227; Shields Warren, "The Pathological Effects of an Instantaneous Dose of Radiation," *Cancer Research,* 9 (1946), 449–453; David Bradley, *No Place to Hide* (Boston, 1948); Robert Divine, *Blowing on the Wind; The Nuclear Test Ban Debate, 1954–1960* (New York, 1978), 3–35; Howard Ball, "Downwind from the Bomb," *New York Times Magazine,* Feb. 9, 1986, 32ff. Richard Pfau discusses Strauss's role in *No Sacrifice Too Great: The Life of Lewis L. Strauss* (Charlottesville, Va., 1984), 164–166, 199–200.

58. Paul Boyer, "Physicians Confront the Apocalypse: The American Medical Profession and the Threat of Nuclear War," *Journal of the American Medical Association,* 253 (Aug. 2, 1985), 633–643; Moss, *Cancer Syndrome,* 58–69; *New York Times,* Oct. 21, 1956.

59. *Cancer Control,* vol. 2, 137–140; Harold Stewart speech, Sept. 1, 1978, Hueper papers, National Library of Medicine; *Washington Post,* Nov. 4, 1976.

60. *Cancer Control,* vol. 2, 142.

61. Cameron, *Truth,* 72; ACS, *Unproven Methods of Cancer Management* (New York, 1971), 6.

62. *Cancer Control,* vol. 4, n.p.

63. Burton Wolfe, "The Cured Cancer Club," *Today's Health,* 31 (Dec. 1953), 24–26.

64. Cameron, *Truth,* 1.

65. Rosemary Stevens, *American Medicine and the Public Interest* (New Haven, 1971), 409–411.

66. As many experts have pointed out, the subject of cure rates (survival rates is a better term) is complicated, and it is often presented in a misleading fashion. With more frequent early diagnosis, for instance, increasing numbers of cancer patients begin the five-year period earlier, thereby increasing the percentage who survive for five years following diagnosis. This does not mean that such patients are "cured." Still, questions of diagnosis aside, most experts agree that surgical advances in the 1940s and 1950s substantially improved five-year survival rates, in part because fewer people died from surgical complications and in part because improved techniques cured some people. But they agree that there has been little improvement since 1960. In the 1980s, as in 1960, roughly one-third of people with cancer (most skin cancers excepted) manage to survive the disease for five years following initial diagnosis. See John Bailar III and Elaine Smith, "Progress against Cancer?" *New England Journal of Medicine,* 314 (May 8, 1986), 1226–1232.

67. Patricie and Ron Deutsch, "These Seven People Were Saved from Cancer," *Ladies Home Journal,* 74 (March 1957), 231.

68. John Eichenlaub, "Lung Cancer: The Growing Specter," *Today's Health,* 32 (April 1954), 18ff.

69. Irma Tedesche, "Figures Count," *Hygeia,* 26 (Nov. 1948), 796–797.

70. Shimkin, *Contrary to Nature,* 389–390; Shimkin, *As Memory Serves: Essays on a Personal Involvement with the National Cancer Institute, 1938 to 1978* (Washington, D.C., 1978), 177; Crile, "The Cancer Problem: A Speculative Review of the Etiology, Natural History, and Treatment of Cancer," *Perspectives in Biology and Medicine,* 3 (Spring 1960), 358–381; Joan Austoker, "The 'Treatment of Choice': Breast Cancer Surgery 1860 to 1985," paper presented to American Association for the History of Medicine, Rochester, N.Y., May 1986.

71. Edward Padolsky, *The War on Cancer* (New York, 1943), 82–89.

72. P. DeKruif, "Fifty Thousand Could Live," *Reader's Digest,* 45 (Nov. 1944), 89–93; Paul Boyer, *By the Bomb's Early Light: American Thought and Culture at the Dawn of the Atomic Age* (New York, 1985), 119–121, 299–333.

73. Stanley Reiser, *Medicine and the Reign of Technology* (Cambridge, England, 1978), 219.

74. *Life* (April 15, 1946), 84; "Control of Cancer Instead of Atomic Bombs," *Science News Letter,* 49 (April 6, 1946), 213–214; *Newsweek* (July 8, 1946), 54; *Hygeia* (Dec. 1947), 916.

75. Pfau, *Strauss,* 100, 105–107.

76. *New York Herald Tribune,* March 28, 1949; miscellaneous clippings, scrapbooks, Sloan-Kettering Cancer Center papers, Rockefeller Archives.

77. Harry Schacht, "Cancer and the Atom," *Harper's,* 199 (Aug. 1949), 83–87.

78. "Atomic Miracle," *Collier's,* 127 (April 21, 1951), 15; Lois Miller and James Monahan, "Cobalt 60," *Reader's Digest,* 61 (Oct. 1952), 19.

79. *Life* (March 31, 1952), 41–42; (Nov. 15, 1954), 59; (Dec. 6, 1954), 10.

80. Perkins, *What Price Civilization?,* 117–119.

81. Shimkin, *Contrary to Nature,* 411; Kenneth Endicott, "The Chemotherapy Program," *Journal of the National Cancer Institute,* 19 (Aug. 1957), 275–293.

82. Use of estrogen against prostate cancer had seemed promising a little earlier, in 1939. See C. Gordon Zubrod, "Drugs That Cure Cancer," *Cancer News,* 31 (Summer 1977), 15–17.

83. David Karnofsky, "New Drugs for the Treatment of Cancer," in Walter Ross, ed., *The Climate Is Hope* (Englewood Cliffs, N.J., 1965), 126–121; Shimkin, *Contrary to Nature,* 401–402.

84. Karnofsky, "New Drugs," 131.

85. Goodfield, *Siege,* 126–149.

86. Elliot Valentin, *Great and Desperate Cures: The Rise and Decline of Psychosurgery and Other Radical Treatments for Mental Illness* (New York, 1986).

87. James Whorton, *Crusaders for Fitness: The History of American Health Reformers* (Princeton, N.J., 1982), 248–249; Edmund Pellegrino, "The Sociocultural Impact of Twentieth-Century Therapeutics," in Morris Vogel and Charles Rosenberg, eds., *The Therapeutic Revolution* (Philadelphia, 1979), 245–266; Alasdair MacGregor, "The Search for a Chemical Cure for Cancer," *Medical History,* 10 (Oct. 1966), 374–385; *New York Times,* Oct. 3, 1953.

88. C. Gordon Zubrod et al., "Historical Background of the National Cancer Institute's Drug Development Thrust," *NCI Monograph,* no. 45 (Washington, 1977), 7–11.

89. Endicott interview, 1964, National Library of Medicine, 19.

90. Claude Stanush, "Medicine's Greatest Hunt—For Chemicals to Starve Out Cancer," *Collier's* (Nov. 23, 1956), 27–31; Steven Spencer, "Can Chemicals Conquer Cancer?" *Saturday Evening Post,* 228 (June 30, 1956), 84; Cameron, *Truth,* 154–158; *Cancer Control,* vol. 4, interview with Cameron, n.p.

91. Michael Shimkin, "Neoplasia," in John Bowers and Elizabeth Purcell, eds., *Advances in American Medicine* (New York, 1976), 345; Vincent DeVita, Jr., "The Evolution of Therapeutic Research in Cancer," *New England Journal of Medicine,* 298 (April 20, 1978), 907–910; Nathaniel Berlin, "The Conquest of Cancer," *Perspectives in Biology and Medicine,* 22 (Summer 1979), 500–551. Quote in Cairns, "The Treatment of Diseases."

92. Greenberg, "What Ever Happened."

93. Harold Stewart interview, 1965, National Library of Medicine, 62; Drew, "Health Syndicate."

94. Greenberg, "What Ever Happened."

95. Moss, *Cancer Syndrome,* 66–70; Hixson, *Patchwork Mouse,* 54–55.

96. Cairns, "Treatment of Diseases"; Moss, *Cancer Syndrome,* 60–65; Michael Shimkin, *Science and Cancer* (Washington, 1980), 93.

97. Crile, "Cancer Problem," 371.

98. Such critics recognized that it was often arbitrary to distinguish between "basic" and "targeted" research: much research cannot be so categorized. What they mainly questioned were "narrow," "trendy" investigations offering little hope of advancing basic understanding of cellular behavior.

99. *Cancer Control,* vol. 1, 41–52.

100. *Cancer Control,* vol. 2, 248–251, vol. 4, 14; Leonard Engel, "Long, Slow Battle with Cancer," *Harper's,* 203 (Aug. 1952), 82–86.

101. David Eddy, *Screening for Cancer: Theory, Analysis, and Design* (Englewood Cliffs, N.J., 1980), 244–245; Louise Russell, *Is Prevention Better than Cure?* (Washington, D.C., 1986), 77–78, 113.

102. Lauren Ackerman and Juan del Regato, *Cancer: Diagnosis, Treatment, and Prognosis* (St. Louis, 1962), 24–25.

103. R. Nery, *Cancer: An Enigma in Biology and Society* (London, 1986), 27.

104. Charles Huggins testimony, NACC, March 29, 1946, box 10, NIH papers.

105. *Cancer Control,* vol. 3, 561, vol. 1, 31. See also J. A. Muir Gray, "The Failure of Preventive Medicine," *Lancet* (Dec. 24, Dec. 31, 1977), 1338–1339.

8. Smoking and Cancer

1. *New York Times,* Oct. 13, 1985.

2. Warnings on American cigarette packs and ads, 1986.

3. Surgeon General C. Everett Koop, 1984.

4. Edward Beattie, Jr., with Stuart Cowan, *Toward the Conquest of Cancer* (New York, 1980), 8; Elizabeth Whelan, *A Smoking Gun: How the Tobacco Industry Gets Away with Murder* (Philadelphia, 1985), 142.

5. Thomas McKeown, *The Role of Medicine* (Princeton, N.J., 1979), 12.

6. *Providence Journal,* June 22, 1986.

7. John Langone, "Cancer: Cautious Optimism," *Discover,* 7 (March 1986), 36–46; *New York Times,* Dec. 3, 1985, Dec. 8, 1986.

8. John Cairns, *Cancer: Science and Society* (San Francisco, 1978), 44; see also Donald Balaban and Paul Stolley, "Cancer Epidemiology," in Barrie Cassileth, ed., *The Cancer Patient* (Philadelphia, 1979), 33–36.

9. Cairns, "The Treatment of Diseases and the War Against Cancer," *Scientific American,* 253 (Nov. 1985), 51–59.

10. *New York Times,* April 20, 1986.

11. *New York Times,* Nov. 11, Dec. 3, 1985; *Newsweek* (Nov. 25, 1985), 76–78; Public Health Service, *The Health Consequences of Smoking for Women: A Report of the Surgeon General* (Washington, D.C., 1980), ix, 3–4, 17–38; Whelan, *Smoking Gun,* 191.

12. William Wild, "Danger Signals of Cancer," *Hygeia,* 4 (Dec. 1926), 699; H. R. Lombard and C. R. Doering, "Cancer Studies in Massachusetts," *New En-*

gland Journal of Medicine, 198 (1928), 481–487; "Cigarette Tar in Cancer," *Scientific American,* 148 (April 1933), 245–46.

13. Whelan, *Smoking Gun,* 66–68; Ronald Troyer and Gerald Markle, *Cigarettes: The Battle over Smoking* (New Brunswick, N.J., 1983), 53–54; Raymond Pearl, "Tobacco Smoking and Longevity," *Science* (March 4, 1938), 217; "Smoking Causes Cancer," *Science News Letter,* 34 (Oct. 29, 1938), 375.

14. James Tobey, *Cancer: What Everyone Should Know about It* (New York, 1932), 271–272.

15. Howard Lilienthal, "Primary Cancer of the Lung," ASCC *Bulletin* (July 1933), 11; *Time* (Dec. 19, 1938), 54; History of Cancer Control Project, UCLA School of Public Health, *A History of Cancer Control in the United States, 1946–1971* (Washington, 1976), vol. 4, 1–3 (hereafter cited as *Cancer Control*); Clarence Little, *The Fight on Cancer* (New York, 1939), 11.

16. PHS, *Health Consequences of Smoking for Women,* 18–19; Whelan, *Smoking Gun,* 66–68; Larry Agran, *The Cancer Connection and What We Can Do About It* (Boston, 1977) 115–122; Lin Bonner, "Why Cigarette Makers Don't Advertise to Women," *Advertising and Selling,* 7 (Oct. 20, 1926), 21, 46; *Newsweek* back covers, 1937.

17. Whelan, *Smoking Gun,* 72–74; Erik Eckholm, "The Unnatural History of Tobacco," *Natural History,* 86 (April 1977), 22–32. Grable, a heavy smoker, died at the age of fifty-six from lung cancer (*New York Times,* July 4, 1973).

18. J. Donnelly, "Carcinoma of the Lung," ASCC *Bulletin,* 25 (July 1943), 74–75; Alton Ochsner and Michael DeBakey, "Carcinoma of the Lung," *Archives of Surgery,* 42 (Feb. 1941), 209–258; *New York Times,* Oct. 26, 1940; Leonard Engel, "Waging the Hot War on Cancer," *New York Times Magazine* (July 25, 1954), 10ff.

19. Whelan, *Smoking Gun,* 79.

20. *Cancer Control,* vol. 2, 170–172.

21. Ernst Wynder and Evarts Graham, "Tobacco Smoking as a Possible Etiologic Factor in Bronchiogenic Carcinoma," *Journal of the American Medical Association* (hereafter *JAMA*), 143 (June 1950), 329–336; Richard Doll and A. Bradford Hill, "A Study of the Aetiology of Carcinoma of the Lung," *British Medical Journal,* 2 (1952), 1271–1286.

22. Evarts Graham to Peyton Rous, Jan. 18, 1951, and Rous to Graham, Jan. 24, 1951, Rous papers, American Philosophical Society, Philadelphia.

23. E. L. Wynder, E. A. Graham, and A. B. Croninger, "Experimental Production of Carcinoma with Cigarette Tar," *Cancer Research,* 13 (1953), 855–864, and 15 (1955), 445–448; E. Cuyler Hammond and Daniel Horn, "The Relationship between Human Smoking Habits and Death Rates: A Follow-up of 187,766 Men," *JAMA* (Aug. 1954); Richard Doll and A. Bradford Hill, "Lung Cancer and Other Causes of Death in Relation to Smoking," *British Medical Journal,* 2 (1956), 1071–1081; Hammond and Horn, "Smoking and Death Rates—Report of 44 Months of Follow-up of 187,783 Men," *JAMA,* 166 (1958), 1159–1172, 1249–1308.

24. *Newsweek* (June 28, 1954), 81.

25. *Newsweek* (June 17, 1957), 98. Twenty-seven years later the Surgeon General estimated that a 25-year-old who persisted in smoking two packs of cig-

arettes a day would live an average of 8.3 fewer years than a nonsmoker. See "Surgeon General's Report: Twenty Years Later," *Cancer News,* 38 (Spring/Summer 1984), 20–21.

26. A. Lee Fritschler, *Smoking and Politics: Policymaking and the Federal Bureaucracy* (New York, 1969), 24–30; Kenneth Friedman, *Public Policy and the Smoking-Health Controversy: A Comparative Study* (Lexington, Mass., 1975), 38–40; "False and Misleading Advertising," Hearings of the Committee on Governmental Operations, U.S. House of Representatives, 85th Cong., 1st Sess. (July 18, 1957).

27. U.S. Public Health Service, *Smoking and Health: A Report of the Surgeon General* (Washington, D.C., 1979), 5–8; Whelan, *Smoking Gun,* 91–94; *New York Times,* March 24, July 13, 1957.

28. *Time* (Nov. 30, 1953), 60, (July 5, 1954), 38, (July 29, 1957), 28; *Life* (Dec. 21, 1953), 20–21, (July 11, 1956), 126. See also Clarence Little to Henry Luce, Aug. 3, 1957, and Luce to Little, Aug. 9, 1957, box 740, Little papers, University of Maine, Orono.

29. George Gallup, *The Gallup Poll, 1935–1971* (New York, 1972), polls of July 2, 1954, July 21, 26, Dec. 20, 1957; Troyer and Markle, *Cigarettes,* 55–56, 69–70, 95–99; *Time* (March 22, 1954), 59. See also Hans Toch et al., "Effects of the Cancer Scares: The Residue of News Impact," *Journalism Quarterly,* 38 (Winter 1961), 25–34.

30. O. Parker McComas to Clarence Little, May 19, 1954, Little to McComas, May 24, 1954, box 734, Little papers.

31. Allen speeches and news releases, Allen papers, Duke University, Durham, N.C.

32. Elizabeth Drew, "The Quiet Victory of the Cigarette Lobby: How It Beat the Best Filter Yet—Congress," *Atlantic Monthly,* 216 (Sept. 1965), 76–80; Friedman, *Public Policy,* 23–28; Thomas Whiteside, *Selling Death: Cigarette Advertising and Public Health* (New York, 1970), 26–27, emphasis his; Whelan, *Smoking Gun,* 15–27.

33. Allen speeches, June 12, 1961, July 6, 1961, Allen papers.

34. Friedman, *Public Policy,* 29–30; Whiteside, *Selling Death,* 2, 14–19; Agran, *Cancer Connection,* 122–125.

35. *Cancer Control,* vol. 1, 43; vol. 3, 848–849.

36. *Cancer Control,* vol. 4, 13.

37. Drew, "Quiet Victory."

38. Stewart interview, National Library of Medicine, March 1965, 57; Stewart to Clarence Little, Jan. 17, 1968, box 734, Little papers.

39. *Newsweek* (Nov. 26, 1956), 48; *Time* (Nov. 26, 1956), 50; Thelma Brumfield Dunn, *The Unseen Fight against Cancer* (Charlottesville, Va., 1975), 61; Michael Shimkin, *As Memory Serves* (Washington, D.C., 1983), 62, 173–174; *New York Times,* July 24, 1957; *Cancer Control,* vol. 3, 610–613.

40. Charles Cameron, *The Truth about Cancer* (Englewood Cliffs, N.J., 1956), 54–66; *U.S. News and World Report* (May 29, 1953), 39.

41. The estimate of one in ten considers "people who smoke one pack a day over a lifetime." *New York Times,* March 10, 1986. Many other experts are more pessimistic. The epidemiologist Richard Peto estimated that one-fourth of "regular

cigarette smokers is killed prematurely by smoking." *Nature,* 284 (March 27, 1980), 297. The variance in estimates depends in large part of what is meant by "heavy" smoking and on the length of time a person smokes.

42. *Newsweek* (April 19, 1954), 94–95; *New York Times,* July 13, 1957; Little, "The Public and Smoking: Fear or Calm Deliberation?" *Atlantic Monthly,* 200 (Dec. 1957), 74–77; box 739, Little papers.

43. *Gallup Poll* (July 21, 26, 1957), 1502.

44. *Newsweek* (Nov. 18, 1963), 65.

45. Little, "The Public"; Whiteside, *Selling Death,* 33–42.

46. *Smoking and Health: Report of the Advisory Committee to The Surgeon General of the Public Health Service* (Washington, D.C., 1964).

47. Kenneth Endicott interview, 1976, in *Cancer Control,* vol. 4, 8.

48. Fritschler, *Smoking and Politics,* 40–42; *Cancer Control,* vol. 2, 177–180.

49. *Smoking and Health* (1964), 20–31.

50. *Newsweek* (Jan. 27, 1964), 54.

51. World Health Organization, *Prevention of Cancer* (Geneva, 1964), 15; Friedman, *Public Policy,* 58.

52. This and following paragraphs rely on Friedman, *Public Policy,* 41–59; Fritschler, *Smoking and Politics,* 28–135; Whelan, *Smoking Gun,* 105–108; Whiteside, *Selling Death,* 46–110; *Cancer Control,* vol. 2, 180–187; and "Cigarette Labelling and Advertising," Hearings before Committee on Interstate and Foreign Commerce, U.S. House of Representatives, 89th Cong., 1st Sess., Cong. hearings (April 1965).

53. Drew, "Quiet Victory," 76.

54. *Cancer News,* 22 (Fall 1968), 13.

55. Whelan, *Smoking Gun,* 142.

56. Surgeon General reports for 1979, 1980.

57. Peter Taylor, *The Smoke Ring: Tobacco, Money, and Multinational Politics* (New York, 1984), xiii–xvii; Beattie, *Conquest of Cancer,* 13–14; Whelan, *Smoking Gun,* 193–202; *New York Times,* March 26, 1986; G. Berry et al., "Combined Effect of Asbestos Exposure and Smoking on Mortality from Lung Cancer in Factory Workers," *Lancet,* 2 (Sept. 2, 1972), 476–479.

58. Samuel Epstein, *The Politics of Cancer* (Garden City, N.Y., 1978), 164–168; *Cancer Control,* vol. 1, 35; Beattie, *Conquest of Cancer,* 98–100.

59. *New York Times,* April 15, 1985.

60. For an accounting of such costs in Britain, see Cairns, *Cancer,* 162–164. See also Whelan, *Smoking Gun,* 146–147. Taylor, *Smoke Ring,* 152, set total governmental revenues from tobacco in 1984 at $22 billion.

61. *New York Times,* June 20, 1986.

62. Agran, *Cancer Connection,* 128–138; Friedman, *Public Policy,* 148–149.

63. Whelan, *Smoking Gun,* 118, 131–132; Taylor, *Smoke Ring,* 277–280.

64. Whelan, *Smoking Gun,* 131–132, 205–206; Kenneth Warner, "Cigarette Advertising and Media Coverage of Smoking and Health," *New England Journal of Medicine,* 312 (Feb. 7, 1985), 384–388.

65. Beattie, *Conquest of Cancer,* 98–100

66. *New York Times,* April 15, 1985. Most writers agreed that low-tar cigarettes were less risky, but never "safe." They also worried that nicotine-hungry

smokers would consume more low-tar cigarettes (or smoke them down to the ends), thereby cancelling the gains afforded by low tar content.

67. *Providence Evening Bulletin,* Dec. 16, 1985.

68. Michael Schudson, *Advertising: The Uneasy Persuasion* (New York, 1984), 179–208.

69. Warner, "Cigarette Advertising."

70. *New York Times,* March 25, 1986. An ACS study concluded in 1986 that the percentage of adult smokers in the United States decreased from 37 percent in 1976 (42 percent of men, 32 percent of women) to 30 percent in 1985 (33 percent of men, 28 percent of women). *New York Times,* Oct. 20, 1986.

71. "Editor's Ashtray: Smokeout Magic," *Cancer News,* 37 (Aug. 1983), 18.

72. *New York Times,* April 20, 1986.

73. *Newsweek* (Nov. 25, 1985), 78.

74. Gallup, *Gallup Poll,* poll of June 13, 1974 (274–275); *Time* (March 8, 1982), 72; *New York Times,* Oct. 7, 1986, Jan. 17, 1987.

9. *Popular Fears, Official Dreams*

1. John Cairns, *Cancer: Science and Society* (San Francisco, 1978), 153; Richard Doll and Richard Peto, *The Causes of Cancer* (Oxford, 1981), 1209; Curtis Bill Pepper, *We the Victors* (New York, 1984), 9. The "observed" survival rate considers those patients still alive five years after they have been diagnosed for cancer. By 1984 it had climbed to 38 percent. The "relative survival rate" also takes into account the normal life expectancy of cancer patients. This is of course affected by accidents and other diseases that might strike people down within five years. By this measure, which counts only the deaths from cancer, almost 50 percent of cancer patients in 1985 will survive for five years. See *New York Times,* Dec. 3, 1985. For debates on this controversial subject, see Daniel Greenberg, "A Critical Look at Cancer Coverage," *Columbia Journalism Review* (Jan.–Feb., 1975), 40–44; *New York Times,* Sept. 18, Nov. 27, 1984; and John Bailar III and Elaine Smith, "Progress against Cancer?" *New England Journal of Medicine,* 314 (May 8, 1986), 1226–1232.

2. Robert Grove and Alice Hetzel, *Vital Statistics Rates in the United States, 1940–1960* (Washington, D.C., 1968), 87; *Statistical Abstract of the United States, 1984,* 78.

3. Richard Doll, *Prevention of Cancer* (London, 1967), 45–47; Doll, "An Epidemiological Perspective on the Biology of Cancer," *Cancer Research,* 38 (Nov. 1978), 3573–3583; Richard Peto, "Distorting the Epidemiology of Cancer: The Need for a More Balanced Overview," *Nature,* 284 (March 27, 1980), 297–300; Committee on Diet, Nutrition, and Cancer, National Research Council, *Diet, Nutrition, and Cancer* (Washington, D.C., 1982), sec. 16(6); Edith Efron, *The Apocalyptics: Cancer and the Big Lie* (New York, 1984), 434–437; Lesley Doyal and Samuel Epstein, *Cancer in Britain* (London, 1983), 8–24.

4. L. A. Fingerhut et al., "Health and Disease in the United States," *Annual Review of Public Health,* 1 (1980), 1–37; *New York Times,* Nov. 25, 1977; Susan Devesa and Debra Silverman, "Cancer Incidence and Mortality Trends in the United States, 1935–1974," *Journal of the National Cancer Institute,* 60 (March

1978), 545–571; James Enstrom and Donald Austin, "Interpreting Cancer Survival Rates," *Science,* 195 (March 4, 1977), 847–851. There were exceptions to this pattern. Blacks had significantly lower rates of skin cancer, and breast and prostate cancers were higher among the rich than among the poor.

5. Crude cancer death rates increased from 120 per 100,000 population annually in 1940 to 149 in 1960 to 163 in 1970 (and to 193 by 1984).

6. *Newsweek* (Feb. 22, 1971), 84.

7. Walter Ross, ed., *The Climate Is Hope: How They Triumphed over Cancer* (Englewood Cliffs, N.J., 1965), vii, 1–6, 51–57. Hutchinson died of cancer in 1964.

8. Adeline Cook to sister, n.d. [1963], James family papers, State Historical Society of Wisconsin, Madison.

9. *New York Times,* May 20, 1986.

10. Jim McIntosh, *Communication and Awareness in a Cancer Ward* (New York, 1977), 93–106; Marie Cohen, "Psychological Morbidity in Cancer: A Clinical Perspective," in Jerome Cohen et al., eds., *Psychological Aspects of Cancer* (New York, 1982), 117–128; Elisabeth Kübler-Ross, *On Death and Dying* (New York, 1969); G. W. Milton, "Thoughts in Mind of a Person with Cancer," *British Medical Journal,* 4 (Oct. 27, 1973), 221–223.

11. Patricia McFee, "Ethical Issues in the Treatment of Cancer Patients," in Barrie Cassileth, ed., *The Cancer Patient* (Philadelphia, 1979), 59–74; John Wakefield, "The Social Control of Cancer," in R. J. C. Harris, ed., *What We Know about Cancer* (London, 1970), 211–232.

12. Wakefield, "Social Control," 211–232; John Pumphrey and Sylvan Eisman, "Patient Adaptation to Terminal Illness," in Cassileth, ed., *Cancer Patient,* 219–231.

13. *Life* (June 22, 1962), 76–84.

14. Mary Kirkpatrick to Rous, June 23, 1962, Mrs. Yockey to Rous, Sept. 18, 1962, *Life* folder, Rous papers, American Philosophical Society, Philadelphia.

15. Ellen Johnson to Rous, June 28, 1962, R. B. Morison to Rous, Dec. 17, 1962, *Life* folder, Rous papers.

16. Alvin Zandt to William Cahan, May 31, 1967, Audrey Toncrey to Cahan, Nov. 1, 1967, box 1, Cahan papers, Rockefeller Archives, Pocantico Hills, N.Y.; Stanley Engelbardt, "Super-Cold: Hottest Thing in Surgery," *Reader's Digest* (May 1967), 131–34.

17. Harriette Thompson to Cahan, May 5, 1967, Mrs. L. J. Mullis to Cahan, July 12, 1967, Mustafa Kareem to Cahan, April 20, 1967, box 1, Cahan papers.

18. Lydia Krupp to Cahan, April 28, 1967, Gerald Rustem to Cahan, July 25, 1967, box 1, Cahan papers.

19. ACS, *Unproven Methods of Cancer Management* (New York, 1971), 9–10, 71.

20. Stearns materials, box 20/33 Diseases file (Ca), Treatments and Cures, NCI, Bethesda, Md. In boxes, Nov. 1985, at NCI office of Kenneth Thibodeau, preparatory to inclusion in Public Health Service Papers, Record Group 90, National Archives.

21. Lillian Silvers to Kenneth Endicott, Oct. 23, 1963, Amanda Simmons to Lyndon Johnson, Jan. 1, 1965, Diseases file, NCI.

22. Antoinette Simmons to NCI, Dec. 1964, Ruby Simpson to NIH, Dec. 12, 1964, G. Joseph Sadyszak to NCI, Sept. 27, 1965, Diseases file, NCI.

23. Joanne Farris to Robert Avery, Nov. 15, 1965, Winifred Dickerson to NCI, June 12, 1964, Joseph Sklar to NIH, April 27, 1962, Tod Ewald to NCI, Nov. 22, 1966, Diseases file, NCI.

24. John Burnham, "American Medicine's Golden Age: What Happened to It?" *Science,* 215 (March 19, 1982), 1474–1479; *Newsweek* (July 19, 1965), 51.

25. Lane Adams, "The American Cancer Society, 1945–1965: A Report on Progress," *Cancer News,* 19 (Feb. 1965), 2–7; History of Cancer Control Project, UCLA School of Public Health, *A History of Cancer Control in the United States, 1946–1971* (Washington, D.C., 1978), vol. 1, 55–57, vol. 2, 452–454, vol. 3, 644–682, vol. 4, 49 (hereafter cited as *Cancer Control*); Pat McGrady, *The Savage Cell* (New York, 1964), 394; William Terry, "Evaluation of Cancer Control Performance," in E. Grundman and J. W. Cole, eds., *Cancer Centers* (New York, 1979), 77–79.

26. Elizabeth Drew, "The Health Syndicate–Washington's Noble Conspirators," *Atlantic Monthly,* 220 (Dec. 1967), 75–82.

27. Daniel Greenberg, "What Ever Happened to the War on Cancer?" *Discover,* 7 (March 1986), 47–64.

28. Stephen Strickland, *Politics, Science, and Dread Disease: A Short History of United States Medical Research Policy* (Cambridge, Mass., 1972), 189–209; Richard Rettig, *Cancer Crusade* (Princeton, 1977), 11; Clarence Lasby, "The War on Disease," in Robert Divine, ed., *Remembering the Johnson Years* (forthcoming).

29. Ernst Mayr, *The Growth of Biological Thought: Diversity, Evolution, and Inheritance* (Cambridge, Mass., 1982), 574–581; Garland Allen, *Life Science in the Twentieth Century* (New York, 1975), 190–197, 225; Edward Sylvester, *Target: Cancer* (New York, 1986), 69–71.

30. *Washington Post,* Nov. 3, 1961; Fogarty speech, Nov. 3, 1961, Legislative file, box 1, Fogarty papers, Providence College, Providence, R.I.; J. D. Watson, "The Cancer Conquerers," *New Republic,* 166 (Feb. 26, 1972), 17–21.

31. Lasby, "War on Disease"; *New York Times,* April 22, 1961.

32. Strickland, *Politics,* 212; *Newsweek* (Sept. 18, 1961), 62.

33. June Goodfield, *The Siege of Cancer* (New York, 1975), 102–123.

34. *Newsweek* (March 27, 1961), 50.

35. David Baltimore, "Viruses, Cells, and Cancer," *Cancer News,* 30 (Summer 1976), 19–21; Goodfield, *Siege,* 43–76.

36. Thelma Brumfield Dunn, *The Unseen Fight against Cancer* (Charlottesville, Va., 1975), 134–139, 162–164; *Newsweek* (April 12, 1965), 68; Fogarty speeches, Oct. 4, Dec. 7, 1961, box 10C, Fogarty papers; Nicholas Wade, "Race for Human Cancer Virus," *Science,* 173 (Sept. 24, 1971), 1220–1222. For such announcements, see Joseph Hixson, *The Patchwork Mouse* (Garden City, N.Y., 1976), 123–126; Goodfield, *Siege,* 181–218; and Lewis Thomas, "Falsity and Failure," in *Late Night Thoughts on Listening to Mahler's Ninth Symphony* (New York, 1983), 108–113.

37. *Life* (July 9, 1965), 70–73, (Nov. 18, 1966), 88–116; *Newsweek* (Jan. 16, 1961), 56.

38. Greenberg, "What Ever Happened"; *Detroit News,* July 4, 1971; Bloomington (Ind.) *Herald-Telephone,* Nov. 18, 1971; *Newsweek* (Dec. 13, 1971), 116.

39. "Cancer—A National Problem," *Clinical Bulletin* (of Sloan-Kettering), 1 (1970), 4; Solomon Garb, *Cure for Cancer* (New York, 1968), 298–303.

40. Greenberg, "What Ever Happened"; Seymour Cohen, "Cancer Research and the Scientific Community," *Science,* 172 (June 18, 1971), 1212–1214; Ralph Moss, *The Cancer Syndrome* (New York, 1980), 15–17.

41. Greenberg, "What Ever Happened."

42. Moss, *Cancer Syndrome,* 15–17; Strickland, *Politics,* 264–265; Rettig, *Cancer Crusade,* 175–176.

43. Major studies are Rettig, *Cancer Crusade;* Strickland, *Politics;* Wyndham Miles, "The National Cancer Act of 1971" (1972?), photocopy in my possession.

44. Goodfield, *Siege,* 156.

45. Goodfield, *Siege,* 151, counted 670,000 for 1975. Of these, 27 percent were research scientists, 14 percent research assistants, 15 percent technicians, 10.5 percent clerical staff, and the rest clinicians.

46. Sylvester, *Target,* 9–12.

47. Nathaniel Berlin, "The Conquest of Cancer," *Perspectives in Biology and Medicine,* 22 (Summer 1979), 500–518; Philip Nobile, *King Cancer* (New York, 1975), 126–128; Barbara Culliton, "Mrs. Lasker's War," *Harper's,* 252 (June 1976), 60.

48. Moss, *Cancer Syndrome,* 18–19; Lucy Eisenberg, "The Politics of Cancer," *Harper's,* 243 (Nov. 1971), 100–105; Rettig, *Cancer Crusade,* 172; Nobile, *King Cancer,* 111–112.

49. Greenberg, "What Ever Happened."

50. Gerald Markle and James Petersen, "Social Context of the Laetrile Phenomenon," in Markle and Petersen, eds., *Politics, Science and Cancer* (Boulder, 1980), 164.

51. *Time* (July 5, 1971), 40; Nobile, *King Cancer,* 14; *Newsweek* (March 15, 1971), 8.

52. Rettig, *Cancer Crusade,* 112–113, 255–256; Robert Bazell, "Cancer Research Proposals: New Money, Old Conflicts," *Science,* 171 (March 1971), 877–879; Barbara Culliton, "National Cancer Plan: The Wheel and the Issues Go Round," *Science,* 179 (March 30, 1973), 1305–1309; Paul Schulman, *Large-Scale Policy Making* (New York, 1980), 114.

53. Hixson, *Patchwork Mouse,* 158–161; Nobile, *King Cancer,* 123–125; Eisenberg, "Politics of Cancer"; *New York Times,* Nov. 25, 1977.

54. Greenberg, "A Critical Look"; *Cancer Control,* vol. 3, 709–720.

55. Sigismund Peller, *Cancer Research since 1900* (New York, 1979), 264.

56. Goodfield, *Siege,* 177.

57. Goodfield, *Siege,* 168; Sylvester, *Target,* 138.

10. The Alliance under Siege

1. Lewis Thomas, *The Youngest Science* (New York, 1983), 205.

2. John Knowles, introduction to Knowles, ed., *Doing Better and Feeling*

Worse (New York, 1977); Paul Starr, *The Social Transformation of American Medicine* (New York, 1982), 380–382; Barbara Culliton, "Health Care Economics: The High Cost of Getting Well," *Science*, 200 (May 1978), 883–885. The cost of medical care rose to $360 billion in 1985, 10.8 percent of GNP. Kenneth Ludmerer, *Learning to Heal: The Development of American Medical Education* (New York, 1985), 272–274.

3. Dr. F. J. Ingelfinger, editorial in *New England Journal of Medicine*, 293 (Dec. 18, 1975), 1319–1320.

4. Renee Fox, "The Medicalization and Demedicalization of American Society," in Knowles, ed., *Doing Better*, 9–22.

5. Barrie Cassileth, "The Evolution of Oncology as a Sociomedical Phenomenon," in Cassileth, ed., *The Cancer Patient* (Philadelphia, 1979), 3–15.

6. Thelma Brumfield Dunn, *The Unseen Fight against Cancer* (Charlottesville, Va., 1975), 188; Thomas, *Youngest Science*, 54; Thomas, "On the Science and Technology of Medicine," *Daedalus*, 106 (Winter 1977), 34–46.

7. Joel Vernick and Myron Karon, "Who's Afraid of Death on a Leukemia Ward?" *American Journal of Diseases of Children*, 109 (May 1965), 395–400; Ro Bagatell, Changing Views of Truth-Telling in Pediatric Oncology, 1960–1986," Brown University seminar paper, copy in my possession; David Hendin, *Death as a Fact of Life* (New York, 1984), 11–13, 208–228; Ernest Becker, *The Denial of Death* (New York, 1973), 26–36, 165–172; James Farrell, *Inventing the American Way of Death, 1830–1920* (Philadelphia, 1980), 22, 222–224; Philippe Ariès, *The Hour of Our Death* (New York, 1981), 589–592; Ariès, *Western Attitudes toward Death* (Baltimore, 1974), 85–107; Leslie Farber, "O Death, Where Is Thy Sting-a-Ling-a-Ling?" *Commentary*, 63 (June 1977), 35–43; Thomas, "On Science," 44; and Michel Vovell, "Rediscovery of Death since 1960," *Annals of the American Academy of Political and Social Science*, 447 (Jan. 1980), 90–95.

8. For persuasive defenders, see Thomas, *The Medusa and the Snail* (New York, 1979), 166; Michael Shimkin, *Science and Cancer* (Washington, D.C., 1980). For chemo, see Vincent DeVita, Jr., "The Evolution of Therapeutic Research in Cancer," *New England Journal of Medicine*, 298 (April 20, 1978), 907–910; Shimkin, *Science and Cancer*, 20; for radiotherapy, *Time* (Dec. 20, 1976), 58; for viral research, John Cairns, "The Cancer Problem," *Scientific American*, 233 (Nov. 1975), 64–78; for cancer centers, Cairns, "The Treatment of Diseases and the War against Cancer," *Scientific American*, 253 (Nov. 1985), 51–59; Curtis Bill Pepper, *We the Victors* (New York, 1984), 13.

9. B. J. Kennedy, "Training Programs in Medical Oncology," *Annals of Internal Medicine*, 78 (1973), 127–130; *Providence Evening Bulletin*, Nov. 29, 1983. Estimate from NCI head Vincent DeVita, Jr. Edward Sylvester, *Target: Cancer* (New York, 1986), 218, placed the number of trained oncologists at 3,000.

10. *Time* (March 19, 1973), 65–66, (March 31, 1980), 61; *Newsweek* (April 7, 1975), 52; Joseph Hixson, *The Patchwork Mouse* (Garden City, N.Y., 1976), 186–193; Philip Nobile, *King Cancer* (New York, 1975), 1–7.

11. David Perlman, "Science and the Mass Media," *Daedalus*, 103 (Summer 1974), 207–222; editorial, *New England Journal of Medicine*, 293 (Dec. 18, 1975), 1319–1320; Dunn, *Unseen Fight*, 179; Hixson, *Patchwork Mouse*, 33–35,

183–184; History of Cancer Control Project, UCLA School of Public Health, *A History of Cancer Control in the United States, 1946–1971* (Washington, 1976), vol. 4, 14 (hereafter cited as *Cancer Control*).

12. *New York Times,* Sept. 30, Oct. 1–3, 1974.

13. Hixson, *Patchwork Mouse,* 115–116; *Newsweek* (Nov. 13, 1978), 133, (May 21, 1984), 13; Nobile, *King Cancer,* 103–109.

14. John Cairns, *Cancer: Science and Society* (San Francisco, 1978), 161.

15. "The Fat-Fiber Connection," *Cancer News,* 30 (Winter 1976); William Blot, "Geography of Cancer," ibid., 32 (Spring 1978), 18–21.

16. NCI and Cancer Research Center, USSR, *Cancer Epidemiology in the USA and USSR* (Bethesda, Md., 1980), 10, 81–84; Paul Marks, "Nutrition and the Cancer Problem," in Myron Winick, ed., *Nutrition and Cancer* (New York, 1977), 7–13; A. B. Miller, "Nutrition and Cancer," *Preventive Medicine,* 9 (March 1980), 180–196; Cairns, "Cancer Problem"; Larry Agran, *The Cancer Connection and What We Can Do about It* (Boston, 1977), 139–140.

17. Lenn Goodman and Madeleine Goodman, "Prevention—How Misuse of a Concept Undercuts Its Worth," *Hastings Center Report* (April 1986), 27–38. Also T. Byers and S. Graham, "The Epidemiology of Diet and Cancer," *Advances in Cancer Research,* 41 (1984), 1–71.

18. U.S. Office of Technology Assessment, *Cancer Risks: Assessing and Reducing the Available Risks of Cancer in the United States* (Boulder, Colo., 1982), 76.

19. Committee on Diet, Nutrition, and Cancer, Natural Resources Committee of the National Academy of Sciences, *Diet, Nutrition, and Cancer* (Washington, D.C., 1982), secs. 1-1, 1-14-16. Also R. Nery, *Cancer: An Enigma in Biology and Society* (London, 1986), 322–323; and Goodman and Goodman, "Prevention," 28–29.

20. Committee on Diet, Nutrition, and Cancer, *Diet, Nutrition, and Cancer,* 2–9.

21. *New York Times,* March 20, 1984. Smoking, they added, acounted for 30 percent of cancer mortality, viruses and other infectious agents 10 percent, sex and reproductive problems 7 percent, and alcohol 3 percent.

22. Amitai Etzioni and Clyde Nunn, "The Public Appreciation of Science in Contemporary America," *Daedalus,* 103 (Summer 1974), 191–205; Gerald Markle and James Petersen, "Social Context of the Laetrile Phenomenon," in Markle and Petersen, eds., *Politics, Science, and Cancer: The Laetrile Phenomenon* (Boulder, Colo., 1980), 151–173.

23. Box 236, Lawrence Spivak papers, Library of Congress, Manuscript Division, Washington, D.C.

24. Gene Smith to Meet the Press, n.d. [1978], Martin Tucker to Meet the Press, June 26, 1978, Box 236, Spivak papers.

25. John Burnham, "American Medicine's Golden Age: What Happened to It?" *Science,* 215 (March 19, 1982), 1474–1479; Renee Fox, "The Evolution of Medical Uncertainty," *Milbank Memorial Fund Quarterly/Health and Society,* 58 (Winter 1980), 1–49; John Powles, "On the Limits of Modern Medicine," in David Mechanic, ed., *Readings in Medical Sociology* (New York, 1980), 18–44; Nor-

man Cousins, "Laymen and Medical Technology," *Annual Review of Public Health,* 2 (1981), 93–99; Leon Kass, "Regarding the End of Medicine and the Pursuit of Health," *Public Interest,* 40 (Summer 1975), 11–42; Thomas McKeown, *The Role of Medicine: Dream, Mirage, or Nemesis?* (Princeton, N.J., 1979), 32; Tobias Kircher et al., "The Autopsy as a Measure of Accuracy of the Death Certificate," *New England Journal of Medicine,* 313 (Nov. 14, 1985), 1263–1269.

26. Kass, "Regarding the End," 1975; Robert Crawford, "Individual Responsibility and Health Policies in the 1970s," in Susan Reverby and David Rosner, eds., *Health Care in America* (Philadelphia, 1979), 247–268; Fox, "Medicalization"; Barbara Gutmann Rosenkrantz, "Damaged Goods: Dilemmas of Responsibility for Risk," *Milbank Memorial Fund Quarterly/Health and Society,* 57 (1979), 1–37.

27. David Harrell, Jr., *All Things Are Possible: The Healing and Charismatic Revivals in Modern America* (Bloomington, Ind., 1975), 5–7, 75, 100–101, 226–229.

28. Burnham, "Medicine's Golden Age"; Fox, "Medicalization"; Starr, *Social Transformation,* 388–389.

29. See June Goodfield, *The Siege of Cancer* (New York, 1975), 221–226.

30. Dunn, *Unseen Fight,* 184–186.

31. Agran, *Cancer Connection,* xiv; Cairns, *Cancer,* 168.

32. *Time* (Aug. 2, 1976), 42, (Nov. 13, 1978), 90; Nathaniel Berlin, "The Conquest of Cancer," *Perspectives in Biology and Medicine,* 22 (Summer 1979), 500–518.

33. Goodman and Goodman, "Prevention."

34. Cairns, *Cancer,* 159–161. Experts have also noted that some screens, as for colon cancer, are of uncertain value and that there is no good screen for lung cancer, the major source of cancer mortality. See also Louise Russell, *Is Prevention Better Than Cure?* (Washington, D.C., 1986).

35. Michael Shimkin, *As Memory Serves: Six Essays on a Personal Involvement with the National Cancer Institute, 1938 to 1978* (Washington, D.C., 1983), 233; final quote cited in Goodfield, *Siege,* 167.

36. *Cancer Control,* vol. 3, 776–796.

37. Richard Rettig, *Cancer Crusade* (Princeton, N.J., 1977), 324.

38. Samuel Epstein, *The Politics of Cancer* (Garden City, N.Y., 1978), 456–464; *Cancer Control,* vol. 3, 866–867.

39. Patricia McFate, "Ethical Issues in the Treatment of Cancer Patients," in Cassileth, ed., *Cancer Patient,* 59–74; Peter Cassileth and Barrie Cassileth, "Learning to Care for Cancer Patients," ibid., 301–318.

40. Jim McIntosh, *Communication and Awareness in a Cancer Ward* (New York, 1977), 46–73.

41. Glenn Mitchell and Arvin Glicksman, "Cancer Patients: Knowledge and Attitudes," *Cancer,* 40 (July 1977), 61–66.

42. Jessamyn West, *The Woman Said Yes: Encounters with Life and Death* (New York, 1976), 100, 133; Morris Abram, *The Day Is Short: An Autobiography* (New York, 1982), 5; Anthony Sattilaro with Tom Monte, *Recalled by Life*

(Boston, 1982), 29, 46. Other published accounts include Stewart Alsop, *Stay of Execution: A Sort of Memoir* (Philadelphia, 1973), and Gerda Lerner, *A Death of One's Own* (New York, 1978).

43. *New York Times,* May 4, 1977; *Newsweek* (April 8, 1985).

44. Sylvia Porter column, *Providence Evening Bulletin,* May 3, 1985. A sensitive account of such feelings is Andrew Slaby and Arvin Glicksman, "Responses of Patients to the Diagnosis of Cancer," in Slaby and Glicksman, *Adapting to Life-threatening Illness* (New York, 1985), 22–59.

45. Arno Karlen, *Napoleon's Glands and Other Ventures in Biohistory* (Boston, 1984), 116–119; Vilhjalmer Stefansson, *Cancer: Disease of Civilization?* (New York, 1960); Paul Rosch, "Stress and Cancer: A Disease of Adaptation," in Jean Tache et al., eds., *Cancer, Stress, and Death* (New York, 1979), 187–212; Frederick Levenson, *The Causes and Prevention of Cancer* (New York, 1985), 25–26.

46. John Thomas, *Alternative America* (Cambridge, Mass., 1983).

47. James Whorton, *Crusaders for Fitness* (Princeton, N.J., 1982), 11–12, 338–340.

48. Regina Markell Morantz-Sanchez, *Sympathy and Science: Women Physicians in American Medicine* (New York, 1985), 32–34, 238–240.

49. Gotthard Booth, *The Cancer Epidemic* (New York, 1979), 134–135, 230; Levenson, *Causes,* 47, 229–233.

50. Paul Rosch, "Stress and Cancer"; Marie Cohen, "Psychosocial Morbidity in Cancer: A Clinical Perspective," in Jerome Cohen et al., eds., *Psychological Aspects of Cancer* (New York, 1982), 117–128; *Newsweek,* (April 19, 1971), 131. See also Basil Stoll, ed., *Mind and Cancer Prognosis* (New York, 1979).

51. Rosch, "Stress and Cancer"; Jean Tache, "Stress as a Cause of Disease," in Tache et al., eds., *Cancer,* 1–9. For a later discussion of laboratory studies, see Steven Locke and Douglas Colligan, *The Healer Within: The New Medicine of Mind and Body* (New York, 1986), 133–154.

52. LeShan, *You Can Fight For Your Life: Emotional Factors in the Causation of Cancer* (New York, 1977), 2–12, 22–34, 65–82.

53. O. C. Simonton et al., *Getting Well Again* (Los Angeles, 1978). See also Constance Holden, "Cancer and the Mind: How They Are Connected," *Science,* 200 (June 1978), 1363–1369; and Locke and Colligan, *Healer Within,* 165–170.

54. B. H. Fox, "Premorbid Psychological Factors as Related to Cancer Incidence," *Journal of Behavioral Medicine,* 1 (March 1978), 45–113.

55. Holden, "Cancer and the Mind"; Peter Medawar, "The Crab," *New York Review of Books,* 24 (June 9, 1977), 10–15; Daphne Panagis, "Psychological Factors and Cancer Outcome," in Cohen et al., eds., *Psychological Aspects,* 209–210; Barrie Cassileth et al., "Psychosocial Correlates of Survival in Advanced Malignant Disease," and "Psychosocial Variables and the Cause of Cancer," *New England Journal of Medicine,* 312 (June 13, 1985), 1551–1555, and 313 (Nov. 21, 1985), 1354–1359; Ted Miller and John Spratt, Jr., "Critical Review of Reported Psychological Correlates of Cancer Prognosis and Growth," in Stoll, ed., *Mind,* 31–37.

56. Gould, *Discover* (June 1985), 40.

57. See Locke and Colligan, *Healer Within,* passim.

58. Holden, "Cancer and the Mind"; *New York Times,* Oct. 29, 1985.

59. Sontag, *Illness as Metaphor* (New York, 1977), 57, passim.

60. Wayne Chambers to "Meet the Press," June 1978, box 236, Spivak papers.

61. *New York Times,* Oct. 29, 1985. See also *Providence Evening Bulletin,* March 26, 1986.

62. James Harvey Young, "The Foolmaster Who Fooled Them," *Yale Journal of Biology and Medicine,* 53 (1980), 555–566; Young, "Self-Dosage Medicine in America, 1906 and 1981," *South Atlantic Quarterly,* 80 (Autumn 1981), 379–390.

63. Young, "Laetrile in Historical Perspective," in Markle and Petersen, eds., *Politics.*

64. ACS, *Unproven Methods of Cancer Management* (New York, 1971), 139–144; Young, "Laetrile."

65. Irving Lerner, "The Whys of Cancer Quackery," *Cancer,* 53 (Feb. 1984), 815–819; *Newsweek* (June 27, 1977), 48; Markle and Petersen, preface [n.p.], *Politics; Cancer Control,* vol. 3, 763–765.

66. C. G. Moertal et al., "A Clinical Trial of Amygdalin (Laetrile) in the Treatment of Cancer," *New England Journal of Medicine,* 306 (Jan. 28, 1982), 201–206.

67. Markle and Petersen, "Social Context of the Laetrile Phenomenon," in Markle and Petersen, *Politics,* 151–173.

68. A critical view of this argument is Barrie Cassileth, "After Laetrile, What?" *Cancer News,* 36 (Autumn 1982), 2–3.

69. Young, "Laetrile."

70. *Newsweek* (July 11, 1977), 4.

71. Markle and Petersen, "Social Context"; Nat Morris, *The Cancer Blackout* (Los Angeles, 1977), 200.

72. "Cancer," by Joe Jackson, copyright 1982 Albion Music.

73. Donald Fleming, "Roots of the New Conservation Movement," *Perspectives in American History,* 6 (1972), 7–91.

74. Frank Graham, Jr., *Since Silent Spring* (Boston, 1970), 145–148, passim; Edith Efron, *The Apocalyptics: Cancer and the Big Lie* (New York, 1984), 31–33.

75. Paule DiPerna, "Leukemia Strikes a Small Town," *New York Times Magazine,* Dec. 2, 1984, 100ff.

76. Michael Gold, *A Conspiracy of Cells* (Albany, N.Y., 1986), 134.

77. Wilhelm Hueper and W. D. Conway, *Chemical Carcinogenesis and Cancers* (Springfield, Ill., 1964), 17. See also *Cancer Control,* vol. 4, interview with Hueper, 6; Hueper, "Adventures of a Physician," in "Occupational Cancer: A Medical Cassandra's Tale," unpublished autobiography, 1976, box 2, Hueper papers, National Library of Medicine.

78. Carson, *Silent Spring* (New York, 1964), 195–216.

79. Carson, *Silent Spring,* 213–216.

80. Epstein, *Politics,* 26. See also Beatrice Trum Hunter, *Food Additives and Federal Policy* (New York, 1975).

81. Agran, *Cancer Connection,* xvi.

82. Jane Brody with Arthur Holleb, *You Can Fight Cancer and Win* (New

York, 1977), 15. The EPA in 1986 published a draft projection estimating that depletion of atmospheric ozone (from use of aerosols and other manufactured chemicals) would increase exposure to ultraviolet radiation and therefore cause 40 million American cases of skin cancer in the next 88 years. *New York Times,* Nov. 4, 1986.

83. Efron, *Apocalyptics,* 68–70; *Newsweek* (Jan. 26, 1976), 62.

84. Hueper, "Environmental Cancer Hazards," *Journal of Occupational Medicine,* 14 (Feb. 1972), 149–153; Irving Selikoff et al., "Asbestos Exposure, Smoking, and Neoplasia," *Journal of the American Medical Association,* 204 (1968), 106–112; Robert Hoover and Joseph Fraumeni, Jr., "Cancer Mortality in U.S. Counties with Chemical Industries," *Environmental Research,* 9 (1975), 196–207; *Cancer Epidemiology in the USA and USSR,* 39–43; Seymour Jablon and John Bailar III, "The Contribution of Ionizing Radiation to Cancer Mortality in the United States," *Preventive Medicine,* 9 (March 1980), 219–226.

85. Cairns, *Cancer,* 85–96.

86. Agran, *Cancer Connection,* 157–161; Epstein, *Politics,* 214–240.

87. Paul Tobin and Jay Turim, "Known and Suspected Carcinogens," in Charles Shaw, ed., *Prevention of Occupational Cancer* (Boca Raton, Fla., 1981), 11–22.

88. NCI, *Decade of Discovery* (Washington, D.C., 1981), 41–44; Cairns, *Cancer,* 162; Mark Rushefsky, *Making Cancer Policy* (Albany, N.Y., 1986), 36–37.

89. Joseph Fraumeni, Jr., "Epidemiologic Approaches to Cancer Etiology," *Annual Review of Public Health,* 3 (1982), 85–100; Toxic Substances Strategy Committee, *Toxic Chemicals and Public Protection* (Washington, D.C., 1980), 9.

90. Epstein, *Politics,* 320–322, 351–359, 383–397; Catherine Damme, "Laws and Regulations: An Analysis," in Shaw, ed., *Prevention,* 143–154; *Toxic Chemicals,* 137–138.

91. R. E. Albert et al., "Rationales Developed by the EPA for the Assessment of Carcinogenic Risks," *Journal of the National Cancer Institute,* 58 (May 1977), 1537–1541; Rushefsky, *Making Cancer Policy,* 85–106.

92. K. Bridbord et al., "Estimates of the Fraction of Cancer in the United States Related to Occupational Factors," (unpublished, National Institute for Occupational Safety and Health, 1978); Epstein, *Politics,* 376–378.

93. Agran, *Cancer Connection,* 33–38.

94. *Cancer Control,* vol. 2, 147–148. It was not until 1986 that the EPA began to take stronger measures against the asbestos industry.

95. Ralph Moss, *The Cancer Syndrome* (New York, 1980), 219–222; *Cancer Control,* vol. 3, 814–815.

96. Hueper interview, 1975, in *Cancer Control,* vol. 4, 9–10; Kenneth Endicott interview, 1976, ibid., 5–6; Rettig, *Cancer Crusade,* 305–306; Nicholas Wade, "Race for Human Cancer Virus," *Science,* 173 (Sept. 24, 1971), 1220–1222; Agran, *Cancer Connection,* 27–31.

97. Epstein, *Politics,* 69–70, 330–346; *New York Times,* Nov. 18, 1977. Nery, *Cancer,* 331, estimated that there were in 1986 some 4 million such chemicals in existence.

98. Epstein, *Politics,* 330–332.

99. Max Singer, "How to Reduce Risks Rationally," *Public Interest,* 51 (Spring 1978), 99.

100. George Morris to "Meet the Press," June 1978, box 236, Spivak papers.

101. Nery, *Cancer,* 177–180, 233–234.

102. Efron, *Apocalyptics,* 83; Thomas, *Medusa,* 165–166; A. C. Griffin, "Mechanisms of Action of Carcinogens," in Shaw, ed., *Prevention,* 39–45.

103. Efron, *Apocalyptics,* 177–182. By 1986 many people worried especially about another natural carcinogen, radon. A by-product of decaying uranium, it seeped into homes, especially in New Jersey and Pennsylvania. Some experts thought that it helped to cause between 5,000 and 20,000 lung cancer deaths a year. *New York Times,* March 10, 1986.

104. "Since Silent Spring," *Newsweek* (July 14, 1986), 72–73; *New York Times,* April 21, 1986.

105. Efron, *Apocalyptics,* 83, 383–393; Richard Doll and Richard Peto, *Causes of Cancer* (New York, 1981), 1227.

106. Medawar, "The Crab," 1977.

107. Singer, "How to Reduce Risks."

108. Cairns, *Cancer,* 46–47. See also *Providence Journal-Bulletin,* Feb. 11, 1984, which focuses on possible reasons why Rhode Island then had the highest cancer mortality in the United States.

109. Some "cancer clusters"—of childhood leukemia in Woburn, Mass., among uranium miners in Utah, of people exposed to radioactive fallout from atomic testing—seemed associated with the presence in these areas of high levels of man-made carcinogens. Experts studying these examples, however, have noted the formidable research problems associated with delineating the precise areas ("clusters") and with identifying the people in those areas to be included in their studies. They have therefore tended to stop short of asserting unambiguous cause-and-effect relationships. See DiPerna, "Leukemia"; *New York Times,* Feb. 10, 20, 1985.

110. Doll and Peto, *Causes,* 1239–1245; Shaw, ed., *Prevention,* 6–8; Frank Thompson, *Health Policy and the Bureaucracy* (Cambridge, Mass., 1981), 250–251; Efron, *Apocalyptics,* 438–440.

111. Cairns, *Cancer,* 163–164; Robert Weinberg, "The Secrets of Cancer Cells," *Atlantic,* 252 (Aug. 1983), 82–88; Doll and Peto, *Causes,* 1196–1212. But see also Devra Davis et al., "Cancer Prevention: Assessing Causes, Exposures, and Recent Trends in Mortality for U.S. Males, 1968–1978," *International Journal of Health Services,* 13 (1983), 337–372.

112. NCI, "Everything Doesn't Cause Cancer" (Washington, D.C., 1979), 5–10.

11. More Promises, More Fears

1. Steven A. Rosenberg et al., "Observations on the Systematic Administration of Autologous Lymphokine-Activated Killer Cells and Recombinant Interleukin-2 to Patients with Metastatic Cancer," *New England Journal of Medicine,* 313 (Dec. 5, 1985), 1485–1492; *Newsweek* (Dec. 16, 1985), 60.

2. *New York Times, Providence Journal,* Dec. 6, 1985; *New York Times,* Jan. 7, 1986.

3. *New York Times,* Dec. 9, 1985. For a sharp criticism of Rosenberg's efforts see *New York Times,* Dec. 12, 1986, which reported on a harsh editorial in the *Journal of the American Medical Association.*

4. ACS, "Research Report" (New York, 1984), 1; ACS, "1985 Cancer Facts and Figures" (New York, 1985), 28.

5. Daniel Greenberg, "What Ever Happened to the War on Cancer?" *Discover,* 7 (March 1986), 47–64. Edward Sylvester, *Target: Cancer* (New York, 1986), 155–157, estimated that funding for the NCI, in real dollars, was no higher in 1983 than in 1973 (after the first large infusion of sums from the "war" on cancer). For figures on funding for drug and alcohol abuse see *New York Times,* Sept. 23, 1986; for AIDS, ibid., Nov. 4, 1986; for the NIH, ibid., Nov. 11, 1986.

6. Office of the President, Office of Management and Budget, *Budget of the United States, Fiscal Year 1985* (Washington, D.C., 1984), 5–108; Spencer Rich, "The Cost, in Dollars," "Cancer" supplement, *Washington Post,* Sept. 30, 1986; "The New War on Cancer," *Business Week* (Sept. 22, 1986), 60–68 (cover story).

7. *New York Times,* Jan. 7, 1986.

8. Lewis Thomas, "Getting at the Roots of a Deep Puzzle," *Discover,* 7 (March 1986), 64–66.

9. ACS, "Answering Your Questions about Cancer" (New York, 1984). An authoritative critique of optimism about cure-rates and other cancer statistics is John Bailar III and Elaine Smith, "Progress against Cancer?" *New England Journal of Medicine,* 314 (May 8, 1986), 1226–1232. Its publication set off yet another public argument among cancer authorities.

10. The NCI estimated that America's total cancer mortality, if unchecked, would increase from slightly over 420,000 in 1984 to 575,000 in the year 2000. "How to Reduce Mortality," *Nature,* 311 (Sept. 20, 1984), 208.

11. *Providence Evening Bulletin,* March 29, Aug. 22, 1985; *Newsweek* (cover story), April 8, 1985; *New York Times,* June 4, 6, 1985.

12. National Research Council, *Diet, Nutrition, and Cancer* (Washington, D.C., 1982); ACS, "Nutrition, Common Sense, and Cancer" (New York, 1985); *New York Times,* Oct. 22, 1985.

13. John Langone, "Cancer: Cautious Optimism," *Discover,* 7 (March 1986), 36–46; ACS, "Research Report" (New York, 1984); *Providence Journal,* Jan. 21, 1986.

14. Sylvester, *Target;* Robert Weinberg, "The Secrets of Cancer Cells," *Atlantic,* 252 (Aug. 1983), 82–88; Weinberg, "The Molecules of Life," *Scientific American,* 253 (Nov. 1985), 48–56; ACS, "Research Report" (New York, 1984).

15. "The New War on Cancer," *Business Week;* Langone, "Cancer"; Philip Boffey, "No More Cancer by the Year 2000?" *Cancer News,* 37 (Spring/Summer 1983), 12–13.

16. *Providence Evening Bulletin,* March 26, 1986.

17. *New York Times,* March 18, June 12, 1986.

18. Weinberg, "Secrets"; John Cairns, "The Treatment of Diseases and the War Against Cancer," *Scientific American,* 253 (Nov. 1985), 51–59.

19. Rich, "The Cost, in Dollars," estimated that total cancer costs in America rose from $50 billion in 1980 to $70 billion in 1986. For statistics on survival rates of poor people see *Providence Evening Bulletin,* Oct. 7, 1986.

20. Bailar and Smith, "Progress?"

21. By contrast, cancer killed an estimated 48,000 in 1900, 158,000 in 1940, and 330,000 in 1970. Crude (not age-adjusted) cancer mortality rates increased from 64 per 100,000 population in 1900 to 120 in 1940, and to 163 in 1970. In 1985 this rate was 193. See Census Bureau, *Historical Statistics of the United States, Colonial Times to 1970* (Washington, D.C., 1970), vol. 1, 58; and *Monthly Vital Statistics Report,* Aug. 1985, 8.

22. ACS, "Answering Your Questions about Cancer" (New York, 1984). According to government statistics, cancer accounted for 18.2 percent of deaths in America in 1970, 20.5 percent in 1975, and 22.7 percent in 1980. Bureau of Census, *Statistical Abstract, 1984,* 78. A later study estimated a total of 472,000 cancer deaths in the United States for 1986 and anticipated that 73 million citizens could expect to develop the malady. *Washington Post,* Sept. 30, 1986.

23. Bailar and Smith, "Progress?"

24. *New York Times,* Sept. 18, Nov. 27, 1984; *Providence Journal,* May 29, 1985.

25. It was 133 per 100,000 population in 1980, compared to 80 in 1900, 120 in 1940, and 130 in 1970. Robert Grove and Alice Hetzel, *Vital Statistics Rates in the United States, 1940–1960* (Washington, D.C. 1968), 87; *Statistical Abstract, 1984,* 78.

26. In 1985 lung cancer deaths totaled 126,000, or 23 percent of total cancer mortality. Other leading sites or kinds of cancer were colon/rectum (60,000 deaths), breast (38,400), prostate (25,500), leukemia (17,000), stomach (14,300), bladder (10,800), uterus/cervix (9,700), oral (9,500), and skin (7,400). Langone, "Cancer," 37–46.

27. Bailar and Smith, "Progress?" (not counting nondangerous forms of skin cancer).

28. Victor Cohn, "The Cancer War: Disputed Victory," "Cancer" supplement, *Washington Post,* Sept. 30, 1986; R. Nery, *Cancer: An Enigma in Biology and Society* (London, 1986), 23–24.

29. John Cairns, *Cancer: Science and Society* (San Francisco, 1978), 22.

30. *New York Times,* June 23, 1986.

31. Cairns, "Treatment of Diseases"; quote by Weinberg, "Secrets," 82. "Years away," for most experts, meant at least a decade or two. See also John Maddox, "Molecular Biology and Cancer," *Nature,* 311 (Sept. 6, 1984), 9.

32. Nery, *Cancer,* 135.

33. Bailar and Smith, "Progress?"

34. *New York Times,* Dec. 8, 1986.

35. See Louise Russell, *Is Prevention Better than Cure?* (Washington, D.C., 1986), 109–113.

36. *Providence Journal,* Sept. 25, 1985.

37. Langone, "Cancer."

38. Weinberg, "Secrets," 82.

39. Cairns, "Treatment of Diseases." Tobacco-related cancer mortality was estimated at approximately one million a year, worldwide.

40. *New York Times,* Aug. 6, 1985.

41. Irving Rimer, "The Mass Media and the Cancer Patient—Some Views,"

Health Education Quarterly, 10 (Spring 1984), 95–100.

42. Sandra Hansen Konte, "How TV Treats Cancer," *Cancer News.* (Spring/Summer 1985), 18–19.

43. Don Colburn, "The Word and Its Myths," "Cancer" supplement, *Washington Post,* Sept. 30, 1986.

44. *New York Times,* Feb. 25, Nov. 28, 1985; *Providence Journal,* Nov. 17, 1985.

45. Similar metaphors were common in other countries as well. Corazon Aquino, who assumed power in the Philippines in 1986, denounced foes in the Assembly as a "cancer" that had "debased" the nation's politics. *New York Times,* March 27, 1986.

46. Jonathan Lieberson, "The Reality of AIDS," *New York Review of Books,* 32 (Jan. 16, 1986), 43–48; *New York Times,* March 16–19, 1987.

47. Cited in Lieberson, "Reality of AIDS."

48. *Providence Journal,* March 24, 1985; *New York Times,* Dec. 23, 1985, Nov. 21, 1986.

49. *New York Times,* Jan. 14, March 18, June 13, 1986; *Newsweek* (Nov. 24, 1986), 30–47 (cover story).

50. Lieberson, "Reality of AIDS."

51. *New York Times,* March 23, Aug. 2, Dec. 9, 1985, Nov. 4, 1986.

52. Shimkin to author, June 4, 1986; Nery, *Cancer.*

53. Michael Shimkin, *Science and Cancer* (Washington, D.C., 1980), 1.

Index

Index